CORNELL STUDIES IN ANTHROPOLOGY

An Eskimo Village

in the Modern World

*Cornell Studies in Anthropology*

This series of publications is an out-growth of the program of instruction, training, and research in theoretical and applied anthropology originally established at Cornell University in 1948 with the aid of the Carnegie Corporation of New York. The program seeks particularly to provide in its publications descriptive accounts and interpretations of cultural process and dynamics, including those involved in projects of planned cultural change, among diverse aboriginal and peasant cultures of the world.

A hunter of Sivokak.

# An Eskimo Village
# in the Modern World

CHARLES CAMPBELL HUGHES

WITH THE COLLABORATION OF

JANE MURPHY HUGHES

Cornell University Press

ITHACA, NEW YORK

This work has been brought to publication with
the assistance of a grant from the Ford Foundation.

CORNELL UNIVERSITY PRESS

*First published 1960*

*Second printing, 1962*

PRINTED IN THE UNITED STATES OF AMERICA

# Preface

THIS study was conducted at one point in time, and the materials were analyzed and written up at another, revised at a still later date, and then finally published at a fourth point in time. During all this, of course, the village of Gambell (or, by its Eskimo name, Sivokak)—the subject of the study—has changed in some ways. A few of these changes are indicated in the final chapter; but for the most part, since it is impossible to collect, analyze, and report data simultaneously with their occurrence, the study has to be presented in the form of the "spurious present," which is now some four years after the event. Therefore, throughout the account, except where otherwise noted, the present mode refers to the year 1954–1955.

Although this is of little importance for some matters, it does make a difference with regard to the picture one gets of Gambell village—in the case of health and illness and the topic of relations with the army base, for example. Determined efforts have been made to improve the health of Alaskan natives since 1955, and thus the portrayal given here does not necessarily hold for Gambell at the present time. In addition, as noted in the final chapter, the army camp has moved away since completion of the study and with it has gone one of the most important foci of intergroup problems.

But the intent of the study was not reportorial in any case. It

was to determine the types of influences, among them health, for instance, which changed the system of belief regarding the Alaskan mainland between the years 1940 and 1955. In this respect the history of the village between 1940 and 1955 is the important focus of attention, and it can offer data for scientific generalizations concerning patterns of change in human groups. Events occurring subsequent to 1955 present an opportunity for further research on the basis of findings contained in this report.

The Eskimo words used in this book are for convenience transcribed in terms of their nearest equivalent in English phonetic symbols. Unless otherwise indicated, the phonetic values roughly correspond to English values, e.g., the letters *g, k, l, n, o, p, s, t, w,* and *y*. Some letters have special English equivalents:

> *a = a* in *idea* or *u* in *fun*
> *ae = a* in *cat*
> *e = a* in *hay*
> *i = ee* in *feet*
> *l = i* in *hit*
> *oo = oo* in *tooth*
> *u = u* in *put*

There are some distinctively Sivokakmeit phonemes which cannot be directly transcribed into the English alphabet, and I have chosen their nearest sound equivalent in English. Thus, the dorsal voiced spirant is here transcribed in most instances by *g* and sometimes by *r*. The glottal unvoiced spirant is indicated by *ch*. There is a glossary of frequently used Eskimo terms.

CHARLES CAMPBELL HUGHES

*Cornell University*
*September 1959*

# Acknowledgments

TO the people and institutions whose help contributed to the completion of this book, I am deeply grateful. Only a small measure of that appreciation can be indicated here.

The first recognition must go to Jane Murphy Hughes for both her professional and personal help during the field period, the analysis, and the time of writing. Without her contributions this would have been a far less thorough study, and I wish particularly to express appreciation for the use of field notes which she gathered.

The background out of which the study of Sivokak grew has been the teaching and encouragement given me by Professor Alexander H. Leighton, to whom I am deeply indebted. The generosity of Professor Leighton and Dr. Dorothea C. Leighton in allowing me to analyze and use for an M.A. thesis the field notes which they gathered in Gambell village in 1940 is especially to be remembered. These field data from 1940 made possible the drawing of an indispensable base line for my subsequent study of sociocultural change.

I am indebted to the Social Science Research Center of Cornell University for the fellowship which made the field period possible and to Dr. and Mrs. Rex L. Murphy for further assistance. The Graduate School of Cornell University kindly supported the final preparation of the manuscript.

This book is a revision of a study submitted to the Graduate

School of Cornell University in 1957 for the Ph.D. degree. To members of the special committee which directed my graduate work, I wish to express my gratitude and acknowledge their guidance: Professors Alexander H. Leighton (chairman), Robert B. MacLeod, and Robin M. Williams, Jr. I also wish to thank Professors Morris E. Opler and Urie Bronfenbrenner, both of whom served on the committee in the early phases of graduate training, for their contributions. For his considerable helpfulness and stimulation extending over several years I wish to thank Professor Robert J. Smith, also of Cornell University. Finally, I am grateful to Professors Lauriston Sharp, John M. Roberts, Allan R. Holmberg, and James L. Giddings for reading a draft of this book and to Professor Joseph M. Stycos for his comments on Chapter III.

I am grateful to Drs. Alexander H. Leighton and Dorothea C. Leighton for the use of photographs of Gambell which they took in 1940.

To Dr. Margaret Lantis I owe a special debt, not only for her suggestions and comments on this book in draft form, but particularly for her encouragement and support extending through the several years of planning, undertaking, and analyzing the study.

Professor Clyde Kluckhohn, under whom I had the privilege of studying at Harvard, will, I hope, see some of his ideas in these pages. For his tutelage I am deeply grateful.

The co-operation given me by the Alaska Native Service and the Alaska Territorial Department of Public Welfare should be noted and my gratitude made clear. I also wish to acknowledge the interest shown in the study by various staff members of the Arctic Health Research Center of Anchorage, Alaska, particularly Dr. Francis H. Fay and Dr. Karl Reinhard, who kindly supplied very helpful data for various aspects of the report. Dr. Fay was good enough to read and comment on sections of Chapter V. For their helpfulness and co-operation during the field period, I wish to thank the Reverend and Mrs. Lowell C. Campbell, Mr. and Mrs. William Benton, Miss Grace Crosson, and Mr. William C. Caldwell, all then of Gambell, Alaska. To the officers of the Village Council of Gambell and to the Sivokakmeit as a whole, few words can convey the extent of my appreciation for their hospitality and good humor in a difficult time of transition.

I wish finally to acknowledge my appreciation to the following publishers and authors for permission to quote excerpts from published works: American Anthropological Association, American Philosophical Society, Basic Books, Inc., Botanical Society of America, Inc., Canadian Department of Mines and Technical Surveys, Canadian Psychological Association, Free Press, Harper & Brothers, Houghton Mifflin Company, Dr. Alexander H. Leighton, McGraw-Hill Book Company, Inc., Dr. Robert B. MacLeod, Dr. Jules H. Masserman, Dr. Thomas Parran, Princeton University Press, W. B. Saunders Company, Charles Scribner's Sons, Dr. Robert J. Smith, Social Science Research Council, University of Pennsylvania Press, University of Pittsburgh Graduate School of Public Health, and University of Toronto Press.

C. C. H.

# Contents

# Illustrations

An Eskimo Village
in the Modern World

The sea ice in winter and the sea itself, open, storm-whipped or basking in sunny calm in summer, are two contrasts in the life of the Eskimos. The third is the *land*. The sea has its vast expanses; but no feeling of vastness surpasses that of the tundra.

—KAJ BIRKET-SMITH

# CHAPTER I

# The Torn Grass

FOR over two thousand years Eskimos have lived on St. Lawrence Island in the northern Bering Sea. During most of that time they were isolated from the Alaskan mainland, one hundred miles to the east, and journeyed instead, when they did contact the world beyond their island, to the coast of Siberia, which lies only thirty-eight miles away to the northwest (Map 1). But such trips were infrequent, occurring only during the spring or summer months, when trading voyages were made. At times even this contact was impossible because of hostilities between the people of Indian Point (Chaplino), Siberia, and those of the principal settlement of St. Lawrence Island, Sivokak, not yet known by its American-given name, Gambell. For the most part, then, the world of these Eskimos was bounded on the north and west by the stormy sea and on the east and south by stretches of tundra reaching to barren mountains and cut by fish-filled streams.

Early on a September morning in 1954 the United States coast guard cutter *Storis,* having traveled westward during the night along the shore of St. Lawrence from the only other native village on the island, Savoonga, anchored off the north beach of the pebble spit which has been formed by countless currents gnawing away at the base of Mt. Chibukak (Map 2). Out on the end of the spit, a mile or more from the mountain, is the modern village of Gambell, off-

*1*

shoot of at least five other village sites which over a span of many
hundreds of years have crept outward from the mountain, always
halting near the beach and moving with the work of the waves
(Figures 1 and 2).

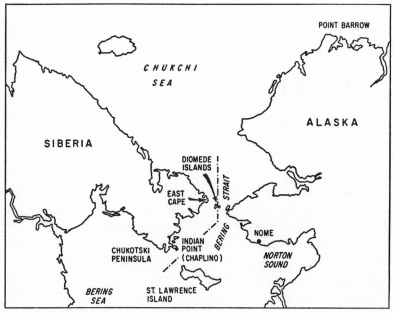

*Map 1.* The North Bering Sea region. (After *Arctic*, vol. VII, no. 3–4.)

The disembarking of its civilian passengers was soon accomplished
and the cutter made ready for departure on the last part of its annual
Bering Sea Patrol. Along with the teachers and nurse it had brought
out from Nome, Alaska, were two anthropologists, coming to study
for a year the social and cultural changes in this village of 300 people
who live in one of the stormiest regions in the world. The village was
one that had been studied some fourteen years earlier by two others
interested in the St. Lawrence Island Eskimos. Drs. Alexander H.
Leighton and Dorothea C. Leighton had spent the summer of 1940
making personality and ethnographic studies in Gambell. In the
intervening period, much had happened to the village. We had
learned something of this through letters from the Gambell Eskimos
and from talking with white people on the mainland. The village,

it appeared, had been affected, like so many other small villages over the face of the earth, by social and economic developments in the outer world and by the changing currents and backwashes of international politics. It had felt, almost at first hand, World War II and was now living in the postwar years of fear and the awesome possibility of mass destruction. It had also felt, again like other villages, some of the effects of the widespread movement of peoples as a result of the war, shown most vividly in changed conceptions of life.

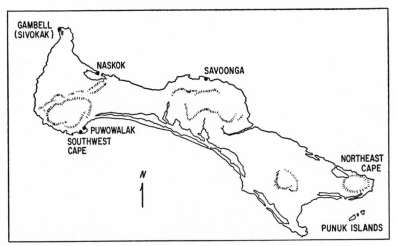

*Map 2.* St. Lawrence Island. (After Geist and Rainey, 1936.)

The fact that there had been a social anthropological study made of the village in 1940 was of crucial significance fourteen years later. The world of the Gambell people in 1954 was in many ways a very different world from that in 1940. Its scale and dimensions had radically altered. Whereas the Eskimos in the decade of the 1930's were still substantially living by the codes of the past, those of just a few years later were having to adapt to many new and different conditions of existence. But more than this was the fact that in the field notes and other data gathered in 1940 there existed an ethnographic base line for a study of that change, one which would not have to be constructed retrospectively years later but could be taken as a cross section at a point in time in the cultural history of the village of Gambell (see Hughes, 1953).

What, then, was this village like in 1940—its conditions of life, its people, and their historical background?

## The People

In their major concerns and general way of life, the St. Lawrence Eskimos are like most other Eskimo groups, especially those of the Bering Sea region. Their habitat, cultural and linguistic forms, and history of contact with the white world show similarities to other groups called "Eskimos," although it is no longer safe to posit a generalized "Eskimo" social structure or cultural pattern, as has been done in practically every introductory text in anthropology. Two compendiums have brought together information on the varieties of Eskimo groups (Weyer, 1931; Birket-Smith, 1936, rev. ed., 1959), and there is no need here to review the ethnographic relationships of the St. Lawrence people. Suffice it to say that St. Lawrence culture is a variant in some important dimensions, such as in kinship and social structure, from the generalized model of an Eskimo group (Hughes, 1958a). It does, perhaps, fit into what we are gradually seeing as a western Alaskan Eskimo type of sociocultural patterning that emphasizes clanlike units and patrilineal descent (see Giddings, 1952).

The Eskimo inhabitants of St. Lawrence Island belong culturally to the Siberian or Asiatic Eskimo groups. A customary distinction is made on the basis of language between "Yupik-speaking" and "Inupik-speaking" Eskimos (Swadesh, 1951). The Yupik-speakers include the peoples of southwestern Alaska, the islands of the Bering Sea, and the eastern tip of Siberia. All the other groups, from Norton Sound, Alaska, to the Ammassalik area of East Greenland, are Inupik-speakers. The closest cultural relatives of the St. Lawrence Island people therefore live on the Chukotski Peninsula, only thirty-eight miles distant, in the village of Ungwaezik (or Chaplino), and in the prewhite days the St. Lawrence Eskimos knew of the Alaskan mainland only indirectly.

Aside from the linguistic differences and the somewhat distinctive kinship and social structure, the St. Lawrence Islanders also notably differed in former times from the Alaskan mainlanders and from some of the Central Eskimo bands in not having the community house, the *kashim* or *kazgii* (see Nelson, 1899).

## The Land and Animals

St. Lawrence Island, about a hundred miles long and averaging twenty miles in width, is the largest island in the Bering Sea. It lies just south of Bering Strait, between 168°45' and 171°50' west longitude and between 63°00' and 63°38' north latitude. The geological backbone of the island is volcanic, although in the western end there are igneous and sedimentary formations. The central portion of the island (the Kukulgit Mountains) contains many volcanic cinder cones and fairly recent lava outpourings, some of these going down to the sea. Much of the terrain, however, is low and swampy, and there are wide stretches of tundra which support a subarctic flora. Inland lakes and lagoons spot the landscape in great numbers, and many streams and rivers drain to the sea.

As noted before, the climate is severe. The terse language of a Weather Bureau summary of climatological data for Gambell sets forth the picture of a very windy, stormy, and foggy island:

Temperatures at Gambell are moderately low, the mean yearly temperature being 24.2°. Extreme low temperatures are rare, due in part to high surface winds, high frequency occurrence of low clouds, high average sky cover and proximity to the Bering Sea. The record low temperature of −30° occurred in February 1947. The all time high is 65° established in July of 1952. Mean yearly precipitation is fairly evenly distributed to all months. Precipitation occurs on approximately 300 days of each year. Total snowfall is not representative of depth of snow on ground as the greater part of snowfall is blown from the ground by high winds. Since prevailing winds are from seaward, NE, very little of the displaced snow is replaced. Mean average wind velocities are high and storms with strong winds may be expected in each month. The all time high velocity recorded at this station is 100 m.p.h. from south, which occurred in October 1946. Average sky cover, sunrise to sunset, is high with approximately 32 days per year with clear sky.[1]

The plant life of the island is termed subarctic. No complete study of it has yet been published, but it includes "varieties of flowering plants as well as plants with seeds, mosses, lichens, grasses, creeping willows, creeping birches, mushrooms, and algae" (Geist and

[1] "Local Climatological Data," 1952, Gambell, Alaska, U.S. Department of Commerce, Weather Bureau, Washington, D.C.

Rainey, 1936, p. 8). One of the most important of the species used for food by Eskimos everywhere is *noonivak (Rhodiola rosea)*, the leaves of which are soured and usually stored for winter use. No trees or even shrubs of any large size grow on the island, although geological deposits have yielded evidence that in Tertiary times the plant cover was markedly different, even containing sequoia, or red-wood (Collins, 1937, p. 14).

Mammals indigenous to the island are the arctic white fox, shrews, ground squirrels, voles, and lemmings (Rausch, 1953). Sometimes polar bears wander onto the land from the ice pack, although they never stay the year round. Reindeer are a recent (1900) addition to the fauna of the island. Occasional visitors are wolves and red foxes from Siberia, cut off by the receding ice pack.

But it is the sea mammals, rather than those of the land, which are of fundamental importance to the St. Lawrence Eskimos—as they are to most Eskimo groups. The Pacific walrus *(Odobenus divergens)* is the most important animal in the diet in terms of bulk as well as taste. Also hunted, however, are the various types of seals —ribbon seal *(Phoca fasciata)*, ringed seal *(Phoca hispida)*, leopard or spotted seal *(Phoca vitulina)*, and the bearded seal *(Erignathus barbatus)*—and the whales, bowhead *(Balaena mysticetus)*, finback *(Balaenoptera physalus)*, and the gray or summer whale *(Rhachianectes glaucus)*. Only a few of the St. Lawrence Islanders regularly hunt the sea lion *(Eumetopias jubata)*.[2]

Bird life is extremely abundant. A complete listing of the many types of birds found on the island is unnecessary here and can be found elsewhere.[3] During summer months the air is filled with swarms of auklets, murres, puffins, and others which make their nests on the rocky cliffs of the island. Loons, cormorants, ducks, geese, snipes, jaegers, gulls and terns, auks, murres, auklets, owls, are all taken for either human or dog food. Birds form an important part of the traditional St. Lawrence Island Eskimo diet, and they have always done so, to judge by archeological evidence.

---

[2] For a brief yet informative discussion of some of these animals, which includes pictorial and descriptive data, see Kenyon and Scheffer's *The Seals, Sea-Lions, and Sea Otter of the Pacific Coast.*

[3] See Murie (1936b), Friedmann (1932), and the more recent study by Fay and Cade (1959) of the bird life of the island.

## Historical Background

It is probable that the first European to sight St. Lawrence Island was the Cossack explorer, Dezhnev, when he rounded East Cape, Siberia, in 1648 on his trip from the mouth of the Kolyma River to the Anadyr River. Russian expansion into eastern Siberia, largely in search for furs, had already begun earlier in the seventeenth century, and it continued after Dezhnev's exploit (although news of his journey was not known to the Russian government until almost one hundred years later).

By 1715 the native peoples of Kamchatka had been conquered, and it was not too many years later that the Dane, Vitus Bering, sailing for the Russian Crown, pushed out into the North Pacific on his first voyage of discovery. Although he did not accomplish his primary purpose—to discover the true nature of the relationship between the Asiatic and North American land masses—he sighted and named St. Lawrence Island, on August 21, 1728 (new calendar). In his journal he recorded the event:

On August 8, when we were in the latitude 64°30′ N., eight men who claimed to be Chukchi (a people known for a long time to the Russians of the country) rowed to us from the shore in a leathern boat and, when near, asked who we were and why we came. On being invited on board, they put one man over, who, with the help of large inflated seal bladders, swam over to have a talk with us. A little later the boat moved up to us and the men in it told us that large numbers of Chukchi live along the shore, that a short distance from here the coast turns to the west, and that not far ahead of us is an island. We located this island, which we named St. Lawrence, in honor of the day, and found on it a few huts but no people, although I twice sent the midshipman to look for them. [Golder, 1922, I, 18]

Russian interest in furs (sea otter and fur seal) stimulated much exploration in the North Pacific area, although most of it centered in the Aleutian and southern Alaskan regions. On his second voyage, in 1741, Bering reached the southern Alaskan coast, and from that time Russian fur traders continued to push eastward along the Aleutian chain from one island to the next, searching for ever more valuable sea-otter banks and fur-seal grounds, subjugating the native Aleuts, and leaving behind them tuberculosis and a decimated people. By 1792 Kodiak Island was the site of a large permanent village, and the Russian Empire in the New World was begun, to continue until the sale of Alaska in 1867 (Stone, 1952).

After Bering's voyages, however, the northern part of the Bering Sea had not been the scene of such intense exploration, and the only official expedition was that of the Russian Lieutenant Synd in 1764–1768. Synd sighted St. Lawrence Island, but mistook the several prominent mountain ranges for separate islands. This happened a few years later also:

Viewed from the distance, the outstanding feature of St. Lawrence Island is the large mass of low rocky mountains about midway between the east and west portions. If, however, the northeast mountain range is also within the line of vision, these two mountain masses, with the low lying tundra between, give the impression of two islands. Consequently Captain Cook, in 1778, was led to believe that there were two islands, and named the easternmost Clerke's Island. [Snodgrass, 1936, p. 331]

In 1791 Commodore Billings, sailing for the Russian Empress, sighted the island, but he, like Cook, did not land.

Through the eyes of early explorers we can learn things about the life of a people that archeological remains cannot tell. Contemporary accounts not only provide valuable ethnographic detail, but at times are case histories in culture contact as well. In a vivid account of this nature, the Russian explorer Kotzebue writes of the time that he landed on the southwestern shore of St. Lawrence Island in 1816 (as quoted in Collins, 1937, pp. 19–20):

We observed people and tents on the shore; and the wish of becoming acquainted with the inhabitants of this island, who had never been visited by any navigator, and also to give our naturalists an opportunity of examining this unknown country, induced me to pay it a visit. Two of our four-oared boats were directly put into the water, and we set out, well armed with pistols, sabres, and guns. . . . At a small distance from the shore, we were met by a baydare, (boat,) with ten islanders, who approached us without fear, calling aloud to us, and making the most singular motions, holding fox-skins in the air, with which they eagerly beckoned us. We easily perceived their arms hidden in their baydare, and therefore observed the greatest caution. After some salutations, according to their custom, which consisted in stroking themselves several times with both their hands, from the face to the belly, their first word was Tobacco!

—of which I had some leaves, handed to them, which they immediately put into their mouths. I afterwards saw them smoking out of small stone pipes, about the size of a thimble; they repaid my presents with different articles of their workmanship. After this friendly barter, I continued my way to the shore, which seemed to frighten them very much, as they ran anxiously to and fro, and some, probably only women, fled into the mountains. Some of them came up to us bravely enough; but their fear, which they in vain strove to hide under the mask of friendship, was visible. At everything we did they laughed without bounds; but as soon as any of our motions excited the least suspicion of hostility, they assumed a fierce look; they prepared themselves partly for flight and partly for resistance. Their friendship, however, returned when they perceived their error, and this sudden change from laughing to seriousness, gave their faces, which were smeared with train-oil, an extremely comical appearance. We landed opposite to the tents, followed by the islanders, ten or fifteen of whom assisted us, with great readiness, to draw our boats on the shore. This place appeared to us to be visited only in the summer, when the islanders employed themselves in the whale, morse [walrus], and seal fishery, as we perceived no settled dwellings, only small tents, built of the ribs of whales, and covered with the skin of the morse, which indicate only a short stay. A deep cellar dug in the earth, filled with train-oil, blubber, dried seals' flesh, and morses' teeth, likewise shows that they only collect their winter provisions here. They gave us to understand, by signs, that their real abode was behind the promontory, in the W., whither they invited us. A second boat, coming from the quarter pointed out, in which two women, dressed like men, looked frightfully with their tattooed faces, confirmed this assertion. How much did I regret not understanding their language, as I should then have been able to relate many interesting things concerning these people. In many respects they resemble the inhabitants of Norton Sound, described by Captain Cook; they are of middle stature, robust make, and healthy appearance; their clothing, which consists of skins, is filthy to the highest degree. My Aleutian, who has passed several years in the peninsula of Alashka affirms, that there is very little difference between these two people, as well in their language as in other respects. We observed several European utensils of iron and copper. Every islander is armed with a knife, an ell (2 feet) long, and adorned with large blue and white glass beads.

While our naturalists were strolling about the mountains, I entertained myself with my new acquaintance, who, as soon as they learnt that I was the commander, invited me to their tent. A filthy piece of leather was spread on the floor for me to sit on; and then they came up to me one after the other—each of them embraced me, rubbed his nose hard against mine, and ended his caresses by spitting in his hands and wiping them several times over my face. Though these signs of friendship were not very agreeable to me, I bore all patiently. To suppress their further tenderness, I distributed some tobacco-leaves, which they received with much pleasure, and were going to repeat all their caresses again. I hastily took some knives, scissars, and beads, and thus happily prevented a second attack. An almost still greater misery awaited me; when, in order to refresh me, they brought forth a wooden trough of whale blubber (a great delicacy among all the northern inhabitants of the sea coasts), and I bravely took some of it, sickening and dangerous as this food is to an European stomach. This, and some other presents, which I afterwards made them, sealed the bond of our friendly acquaintance. My host, the proprietor of the tent, and probably the chief of his countrymen present, after our meals ordered a dance; one of them stept forwards, made the most comical motions with his whole body, without stirring from his place, making the most hideous grimaces; the others sang a song, consisting of only two notes, sometimes louder and the time was beat on a small tambourine. . . . The island is called by the inhabitants, Tschibocki; and the country to the east (America) Kililack. The part which we saw had a most dismal appearance; it consists of pretty high mountains, covered with snow. Not a single tree, not even a small bush, adorns the gray rocks, only short grass sprouts up here and there between the moss, only a few stunted plants rise above the ground, and yet many a flower blows here. The arms of the islanders, which they use for the chase as well as war, consist of bows, arrows, and lances; the two latter are furnished with a broad well-wrought iron head: these, as well as their other European utensils, we afterwards learnt they received from the Tschukutskoi. They do not appear ever to have seen any European, to judge by the amazement with which they beheld us. Nothing attracted their attention so much as my telescope; and when I showed them its properties, and they really saw quite distant objects close before their eyes, they were seized with the most extravagant joy.

Following the visit of Kotzebue and that of his colleague, Shishmareff, in the first quarter of the century, St. Lawrence Island was again relatively isolated from contact until the great period of the North Pacific whale fishery in the last half of the century. Whalers and trading ships often stopped at the island to barter, carouse, and even hire some of the Eskimos as hands; but in general these visits

have left nothing of value in historical or cultural records of the
time.

A few paragraphs from a survey of the fur-seal fishery, however,
made soon after Alaska was purchased by the United States, briefly
describe the natives of the island in the early years of the 1870's. The
notes were evidently collected on only one short summer's visit, but
the author observed:

The natives on the island cannot be much over three or four hundred in
number, and are living in five settlements, about equidistant, around the
coast. They are well formed and hearty, genial and good-natured. They
are of Mongolian cast and build, strongly resembling Chinamen. . . . They
met us in an unaffected, free manner, showing no fear or hesitation, and,
coming upon deck, commenced a vociferous cry for tobacco, and that
alone; yet they were civil and curious; three or four women usually came
in each baidar with them, paddling like the men; the boats, about 14 feet
long with 4 feet of beam, consisted of a frame, very neatly lashed together, of pine, with whalebone fastenings, over which walrus-hide was
stretched; they propelled it with paddles and oars, which were also well
made. They live in summer-houses made of walrus-hides, weighted down
by logs and stones so as not to be blown away; and close by are the winter-
houses, which are under ground, with a tunnel entrance. The food of
these people is whales' blubber, cut in large chunks, of the strongest,
rancid odor; mullets from the fresh-water lakes, and caught in nets of
walrus-thongs; murres, small waders, walrus and hair-seal meat, varied
by geese and ducks. . . . They were poor, and had nothing for trade but
clothing made from the intestines of the walrus, walrus-teeth, and some
whalebone; but they had an ample supply of food, such as it was, and
their desire that we should taste of it was almost equal to our determina-
tion not to do so. They were exceedingly anxious to trade, and I noticed
that the women seemed to have equal rank with the men, doing more
than half the talking, and barter solicitation; they seemed to be warmly
attached to one another. [Elliott, 1875, pp. 222–223]

Of considerable interest is mention of the presence of only
three or four hundred people on the island. Another is the statement
that there seemed to be sufficient food. These assertions contrast
with the conditions said to have developed just a few years later,
during the time of the Great Starvation.

This major event, from which the population of St. Lawrence

Island has never recovered, occurred in 1878–1879. During the late fall and winter, and through the spring as well, over two-thirds of the island's estimated population of 1,500 died.[4] One reason advanced by white authorities who investigated the tragedy the following summer is that the Eskimos got drunk from liquor acquired in trade with the last of the whaling ships to stop on their way homeward in October and that the hunters thereby missed the walrus herds going by on the November ice. The ensuing starvation and deaths were thought to have resulted from that prolonged debauch. Whether it was more from starvation and sickness, as Collins (1937) suggests, whether it actually was from drunkenness, or whether it was from capricious weather conditions, as some modern St. Lawrence Islanders claim, probably can never be answered for certain. But the facts stand that during the winter of 1878–1879 several villages scattered around the island were completely decimated, and Captain H. L. Hooper, of the U.S. revenue cutter *Corwin,* who investigated reports of the famine in the summer of 1880, found large numbers of people lying where they had died. On another trip to the island the next summer he was accompanied by the naturalists Edward W. Nelson and John Muir, and the latter described something of what he saw in the following poignant passage:

A few miles farther on we anchored before a larger village, situated about halfway between the east and west ends of the island, which I visited in company with Mr. Nelson, the Captain, and the Surgeon. We found twelve desolate huts close to the beach with about two hundred skeletons in them or strewn about on the rocks and rubbish heaps within a few yards of the doors. The scene was indescribably ghastly and desolate, though laid in a country purified by frost as by fire. Gulls, plovers, and ducks were swimming and flying about in happy life, the pure salt sea

[4] Note the discrepancy between this population figure and that given by Elliott as the population of the island some five or six years earlier. The difference may be due to Elliott's faulty reporting, since he was on the island only a short time; or it may be that the much larger population, which is inferred to have existed by the many large village sites around the island, was successively killed off by several famines during the 1870's. Present-day informants speak of not just one great famine, occurring in 1878–1879, but of several, although the others were not so severe. In all events, however, Elliott's population figure is probably an underestimate; for Hooper, who investigated the 1878–1879 famine, counted several hundred bodies the following summer (Hooper, 1881, pp. 10–11).

was dashing white against the shore, the blooming tundra swept back to the snow-clad volcanoes, and the wide azure sky bent kindly over all—nature intensely fresh and sweet, the village lying in the foulest and most glaring death. The shrunken bodies, with rotting furs on them, or white, bleaching skeletons, picked bare by the crows, were lying mixed with kitchen-midden rubbish where they had been cast out by surviving relatives while they yet had strength to carry them. [Muir, 1917, pp. 108–109]

At least one old man vehemently claimed in 1955 that liquor was in no way responsible for the terrible event. His contention is that the winter ice, carrying the walrus as they migrated to the south, was kept from the island by southerly winds until late in January, so that the period from November to January was one of extreme starvation. Normally after the birds and spotted seals depart for the south during October and November, the slack in food supply is taken up by walrus meat acquired during the brief fall hunting season.

Whatever the facts with regard to the role drunkenness played in preventing the fall walrus hunting (see Hooper, 1881, p. 11; Collins, 1937, pp. 23–24), it is nevertheless true that for many years whaling ships made profit by trading rum or whisky to the natives in return for baleen, sealskins, and ivory. Very likely other factors were also involved in the famine, however, such as poor weather conditions. And, too, once famine had begun, no doubt its effects were quickly compounded by illnesses of many types, so that one cannot simply say that liquor was the "cause" of the famine.

Food shortages and famines are not unusual in Eskimo groups, and old people in Gambell still recall several times of extreme scarcity. There is even a term in the medical lexicon of the people differentiating between "starvation" and "poorly nourished." So conditions of food shortage are not unusual. But this cannot alter the extremely traumatic effects of the 1878 famine, for it is even today vividly remembered by old people who, as children, lived through it.

To summarize now, briefly, the history of the island since the great famine—further details are discussed in appropriate places in later chapters—in 1894 the first permanent agency of contact with the mainland was established by the Presbyterian church, a combined school and mission. The first teacher-missionary was V. C. Gambell, after whom the village of Sivokak, where the school was built, was renamed in 1898 following the drowning of Gambell and his family.[5] Since that first mission, there has usually been a teacher or missionary in Gambell each year, although on some occasions the post could not be filled.

Reindeer were introduced to the island in 1900 under the direction of Sheldon Jackson, a Presbyterian missionary who became the U.S. General Agent for Education in Alaska, and in 1917 a permanent village was begun out of what had been, for a few years, a herders' camp. This is now the only other village on the island, Savoonga, located on North Cape, in the center of the island. It is slightly smaller than Gambell, having a population of approximately 250 people. There are, in total, about 550–600 Eskimos on all of St. Lawrence Island at the present time.

Following the decline of the market for baleen (occurring roughly about 1900), the St. Lawrence people lost one of their very valuable economic assets as far as the mainland was concerned. There had been times when they received as high as $3.50 to $4.00 per pound for baleen from the bowhead whales they captured. Interest in the skins of the arctic fox continued, however, and during the peak market of the 1920's some St. Lawrence Eskimos were rich men. At one point a single pelt was bringing over $60 on the market (Steffen, 1958), and during one year in the early 1930's a Gambell man made seven to eight thousand dollars from his catch.

The history of contact during the 1930's is that of an island fairly isolated, trading its valuable economic resources for those items of white culture which could be used to pursue basically Eskimo goals, such as better hunting, warmer houses, and extra food supply. The reindeer herd had grown large, and it provided a continual source of security in case the sea-mammal hunting failed, as it sometimes did. The social organization was still patterned on inherited forms, and the major processes of social life were still directed with reference to basic kinship groupings. A native-owned store had been started early in the century, and it began to prosper during the 1920's and 1930's and served as the principal channel for the incoming of the white world's economic goods. A native village

[5] A photograph of Mr. and Mrs. Gambell is contained in Elliott, 1898, opp. p. 588.

council, organized on an elective basis, was instituted in the late 1920's, and it grew into a responsible community organization during the following decade. The council was organized under the authority of the Indian Reorganization Act (Wheeler-Howard Act of 1934, made applicable to Alaska in 1936) and given the rights of self-government in all those matters which do not contravene the constitution of the United States or that of Alaska.

## Gambell Village in 1940

In 1940 St. Lawrence Island was thus fairly isolated from the white man's world. Annual visits by one or two small trading vessels operated out of Nome or other coastal towns by Alaskans, a yearly journey by the Native Service supply vessel, and occasional trips by coast guard cutters or commercial ships were the only major modes of contact with the outside. A rare flight to the island by an airplane and short-wave radio communication completed the types of links with the American shore. With the Siberian coast, contact consisted only of journeys in small boats across the water separating the Gambell people from their relatives living at the foot of the Siberian headlands, which on a clear day can be seen in the distance from St. Lawrence Island.

As approached from the direction of the sea, the village was seen as a cluster of wooden houses arranged roughly in three straggling rows running parallel to the western beach (see Figure 3). In front of the houses and typical of practically all Eskimo settlements were the many whale-bone racks within easy reach of the water, onto which whaleboats and skin-covered native craft were lashed (Figure 4). The center of the village was clearly the square bounded by the newly constructed schoolhouse and teachers' quarters, the community store, the nurse's residence and dispensary, and the Presbyterian mission, the oldest building in the village and the first permanent white construction, which dated from the late 1890's and for many years served as church, school, and community meeting hall.

The fifty or so Eskimo houses were constructed of lumber imported from the mainland, and they could be grouped by a casual glance into two types: a dwelling resembling any small frame house one might see in a rural area on the mainland and a structure which, though square at one end, tapered to a blunt point at the other where, facing the sea, a small raised doorway was placed. The first type of house was typically the summer dwelling place, and the second was the structure in which a family spent the winter. Most families had a house of each kind. It was not until the summer of 1940 that the last remaining example of aboriginal design in houses was destroyed—a walrus-hide and moss-insulated, loaflike structure built over a framework of driftwood.

Stretching away from the village was a grass-covered gravel spit leading eastward to the mountain behind. Nothing marred the smoothness of this green plain except the two or three archeological sites—remains of old villages—in which the Eskimos dug for specimens to send outside for sale or to use in their ivory carvings.

The mountain itself served as the most prominent landmark for miles in every direction. It was the bearing by which boat captains steered when out hunting on the sea or which trappers returning from their camps in a blizzard tried to glimpse, for it marked home. It was also a lookout for game, the source of vegetable plants which supplemented an otherwise largely meat diet, a place of the spirits dwelling among the grotesque rocks and fog of the summit, the site of altars at which sacrificial foods were burned, and the final resting place for the dead. On it also was located the site of the oldest known habitation on the island, whose stone-floored house remains were buried under the talus slopes at the mouth of a hillside spring.

In such surroundings the people of Gambell, the Sivokakmeit, lived.[6] They took from the white mainland many items which were

[6] The term used in referring to the people of Gambell is taken from the aboriginal name for the village and the island, Sivokak. In consonance with the usual system for designating the different Eskimo groups, people living there are called Sivokakmeit—"people belonging to Sivokak." In a strict sense this term actually applies to but one or two living individuals, the only descendants of a group who are said to have been the "original" St. Lawrence Islanders, inhabiting the point where Gambell village is now located. All other present clan groups have moved to Gambell either from the Siberian shore or from elsewhere on St. Lawrence Island, and consequently the "real" group designations of these clans are based on the local sites from which the ancestors came. However, informants in the village now do occasionally use the term "Sivokakmeit" in referring to the present-day inhabitants, and this will be used throughout the book for ease of reference as well as etymological value. But its qualified ethnographic validity should be noted. For a more extended discussion of the various clan groups having ancestral homes elsewhere but now functioning as

*Figure 1.* Winter sea ice, with Gambell village and Mt. Chibukak in the distance, 1955.

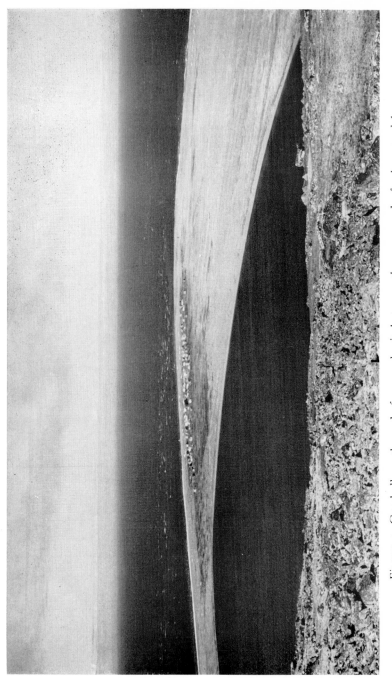

*Figure 2.* Gambell, on the end of a gravel spit, between the ocean and a fresh-water lake.

of considerable use to them in their lives as Eskimos. Thus one saw outboard motors standing alongside both the *angyaks* (native craft) and wooden whaleboats, the latter of which had been acquired years before from whaling ships. Rifles and ammunition were part of every hunter's equipment, as well as knives, saws, and tools of every description. Metal pots and pans had largely replaced wooden, clay, or baleen vessels; and though the seal-oil lamp was still always used, especially in winter, kerosene-burning pressure lamps were likewise found in most homes. Clothing cut in mainland fashion and made of cloth fabric was frequently seen, although for the most part clothing was made from the skins of animals hunted or tended by the people: seals and reindeer. The imported mainland style of clothing was used principally in the summer and was worn along with many items of native origin, such as skin boots. In matters of dress the women tended to be more conservative than the men, but they had taken up gaily colored cotton print material to use as the overgarment or "snow shirt" protecting their parkas (see Figures 6, 15, and 16).

This topic of clothing styles as well as other aspects of life comes out in excerpts from field notes taken on the day of the Leightons' arrival at Gambell in June of 1940:

All the village was gathered in clumps on the beach watching us. Five boats full of natives came out powered by outboard motors set down through a square hole in the stern half of the boat. The natives swarmed up the ship's ladder, each with a little package, some skin, some cloth, some carrying it in their teeth, some slung over their backs. They were all men that came out. They were helped aboard by the sailors. They began to bring out carved ivory from their bags and went into business with the crew. Money, candy, chewing gum and cigarettes seemed to be the prized articles. The men wore yellow canvas parkas over their fur suits. They were all smiles and cheerfulness. . . . After an hour or so the captain came ashore, and escorted by one of the Eskimos we went through the village with him. We noticed that a number of the boat racks were made of whale jaws; there were dogs tied up everywhere [see Figure 5]; there were lots of fresh walrus skulls with tusks still attached lying around, some being chewed on by dogs. There was one whale scapula

effective social subdivisions of Gambell village, see Chapter VI. The orthography used here for Eskimo terms is only an approximation and is described in the Preface.

which the Eskimo and the captain said covered the entrance to a meat cellar. There were many barrels of smelly oil sitting around, probably mostly seal; most houses had a rack of meat drying outside. . . . Most of the women wore cotton parkas of brightly-colored prints, apparently over fur clothes. They wore mukluks or some kind of skin boots, and many had on wool socks. Their hair was in two braids, interlaced with strings of red and white beads. Most of them had more or less tattooing on their faces, straight lines between the eyes and on the chin, or fancy patterns on the cheeks. . . . Many of the men had sealskin pants on. Most had ordinary haircuts, but some were tonsured. The children were all dressed like small adults. They looked very cute with their little fur ruffs around their faces. Most of them said "Hello," but didn't say much else.

By 1940, therefore, the culture of the Sivokakmeit had been affected in important ways by earlier contacts with the white world. The advent of a commercial market for fox skins had encouraged the trapping of what had theretofore from the Eskimos' point of view been a worthless animal; the demand of the industrial world for baleen has already been noted as having made possible the acquisition by the Eskimos of many items of white culture; further, the ready market on the mainland for ivory carvings from St. Lawrence Island —the excellence of which had by 1940 long been well known—influenced other complexes of behavior oriented toward Alaska. One of the most important, even if indirect, effects of outside contact was the introduction of reindeer in 1900, since new residence and settlement patterns were required as well as the instilling of sentiments toward game different from those in connection with the maritime mammals. Throughout all this, of course, technological items from the white world made important contributions to the Eskimo way of life.

Yet on the whole the changes that had been made were those of substitution and increase of content rather than change of configuration. In 1940 the Sivokakmeit were still living much the same as had done their ancestors before them. They were hunting walruses, seals, whales, polar bears, and birds. They were fishing and still collecting the leaves, stalks, and roots of plants growing on the hillside. They were eating, therefore, the meat and vegetable products their sea and island provided, supplemented with only relatively few of the white man's staples and luxury goods—except for that ubiquitous item, tea, of which they drank great quantities.

In its basic outlines, the social organization of the village had been relatively unchanged by contact with the white world, even though there were institutions adopted from the mainland, such as the village council, the school, the mission, and the store (see Figure 7). Ancient patterns of kinship prevailed, and everyone was reckoned a member of his father's clan. Traditional sentiments of reciprocity and sharing of food and other goods were still strong. Eskimo religious rites and beliefs were held by about half the village. The remaining people were Presbyterians, served by the mission which had first been established in 1894. The only white people permanently living in the village consisted of a trinity well known in culture-contact literature, the schoolteacher and government representative, the missionary, and the nurse.

There was no emigration from the island to the mainland of Alaska, although a few Eskimos had made occasional trading voyages, and some had even sailed on whaling ships in their youth. Further, to judge from the best evidence available, there seemed little desire to leave the island. Although theirs was indeed a harsh environment, the sentiments and range of knowledge of the group transfigured it into the best of all worlds. In effect, in 1940 Gambell was substantially an Eskimo village, manifesting traditional Eskimo sentiments and subscribing to Eskimo norms, although it was a village which had had some contact with the white world. But by comparison with what was to come, that contact had been of an intermittent and narrowly circumscribed nature, and the white mainland had apparently failed to touch the mainsprings of this people's way of life.

## The Village in 1954

Evidence of significant shifts in the Gambell Eskimos' way of life presented itself even before we had reached the village on the mile-long journey from the point of landing. As noted before, in that summer fourteen years earlier the entire gravel spit stretching from Mt. Chibukak out to the sea was covered with grasses and other plants, making a thin matting of vegetation over the loose pebbles underneath. This was green in the infrequent summer sun and provided a firm base for the women who walked almost every day to the mountain to pick *noonivak* or other vegetation for food. It was also clean and clear of the rotting metal debris of white culture. But now most of the covering was gone, turned over and churned under by tractors of the construction crews and military bases. Walking now was done only with considerably more difficulty on an insecure, shifting base.

The destruction of the thin edge of green on the seaworn pebbles was merely a symbol of a much larger set of circumstances which had come to Gambell in the fourteen years. Now hundreds of empty oil drums, rusted and filigreed by the rains, snows, and sea spray, dotted the gravel spit, providing mute testimony to one of the most far-reaching of changes in the way of life of the Eskimos, a people who traditionally had gotten heat, light, and some food from sea-mammal oil. Near the base of the mountain were the abandoned shelters of a small military site, rapidly deteriorating under the joint action of the wind and the search by local inhabitants for usable materials in an ungenerous environment. Some distance from the abandoned site there was another, functioning military camp, a more recent example of the enlarging world of the Gambell people. As we approached closer to the village, we came across twisted and bent sections of steel matting, intended, a couple of years before, for an airplane runway to link Gambell regularly with the outside world. But before the steel strips could be laid down after being unloaded and neatly piled on the beach, a sudden storm with very high waves had scattered them up and down the shore line, twisting and buckling the heavy steel and leaving some of it sticking upright from the gravel.

Some pieces of the matting were saved, however, and had been joined together to form a solid walking surface over the shifty gravel. This walk extended from the village itself to the beach and went past a series of well-constructed, white wooden houses which were also a symbol of further changes in the Gambell scene since 1940. The houses and buildings were the remnants of a weather station and Civil Aeronautic Administration (CAA) site which had operated in the village for some ten years just prior to abandonment the summer before our arrival. Entire white families had occupied the houses, and, for the Gambell people, this was an example within a few hundred feet of what the white world across the water was like. The buildings and houses were now standing empty, and, like everything else in this harsh corner of nature, were already showing marks of a losing struggle against wind, cold, and sea.

On that day of arrival, a Sunday, all was excitement in the village. Not only was a ship coming, with news, interesting passengers, the new teachers, the returning nurse, and possibly medical help from doctors or corpsmen aboard the vessel, but also something else was happening that day. The time for the annual encampment of the local National Guard unit—a new organization since 1940—had arrived; and all during the day, airplanes were landing on the metal airstrip which had finally been constructed near the shore with a second cargo of steel matting. Many of the younger men of the village were leaving their families to attend a two-week encampment on the mainland, an experience of which they had not dreamed in 1940. Army-style clothing was everywhere in evidence. The guardsmen were of course in uniform, and most of the other young men, too, and many of the older ones, were wearing various bits of army-type clothing—jackets, trousers, boots. Even some of the girls wore the ill-fitting khaki jackets instead of their traditional parkas.

In the midst of all this activity, not many took notice of the coming of anthropologists, at least not at first. It was in a military vehicle that we were transported from the beach, and it was without any formal greeting or welcome to the village that we found our way to the small wooden house which had been rented by mail from an Eskimo family. The arrival of white people was by now a commonplace happening in the village, something that definitely was not the case in 1940.

Yet in the bewildering array of new faces, sights, and experiences with which we were confronted that day, there was also a brooding sense of familiarity about the place and people—akin to a *déjà vu* sensation. There still, on the horizon behind the village, lay Mt. Chibukak, like a great, protecting mother watching over the settlement. At its base, filled from mountain springs, was the same lake from which the village had gotten its water years before. The sea stretched to the north and west, its waves on the shore still rolling the gravel in a shimmer of sound.

Most of all, perhaps, there was something familiar in the village itself despite the military bases and CAA site. The schoolhouse was as it had appeared in photographs taken in 1940; the nurse's quarters remained much the same; and the store and mission had not changed except for a coat or two of paint. Even many of the houses seemed to have undergone only minor alterations, although there were new buildings scattered about (and there were now the army base and the Civil Aeronautics Administration buildings). The houses were arranged in the same three or four rows running parallel to the beach, and whale bones still supported the overturned *angyaks* and wooden whaleboats. Perhaps one of the most familiar of all scenes was that of dogs staked out on long chains behind the houses, usually looking up hungrily toward one of the nearby meat racks (as in Figure 5).

There were obvious changes from 1940 in the people who greeted us during those first few days. Not only were they wearing different types of clothing from what had been the mode fourteen years before; they met the arrival of white people differently, and the inevitable marks of time had left changes in them. In addition, there were many faces missing from those which had figured in the photographs and moving pictures that had been taken by the Leightons. As we found out very soon, the death rate in the village, among both the elderly and the young people, had been very high since 1940. Yet even with these differences, there was a sense of the familiarity of these people to us, and we were accepted as acquaintances by many of them. We had, of course, grown to know many of them indirectly—through studying field notes and photographs—and we had carried on direct correspondence with some of those whom the Leightons had known particularly well. There may also have been the feeling that we were coming as friends of people who with their medical training had been able to give much needed assistance. In a village where health problems are severe, such kindness has enduring ramifications.

In a short time it also became evident that there was some continuity in the midst of change in aspects of the village's social life. The role of the church as an important center of activities, the school, in which public meetings and recreational events were held in addition to instruction, and the store, serving not only as dispenser of goods but as a visiting and gossiping center for the men, were examples. Above all, there was a familiar note in the importance of kinship and clan membership in regulating the social life of this community. Living as we did in the "compound" of one of the extended families, it soon became quite clear to us that social divisions on the basis of group affiliation still existed, even, to some extent, for adopted outsiders. The extent to which these patterns had changed since 1940 became apparent only after a much longer time and study in the village.

This perplexing combination of the familiar and the new, the known and the unknown, was the occasion, then, of the year's research.

## The Research Problem

With such knowledge as that above, the restudy of Gambell following a period of years seemed a natural consequence. World War II had intervened since that first visit of the Leightons; there had been much more contact of the St. Lawrence Islanders with the outside, and undoubtedly many more of them had visited the mainland. But beyond these few facts, before actually going to the island we could learn little in detail about the types and magnitude of changes that had occurred.

For a generation now anthropological literature has been concerned with studies of the effects of culture contact, especially that between a large, industrialized society and the small, typically tribal nonliterate group. In some cases the small group adapts itself to the new conditions, sometimes effecting adequate substitution of content while basic cultural forms remain unchanged, at other times retaining social integrity while the patterns themselves alter. In other cases, of course, the group crumbles and its culture is shattered.

The solid basis of knowledge of the situation in 1940, in addition to the fact that contact of a fairly profound nature had occurred since that time, presented another "experiment of nature," an opportunity in which could be seen the effects of increased outside contact in a particular village as well as the historical and cultural roots of some of those effects.

The utilization of this "experiment of nature" for the investigation of sociocultural change was thus the primary impetus for a return to St. Lawrence Island fourteen years after it had first been studied. This orientation was at the heart of the research problem, and it involved a detailed examination of social and cultural facts, an evaluation of the directions and intensity of changes that had occurred, and, finally, some assessment of their implications. A few words in description of methods used may help the reader to evaluate the evidence and conclusions subsequently presented.

Several kinds of data have been employed. On the whole, these were based on traditional anthropological field techniques, and they resulted in approximately 5,000 typewritten pages (5 by 8 inches in size) of field-note material plus supporting data, such as kinship charts. The notes included daily records of multiple observations of community life and personality expression; participant observation in many community activities, such as hunting and trapping, picking of greens, and other subsistence work; attendance at public meetings of the village and council, at church, and at social and recreational affairs throughout the year; and verbatim interviews.

The main technique consistently used was, of course, the key-informant method.[7] In all, approximately 16 "principal" key informants, both men and women, and 10 secondary informants were used during the year. These informants came from the major patriclans and were distributed throughout the power structure of the village. In addition to the above-mentioned informants, there were also special interviews on particular topics, for which different individuals often were used. Since practically all the men spoke English sufficiently well to carry out an interview, an interpreter was rarely used with them. With the women, however, an interpreter was much more frequently employed.

The interviews included those on general topics pertinent to this study of sociocultural change; more specialized topics within that broad rubric whenever necessary (e.g., kinship patterns and kinship diagrams); and interviews to fill in essential ethnographic data for a long-term perspective on changing institutions. There were also special interviews on folklore and on child-rearing patterns, on health patterns and mortality data of all people listed in the 1940 census, on the free associations of a sample of women about selected magazine advertisements showing aspects of life in the white world, and on changes as elicited by photographs showing the village and its people in 1940.

[7] For a summary article discussing this method, see Tremblay, 1957.

Small random samples of the village's adult population and total households were used for surveys of health and of diet patterns. Observations on household equipment and appurtenances were systematized to a certain extent by a check-list type of schedule made up in the field that included presence or absence of certain traits (e.g., electric lights) and ratings on other qualities (e.g., cleanliness of floor, etc.).

Finally, 4 Rorschach tests were given to individuals for whom life histories were also recorded (of which there were 9 in all); and we have several sections of diaries of daily household routine, kept for 3 or 4 weeks at a time at irregular intervals through the year by women of the household. The last major source of verbal data consists of copies of pertinent records found in the school and in the church and offered for use by the proper authorities in each case.

Photographs taken as additional sources of data consist in approximately 800 feet of 16 mm. movie film, mainly on hunting; 500 color transparencies; and 850 black-and-white negatives of all aspects of village life.

The first two or three months of the field period were given over, largely, to observation and to participant observations, with relatively few focused interviews. Such observations continued throughout the remainder of the year, but they were increasingly supplemented with key-informant interviews. The typical research day, during the spring and summer, consisted of a morning taken up with completing the previous day's notes and daily entries of observations and with the necessary household chores. The afternoons and evenings were used for interviews, and often, particularly toward the end of the field period, we were able to secure a total of four separate interviews in a day (each lasting an hour or an hour and a half). Practically all such interviews were verbatim reports, since we carried typewriters with us to the informants' homes. During the winter, and especially during the spring, the entire day was often given over to accompanying a boat crew on the hunt over the ice or through the meandering floes.

This description of methods may easily fail, however, to convey the deeper feeling of what life is in an Eskimo village. Such an understanding—which, with that of method, is relevant to the interpretation of evidence—one may find in the thoughts of the investigator which are usually kept in a private journal and have no part in a formal research report.

The anthropologist gathering his data does not work in separation from others of his kind. He does not seclude himself in a library or laboratory. Rather, he daily works with people, often in a small village, where he is close to what in one sense is his "problem," what in another sense are his neighbors. Whatever else he may be, he is a *person* in the village, one with domestic tasks and requirements and (presumably) the normal human complement of needs and reactions; these attributes are often as important in the success or failure of his research as is the quality of ideas and material obtained. The nonanthropological aspect of anthropological research may in fact even be accentuated under severe conditions, such as those in the arctic.

The hospitality and courtesy of the Eskimos to outsiders is well known. This was no less true of the Gambell people than of other groups, and any study of the kind we undertook would have been impossible without the generosity of the villagers and their leaders. To say that there were no disagreements or misunderstandings, however, would not be true. Such inevitably arise in any human relationship, especially when it must transcend both cultural bounds and the confusions inherent in a rapid change and blurring of cultural structures. But of the friendships made with these people and the high respect engendered for them, there can be no full telling.

The story of this research in Sivokak is only partially one of an anthropologist setting out each day with notebook and pencil in hand. It is, before that, a story of accomplishing such household tasks and chores as are required to maintain oneself in the arctic. Carrying water or ice to melt for water; shoveling snow away from windows and doors several times a day during the height of winter; attempting to weatherproof a house built originally for summer living by piling snow all around the outside; putting a year's supply of tinned foods upstairs in a small attic from which cans of vegetables, fruits, or meat must be brought down into the warm room below for thawing several hours before a meal; digging through ten to twelve feet of snow to uncover barrels of oil when the temperature has dropped to 20 or 25 degrees below zero and the stove is perilously low on fuel—these activities are not properly part of an ethnographic account of a group, but they contribute vitally to the completion of that study.

There is also the recounting of such things as straightening out bent nails and of saving scraps of wire, string, or paper against a day of need, because no supply is to be had in the local store; of acquiring skin clothing in order to accompany hunters out over the winter ice, as well as to move around the village comfortably; of borrowing a neighbor's wood saw to cut off steaks for supper from a frozen reindeer carcass. But one sees, too, a village where there is illness after illness throughout the year; where almost a third of the people have known tuberculosis and unknown other sicknesses; where, everyday, one visits or hears of someone who is sick and, at times during the year, also short of food.

A full account of this social anthropological research in Gambell would also include problems of attempting to take photographs of fox trapping in temperatures as low as —35° with winds of 40–50 m.p.h. and of finally giving up in despair because of freezing hands; of trying to photograph techniques of skinning foxes inside the trapping cabin, but of giving that up too when flash equipment froze; of learning, through experience, the aptness of often repeated warnings that the only way to keep warm in the arctic is by running and exercising the body so that it will produce its own heat and not by sitting on a sled as it crosses the island through the crisp, cold moonlight of a February night; of falling through the Bering Sea ice in January. And finally there comes the realization, on returning home after ten or twelve hours of hunting—tired, aching, hungry, and cold—that such a day is frequent and routine for one's Eskimo companions.

One would also recount the interviews conducted while a typewriter is balanced on outstretched legs and stories are taken down by the light of a single flame and the heat of a kerosene lantern; the six weeks of being snowbound, with no mail coming in and no possibility of getting sick people out to a hospital; and the topsy-turvy days of June, with sunlight to 1:00 A.M. and daybreak at 1:20 A.M. and children playing at midnight on the lingering banks of snow as their fathers prepare to hunt the last of the spring walrus or the first of the returning summer birds.

This account of social anthropological research in an Eskimo village is, in short, that of sharing, albeit only partially, in life as it is lived by Eskimo families and in nature as it is experienced by these people of the north. For them, in 1940, there was some knowledge of, but no longing for, the outside world, and to them, during many centuries, this island was the limit of hopes and the center for life's satisfactions.

# CHAPTER II

# A Clearing Away of Idols

THE story of the small Eskimo village of Gambell has several facets. From one viewpoint there are its unique past and its inherent drama as a Yuit settlement straddling the line between the Old World and the New, lying very near and possibly being part of the migration route by which the great land masses of the Western world were populated (see Byers, 1957; Hopkins, 1959). The village can be seen as a small group of people isolated for many hundreds of years, possibly a few millennia, from all but a handful of other human beings living on the easternmost tip of a huge continent stretching outward for thousands of miles. Something of this image was brought out in the previous chapter.

But Gambell as a village in a changing world has another aspect as well. It can contribute to the growing social science literature that deals with the impact of the industrialized world on the small community which, usually in too short a time, must develop techniques of adaptation as a sociocultural integrate or have its social structure overwhelmed and its people absorbed. Both interests, that in Gambell as a unique village with a unique past and present and that in Gambell as a "specimen in a series," another case having relevance to a scientific problem, have been involved in the present study. It is only the second that is featured here, however.

As stated in Chapter I, this is a study in sociocultural change centered particularly on a fifteen-year time period in the life of the village. Such a purpose involves three phases: (1) a detailed knowledge of the facts of history in those fifteen years, a chronology of happenings in Sivokak from 1940 to 1955; (2) discernment of the gross patterns that are apparent in that mass of data; and (3) analysis of the factors involved in bringing about the changes that are evident. In broad outlines, Chapters III–VI will be concerned with presenting the chronology of stability and change. The last two chapters will treat major themes in change and will analyze shifting orientations and behavior patterns.

Such a line of interest—in the changing culture rather than in problems of cultural statics—has been influenced by directions taken in much contemporary social anthropological research.[1] In the programs being conducted by the Department of Sociology and Anthropology at Cornell University, for example, the impact of the world of machines and massive social structures on the small, hand-and-muscle world of the village is being studied in several different places on the continents of North and South America and Asia. Several broad, consistent patterns of change over the past generation were seen in the preliminary research accounts of small rural groups in Peru, Japan, India, Burma, Thailand, Northeastern North America, and the American Southwest (among the Navaho). These patterns of sociocultural change are:

1. A trend away from an economic system that was primarily self-contained and independent, toward a cash economy with dependence on a larger social group such as the state or the nation.

2. A similar shift in governmental and political affairs from relative local autonomy to dependence on higher authority in the larger social group.

3. Changes in values, ideologies, and social usages which, although they constitute a break with the traditional and are increasingly influenced by outside forces, are not altogether in harmony with the economic and governmental trends noted above, or consistent with each other within a given community.

4. Progressive secularization of life, with an increasingly sharp line drawn between religious and other human activities such as work, governing, and recreation. [Leighton and Smith, 1954, pp. 81–82]

[1] See, for example, a bibliography of sources dealing with culture change compiled by Keesing, 1953. A recent article on this subject is R. J. Smith, 1957

The general theme underlying all these trends forms the most important specific focus for the present study: the nature of the relationship between the small sociocultural world and the mainland. A crucial aspect of this is the way the outside world is perceived by the people on the island—its meaning for them. More will be said about this phenomenological point of view later. The relationship between the village and the outside has both material or "hardware" aspects—clothing, weapons, food—and ideational aspects, such as new conceptions and sentiments of what is adequate and satisfying in life. Although ultimately it is the latter which are of most interest here, in order to establish some of their relationships to other empirical events one must look also at the interchange of material artifacts and the movements of people between the island and the mainland.

The initial form of presentation of relevant data will be that of social history within a given time period, constituting a survey of the range of factors which conceivably may be involved in sentiment change. But in order properly to assess any situation of change and in some way measure it, one must know what it is that has changed —a platitudinous point on the face of it, but it is well to remember that "sociocultural change" is not something occurring in the abstract. The empirical referents of the term are shifting patterns of behavior and thought, and it is with these that one begins in order to study those discrepancies in patterns taken at two points in time which we call changes. For an apprehension of departures from established patterns of behavior and thought, a background must be laid, a base line drawn. It is in accord with this imperative, therefore, that ethnographic descriptions of principal sociocultural patterns will be given at various places throughout the succeeding four chapters. These come from my own knowledge of the culture, as systematized in the Leightons' 1940 field notes and our 1954–1955 field notes, and from the literature.

Such an introduction of descriptive historical data is particularly necessary in this case, for published ethnographic knowledge in English of the St. Lawrence Eskimo is very limited. Until the present study, only one specifically social or cultural anthropological article concerning the St. Lawrence Island Eskimos existed in published form, that of Moore in 1923. Since that time works by myself and others have helped fill the gap in the literature (Leighton and Hughes, 1955; Hughes, 1957a, 1957b, 1958a, 1958b). There are a number of relevant sections found in works devoted to other topics, such as archeology (Collins, 1937; Geist and Rainey, 1936) and travel (Muir, 1917). References of varying quality are also found in an annual report of the Bureau of American Ethnology (Nelson, 1899), in other governmental reports of various types (Elliott, 1875, 1898; Hooper, 1881; Doty, 1900, 1901; Jackson, 1900, 1901, 1902; Lerrigo, 1901, 1902), and in popular magazines (Gambell, 1900; Geist, 1937; Smith, 1937; Nelms, 1945, 1946). A full and adequate ethnography of the St. Lawrence Islanders, however, is yet to be drawn together, that compiled by myself being only preliminary (Hughes, 1953).

## Conceptual Background

In this book no attempt is made to develop new theory; that is not the purpose. Nevertheless, hypotheses and propositions of "the middle range" do emerge in the latter part of the book—after the data have been examined—as being an important concern; and the principal theoretical relevance of the material is to the corroboration and refining of certain propositions.

This is not to say that the approach to the field and the gathering of data were done without benefit of any guiding ideas or approaches. I have worked within the framework of some commonly accepted dynamic concepts of modern social anthropology and other social sciences, particularly those in which the ideas of function, system, adaptation, and striving are crucial as relating to personality and man's behavior in groups.[2] It would seem that there is much truth in Herskovits' remark:

Today we are all functionalists, certainly in our field research. We probe for the relations between the institutions of the culture, as they channel the behavior of those who live in accord with them, without giving a thought to the debates that marked the introduction of the term, or the

[2] Such general concepts as these are, of course, protean in modern social science. A few of the sources pertinent to this point are the following: Parsons, 1951; Firth, 1955; Leighton, Clausen, and Wilson, 1957; Merton, 1957; Radcliffe-Brown, 1957. See also the publications of the Society for General Systems Research.

attempts to provide theoretical depth for what we have come to see as essentially a perceptive methodological instrument. [1959, pp. 394–395]

Nevertheless, two or three points of emphasis might be highlighted as being particularly important in this case. One of these is the attention given to what Malinowski would call the "derived imperatives"—culturally developed and learned modes of coping with basic requirements of experience which in themselves become fully as imperative for the organism as the basic needs. A simple illustration is that sometimes it is not so important that a man have food (basic need) as a particular kind of food (culturally derived need). In the Eskimo case, this may mean turning to white man's canned goods rather than using seal oil. Of particular importance are those more overarching needs which also come from man's ability to transcend the immediate situation. As MacLeod has aptly remarked:

The human organism is a biological organism, the human mind a product of the evolutionary process. If we are to understand why people behave like human beings, i.e., like social beings, we must first understand why they behave like animals; for man brings to the problem of surviving in human society the residues of ages of struggle for survival in less complex but more brutal environments. [But] what is unique about man is the developing capacity for objectification. With the increasing modifiability of the instinctive patterns man's behavior becomes increasingly regulated by objects, ideas and ideals that are no longer simply and directly dictated by the instincts. The sentiments, then, the most powerful of which is centered about the idea of self, become the real regulators of social behavior. [1951, pp. 218–219]

Speaking particularly of the phenomenological aspect of existence, he notes in another place:

Once we free ourselves of the compulsion to explain away the facts of direct experience by reducing them to atoms or tracing them back to non-observable origins we realize that the self is just as compelling, just as inescapable a datum, as is the perceptual object. When "I need friendship" it is the "I" that has the need. If we analyze away the "I" we lose the meaning of the motivation. [1949b, p. 63]

Such needs as these are closer to the "surface" of experience, yet are equally as compelling as any which may be abstracted as "basic."

In the foreground of my approach to the problem of sociocultural change in Gambell was a body of concepts and a functional frame of reference often called the "psychobiological" approach to the study of man. It is an orientation and not a theory, except insofar as basic assumptions of entity, structure, and process are the initial stuff of theory. My influences in this direction came most strongly through the teaching of Alexander H. Leighton, himself a student of the Swiss-born psychiatrist, Adolf Meyer, from whom the term and method of study of psychobiology derives.[3]

The psychobiological frame of reference is similar to that of the functionalists in social anthropology—especially those following Malinowski's preoccupation with the individual rather than Radcliffe-Brown's centering on the level of the group structures and group needs—since one of its basic assumptions is that man must be studied as part of animate nature. Psychobiology is perhaps more insistent, however, that such study be accomplished with concepts true to the characteristics of those integrates which maintain themselves against the environment by constant work and not with concepts more applicable to nonstriving phenomena. The processes of man's adaptation in the light of patterns of energy intake and expenditure, including the reworking of these in complex symbolic networks, are the basic point of focus in the psychobiological approach to the study of man.

Compared to anthropological functionalism, the psychobiological frame of reference also places far more importance on the integrated aspect of the functioning of the whole organism and on the artificiality of the division of man into "psychological" and "biological" and "cultural" needs. As Meyer would have it, "psychobiology starts not from a mind and a body or from elements, but from the

[3] For a work which shows the influence of Meyer's teaching, see Leighton's *My Name Is Legion,* as well as his earlier works, *The Governing of Men* and *Human Relations in a Changing World.* Another student of Meyer, Norman Cameron, has used the same conceptual approach to human behavior but labeled it "biosocial" and in his book *The Psychology of Behavior Disorders* illustrates the range of phenomena of interest and types of analysis undertaken with this point of view. See also Oskar Diethelm, *Treatment in Psychiatry;* Wendell Muncie, *Psychobiology and Psychiatry,* a text which embodies Meyer's teachings; and Jules Masserman, *Principles of Dynamic Psychiatry.* A recently published statement of Meyer's own expression of concepts of "psychobiology" is found in Adolf Meyer, *Psychobiology: A Science of Man.*

fact that we deal with biologically organized units and groups and their functioning." [4] Man lives, reacts, formulates in terms of a total organism, not separable parts; and such phenomena as processes of affect and cognition are inextricably involved in the adaptive pattern. Any research problem which too early and too narrowly defines the variables of interest generalizes to what is only a parody of human behavior. To quote Meyer again, speaking of the "psychobiologists":

We therefore demand that we take the mental functioning as a general part of the functioning of the organism and have the courage to make ourselves responsible for the total functioning. Psychobiology claims that anything that is part of a person—his hopes and his fears, his motivations and urges, his attitude toward right and wrong, and even his religious conceptions and beliefs—is as much a property and quality of the person as anything that can be weighed in the scales or measured by the yard. [In Lief, 1948, p. 547]

Especially significant in the psychobiological frame of reference is the emphasis placed upon man's probably unique capacity, the ability to forge and manipulate and accept as "real" the things of his imagination—symbols. In the adaptation and integration of the total organism, conscious mental functions, especially the capacity for symbolization, play a crucial role, more important than in any other animal species. This key function of symbols and ideational products in human group life has also long been stressed in anthropology. Culture is part of, perhaps the most important part of, the series of mechanisms by which man adapts himself to his environment. But it should also be noted that cultural facts themselves come to constitute part of that environment which imposes demands upon the organism.

The primary conceptual method of studying a problem using the psychobiological point of view is the inductive approach, with a minimum of specification and premature restriction of phenomena of interest. At this stage in the development of scientific knowledge of human behavior (of either an individual or a group), we must

[4] Lief, 1948, p. 591. By permission from *The Commonsense Psychiatry of Dr. Adolf Meyer*, edited by Alfred Lief. Copyright, 1948. McGraw-Hill Book Co. All Meyer quotations found in the present chapter are from this book and are quoted with permission.

gather a wide range of data concerning the functioning of the unit in response to the many-faceted demands of the environment. Searching out the "stubborn facts of nature" is therefore not to be eschewed; on the contrary, it, in conjunction with thought and concept, is the only path to uncovering the relevant factors affecting the total psychobiological integration of the organism in many complex patterns. Such "facts" may form part of the subject matter of a wide variety of disciplines, all the way from physiology and allied fields through psychology, anthropology, and sociology. But the lines separating disciplines, each with a distinctive type of question and concept, are not as important as the bringing to bear, on a particular problem of human adaptation, evidence gathered at many points on the entire arc along which a personality or a group meets its environment. As Meyer stated this in another place:

Man meets a world of fact, to be studied for what it is and does, whether the inquirer is there or not; to be studied by observation of the material accessible to common experience, with a genetic-dynamic background and a willingness to accept and use all the facts according to their role and importance in working and thinking in terms of an experiment upon man or nature. [In Lief, 1948, p. 591]

Academic purity is therefore to be sacrificed to an understanding of man, the animal with a conscience.

Masserman has attempted a statement of the basic principles of psychobiology, and we may take these as summarizing the present discussion. He noted them as follows:

I: Behavior is to be regarded as a psychobiologic expression of the whole organism, and not as a compendium of the sum total of separate "physical" and "mental" part-reactions.

II: Behavior is both constitutionally and developmentally patterned and must therefore be studied in the historical "long-section" rather than [only] in the phenomenologic "cross-section" of the current moment.

III: The determinants of behavior are considered . . . to be pluralistic in the sense that all possible factors—genetic, physiologic, pathologic, experiential—were to be investigated and given their proper etiologic weight. However, it is to be kept in mind that these influences do not act separately, but as vectors in an environmental field to which, in turn, the individual reacts as a whole. [1946, pp. 97–98]

At least some aspects of the approach to understanding human behavior which was just outlined have important similarities to a movement in modern European philosophy and, to a lessor extent, in American philosophy and psychology. This is the "phenomenological" or "existential" point of view, and a few words might be said in noting the relationship, although obviously detail must be spared.[5]

Phenomenology (or existentialism, both of which, though they are from different philosophical backgrounds, converge on the same basic problems and approach to knowledge) as a movement in philosophy began during the latter part of the 1800's and the early years of this century with the writings of Kierkegaard, Nietzsche, Husserl, Heidegger, Jaspers, and a number of other scholars, most of them German. Philosophical, artistic, theological, psychological, psychiatric, and even political thought has felt its influence. As one writer puts it, the term refers to "the endeavor to understand man by cutting below the cleavage between subject and object which has bedeviled Western thought and science since shortly after the Renaissance" (May, 1958, p. 11). It is an approach, a point of view, in which man is seen as a part of nature, interacting with it in terms of meaning relationships, structuring it by his participation in it. The individual's "experiencing of experience," as it were, is at the center of the existential or phenomenological frame of reference: "The phenomenological approach does not merely permit the inclusion of meaning as a fact of perception; it reveals meaning as the very stuff of experience" (MacLeod, 1951, pp. 227–228). The Cartesian assumption of an unambiguous distinction between objective and subjective, a principle of Western science, is therefore seen to be outmoded for an understanding of the nature of the human world.

For a social science, this means that new and more fundamental assumptions concerning the data must be made. The most basic of these assumptions is well stated by MacLeod in his paper, "The Place of Phenomenological Analysis in Social Psychological Theory":

[5] The discussion that follows is taken primarily from Tillich (1944), MacLeod (1947, 1949a, 1951), May (1958), and Grene (1959). A review of the concepts and history of existential thinking is found in Barrett (1958).

The main thesis is that if we are to understand the social behavior of man we must understand the structure of the social world to which he is responding—not merely the social world as independently defined by the omniscient sociologist, but the social world as it is actually apprehended by the behaving individual. [1951, p. 222]

In another place he once again stresses the importance of phenomenology as an approach, not as a theory:

The essential thing about psychological phenomenology is that it is not a school or a system but an approach. A phenomenon is by definition an appearance. Psychological phenomenology is the attempt to suspend biases and to observe and describe faithfully that which appears [p. 226]. Phenomenology is, however, not psychology. Phenomenology is sheer description. Psychology is a science, which attempts to explain; and to explain it must have constructs. There is nothing in the descriptive analysis of experience that can decide whether the explanatory constructs are to be quasi-psychological, quasi-sociological, quasi-biological, or quasi-mathematical. All the phenomenologist can do is insist that the system of constructs be flexible enough to deal with experience in all its richness and variety. No set of constructs thus far proposed has been able to do this. [Ibid., p. 228]

The implications of this approach are obvious. We are to try, insofar as possible, to understand the meaning for the people themselves of the behavior and thought patterns which we take as data. This does not imply an abdication of the need to be "objective"; rather, it enlarges the scope of concepts of process and interrelationship and methods of analysis which must be brought to bear in the effort at scientific understanding.

Relevant to the study of the individual in his sociocultural setting, MacLeod has pointed to the types of problems for which the phenomenological frame of reference is necessary:

Insofar as our learning-oriented theories are couched in a quasi-mathematical language without phenomenal content, they are, I am afraid, beyond hope. If, however, their primary concern is to discover how it is that the individual incorporates within his own behavioral system the characteristics of a culture, then there is clearly a role for phenomenology. How are the variables of a culture, its values, its customs, its prohibitions, represented in the psychological field? What is the phenomenal counterpart of an attitude, of a social role? What is the meaning for the individual of reward and punishment? And, above all, through what changes do the structures and relationships of the phenomenal world pass as the individual becomes a social being? These are all phenomenological questions of first importance. [1951, p. 239]

Particularly in this passage can be seen the conceptual congruities between the phenomenological point of view and the historic insistence of anthropology that it is not merely food habits or even forms of emotional expression which differ culturally among the peoples of the world, but, and this is more crucial to the sciences of man, the structure of the perceived world, the meaning for a people of their particular place in existence. Some of the most forthright statements in anthropology in this respect have come from Hallowell. In the preface to the book which is a collection of his writings over a number of years (*Culture and Experience*), he states:

A human level of existence implies much more than existence conceived in purely organic terms. Even if a naturalistic frame of reference is fully accepted, physical anthropology cannot give a complete answer to this question. The unique qualitative aspects of a human existence that arise out of conditions of human experience which are not simple functions of man's organic status alone, and that have variable as well as constant features, must be thoroughly explored in all their ramifications and given more explicit formulation.

Perhaps Franz Boas had some such problem in mind when he commented that one of the central questions of anthropology "was the relation between the objective world and man's subjective world as it had taken form in different cultures." At any rate, it seems to me that although we now know a great deal about man's organic status, seen in evolutionary perspective, about his capacity for the symbolic transformation and articulation of experience, and the wide variations in his sociocultural mode of life, the full significance of this knowledge cannot be brought to a logical focus without reference to an implicit psychological dimension. For a human level of existence not only necessitates a unique biological structure and a sociocultural mode of life, it necessitates a peculiar and distinctive kind of psychological experience in which a unique and complex integration occurs between responses to an "outer" world of objects and events and responses to an "inner" world of impulse, fantasy, and creative imagination. Besides this, a human existence is one in which potentialities for readjustment, reorientation, change, are constantly present. [1955, p. viii]

I have quoted at some length in order to let this cogent statement stand as the best expression of one very strong line of interest in anthropological studies. Here is stated in a clear way what many others conceive, use, and perhaps only partially express.[6]

Also evident in the preceding discussion are the agreements in point of view between existential or phenomenological assumptions and the psychobiological approach to understanding.[7] The central area of overlap is in the great degree to which the facts of existence for the individual, as these present themselves, are made the starting point (though not the terminus) of inquiry. This involves recognition of the incredible proliferation of symbols and the "meaning-function" of experience. Another aspect of similarity is in the conception of the whole organism as being involved in behavior— emotion, cognition, and instinctual urges all entering into the undifferentiated flow of behavior of man in a social context. It is felt that the fragmentation of empirical processes for the purpose of understanding a particular aspect of the whole cannot lead to an understanding of the behavior of the whole. As Cassirer said of the "autonomous sciences" developing out of the nineteenth century's spurt in natural inquiry:

Each theory became a Procrustean bed on which the empirical facts were stretched to fit a preconceived pattern. . . . Owing to this development our modern theory of man lost its intellectual center. We acquired instead a complete anarchy of thought. . . . Theologians, scientists, politicians,

[6] Other of Hallowell's works which are pertinent to this point are the following: "Personality Structure and the Evolution of Man," "The Self and Its Behavioral Environment," especially pp. 79, 83–84 (both contained in *Culture and Experience*), and "Culture, Personality, and Society" (in *Anthropology Today*, ed. by A. L. Kroeber). Finally, there is his article "Cultural Factors in the Structuralization of Perception," in Rohrer and Sherif, eds., *Social Psychology at the Crossroads*. Aside from Hallowell, anthropological literature is replete with statements of this point of view. Some illustrative references are Kluckhohn, 1945, pp. 97 ff.; Kluckhohn and Leighton, 1946, p. xviii; Sapir, found in Mandelbaum, 1949, pp. 544–559; Malinowski, 1953 ed., pp. 22–24; La Barre, 1954; and Redfield, 1955, chap. vi.

[7] Meyer's Swiss background and European training very likely exposed him to influences of the German existential thinkers, although this is not clearly stated. However, a student and co-worker of Meyer, J. C. Whitehorn, does make explicit the need to search for the meaning of behavior in the psychobiological approach to the study of behavioral processes. See his article "Concerning Emotion as Impulsion and Instinct as Orientation."

sociologists, biologists, psychologists, ethnologists, economists all approached the problem from their own view points. . . . Every author seems in the last count to be led by his own conception and evaluation of human life.[8]

There is evidence of concern in modern social science with overriding the encrusted boundaries of "disciplines" and of working toward a view of man which will more accurately approximate his condition in nature. To this end there are many contributors. Not the least important are anthropological studies showing the diversity of man's manners and mentation and range of functioning; psychobiological studies of the individual who behaves as a total, integrated organism adapting to an environment made immensely more complicated and rich by his own imagination; and, behind both of these, the philosophical approach of phenomenology or existentialism, which insists that we begin at a fundamental level hitherto not sufficiently considered, with that which *appears*. We may then move to a comparison of such "appearances" with what we may independently define as "reality."

This book is therefore mainly an inductive study in the long tradition of anthropological and archeological formulation, with a psychobiological frame of reference. It centers, however, not, as Meyer's work did, on personality in a sociocultural matrix, but rather on that matrix itself and its functioning as an integrate unit of nature. In Northrop's phrase, the study falls in the "natural history stage of inquiry" (1947, p. 36). Anderson has a nice statement of this approach to a problem:

Confronted with any large and complex problem, in any field, the scientist who has had effective training in Natural History knows more or less instinctively what to do. Everything looks chaotic at first but we do not live in a chaotic universe. There may be confusion in our minds but there is no chaos in the way the world is running. Faced with such a problem, the properly trained scholar looks around for significant repeatable patterns in the data and reasons back and forth from observation to hypothesis until he has found his way into it. The finicky pointer reading data, single sense impressions, lengths, widths, weights, so useful for precise analysis, are best deferred until we know what kind of a problem we are up against. [1956, p. 883]

[8] Quoted in May, 1958, p. 22.

The problem in this case is, quite obviously, "large and complex," and the methods used can broadly be classed with those which search for "significant repeatable patterns" in the attempt at understanding sociocultural processes. The study will not entirely stop at the point of discerning relevant antecedent factors involved in changing sentiments about the mainland, however. On the basis of trends seen in the data, certain assumptions concerning future patterns of change can also be attempted.

The sciences of man are unique among the various fields of study labeled "science" in at least one respect: both that which is studied and he who frames the inquiry belong to the same class of nature. This has one very practical consequence, aside from many intriguing theoretical and philosophical questions. It means, for one thing, that the natural course of existence of the pertinent phenomena— man's behavior over a span of several decades—requires as long a time to become manifest as does the life of the person doing the research. The problem of immensity of the time scale with which a science works is found not only in social science, of course. Indeed, the latter's problems in this respect are minor compared to those in astronomy, geology, or paleontology, for example. Also in common with the latter fields, in the sciences of man the opportunities given for direct experimentation and replication are few indeed, if possible at all.

Nonetheless, the importance of the longitudinal study in human behavior for both the individual personality and the social group is recognized and accepted, though in terms of predominance of type of research done it is the synchronic rather than the diachronic study which prevails in current social anthropological, sociological, and psychological research. Scott once pertinently remarked, with regard to the formation of the Ramah project of the Department of Anthropology of Harvard University, that "if biologists have found it profitable to spend their lives following the events in colonies of *paramecia*, it is likely that the sciences of man would be rewarded by intensive, longitudinal observations of a single community" (Leighton and Leighton, 1949, p. v). Such is the point of view adopted here. A definite commitment to long-term observation of phenomena and "continuity in social research" was part of the conceptual approach to the study. It was one of the main reasons for building further work in Gambell on a base which had already been laid some fifteen years before. It also figured in the attempt to reconstruct the history of event, reaction, and synthesis in cultural forms over the years intervening between 1940 and 1955.

For reasons of convenience, the data gathered on patterns of sociocultural change from 1940 to 1955 must be grouped into categories. Any categorization is, of course, only a construct of the observer made to fit certain needs. These needs either may explicitly derive from a theory or may be less formal and more devoted to pragmatic uses. In the present case, the categorization falls about midway between those systems which clearly have no relevance to the possibly theoretical implications in the data and those which are based on a theoretical structure. The data are organized for presentation in terms of demography, health, subsistence, and social relationships. Such a division comes both from the general types of categories used in the study of human behavior and from the specific emphases of the psychobiological and functional points of view discussed above. Insofar as any set of categories only organizes data for the purpose of ease in handling evidence in the search for explanation, arguments as to labels or specific groupings are fruitless. The adequacy of the categorizing in this or any case can best be judged by the use to which the evidence is put.

Along with the detailing of "objective" facts concerning each of the four areas of interest during the fifteen years, attention is also given to salient sentiments which are relevant to these chosen aspects of sociocultural life. Sentiments are defined for this purpose as "ideas charged with affect and exhibiting a tendency to recur." [9] This interest in sentiments flows quite naturally from the psychobiological emphasis in the background of the research, with the inclusion of feeling and affect as determinants in the actions of the adapting organism. An explicit emphasis on sentiments related to these areas is likewise an attempt to utilize the phenomenological frame of reference; for in the following chapters I shall endeavor to determine, for instance, not only what is "abstractly true" (such as mortality or sickness rates), but also "what is *existentially* real for the given living person" (May, 1958, p. 13), such as the meaning

[9] Leighton, 1946, p. 383. For a more extended and recent discussion of the concept of sentiment as used here, see Leighton, 1959, chap. vii. See also Adams, 1953.

of an extremely high death rate for him as a personality whose social world is disrupted by the early and unexpected death of friends and relatives.

Insofar as possible, then, in the following chapters something will be said about principal sentiments which the Sivokakmeit manifest concerning the facts of birth, death, and migration; about health problems; about the search for food, clothing, and heat; and about social relationships and changes in the types of people met and intensity of contact with them over the fifteen years. A brief discussion will end each chapter in the presentation of evidence. The remaining two chapters will take up the task of seeing the "general in the particular," of formulating more abstract patterns of change which might be incorporated into theories dealing with human behavior. Such a process will best accord with directives of Francis Bacon, still cogently applicable to the study of the complex thing which is man:

> One method of delivery alone remains to us; which is simply this: we must lead men to the particulars themselves, and their series and order; while men on their side must force themselves for a while to lay their notions by and begin to familiarize themselves with facts.

> The formation of ideas and axioms by true induction is no doubt the proper remedy to be applied for the keeping off and clearing away of idols.

Therefore, in the words of Meyer, "Shall we begin . . . the best we can with the facts met?"

# CHAPTER III

# Birth, Death, and the Community

BEFORE anything else, a human group is a biological population, subject to the universal processes of death and reproduction. It is on such a base that any social or cultural system has its foundations. The facts of population—size, age and sex distributions, growth, diminution—are therefore of interest from a number of points of view to the anthropologist studying a village. Many sociocultural patterns are directly influenced by the numbers and sex of human beings available for their performance and perpetuation. A tribe which loses many of its young men in a catastrophic war expedition, for instance, will very likely undergo change in family structure, division of labor, kinship and inheritance patterns, and other areas of life in which there is normally some contribution made by both sexes. Likewise a society which somehow lengthens the span of years given to man must develop special cultural patterns for dealing with added numbers of people past their prime. It must either allow space for them in already-functioning institutions or develop some Floridian haven for quietly easing them out of its way.

Another aspect of the influence of population on a cultural and social system can be found in the case of a generally burgeoning population (i.e., one in which not only the old are kept alive longer, but the birth rate increases and/or the infant mortality is lowered). By the very fact of sheer increase in numbers, the nature of social relationships is so changed that new forms of communication and regulation arise (Firth, 1951, p. 47). Kluckhohn also notes:

A plurality of individuals (of such and such numbers, etc.) continuously interacting together, produces something new which is a resultant not merely of previously existing cultural patterns and a given impersonal environmental situation but also of the sheer fact of social interaction. Suppose that two random samples of, say, 5000 and 500 persons are set down on islands of identical ecological environment (but of areas varying proportionately with the sizes of the two groups). After a few generations (or a shorter interval) one could anticipate that two quite distinct cultures would have evolved—partly as a result of "historical accidents" but also as accommodations to the contrasting number of actual and potential face-to-face relationships. Patterns for human adjustment which were suitable to a society of 500 would not work equally well in the society of 5000 and vice versa. [1945b, p. 633]

The growth of bureaucratic structures can be attributed at least in part to the sheer increase in numbers of people whose actions must be co-ordinated to some given end (Williams, 1951, pp. 179–180).

But the relationship is of course reciprocal, as Davis notes (1948, p. 552). Cultural and social patterns may themselves be crucial influences in determining the facts of population. Birth control or patterns of infanticide, social encouragements to fertility, health beliefs and practices, preferential mating behavior—these are obvious examples. Another, perhaps less obvious, illustration is in the area of shifts in population strongly influenced by or attributable to sudden and extensive change that disorganizes an entire culture and thus affects fertility. A rapid change of this type occurred in Melanesia and is believed by Rivers (1922) to have influenced the subsequent depopulation of many islands.

My present interests in examining the facts of population cannot be so easily placed or so thoroughly examined in this paradigm of reciprocal relationships between culture and population. For one thing, there are two broad cultural systems involved, the traditional Eskimo set of beliefs and practices and those of the mainland. Secondly, however, the relationship between cultural and populational factors forms only part of the background for the primary task, which is a survey of antecedent factors involved in the shift of sentiments relating to the mainland over a fifteen-year period. In such a light, population factors play a contributing role and are not the center of analysis. Given the fact, for instance, of a very high infant mortality rate or an abnormally high adult death rate, the question asked here is: what relevance has this for changing a system of belief? Posed in this way, the inquiry concerns the influences of population on culture. But the reciprocal relationship can also be seen in these materials—the influence of culture on population. When, for example, along with a high death rate in a village, there is knowledge or supposed knowledge of a much lower death rate elsewhere, leading to emigration, then the direction of influence is reversed—from cultural factors to population.

The concern here is therefore not with tracing priority in relationships between culture and population, but rather with laying a factual groundwork for inferences relevant to a larger issue. The fact that there is an interrelationship between culture and population is the important point. Accordingly, in this chapter I shall work toward a descriptive understanding of birth and death rates and migration patterns—and changes in these—over the fifteen-year period under scrutiny. This is done in the hope that it will afford a partial entry into fuller understanding of the shifting pattern of sentiments about the mainland between 1940 and 1955.

But intervening between a demographic statistic and human behavior is a perceptual and motivational complex which may treat an objective datum, such as mortality rate, in a variety of ways. Whatever else may be involved, behavior is always a function of perception and affect, more particularly when vital needs are concerned. Therefore, something must also be said in this chapter about the meaning of these demographic variables for the people in whose lives they operate. Such meaning can best be comprehended by use of the concept of sentiment.

## Sources of Data on Vital Statistics

The vital statistics upon which the following demographic estimates are based were derived from several sources. The first type of data consists of compilations of the village population recorded at four points in time. In the summer of 1940, a "census" was constructed by an Eskimo at the request of the Leightons which contained a listing by name and household of all people considered residents of Gambell at that date. In the years 1946, 1950, and 1954, the Alaskan Native Service teachers in Gambell compiled similar listings of the entire population by name, sex, and household. These latter listings, however, were more complete than the 1940 census, for they included the date and place of birth for each individual, his marital status and relationship to the head of the household, and his relative proportion of Eskimo descent. It should also be noted that changes in the population subsequent to each of the 1946, 1950, and 1954 censuses were written on the lists, apparently by each teacher. Thus, if any individual in one of the quadrennial censuses died prior to the subsequent counting, his name was crossed out and the date of death noted. Similarly, dates of new additions to the family by birth were also inserted, as well as the sex of the infant.

Although these appended notes on population change were not complete in all cases and had to be corroborated by other data (see below), they did form the basis for a charting of population size by year. By a collation of the censuses I was able to construct a list of all births occurring each year from one quadrennial census to the next. All these data—the 1940 population listing, those of 1946, 1950, and 1954, and the emendations added by the teachers—were used in a final collation of pertinent information for each individual who was alive in 1940 or was born after that year. This latter collation, to be described below, was accomplished by Jane M. Hughes, who prepared the various data for punched card machine analysis.

A second form of data gathering which contributed to the demographic materials was the systematic interviewing of a key informant undertaken by Jane M. Hughes, using the 1940 census as the starting point. With that population as the basis of discussion, the following types of data were obtained for each person listed therein: health history since 1940, date of death (if relevant), cause or reputed cause of death, migrations, marital history, additions to the family by either birth or adoption, deaths of children born since 1940, dates of additions to family, and other types of personality and sociological data. For the study of Gambell, there were in all some relevant 495 individuals on whom data were obtained. Much of the material relates more to the next chapter than this one; but I will note

*Figure 3.* Gambell village seen from the air in 1940.

*Figure 4.* The walrus-hide hunting boat (the *angyak*) in 1940.

*Figure 5.* Heavily laden meat racks and hungry dogs in the summer of 1940.

here that in some cases the key informant provided the necessary information on year of birth or death when this was lacking from the Native Service census materials. Moreover, since the key informant was intimately acquainted with personal affairs of this nature in the village, she was able to note some thirteen births to Gambell women which had not been recorded on the censuses, apparently because the infants had died before the teacher was able to enter them on the household list.[1]

A final source of data on facts relevant to population consisted in health and death records kept by the Alaska Native Service. Such records, though incomplete, did give a corroborative date of death in a number of instances.

These three types of data form the basis for the demographic estimates in the present chapter. In the course of coding the information for analysis, they were brought together, discrepancies were adjudicated, and the final outline of material was transferred to IBM cards for each individual appearing in the 1940 census (and for additions to each household, as well as for those new households which appeared subsequent to the 1940 population distribution). Thus, in effect, demographic data were obtained for all individuals who comprised, continue to comprise, passed from, or were added to the population of Gambell from 1940 to 1955.

Only some of the more common demographic measures will be used in the following pages, and elaborate refinements are not attempted. Because of the lack of annual censuses giving a contemporaneous criterion population, it is difficult to compute fertility or mortality rates by specific year, even though data on annual frequency of births and deaths from 1940 to 1955 are available. With certain assumptions about the village population based on its known size in 1940 and 1954, however, annual fertility and mortality rates can be roughly estimated.

For some of the over-all population characteristics, the fifteen-year time span will be used as a single unit covering which rates are calculated. Actually, for some measures this must be done, since in a population as small as that dealt with here wide fluctuations from one year to the next occur. These fluctuations are meaningful from

[1] See the Appendix for further details of the key-informant interviewing on demography and health, as well as reliability checks.

one point of view—that of their psychological effect. But for purpose of establishing long-term demographic rates, relatively more representative figures can be obtained by using a longer time and population series.

It should be emphasized at the outset that this is not to be thought of as a "population study," for the data are too crude and few for that. It is, at best, a series of systematic estimates of certain demographic features.

## Population Characteristics

### AGE AND SEX COMPOSITION

The population of Gambell in the summer of 1940 was 293 people. This breaks down into the age and sex categories shown in Chart 1.[2]

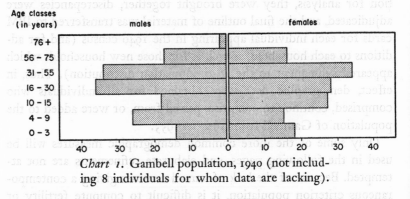

Chart 1. Gambell population, 1940 (not including 8 individuals for whom data are lacking).

The 1954 census listed 317 individuals, distributed in Chart 2 in a manner to approximate the age and sex categories of Chart 1. The 1954 census included people who were still considered part of the

[2] The age groups here are somewhat unorthodox, because of the difficulty of fixing a more exact age. The 1940 census gave no age data, and this had to be ascertained by other means (e.g., checking back from the 1954 census to obtain age in 1940). If the individual had died since 1940 and was not listed on the 1954 census, his age was ascertained as accurately as possible with the use of data in the field notes. This is the main reason for the broad age categories, corresponding, roughly, to "infant," "child," "youth," "young adult," "adult," "old," and "very old." In the calculation of various demographic measures which follow later in this chapter, the standard age classes will be used, since they are based mainly on more recent censuses containing more complete information.

village population even though they might have been at a hospital or school on the mainland.

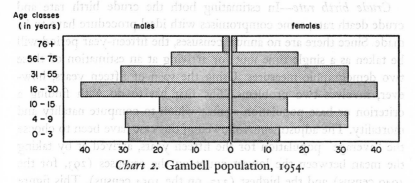

Chart 2. Gambell population, 1954.

In 1955 another census was prepared which lists a population of 291 individuals.[3] However, this figure, lower than that of 1954, included only those people actually in the village at that time. The age and sex pattern of the 1955 census is generally similar to that of 1954, although there is some difference in the younger age groups (11–19, 20–29, and 30–39 years). As will be seen in this and the following chapter, many of the people going out to the hospital are in those age groups. The 1955 census will be used only for computing one or two demographic measures, and the "standard" village population for the research year will be 317, that which is listed in the 1954 Alaska Native Service census.

Since 1940, as shown in Charts 1 and 2, there has been a slight shift in the age-sex composition of the population toward a more normal-shaped population pyramid. In 1940 there were comparatively fewer people in the age categories of "child" and "youth" than there are now. What this means is not clear, but it may indicate higher fertility or lower infant and child mortality at the present time than prevailed in 1940 and before that, since immigration has been negligible. In view of the evidence concerning sickness and its treatment, it is at least a reasonable hypothesis that infant mortality is lower, although even if true, the infant mortality rate over the last fifteen years was still very high.

[3] Listed in a memorandum dated February 5, 1956, prepared by Dr. Karl Reinhard of the Arctic Health Research Center, Anchorage, Alaska.

FERTILITY

*Crude birth rate*—In estimating both the crude birth rate and crude death rate, some compromises with ideal procedure have to be made. Since there are no annual censuses, the fifteen-year period will be taken as a single time unit for arriving at an estimation of these two demographic measures. Using the span of fifteen years, however, involves two problems. The first has to do with finding a criterion or base population against which to compute natality and mortality. The adjustments followed in this case have been to choose the "average" population for the fifteen years, arrived at by taking the mean between the lowest count on the censuses (293, for the 1940 census) and the highest (317, on the 1954 census). This figure is 305, representing a "base" population for each of the fifteen years. The second necessary adjustment is to calculate a yearly average of both births and deaths over the fifteen years, arrived at by using the total number occurring from 1940 to 1955.

Although it may seem as if the compromises involved with these data will too greatly distort any subsequent demographic rates and make them useless, the estimations are probably not too much in error. Indeed, they strongly resemble rates for the Alaskan mainland native population arrived at through much more systematic data (see below, pp. 55, 59–60).

According to the system outlined above, for the fifteen years taken as a unit, the crude birth rate in Gambell was 40.4 per 1,000. This figure is considerably higher than that for the United States for 1953, which was 24.9.[4] Gambell's crude birth rate is of a magnitude characteristic of those of economically underdeveloped populations (Brockington, 1958, chap. iv), which in recent years were, for example, 51.3 in Guatemala, 49.2 in Burma, 45.7 in Nigeria, 45.0 in Mexico, 35.1 in Puerto Rico, and 33.6 in India. On the other hand, the crude birth rate in other economically and medically developed

[4] Unless otherwise indicated, the comparative demographic statistics given in this and the following chapter are taken from either the *1955 Statistical Yearbook* or the *1954 Demographic Yearbook*, both published by the United Nations Organization. In the following pages, these two sources will be abbreviated as *Demographic Yearbook* and *Statistical Yearbook*. The crude birth rates given above are taken from the *Statistical Yearbook*, pp. 37–39, and refer to the year 1953.

countries besides the United States is considerably lower. As examples, in Canada it was 28.2, in Argentina 24.6, in Japan 21.5, in France 18.8, in Denmark 17.9, in the United Kingdom 15.9, and in Austria 14.8. These figures have been selected to illustrate the range of variation in birth rate against a background of economic and public health development or the relative lack of it. They do not imply a systematic sampling or division of countries into these two categories; but there is little question that Gambell's rate is quite expectable given its social and medical conditions at the present time (Brockington, 1958).

*Fertility ratio*—Another demographic measure is the fertility ratio or the "effective fertility" (Smith, 1948, p. 197; Goode and Hatt, 1952, p. 309). The fertility ratio is calculated by dividing the total number of children under 5 years of age by the total number of women in the childbearing span of life (15–49 years). The resulting quotient is then customarily expressed per 1,000 of the population for purposes of standard comparison. This measure does not depend upon accurate annual birth registrations. For this reason alone it would seem especially applicable to non-Western areas, where accurate vital statistics are not usually kept. Furthermore, since sex differences are eliminated as well as overconcentration in either the young or old age groups of a population, it is a more sensitive index of population replacement than is the crude birth rate.

On the basis of the 1954 Native Service census, Gambell is characterized by an extremely high fertility ratio. The number of females between 15 and 49 years—the potential mothers—is 69, and the number of children of 5 years and under in the population is also 69, resulting in an "effective fertility" of 1,000 per 1,000. In the census figures collected a year later by the Arctic Health Research Center (the 1955 census mentioned above), the fertility ratio drops a little, to 770 per 1,000. But it is still high enough to give evidence that we are dealing with a young and reproductively vigorous population, for other illustrative ratios from underdeveloped areas of the world tend to be somewhat lower. In the native population of Costa Rica, for example, the ratio was 686; in Guatemala, 666; in Algeria, 633; in Mexico, 626; in Tunisia, 622; in Burma, 559; in India, 549, and in Egypt, 546. Mozambique with a ratio of 777, the Dominican Republic with 749, and Puerto Rico with

725 approached the effective fertility of Gambell during this time (*Demographic Yearbook*, pp. 236–240). Characteristically, as with lower crude birth rate, the more economically advanced countries tend also to have a lower effective fertility than do the under-developed populations. This ranges from 278 in France, 293 in Austria, 335 in Switzerland and the United Kingdom, and 393 in Denmark to a few which are higher, as 467 in Ireland, 473 in the Netherlands, and 527 in Japan (*ibid.*). In the United States in 1950 the fertility ratio was 417 per 1,000, considerably lower than that for Gambell in 1954–1955.

Although the data are not amenable to the calculation of effective fertility for the 1940 listed population (the age groups of the women being more difficult to determine with any accuracy), it would appear on the basis of the general age and sex distribution that there has been a rise in effective fertility since that time (or else, as noted before, a drop in infant and child mortality). Even in 1940, however, the rate was no doubt well above that found in modern industrialized societies.

*Age-specific fertility rates*—The very high fertility ratios dis-cussed in the previous paragraph can be made a little more specific through use of another demographic measure. Data at hand permit a counting of all births occurring in a given year (August 31, 1954, to August 27, 1955) to women of different age groups, the latter data being taken from the 1954 ANS census. The resulting calcula-tions are the "age-specific fertility rates" for Gambell females in 1955. For women from the ages of 20 to 29 (there were no births to women under 20 years), the rate was 357 per 1,000; for women from 30 to 39 years, 428; and for women from 40 to 49 years, 133 per 1,000. A comparative figure for this measure which may help put it in some perspective is that of the United States, which had rates of 190 for women from 20 to 29; 84 for women from 30 to 39; and only 7 per 1,000 for women from 40 to 49 (*Demographic Yearbook*, pp. 283–294). On the other hand, the Dominican Republic, as an example of an underdeveloped area, had rates of 310, 255, and 98 for these three age classes (*ibid.*). The previously noted difference between birth rates and fertility in the underdeveloped as against relatively more developed countries is therefore also reflected in this demographic measure. Noteworthy, even so, is the unusually high rate for women over 40 years in Gambell.

On the basis of the data just given, Gambell's birth rate and fertility characteristics seem exceptionally high, so high, in fact, that one may be tempted to doubt the validity of the figures used. It will be helpful, therefore, to introduce a comparative note which will lend confidence to the demographic statistics for Gambell village. This will also apply below, in the discussion of death rates.

*Corroborative data: crude birth rate*—Results of an extensive study of demographic and health problems in the then Territory of Alaska [5] corroborate the general picture of high fertility presented for Gambell people. Referring to the mainland of Alaska as a whole, this report says:

While in 1950 the mortality for Alaska as a whole was only slightly higher than that of the States . . . the birth rate equalled 29 per 1,000 population in contrast to 24 for the States. The higher birth rate in Alaska was found for whites as well as for the natives—25 per 1,000 population in the former and 40 in the latter. [Chap. ii, p. 48]

It may be recalled that Gambell's crude birth rate over the fifteen years was 40.4 per 1,000. The higher fertility of the native woman as compared to that of the white woman is quite evident on the mainland:

The reproductive pattern of the non-whites—mostly natives—was different, with higher fertility at all ages than observed among the married women of the States or among the Alaska whites. [*Ibid.*]

Thus it is seen that Gambell's birth rate is as high as the average for native villages in Alaska. In terms of the high fertility in Gambell, then, we would expect a growth in population unless early death caused by sickness or accident intervened.

[5] Alaska Health Survey Team, Thomas Parran, Chief, *Alaska's Health: A Survey Report to the United States Department of the Interior*, 1954. The survey did not specifically include Gambell; but because of many similarities of Gambell to the mainland, the gross patterns found on the mainland are generalizable to Gambell. The mainland figures are presented here also as further indications of the fact that Gambell's high fertility and mortality rates, though very high, are not likely to be much exaggerated by the somewhat crude data with which we have to work.

DEATH

*Crude death rate*—Not only is the Gambell crude birth rate higher than that for the continental United States, but also higher— as might be expected—is its crude death rate (31.3 per 1,000), calculated in the same manner as the crude birth rate. For the continental United States, the corresponding crude death rate was only 9.6 per 1,000. Other countries of a social and economic development comparable to that of the United States had similarly low rates—France, for example, with 13.0; Belgium, 12.1; Austria, 12.0; the United Kingdom, 11.4; Denmark, 9.0; Japan, 8.9; Argentina, 8.7; Canada, 8.6; Norway, 8.5; and the Netherlands, 7.7, per 1,000 (*Statistical Yearbook*, pp. 42–45). Some countries with a lower stage of economic and public health development have also had relatively low crude death rates in recent years, such as India, with 13.6; Nigeria, 13.4; Costa Rica, 11.7; Nicaragua, 10.2; and Tunisia, 8.3, per 1,000. But other countries were perhaps more characteristic of the trend in underdeveloped areas, such as Burma, with 33.5, and Guatemala, with 23.2 per 1,000 (*ibid.*).

Death is thus a very prevalent occurrence in Gambell. Over the fifteen years up to 1955, approximately 91 per cent of the fifty or so households had at least one member of the household die. The average number of deaths among those houses so affected was 3.4. But there were some houses that had as many as 6 or 7, and one household suffered 14 deaths over the fifteen years.

*Infant mortality rate*—The infant mortality rate is one of the most widely used demographic and public health measures. In fact, it alone is often used as a general index of the health level of an area, for it is markedly sensitive to environmental influences.[6] For Gambell over the fifteen years this rate was 169.4 per 1,000 live births. The rate is calculated on the basis of the fifteen-year time unit, instead of annually; the figure is derived from the total number of cases dying at one year or less (31), divided by the total number of live births over the fifteen years (183). This is an average; the yearly totals fluctuate widely, and these will be given later in the chapter.

[6] Anderson, 1958, p. 11. See this article for a recent summary and review of studies dealing with the influence of sociocultural factors on the infant mortality rate.

The comparable infant mortality rate for the continental United States for 1953 was 27.8 per 1,000. The Gambell rate even exceeded that of India for the four-year period 1941–1945, which was an average of 161 per 1,000 per year (Davis, 1951, p. 35). Some other comparative rates for underdeveloped areas ranged from 62.8 in Puerto Rico, 81.7 in Nigeria, 95.2 in Mexico, 113.1 in Costa Rica, 127.1 in Egypt, and 127.9 in Sierra Leone to highs of 197.0 in Aden and 230.5 in Burma (*Statistical Yearbook*, pp. 47–49). Contrastingly low rates were found in the developed countries. The United Kingdom, for example, had a 27.6 per 1,000, a rate which was similar to that found in Denmark (27.2); the Netherlands and Norway had rates of 22.1 and 22.0, respectively; Canada's rate was 35.4; Ireland had a rate of 39.4; France, 41.9; Japan, 48.9; and Austria, 49.9, per 1,000 live births (*ibid.*).

Thus the measure of years given many Sivokakmeit is short indeed. What effects can such an extremely high infant mortality rate have on the sentiments of the Gambell people toward the white world?

*Age-specific mortality rates*—It is also important to examine the differential patterns of mortality in various age sectors of the population. But because of the small numbers involved in the Gambell population, it is necessary here to take an average over a number of years to establish mortality rates in different age categories. For instance, if only a single year were taken, there might be no deaths in some age categories. The procedure followed for estimating age-specific mortality rates has therefore been to take the figures of age at death for the entire study period and divide this by 15 to get a yearly average for the various age categories. There was a problem with 5 cases for which age at death was not clearly known; but in order to handle this, the figure was also divided by 15 (yielding .022 individuals) and the result evenly distributed over the assumed yearly average by adding it to each of the age categories. Although it is recognized that this is a somewhat contrived procedure for ascertaining age-specific mortality rates, and hence no doubt has distortion and error, nevertheless for purposes of outlining the gross tendencies involved, it may be accepted as useful. With the frequencies thus calculated, what are the death rates for various age classes, using a breakdown into criterion age groups taken from the

1954 census? (Note that the 1954 census is divided into somewhat different age classes for this purpose than was previously done for its use in the population pyramid, Chart 2.)

*Table 1.* Age-specific mortality rates for Gambell, 1940–1955 (per 1,000)

| One year or less | | 110.1 | 30–39 | | 34.3 |
|---|---|---|---|---|---|
| 2–5 | | 16.4 | 40–49 | | 17.8 |
| 6–10 | | 12.0 | 50–59 | | 52.0 |
| 11–19 | | 37.7 | 60–69 | | 32.5 |
| 20–29 | | 8.8 | 70 and over | | 68.0 |

Of particular note in Table 1 is the high death rate for young people in Gambell (age group 11–19 years). In this age category the Gambell death rate is 44 times greater than that for the United States in 1951 (*Demographic Yearbook*, p. 532). As will be seen in the next chapter, during the fifteen-year period most of these young people died from tuberculosis.

Since 1940 there has been much loss of older people in the population. This is expectable in any society, but it takes on considerable significance in a changing group, where the power and prestige of the traditional way of life have their most potent symbols in the elders of a village. As Durkheim reminded us long ago in a passage which is still very perceptive, though we would now quarrel with some of it:

What especially gives force to tradition is the character of the persons who transmit it and inculcate it, the old people. They are its living expression. They alone have been witnesses of the acts of their ancestors. They are the unique intermediary between the present and the past. [Durkheim, 1933, p. 293]

In over-all terms, 22 per cent of the people who were living in the village in 1940 died before 1955. And in the group of people who were the elders in 1940 (i.e., over 56 years of age), those who were "the unique intermediary between the present and the past," two-thirds have died in the last fifteen years (see Table 4 in the Appendix). The social effects of mortality are not seen just in mortality rates. Table 2 shows how death disrupts established family patterns when the adult who dies has growing children dependent upon him in any of the various types of parental role situations found on St. Lawrence Island.

*Corroborative data: crude death rate*—Turning again to the survey of Alaska's health (the "Parran Report" mentioned above) in order to compare Gambell's death rate with other Alaskan native populations, we find that it was almost twice as high over the fifteen years as that of mainland natives:

*Table 2.* Family status at death *

| | No. | % |
|---|---|---|
| Deceased was child or infant | 62 | 43 |
| Deceased was single adult | 25 | 18 |
| Deceased had children dependent on him | 43 | 30 |
| Deceased had no children or children were grown | 6 | 4 |
| Deceased was widow(er), with either small or grown children | 6 | 4 |
| Not ascertainable | 1 | 1 |
| Total | 143 | 100 |

* This table includes all those individuals who, born after 1940, died before 1955 (38 cases); this explains the difference from the figure of deceased in Table 4, Appendix.

The crude death rate for Alaska in 1950 was 9.7 per 1,000 population, hardly different from the 9.6 per 1,000 rate of the United States. But a more accurate view of the health conditions in Alaska emerges when we examine the crude death rate of the natives—the Aleuts, the Eskimos, and the Indians—which in 1950 was a remarkably high 17.0 per 1,000, nearly twice that of the rate for the population of the United States or Alaska generally. [Chap. iii, p. 2]

The report goes on to say something about health conditions, which are the substance of the next chapter but can be anticipated here: Undoubtedly this is an underestimate of the native death rate. Nevertheless, it effectively reveals that the health status of the native is far inferior to that of the population of the United States, and also to the Alaska white whose crude death rate was only 7.1 per 1,000 population for the same period. [*Ibid.*]

And a pattern that we have seen very apparent in Gambell is pointed up in the following:

The higher mortality of the Alaska natives as contrasted to the mortality of the whites and non-whites in the States and the whites of Alaska becomes strikingly more apparent when we examine the age specific mortality rates. . . . For the groups below 45 years of age the mortality of the natives is two to three times as high as that of the States non-whites, and three to four times as high as those of the States whites and the Alaska whites. [*Ibid.*]

No comparison of age-specific death rates of Gambell with those of the United States has been made, but the generalization pertaining to the Alaskan mainland would no doubt hold true of Gambell as well.

*Corroborative data: infant mortality rate*—As one might expect, the infant mortality rate for the Alaskan territory as a whole is also higher for native groups than for whites:

The infant death rate in Alaska generally in 1950 was 52, nearly twice the rate of the United States which was 29. Among the Alaskan whites, the rate was only 24 per 1,000 live births—again, this group including births and deaths of the military. On the other hand, the native infant death rate in 1950 was a phenomenal 101 deaths per 1,000 live births under one year of age, a rate about equal to that reported in the United States in 1900. The native rate is more than three times that observed in the United States in 1950, and four times that observed for the whites in Alaska. [Chap. iii, p. 3]

Another note has relevance for the subsequent chapter:

To a large extent, infant mortality indicates the effectiveness of community health activities and facilities. These data show that for the whites of the Territory health activities and facilities—when we include those of the military—were as adequate as activities and facilities in the United States. Not so, obviously for the native population. [*Ibid.*]

Thus Gambell's infant mortality rate was half again as high as that for the native populations of Alaska as a whole.

### THE BALANCE

*Crude rate of natural increase*—What is the net result of the cycle of birth and death in this village? The data unfortunately do not allow construction of a life table or net reproduction rate, but one measure can be computed.

As can be seen by comparing the 1940 and 1954 censuses and the crude birth and death rates, there has been an increase in population of the village since 1940. Such a rise can be expressed as the "crude rate of natural increase." To calculate this the crude death rate is subtracted from the crude birth rate (40.4 minus 31.3), which yields a crude rate of natural increases of 9.1 per 1,000. This compares with a similar measure for the continental United States in 1953 of 15.3 per 1,000.

The increase in population is seen in both a larger village unit and a greater number of emigrants. The total number of Gambell villagers as of 1955, including present residents, immigrants, and those who, though living elsewhere in 1955, were originally from the Gambell population, is 347. This contrasts with the 293 having the same demographic definition in 1940.

Although in recent years sanitation and health levels have risen, and with them apparently population growth, it still remains true that for many years Gambell had a difficult time in maintaining itself and providing generational replacement. For a number of decades it was able only to maintain a stable population of approximately 250–300 people, and the adoption of orphan children from the mainland helped in retaining this population level. Since the great famine and sickness of 1878 the population of the island has not risen appreciably above 600 people, a little more than half of them now in Gambell.

INCONSTANCIES

*The pattern of birth and death over the last fifteen years*—It was mentioned above that the crude birth and death rates pertained to the entire fifteen years taken as a unit. These rates were not constant from one year to the next, however, and it is important from a psychological point of view to see their fluctuating character. In estimating these yearly rates, certain assumptions have to be made as to annual population. In addition to the small numbers that one works with here, the assumptions make for considerable random variability when rates are computed and they therefore call for qualified acceptance at face value. The main purpose of these rates is not that of demographic statistics, but rather that of being some indication of the fluctuations in the only social environment that (until recently) is of direct significance to the people of Gambell.

There are no census data on an annual basis for the fifteen-year period. We do, however, have censuses for the beginning and the end of the fifteen years. The first is that for 1940, listing 293 individuals in the village; and the second, the Alaska Native Service 1954 census, lists 317 inhabitants. Thus, there has been a slight increase since 1940 in the resident population of the village. I will assume that the increase has been gradual over the fifteen years and that the migration factor has not seriously changed the broad pattern of reproduction. In this way, by taking the difference between the two populations (24) and dividing by 15, we can get an assumed yearly increment of 1.6 individuals. Additively, then, the 1940 population is 293; that of 1941, 294.6; that of 1942, 296.2, etc. The procedure, obviously inexact to some degree, is at least probably accurate enough to give a reasonable sense of assurance that the rates are not grossly distorted. This is particularly true when we see how much the actual frequencies from one year to the next contrast with each other.

*Table 3.* Estimated Gambell annual crude birth rate, 1940–1955

| Year | Adjusted population | No. of live births | Crude birth rate (per 1,000) |
|------|--------------------|--------------------|------------------------------|
| 1940 | 293   | 4  | 13.7 |
| 1941 | 294.6 | 7  | 24.1 |
| 1942 | 296.2 | 4  | 13.5 |
| 1943 | 297.8 | 5  | 16.8 |
| 1944 | 299.4 | 14 | 46.8 |
| 1945 | 301.0 | 8  | 26.6 |
| 1946 | 302.6 | 15 | 49.6 |
| 1947 | 304.2 | 9  | 29.7 |
| 1948 | 305.8 | 15 | 49.1 |
| 1949 | 307.4 | 16 | 52.0 |
| 1950 | 309.0 | 17 | 55.0 |
| 1951 | 311.6 | 19 | 60.9 |
| 1952 | 313.2 | 11 | 35.1 |
| 1953 | 314.8 | 14 | 44.4 |
| 1954 | 316.4 | 13 | 41.1 |
| 1955 | 318.0 * | 13 | 40.0 |

* These figures obtain only through August 27, 1955, when the fieldworkers left Gambell.

The fluctuations in births and deaths from one seasonal round to the next are shown in Tables 3 and 4. And likewise there are inconstancies in the annual infant mortality rate (see Table 5). It thus appears that there have been considerable variability and unpredict-

*Table 4.* Estimated Gambell annual crude death rate, 1940–1955

| Year | Adjusted population | No. of deaths | Crude death rate (per 1,000) |
|---|---|---|---|
| 1940 | 293 | 8 | 27.3 |
| 1941 | 294.6 | 11 | 37.3 |
| 1942 | 296.2 | 2 | 6.8 |
| 1943 | 297.8 | 22 | 73.9 |
| 1944 | 299.4 | 25 | 83.5 |
| 1945 | 301.0 | 3 | 9.9 |
| 1946 | 302.6 | 7 | 23.1 |
| 1947 | 304.2 | 6 | 19.7 |
| 1948 | 305.8 | 7 | 22.9 |
| 1949 | 307.4 | 8 | 26.0 |
| 1950 | 309.0 | 7 | 22.7 |
| 1951 | 311.6 | 6 | 19.3 |
| 1952 | 313.2 | 12 | 38.3 |
| 1953 | 314.8 | 11 | 34.9 |
| 1954 | 316.4 | 4 | 12.6 |
| 1955 | 318.0 * | 2 | 6.3 |

ability in the crude birth rate and crude death rate and, more
especially, in the infant mortality rate.

*Table 5.* Estimated Gambell annual infant mortality rate, 1940–1955

| Year | Births | Infant deaths | Rate |
|---|---|---|---|
| 1940 | 4 | 4 | 1000.0 |
| 1941 | 7 | 5 | 714.3 |
| 1942 | 4 | 0 | 00.0 |
| 1943 | 5 | 2 | 400.0 |
| 1944 | 14 | 0 | 00.0 |
| 1945 | 8 | 0 | 00.0 |
| 1946 | 15 | 4 | 266.7 |
| 1947 | 9 | 1 | 111.1 |
| 1948 | 15 | 0 | 00.0 |
| 1949 | 16 | 2 | 125.0 |
| 1950 | 17 | 3 | 176.5 |
| 1951 | 19 | 3 | 157.9 |
| 1952 | 11 | 3 | 272.7 |
| 1953 | 14 | 4 | 285.7 |
| 1954 | 13 | 0 | 00.0 |
| 1955 | 13 | 0 | 00.0 |

## Sentiments regarding Birth and Death

Sentiments of the Sivokakmeit about the phenomena of birth and death seem particularly sharp and clear by comparison with mainland culture. The occurrence of either is an event far more public and much more in the people's awareness than in mainland culture. Children are greatly loved and wanted, and having many children has traditionally been the woman's chief joy in life. This is not surprising, but there are some particular emphases in Sivokak culture which are noteworthy. For one thing, the practice of infanticide, even of females, was apparently never institutionalized in St. Lawrence culture as it was in some Eskimo areas. In addition, by contrast with some other Eskimo groups, orphans are particularly to be loved. Very permissive socialization techniques, much display of affection and indulgence, general lack of punishment, and widespread adoptive patterns all illustrate the "social encouragements to fertility" and love of children found in this culture. One female informant phrased it thus: "Eskimos think children are a joy in the home, a little joy in the home." Another said, "I've never heard of anybody not wanting any more babies. As many babies as they can have, that is the way."

In the traditional culture, the background for such statements was formally signaled at the girl's pubescence, when she underwent a ceremony which emphasized the importance of having children. In this rite, the girl's body was stroked and "shaped" by an older woman so that it would be beautiful and attractive. The girl observed certain of the prescriptions applicable for a pregnant woman, such as remaining in bed unwashed for several days and wearing a special binder which the parturient used at the time of delivery. She also held a doll in simulation of an infant during this time.

Although the public celebration of this ceremony has passed from the culture, the sentiments which it supported still remain. Indeed, the traditional cluster of sentiments regarding fertility and the importance of children has not seriously changed during the fifteen years since 1940. Only the passage of time will make clear how much some of the young people, particularly the girls, have been affected in this matter by contact with the outside. The influence of the mainland "small-family ideal" may make itself felt in their easier acceptance of contraceptive devices, against which there seemed to be general antipathy in 1954–1955.

To the empirical fact of death—final, irrevocable, yet totally expectable—the human intellectual and especially emotional systems must make some adjustment. The Sivokakmeit characteristically display an initial restraint and overt equanimity expressed by one woman whose husband had just died as, "Inside, my heart hurts, but outside I smile." The title of a recent book on the Central Eskimo illustrates this grim resignation to irrevocable fact as a widespread Eskimo reaction (*Ayorama*, meaning "it can't be helped"; see De Coccola and King, 1956). The same words were used by a Gambell person in 1940 in reacting to the death of his wife. As recorded by the Leightons, "we left as quietly and quickly as possible. Outside, Donald [7] was walking up and down with his baby. He asked if it was all over [i.e., had the death yet occurred] and when we said yes, he said, 'Well, it can't be helped.' "

Traditional St. Lawrence sentiments toward death were complex. On the one hand, there were the resigned acceptance of a grim fact of nature and a quality of fatalism in the emotional readjustments necessary after the death of a loved one. The occurrence of death, as well as the realization that one's loved ones and oneself, too, would someday die, was a fact that on the whole was met with an overt calmness. No doubt a strong support for this system of sentiments was the belief in the reincarnation of the deceased in the body of a newly born baby (see Chapter VI).

But there was another aspect of traditional belief which is also important and shows the great concern with death. This is the belief in ghosts or at least in a potentially malevolent return of the soul of the dead one or of the spirits that caused his death. The danger involved appears to have come from the harm the ghost itself might do as well as from its general contaminating influences in a household of the living; and there was a series of ritual precautions which seem designed to prevent such a return. They can be interpreted as efforts to break as quickly as possible the tie that bound the deceased to earthly wants and earthly activities.

Following Durkheim's brilliant analysis of the functioning of

[7] This name and all other personal names used in quotations from the field notes and records are pseudonyms.

religion in society (in his *Elementary Forms of the Religious Life*), one may assume that rituals serve to give coherent symbolic expression to, and "revivify" fundamentally important sentiments in, the life of the group. In this connection we may therefore briefly look at illustrative data from ritual observances of the traditional culture which pertained to the question of separating the world of the living from the much-to-be-feared world of the deceased. (It should be recalled that even as late as 1940 at least half the village was still practicing Sivokak religion.)

One expression of the insistence on the division occurred during the funeral rites. Following a death, many of the deceased's personal effects were ritually broken at a special "Destroying Place" near the village. After that, the body was carried to its burial place on the slopes of the mountain, and the reindeer-skin covering and all clothing on the corpse were slashed into small pieces, leaving the body naked in the fog and wind. No clear explanation of this action has been advanced, but one old informant averred that it was in order that the corpse would quickly disappear.[8] In any case, it is true that animals make short work of the bodies.

On their way back to the village after depositing the body, the group of pallbearers ritually stepped over a series of small stones which were thrown down by their leader, who also uttered prayers to the effect that each stone was a high mountain rising up to all horizons, stretching to the sky, "so that no harm will come from behind." When they reached the village, the pallbearers first went to the beach and rolled in the gravel. It was believed that unless they (symbolically) washed themselves, the animals of the sea would thereafter be offended by such close contact with the dead—and presumably not allow themselves to be killed by the hunter. Following this, the pallbearers went to the house of the deceased, where each one stood over a small fire and let the smoke rise up through his clothing. A woman relative of the deceased gave each of them a piece of sinew with a bead attached; the recipient wore this on his

[8] In a recent Russian novel which describes the life of the culturally related Maritime Chukchis living on the Chukotski Peninsula just opposite St. Lawrence Island, the author specifically notes that the burial shroud and clothing of a dead person are slashed in order to make it easier for animals and birds of prey to get to the body (Tikhon Semushkin, 1948, p. 78).

belt to ward off sickness. He also received a small piece of the walrus-skin rope that had been used to tie up the reindeer-skin bundle containing the corpse. With this he went to his meat rack, tied the walrus rope around all four posts in succession, and, at each post, grasped it and shook himself. Turning around, he grasped it behind his back and again shook himself. Then, picking up some seaweed, he went to his own house, and before he could enter, a woman threw some burning grass in his direction. The pallbearer avoided this, shook himself once more, and entered. Inside the sleeping room he disrobed and washed himself with water and the grass which comprised the insole of his boot. Next he built a small fire and placed the seaweed upon it. In the smoke from the smoldering seaweed he fumigated his clothing and himself, and his duties and ritual precautions against danger were now finished.

Meanwhile, however, the mourning family had to endure moderately severe piacular rites. They had to turn their clothing inside out and remain in the sleeping room of the house for five days with all lamps burning. They could do no work, could not disrobe, and were not allowed to raise the deerskin curtain for fresh air. After this initial period of mourning, they went to the mountain where the corpse was left; and when they returned to the village, they went through the same ablutions which the pallbearers had completed (e.g., bathing themselves with grass from their insoles and smoking their clothing in a seaweed fire). Following another period of days of less severe restriction upon their activities, such as not working, their mourning was completed.

It is perhaps indicative of the community's concern that until the immediate family went to the mountain after their initial period of mourning (and what they did there is not clearly known, but presumably they performed some sort of last rites) no one in the village could do any work at night. It was believed that in the few days just after death the spirit of the dead person was always brought back to the village by the spirits which had caused his death; and these spirits, hovering just above the ground, went from house to house and stopped briefly above all the sleepers. If anyone in the dwelling were working, the killing spirits might leave the dead soul there or even materialize the decaying corpse. In any case, sickness and harm would result.

One may, it seems to me, interpret many aspects of this ritual pattern as being attempts to make the line between living and dead definite and irrevocable.[9] The destroying of personal effects of the deceased, the slashing of clothing and bodily covering, the placing of pebbles to make high mountains, the fumigating of clothing and person in smoke, the ritual washing, and, perhaps as dramatic as anything, the preventing of the deceased soul's seeing homely and familiar actions if he returned to the village on those nights just following death—all these can be seen as actions intended to make unambiguous the status of the living as opposed to the dead. It was not that the deceased person had not been loved in life or that his memory was no longer revered, but that there was danger in association of his soul with living people.

Thus death was to be feared on at least two levels: (1) the loss of loved friends and relatives, which called for profound emotional readjustments—a part of which might be assuaged by the reincarnation belief—and (2) fear of the possibly malevolent return of the shade of the dead person. These sentiments were expressed in actions intended to render clear to both the survivors and the departed soul that there was a dividing line between the living and dead worlds which must be respected by both. There were, in addition, attempts to "decontaminate" oneself from participation in a funeral—the peripheries of the world of the dead—and a reiteration of the insistence that the animal world must be accorded proper ritual respect.

The ceremonial complex just described does not, of course, exist in the present day, with its Presbyterian funeral services. But all indications are that many sentiments of the fear of the dead still linger, and it is understandable that the feelings formerly expressed (and generated) in the rituals cannot have disappeared so quickly from a group in which a heavy burden of death must be intellectually and emotionally accepted.

There were two funerals during the year of research. In common with the ancient practice, both of them were held as quickly as possible, within twenty-four hours after the death. The types of

[9] Lantis (1947, p. 121) feels that such a separation of the survivors from the deceased is one of the common features of the funeral complex in Alaskan Eskimo ceremonialism.

reactions to death and some of the habits connected with it, already discussed as found in 1940, were likewise seen fifteen years later —a marked emphasis on the sentiment that "it can't be helped," a withholding of grief and an attempt to make the affair ostensibly as matter-of-fact as possible, the washing and dressing of the body by close female relatives, and, following the ceremony in the church, the quick transit to the mountainside by sled. It also tends still to be true that people of distinction are buried relatively higher on the slope than individuals of lesser prestige, such as women. Sometimes also, apparently, articles of value are destroyed about the coffin, as was done in the aboriginal funeral pattern.

Coffins for the deceased are made by the Welfare Committee of the village council (see Chapter VI), and the pallbearers consist mostly, though not exclusively, of clan relatives of the dead person, if one may judge by the two funerals witnessed. Following the death, there is no commonly accepted period of mourning by the family or relatives.

There is another aspect of the phenomenon of death and its cultural interpretation which is of interest, for it pertains to the interlocking of Christian theology with areas of Sivokakmeit life which are especially vulnerable. In traditional St. Lawrence belief, the afterlife did not promise much to the inhabitant of the present world. Beliefs about the nature of the afterworld, who went there, and qualifications for entry were confused and uncodified. There were, as in other Eskimo cultures, several "spheres" of the afterlife, with entry depending upon one's status at death and not upon one's ethical behavior in life. Some evidence exists that at least part of the attraction in becoming Christian is the clear and unequivocal nature of a promised afterlife to those who qualify. In a life situation in which there is a great deal of death and the omnipresent probability that one will be cut off from family and friends, belief in the possibility of a reunion with them after death is potentially very attractive. This very sentiment has been verbalized by the Sivokakmeit themselves, and it has a reasonable congruence with some of the major structural features of the Eskimo belief system and their life situation.

Today, as noted above, a deceased person is buried on the day of death or, if that is not feasible, the next day. But although the funeral is hastened, the dead person is not forgotten. Sentiments of one

elderly man are recorded in the following passage: "He said that
sometimes he can't go to sleep at night, because he thinks of the
people he has known who are dead now; he tosses and turns all
night. He said that he has done a lot of mourning in his life. He
thinks of his wife and of the other people." In 1955 a movie was
shown to the village which had been filmed in the summer of 1940
by the Leightons. The Gambell people had not earlier seen this film,
which showed many aspects of life in the village some fifteen years
before and many people who since had died. A statement made to us
by a number of people following the public showing summarized
many other sentiments heard throughout the year: "Thank you
for bringing our sons and daughters back to us." And an elderly man,
discussing death, said, "All over the world, he fall down. Too
bad. . . . We like a little more [time]."

Thus, in a world in which the elements of nature seem to combine
overwhelmingly against human desire and in which the animals
must be killed and their flesh consumed in order that man may live,
the hazards of life and the imminence of death hover about the
Eskimo from his earliest days. Death from hunting accidents, from
drifting away on the ice, from drowning, from being lost in a
blizzard, and, most of all, from sickness—these are ever-recurrent
themes in the life stories of the Sivokakmeit. There is no one who
has not lost either siblings, childhood friends, parents, spouse, or
children through some form of premature death. Thus what out-
wardly may appear unfeeling in face of the death of a person with
whom one has had close affectional ties is actually a withholding
of emotion, a culturally-encouraged inhibition of prolonged expression of grief. And with this loss there appears to come a
heightening of social bonds that remain and emphasis on simply
being with people and on public expressions of solidarity. This was
clearly expressed by a phrase heard more than once, "It's not good
for people to be by themselves—too much thinking."

## The Movement of Peoples

It is impossible to make numerical statements about migration of
the Gambell people prior to 1940, but it is clearly known from field-
note materials that the principal movements of population were
confined to the island itself. People moved to and from their

trapping or hunting camps, for instance, or from one village to another. There had been almost no emigration of a permanent nature to the Alaskan mainland, although a few men had worked on whaling vessels and others had made trading voyages to Nome. The annual trips to Siberia have also been mentioned. During the 1920's and 1930's, one or two families of King and Diomede Island Eskimo came to Gambell from Nome to live for a year or two. Other immigrants of a more permanent nature were native orphan children adopted from Nome.

Since 1940, however, the migration patterns have changed markedly. At first it was the young men leaving for the army, but during the last few years the stream of sick people (mostly tubercular patients) going outside to the mainland hospitals has greatly increased. In addition, there have been more people who have decided to settle permanently on the mainland. Some of these individuals who go outside add to the total migratory turnover of the population by returning to Gambell and then visiting the hospital again for a second or possibly a third time.

Through the systematic census interviewing by use of a key informant, which has already been mentioned, the general mobility pattern of living people who are from Gambell was obtained (see Table 6). It refers to the situation in 1955 and does not include as emigrants those individuals then in hospitals. The significance of the total number (347) in relation to the population increase of the village since 1940 has been discussed above.

*Table 6.* Estimated mobility status of Gambell people, 1955

|  | No. | % |
| --- | --- | --- |
| Native, resident of Gambell | 282 | 81 |
| Permanent emigrant | 31 | 9 |
| Emigrant, but returned to Gambell | 26 | 8 |
| In army or school | 8 | 2 |
| Total | 347 | 100 |

Migration to the mainland has now become of vital concern to many Sivokakmeit. The thirty-one people listed as "permanent emigrants" include at least two family groups who have migrated to the mainland for better jobs. In both cases, going to the hospital was the first step in the process of family emigration. Some people decided to remain on the mainland after leaving the hospital; and in another case a man took his children with him and looked for a job so that the family could be nearer their mother, who was hospitalized. In other cases, leaving the island to attend the native high school has proved to be the bridge to permanent emigration. Some of the young people have decided to remain on the mainland and find jobs there following graduation.

*Table* 7. Movements to the hospital

|  | No. | % |
|---|---|---|
| Is in hospital now . . . . . . . . . | 19 | 5 |
| Has been in once . . . . . . . . . . | 47 | 14 |
| Has been in twice or more . . . . . . . | 14 | 4 |
| Has never been in . . . . . . . . . | 267 | 77 |
| Total | 347 | 100 |

The extent to which journeys to and from the hospital contribute to the total movement to the mainland can be seen in Table 7. I will return to the subject of hospitalization in the next chapter, when considering the relation of ill-health to the changing pattern of sentiments toward the mainland.

## Sentiments about Migration

In a survey conducted in 1955,[10] two questions bearing on migration were included. To the first question, "Have you ever wanted to move away from here very much, but didn't?" the 25 respondents answered in the following manner: 10 replied "no"; 12 answered "yes"; and 3 gave no answer. The second question posed a hypothetical situation: "Suppose the head of the household had a chance for a job in a place on the mainland for more money than he is making now—what do you think he ought to do?" This was followed by a series of alternative responses. Some 14 people chose the alternative "take the job and move." Only one indicated that

[10] The survey was mainly concerned with health, although some other general questions, such as those cited, were also asked. A small random sample consisting of 20 informants 18 years of age and over (approximately a 15 per cent sample) was initially chosen; but 5 additional protocols taken from people for whom life histories were being recorded have been added in the total above. The sample is small, but it gives some complementary materials to the great mass of observations and recorded sentiments in the field notes which echo the same theme.

he would "move away with the family but try to keep a place here as a permanent home." There were 4 who agreed that they would "take the job, but let the family stay on living here"; and another 4 said they would "turn down the job." Two failed to answer this hypothetical question. In all, the aspirations toward emigration are obvious in these responses.

A statement made in 1955 by one of the leaders of the village—a principal "opinion setter" for many people—is particularly important in epitomizing patterns of feeling that are widespread. He said, summarizing an entire complex of motivations toward emigration: "Sometimes I get tired. I think that if I could find a job somewhere and find a place where my children could get a good education, and have good doctors and nurses, I would leave the island."

In Chapter V, I will have more to say about the importance of the "job" as a reason for emigration. But note here the three main points of his statement: (1) subsistence, (2) education, (3) health. These themes were heard over and over again throughout the year from people wanting to go to the mainland.

Sentiments toward emigration in 1940 were quite different. An observation by an elderly man at that time who was an important leader, a setter of standards for many of the population, can serve as an example. This elder, a shaman and a man of wealth, who had traveled to the mainland several times on trading voyages in his younger days, said in referring to the outside: "Too many people. All the time soldiers, lawyers—too much law. This is the best place. Here nobody starve—when catch whale, cut 'em up, each house get piece. If some people no go to corral for reindeer, others bring back many hides, give them some." The fact also that no one ventured to go "outside" even though transportation was available is presumptive evidence for his generalization.

## Summary

The major features of Gambell's demographic pattern over the fifteen years can be summarized briefly as a high birth rate, a very high infant mortality rate, a high death rate (particularly among the young people), and an increasing though not yet great emigration to the mainland. The last, however, is accompanied by decided aspirations toward emigration on the part of many people. What all these features amount to is, in effect, a considerable turnover in the population, though its size still remained fairly small, and a comparative inconstancy in the physical composition of the social environment of the native village itself. The latter is also shown dramatically by the fluctuations in birth and death rates from year to year. There is, above all, general concern with the fragility of life and the fear of death.

# CHAPTER IV

# Into a World of Sickness

TWO statements set the frame for an examination of health as a factor in the sociocultural processes of Gambell village:

The indigenous peoples of Native Alaska are the victims of sickness, crippling conditions and premature death to a degree exceeded in very few parts of the world. Among them, health problems are nearly out of hand.

The child is born into a world of sickness from the other world.

The first statement is that of the outside observer, a conclusion based on the extensive Parran survey of Alaska's health problems mentioned above. The second is the succinct expression of a modern Sivokakme, an individual born and reared in the midst of the type of conditions described by the outsider. This general pattern will therefore be followed in the present chapter—first, an examination of some aspects of sickness and health and, second, an inquiry into the sentiments of people with regard to these facts.

In order to obtain as systematic health data as possible for studying certain of the sociocultural effects of morbidity, a key informant, as noted before, was interviewed about salient health experiences of everyone in the village, using the 1940 census as a base. The material was supplemented where possible with health and death records and general knowledge provided by us. Another technique used in studying sickness in Gambell was an approximately 15 per cent

75

random-sample survey of the village, consisting of 20 individuals 18 years of age and over. These respondents were asked 43 questions in a schedule concerning sickness experience in their lifetime, including a number of questions bearing on psychophysiological complaints.[1] In terms of sampling criteria, the respondents involved were probably too few to allow strict generalization to the entire universe of adults in the village. In fact, generalization was not the original intention of the random-sample survey. Such use was conceived to be supplementary to the mass of other data converging on the delineation of health problems in the village. In this light, for the purpose of making statements based on the survey material 5 additional protocols were added. These protocols were taken from 4 men and 1 woman for whom life histories were recorded. For the systematic assessment of health experience of living people, the survey and general observations have in the main been used. Indeed, with the general lack of useful health records or death certificates, the only systematic statement that can be made concerning sickness factors in death over the fifteen years comes from the data of the key informant, who was found most useful in providing information concerning the main cause of death.

Obviously such a brief survey of morbidity as was possible using these types of data is not intended as an epidemiological study. Nonetheless, even a cursory assessment of the material is of assistance in outlining the impact which health factors may have on changing a system of belief. It should also be emphasized here that the picture of the health situation which comes from these data pertains to 1940–1955. In some respects there have been marked improvements since then, particularly in the treatment of tuberculosis. But the fact of improved treatment subsequent to 1955 in no way diminishes the force of concern with health and sickness or their importance with relation to the mainland up to 1955.

## Morbidity and Mortality in Gambell

Some of the substance of the present discussion was presaged in the preceding chapter. There it was noted that Gambell's infant

[1] Adapted from the health section of the Family Life Survey of the Stirling County Study, Cornell University. See vol. II of the Study, *People of Cove and Woodlot: Communities from the Viewpoint of Social Psychiatry* (1960), by C. Hughes, Tremblay, Rapoport, and Leighton.

mortality rate over the fifteen years from 1940 to 1955 was extremely high. This has important implications for an assessment of health, for "infant mortality has long been regarded as a reliable index of the economic and health level of a population and one readily affected by shifts in socio-economic circumstances" (Jaco, 1958, p. 9).

It will also be helpful, in this assessment of Gambell's recent health history, to chart as accurately as possible with crude data the types of diseases to which the population has been subjected and the chronological pattern in which sicknesses have affected the village. In the fifteen-year period since 1940, for example, there were three fairly major epidemics. Thirty-two per cent of the deaths since 1940 occurred in the years 1943–1944, when there were epidemics of influenza and whooping cough. There was also an epidemic of measles in 1953 which was not as severe as the first two.

As for the general question of main cause of death over these fifteen years in Gambell, it is clearly the communicable diseases which have been most destructive, as shown in Table 8. Tuberculosis, in particular, was extraordinarily prevalent, so prevalent as to make almost unnecessary any discussion of other causes of death. A note of caution should be added here, however, for the data do not tell of the complicating factors of other types of diseases which no doubt often contributed to debilitation and death, such as the degenerative diseases or, especially in this region, the nutritional disorders or diseases of deficiency. For purposes of orientation, whenever it is possible some comparative mortality rates have been included for the United States for 1954; [2] but because of the nature of the basic data, no general comparisons will be made in this instance. As with the estimation of crude birth and death rates in the previous chapter, a population figure of 305 will be taken as the "average" village population for the fifteen years against which the estimated mortality rates are computed.

In the United States, by contrast to the Gambell population, 87 per cent of all deaths in 1954 were caused by cardiovascular-renal diseases, malignant neoplasms, accidents, certain diseases of early infancy, influenza and pneumonia, diabetes mellitus, congenital mal-

---

[2] Taken from U.S. Department of Health, Education, and Welfare, *Vital Statistics—Special Reports*, vol. XLIV, no. 10 (August, 1956).

formations, and tuberculosis, in that descending order. In Gambell, on the other hand, tuberculosis and other infectious diseases were much more important, the death rate from tuberculosis alone being one hundred times greater than that in the United States in 1954. Clearly, better data on the great bulk of deaths due to unknown causes in the Gambell population would alter the disease rates

*Table 8.* Crude death rates for estimated main cause of death, 1940–1955

| Cause | No. | Gambell est. rate (per 100,000) | U.S. (1954) |
|---|---|---|---|
| Tuberculosis | 49 | 1,067 | 10.2 |
| "Probable tuberculosis" | 5 | 108 | — |
| Whooping cough | 12 | 261 | 0.2 |
| Accident or physical trauma | 8 | 174 | 55.9 |
| Died at delivery (neonatal) | 6 | 130 | 17.8 |
| Influenza and respiratory disorders | 6 | 130 | 1.7 |
| Pneumonia | 5 | 108 | 23.8 |
| Cardiovascular disorders | 5 | 108 | 484.6 |
| Malignant neoplasms | 4 | 87 | 145.6 |
| Measles | 3 | 65 | 0.3 |
| Meningitis (probably nonmeningococcal) | 3 | 65 | 1.1 |
| Congenital malformation | 2 | 43 | 12.5 |
| Causes unknown; inadequate data | 35 | 763 | — |
| Total | 143 | | |

described above. But it would probably not change its essential outlines, for as already brought out the conditions of health and well-being in Gambell do not differ greatly from those found in many "underdeveloped" areas of the world, which tend to be relatively more subject to infectious diseases than degenerative types of illness (Brockington, 1958, chap. iv, esp. pp. 41–42).

As noted in the previous chapter, one of the clearest findings is the comparatively early death of much of the population (Table 1). In addition to the high death rates shown, other data indicate that 53 per cent of the people in this population (not counting stillbirths) died before reaching 20 years of age. The effect of tuberculosis, in particular, in producing such a high death rate among the younger people is especially pronounced. For the fifteen-year period, on the basis of the relationship between age at death and a diagnosis of tuberculosis as main cause of death, one finds that 31 per cent of the deaths from tuberculosis fall in the 11–19 year-old age group and that almost half the people dying from tuberculosis were under 20 years of age (Table 9).[3]

*Table 9*. Relationship between age at death and tuberculosis as main cause of death

| Age | Tuberculosis main cause | % |
|---|---|---|
| One year or less | 2 | *4* |
| 2–5 | 2 | *4* |
| 6–10 | 5 | *10* |
| 11–19 | 15 | *31* |
| 20–29 | 5 | *10* |
| 30–39 | 9 | *19* |
| 40–49 | 4 | *8* |
| 50–59 | 4 | *8* |
| 60–69 | 0 | *—* |
| 70 and over | 3 | *6* |
| Total | 49 | *100* |

Sickness has had effects on the social and political structure as well as the age distribution. To some extent, the power of the basic divisions of the village, the clans (see Chapter VI), depends on sheer number of members. Some years ago influenza greatly weakened one of the clans, the Meruchtameit, so that it now is only the third most powerful clan in the village; and since 1940 another of the clans, the Aimaramka, has been particularly hard hit by tuberculosis. Since 1940 also two other clans have completely disappeared as effective social groups through decimation by sickness that led to death. The numbers involved in the last two instances were small, but the dying out of a clan has effects far more pervasive than the mere subtraction of numbers. It means social realignments, changes in kinship patterns and other types of human relationships, and the loss of a distinctive subcultural lore.

The question of sickness experience of living people in Gambell is,

[3] For a similar statement concerning both the high death rate from tuberculosis among Alaskan natives and the early death of the population, see F. S. Fellows, "Mortality in the Native Races of Alaska, with Special Reference to Tuberculosis," *Public Health Reports*, XLIX (March 2, 1934), 289–298.

therefore, one of major importance. Short of having continuously kept health diaries, however, or a series of periodic epidemiological surveys, information on the subject is always circumscribed in one way or another. Neither such diaries nor epidemiological surveys were available for Gambell at the time of this study,[4] and so other means of estimating sickness experience were employed. One such means was general observation of the types of sicknesses, especially contagious and infectious diseases, which affected the village throughout the year. Another was use of the special key informant mentioned previously. Both these means of obtaining epidemiological data are, of course, crude and inexact in many respects. But their results point up once again the high prevalence and severity of the infectious diseases, especially those of the respiratory and gastro-intestinal systems. On the basis of the key-informant data, for example, it can be estimated that the prevalence of current or past tuberculosis in the village was 24 per cent in 1955. It is of interest in this connection that x-rays in the spring of 1955 showed some 42 individuals who had signs of possible tuberculosis—42 out of ap-proximately 310 people then in the village. Some of these 42 cases had previously been suspected of having the disease. The 42 cases were additional to 19 already hospitalized at that time, most of them for tuberculosis, thus making approximately 20 per cent the esti-mated prevalence of the disease among the population—fairly close to the 24 per cent noted above.

A common disease for which no morbidity or mortality statistics are available, and one of which the local people are generally un-aware, is echinococcosis, or "hydatid disease," caused by a minute species of cyst-forming tapeworm, *Echinococcus granulosus*. Tests administered during the winter of 1955 showed a very high propor-tion of the people, especially males, who had the disease. Although the particular type of test used was later considered somewhat in-accurate, it is certain that many Gambell people are afflicted. One of the reasons that it does not appear in mortality statistics from Gambell has been the difficulty of adequate diagnosis as to the main cause of death.

[4] Beginning in 1955, under the direction of Dr. Karl Reinhard of the Arctic Health Research Center of Anchorage, Alaska, epidemiological data have been collected concerning the health situation of the St. Lawrence Islanders. It is ex-pected that results of these surveys will soon be available.

*Figure 6.* Family life in 1940.

*Figure 7.* The native store in 1940.

*Figure 8.* Games in celebration held on July 4, 1940.

Another method of obtaining data on sickness experience of living people was the survey questionnaire given to some 25 respondents, which has been referred to above. In response to the question, "What sorts of serious illnesses have you had during your lifetime?" out of the 25 respondents no one had been free of a serious illness; 10 people had had only one serious illness; 3 people had had two such sicknesses; there were 6 people who had had three illnesses; and 6 people had suffered four or more serious illnesses. In all, no one had been unaffected by major sickness, and fully half of the respondents had had at least two serious illnesses.

Following that question, a check list was presented to each person who was then asked whether he had ever had any of a number of specific complaints. The results are presented in Table 10 in terms of the principal anatomical and physiological systems involved, with the total number of complaints for the 25 respondents being 189— almost 8 per person.

*Table 10.* Types of sickness in lifetime

| Type of complaint | No. of complaints | % of total |
|---|---|---|
| Diseases of respiratory system | 42 | 22 |
| Diseases of gastrointestinal system | 25 | 13 |
| Diseases of musculoskeletal system | 21 | 11 |
| Diseases of organs of special sense | 19 | 10 |
| Generalized infectious diseases | 16 | 9 |
| Diseases of the skin | 16 | 9 |
| Tooth troubles | 15 | 8 |
| Diseases of genitourinary system | 10 | 5 |
| Bodily injury | 10 | 5 |
| Diseases of cardiovascular system | 8 | 4 |
| Other | 7 | 4 |
| Total | 189 | 100 |

An important item corroborative of data presented earlier is that 7 of the 25 respondents reported that either formerly or currently they had tuberculosis. This rate, 28 per cent, again roughly corresponds to the 20 per cent and 24 per cent prevalence estimates presented earlier. It is clear that none of these three figures may be completely valid; but the fact that they all converge upon an estimate of some 20–30 per cent of the people with either current or past tuberculosis is of considerable importance.

One question was asked pertaining to a summary evaluation by the respondent of the effect that sickness had had in his life. This question did not prove altogether satisfactory, and it is reasonable to assume that at least part of the difficulty was unfamiliarity with such a question, posing as it did a cognitive problem in a framework in which the respondent was not used to thinking. The question was therefore not asked in several cases. Usually such cases were people who had had an overwhelming amount of sickness in their life and had seen many of their family die from sickness; and it was not considered appropriate to follow up this recitation of the effects of illness in their life by asking if all that had made much of a difference. Nevertheless (with those who were not asked the question left out), 36 per cent of the respondents felt that sickness had made some or a very great difference in their life (Table 11).

*Table 11.* Evaluation of effects of sickness in lifetime
Question: Looking back over your life, would you say that the illnesses of you and your family or others in your home have made much of a difference in your life?

|  | No. of replies |
|---|---|
| Very much . . . . . . . . . . | 4 |
| Some . . . . . . . . . . | 5 |
| Very little . . . . . . . . . | 3 |
| None . . . . . . . . . . | 2 |
| Not answered (for various reasons) . . . | 11 |
| Total | 25 |

During the research year from September, 1954, to September, 1955, daily field notes record many periods when sickness in the village seriously interfered with normal activities. Several times, particularly from December through May, epidemics of colds, influenza, or other respiratory or gastrointestinal disorders affected practically all the village. At such times church services, public meetings, showing of moving pictures or scheduling of other recreational events, and especially hunting activities were all adversely affected. Indeed, during the spring, when the principal hunting for the year must be done, there were several times when only a few of the eleven hunting boats could go out because most of each crew were sick. The boats which were launched were manned by makeshift crews assembled from various clans. This practice is one that in normal times never occurs.

On other occasions throughout the year men often went out hunting even though they were sick with colds, influenza, or tuberculosis. As long as they were able to move and there was game to be found, it was important not to let the possibility of a successful hunt pass, especially in a year of scarcity such as 1954–1955. Needless to say, the long, tiring march over the ice and the exposure to bitter cold greatly retarded recovery.

## Converging Evidence

The Parran report mentioned in the last chapter is helpful in giving materials on the health of both native and white communities on the mainland of Alaska. Bearing in mind that there are differences between some of the mainland communities and those on St. Lawrence Island (such as lack of a hospital in Gambell), one nevertheless finds that the gross pattern of high incidence of sickness and of particular types of sickness is found in both places. Thus, most of the illnesses are accounted for by "acute communicable diseases, acute upper respiratory infections, accidents, tuberculosis, gastro-enteritis and gastro-intestinal symptoms, inflammatory diseases of the eye, and diseases of the ear and mastoid" (chap. iii, p. 11). It is also noted that when medical facilities are available, they are much used by the native population. Some of the conclusions of the report, which bear on the health pattern of Gambell and show it to be part of a larger phenomenon all over Alaska (though more extreme in some details), are the following:

Differences in morbidity are consistent with the differences in mortality between Alaska natives and the population of the States, pointing out clearly that the natives have many more health problems than do the people of the States; that they are problems which affect principally the children and young adults. [Chap. iii, p. 10]

These findings clearly indicate that natives utilize available medical facilities to a greater extent than does a metropolitan population—due in part to a higher sickness rate. These natives are not the strong, healthy specimens that we usually associate with primitive peoples. On the contrary, they have considerable sickness, and except for accidents and acute upper respiratory infections, about which we know little in terms of effective control, the bulk of the higher sickness is a consequence of the high incidence of those diseases which we do know how to control. The fact that the rate is high for such diseases reflects the great need for increased public health efforts in applying the knowledge we now possess. [Chap. iii, p. 11]

And, finally, a cogent summary statement is made of the effects of sickness and the extent of medical care in the Alaskan native population as a whole:

Although much of the data on Alaska's health conditions are fragmentary and incomplete, they are sufficient to reveal a situation which is grim and which does not redound to the prestige of public health in this country.

In the scattered small villages of the Territory, we find that children and young adults are subject to a high rate of disability and mortality from infectious diseases, some of which is due to lack of immunological resistance, but much of it is the consequence of inadequate health service, compounded by ignorance and poverty and all their effects.

In that portion of the population which lives in the more urbanized centers, has the advantages of education, is conditioned to hygienic and sanitary practices, and has health care available either in the Territory or the States, we find mortality from most preventable diseases comparable with that in the States. However, we find here much higher mortality rates from homicide, suicide, alcoholism—all manifestations of social stresses and emotional instability. [Chap. iii, p. 18]

As demonstrated in the preceding materials, which include crude but probably not too unreliable estimates, Gambell has been, if anything, more extreme than the mainland in its susceptibility to and mortality from some types of sickness. The next question to consider is that of facilities for the prevention and treatment of sickness in the village.

## The Background of Sickness

Unhygienic and unsanitary conditions provide the breeding ground for disease. These have changed to some extent in Gambell village since 1940. I shall examine briefly housing, clothing, and cleanliness patterns.[5]

[5] Many of the paragraphs in this section are taken from a memorandum submitted to the U.S. Public Health Service, "Suggestions for Improving Public Health in Gambell, St. Lawrence Island, Alaska," drafted by Alexander H. and Dorothea C. Leighton and Charles C. and Jane M. Hughes, April, 1956.

In 1940 the Eskimos lived in two types of houses, a summer house of lumber of much the same construction as that found in the States and a winter house that consisted of a large unheated entry shed and an inner, heavily insulated, well-warmed living room. This room was usually lined with oilcloth and had a walrus-skin floor, and the large opening to the cold shed was covered with a thick skin curtain. Heat and light were furnished largely by seal-oil lamps, though even in 1940 many families had gasoline lamps, and during that summer a community electric-light plant was installed.

All the usual domestic activities took place in the inner room: the whole family (from 2 to 10 or more persons) ate, slept, washed, cooked, sewed, carved, played, and excreted there (see Figures 6 and 11). Damp clothing was dried on racks, various types of food were fermented, and a kettle was usually hanging over one lamp either to melt snow or to boil water for tea. This inner room usually measured about 16 feet wide by 6–7 feet deep by 6 feet high. There was little furniture, necessarily, and at night a communal bed was made up by spreading heavy skins on the floor for a mattress and using lighter ones for a blanket.

The summer house was in many ways similar to a lower-middle-class frame dwelling in various rural sections of the United States. It contained some of the usual types of furniture (such as chairs) and often was heated by a kitchen stove. Beds with blankets and pillows were common. In many families most of the members moved into the summer house when the weather was warm enough. The older practice had been to dismantle the wooden-frame and walrus-hide winter house entirely, and then the family spent the summer in a skin tent, rebuilding the winter house when the weather became cold in the fall.

A sick person could not be cared for very adequately in the family room of the winter house, and serious problems arose with communicable diseases. It was impossible to isolate the patient from other family members in such a small area. Even in a summer house, a sick person had to be moved near the stove to be kept warm, since few houses had any provision for heat except in the kitchen.

When the winter house was occupied in the summertime as well, the inner room was not kept very hot; but in the winter it was said to average 80°F. or better. In many families underclothing was kept on, because of Christian mission influence, but sometimes nothing was worn in this inner room. Personal hygiene was not maintained at a very high level, since water had to be hauled from the lake in summer or melted from snow or ice in the winter. The understandable habit was to use a minimum. The custom of washing in urine was still practiced by a few of the older people, though most of the middle-aged and younger people preferred soap and water. Urine had the advantage of being easily available and of removing the ever-present oiliness. Up to the recent past, the only dishes used had been wooden platters, which were still in evidence for all meat and blubber. The mother of the family cut up the meat with her broad-bladed woman's knife (*oolak*), and it was then eaten with the fingers. Sometimes, too, a large piece of meat was held in the teeth, and enough for a bite was cut off with a hunting knife by the eater. In any case, individual plates, spoons, or forks were rare. Usually, for instance, a cup was shared among a number of persons. Cooking and eating utensils and a few cooking supplies were kept in boxes along one side of the room. Meat and blubber were left in the cold outer room or in meat cellars underground. There was usually some sort of washbasin available, and a number of chamber pots of various sizes and shapes, covered or uncovered, stood about. The latter were emptied daily but not washed out in the process.

Gasoline-powered washing machines were fairly common in the summer of 1940 and were used a good deal. The preceding year the new school had been built in the village, and it included a laundry room and shower rooms for both men and women, which were very popular.

As noted in Chapter I, the houses of the village were arranged in rows more or less parallel to the sea, stretching along the highest part of the gravel beach. There was a reasonable amount of space between houses, but this area was used in many cases for tethering the dogs. Consequently the ground between houses was strewn with refuse and dog droppings. The teacher in 1940 had started a campaign to clean up the village, which resulted in a temporary diminution of the rubbish and bones and animal wastes commonly in evidence. At times since 1940 the mayor of the village also made efforts to get people to keep the village clean.

By 1955 the two-house (summer and winter) living pattern had disappeared almost entirely. Some new houses have been constructed after mainland models (see Figure 10); some old-style winter houses have been remodeled so that the interior living portion is much larger; and a few of the small, one-room houses remain. The over-all impression of the 1955 village is one of diversity—both in the way the houses look from the outside and in the kind of routine that goes on inside.

There were two houses in 1940 that still used the walrus-skin covering. But by 1955 there is little evidence of skin for insulation, either indoors or out. Only two houses still use the walrus-skin floor. For the most part, the improved houses do not have the old-style moss insulation or any effective substitute. Thus there are more rooms to heat and, at the same time, more places for winds to blow in and warmth to seep out.

Only three of the sixty houses still use the seal-oil lamp. For the other houses, fuel oil, driftwood, or coal are used for heating; and many men have to earn enough money somehow to buy both the fuel oil and the heaters. A barrel of fuel oil costs anywhere from $25 to $35, whereas blubber—which was the Eskimo's fuel and often-times his food in the old days—is usually pitched back into the sea when the animal is cut up on the ice or thrown away on the ground at home. The size of the new house which uses fuel oil exclusively is deceptive, for not every room can be heated. Although there is more space for the storage of food and clothing, during the winter months the family still huddles in one tiny room.

Much of the floor culture has disappeared in the new houses. Where the influence of the white man's way of living is particularly strong, many activities have been elevated to the height of chair, bed, and table, but there are still many homes where all the indoor processes of housekeeping and family life are carried on at floor level. A few houses boast cupboards and the more elaborate cooking equipment that is required for preparation of white people's food. On the other hand, all families still use the wooden dish for the main meal of meat, although some do so with considerable em-barrassment if white people are watching. Linoleum has greatly eased a major cleaning problem in some homes by making floor scrubbing easier. Next door to one so furnished, however, is probably an old-style house where a sea gull's wing is used as a broom and where the years of eating, sleeping, cleaning boots, scraping skins, and performing other tasks on unfinished wood boards makes brushing up a surface operation at best. Two houses have sinks which drain into the underlying gravel. These, of course, can be used only in the summertime and do not alleviate the problem of water scarcity. Suitcases are used for storage in some homes, but the older habit of hanging clothes from the rafters is still more common.

The lake which supplies the village with water is contaminated with *Echinococcus granulosus*, and there has been some effort on the part of the nurse to encourage people to boil or disinfect water in order to prevent infection from this cyst-forming organism. Some people say that they disinfect their water with chlorine pills procured from the army; but the link between dropping a pill in a quart of water and the health of the child who drinks it is usually not understood, and consequently it is an easily forgotten procedure.

There are numerous examples of how difficult it is to carry out habits of sanitation even when there has been some instruction on the part of teachers and nurses and high motivation on the part of the Eskimos. For example, one frequently sees babies' wet diapers hung over the heater to dry without first having been washed or even rinsed out, and this is apparently the predominant pattern. It is true that on the days when weather permits easier access to the water supply some people expend much effort in trying to keep clean; but the important point is the irregularity of this and the difficulties involved. It is a major activity which takes time and energy away from the more fundamental requirements of providing the sustenance necessary for life itself.

The school showers and laundry have been discontinued because it was impossible to keep the well clear and open. The village power plant is no longer in operation, reputedly because of mismanagement and inadequate care. A few people own private power units today and either give electricity to their relatives or sell it to their neighbors, but it is notable that in many homes there are washing machines now standing idle which were bought when the village sponsored electricity. For approximately ten years a Civil Aeronautics unit functioned near the village (see Chapter VI), and during much of that time water was pumped from the lake through a pipeline to the CAA site. This pipeline had three outlets in the village. There was constant difficulty from freezing of the pipes; but for several years, apparently, at least one tap was kept open and the village was allowed to use it. Now this practice has died out.

Clothing styles have changed considerably, as noted before. Children appear at the Christmas program or at the Fourth of July celebration in new clothing bought through mail-order houses, and even adults sacrifice warm and practical clothing for fashion and prestige. Due regard must be given to water shortage and the size of families for which one mother has to wash; it is not uncommon for a suit of long underwear to be worn, day and night, until it is imperative to buy a new suit (a doubtful improvement over the old custom of at least letting the air cleanse the body when no clothes were worn inside the house). Many women have given up making and wearing warm fur boots, although they still sew skin clothing for the hunters. As one informant said, "Ever since we found out about lined galoshes, the ladies around here have been getting lazy." Especially to the younger generation of girls, the woman's parka of blanket or other cloth material is less attractive than a store-bought jacket, though no one doubts the greater advantage of the parka in keeping out the cold.

Disposal of human waste is essentially what it was in 1940: the excretory pots are emptied when convenient, and each house has an open trash area either out toward the sea or back toward the mountain. It is impossible, therefore, to go to the shore or to the mountain without getting near the disposal areas, and they pose a considerable public health danger.

Changes in diet have a direct bearing on health; and there seems little question that the traditional Eskimo diet, if not unbalanced by the incorporation of white man's foods, was healthful. Now, however—and for a number of years—dietary changes of a significant nature have begun to occur, and much less healthful food is wanted and eaten.

## The Treatment of Sickness

The great bulk of what is known about aboriginal medical techniques for St. Lawrence and other Eskimo groups has to do with the shamanistic pattern. Sickness was one of the two or three foci of intense social concern; and it was the duty of the shaman (or *aliginalre*—"holy man") to call upon all his spiritual and ritual powers to safeguard health and cure the sick. In his spiritual-medical armamentarium were included some practices that could be called "empirical medical techniques." It is these latter to which some attention will be given in this brief section. The importance of mentioning them in the present chapter lies in the fact that they were apparently not well developed and not completely adequate to the task at hand. Certain reservations must be entered, however; for to my knowledge, no study has been made of St. Lawrence Island pharmacological and medical techniques.[6] Treatment of the total complex of behavior patterns that were oriented toward the curing of the sick, including ritual and supernatural techniques, cannot be given here.[7]

One of the most important aspects of the aboriginal medical techniques was that much of their strength lay in the preventive function. All people, and especially the males, were urged and trained from their earliest days to build their bodies to be strong enough to withstand cold and fatigue. The older generation of men now living in Gambell remember being waked by their fathers early in the morning and made to do strenuous exercises before breakfast— running, doing calisthenics, carrying weights, practicing with weapons, and wrestling. This concern was expressed in the dictum that a man must build his body and care for it; one elder in the village now recalls his father's advice and passed this on as: "Take care of yo' body." The importance of strength and hardihood in the older culture is shown by the fact that different degrees of skill and prowess were institutionalized into formal titles. For instance, *oomellk* [8] means "strong man" and *Iknaekunre* means "*very* strong

---

[6] For a study of ethnobotany on the Alaskan mainland, see Oswalt, 1957.

[7] Patterns of ceremonialism in which sentiments relating to sickness and health are very prominent have been described for the Eskimos living on the Siberian coast just across from St. Lawrence Island. These are found in the article "Eskimosskie Prazdniki," in I. K. Voblov, *Sibirskii Etnograficheskii Sbornik*, 1952. For an English translation, see Hughes, 1959.

[8] Note the similarity of this term to that for a somewhat comparable role at Point Barrow, *umialik*—literally, the "man who owns a boat," though the term generally refers to a man of wealth and hence power. Cf. Murdoch, 1892, p. 429. See also Nelson, 1899, p. 306.

man and wrestling man"; *sookaellngak* is a man who excelled in running; and *paenaethllk* meant one who was a skilled lance man.

It is significant to note that this emphasis on training one's body has changed. Its importance is still recognized, but, as one fifty-year-old man said, "We're getting lazy." The young men do not exercise now, and the old men deplore the failure to carry out the rules for life which they received from their fathers.

Certain aspects of the shaman's role were also "preventive" in nature. Thus, the shaman would warn of the possibility of contracting measles or tuberculosis or some other contagious disease, if certain proscriptions were not rigorously followed. Other practices of a similar nature were those of changing the name of a child who had been visited by many sicknesses, in order that the spirits which caused illness would not recognize him and therefore would not plague him further, or having a girl child wear boy's clothing, or tattooing the face. In both the empirical and the symbolic phases of the orientation to sickness there was a strong attempt to ward off its occurrence.

Once sickness had struck, however, the battery of empirical medical techniques was severely limited. For cuts, blubber was wrapped on the wound; for physiological upsets of various types, roots, leaves, and other parts of plants were taken, with apparently different degrees of success. Several vegetable plants were known to have cathartic and purgative effects, and a couple of plants were eaten to help soothe the throat during a cold. Urine was a common medicine, particularly for skin diseases such as rashes. But, in all, empirical medical techniques of the aboriginal St. Lawrence Eskimos cannot be said to have been well developed.[9] Their real effectiveness lay in the strength of a well-developed human body having sufficient reserves to overcome noxious agents. Even so, many people in the village today feel that "in the old days, people were more healthy," and the sentiment was frequently verbalized thus.

The treatment of tuberculosis deserves special mention here be-

[9] This is said on the basis of, admittedly, incomplete interviewing on the subject. There is probably little doubt that the St. Lawrence Islanders' knowledge of anatomy was fairly good, engaged as they are in the hunting and butchering of maritime mammals. But it is not so likely that they knew very much about the complexities of internal medicine.

cause of the great prominence of the disease today. Although one cannot be certain of its veracity, some Sivokakmeit say that tuberculosis was first introduced to St. Lawrence Island by contact with the Siberian shore. This is quite likely, and whatever the date (which must have been no more ancient than 100–150 years ago, since it was first introduced among the Aleuts about 200 years ago by the Russian fur traders), empirical native techniques for dealing with it were developed. These consisted of comparative isolation of the tubercular person and the requirements that he eat with special utensils which only he used, that he carry a walrus-skin bag or some other kind of container for spittal, which was then burned, and that he generally take care to prevent spreading the disease. Since these requirements would appear to be based on a belief in the germ theory of disease contagion, it may be that they were introduced into St. Lawrence culture only after the permanent establishment on the island of an American teacher, i.e., sometime after 1894. Such practices might also have been based on beliefs in the efficacy of contagious magic. But whether the pattern was developed indigenously or not, the fact remains that today many Sivokakmeit contrast this careful and responsible behavior on the part of the tubercular person of old with the generally unthoughtful and careless behavior of many tubercular patients of today, who are not careful to eat from special utensils, guard their spittal, or stay away from crowds.

It seems clear that aboriginal empirical medical techniques had little real effectiveness in dealing with the epidemic or highly contagious types of diseases, other than setting an example of patterns of circumspection for the tubercular person. Without a germ theory of disease or comprehension of the highly dangerous health situations existing in small and crowded houses with little water, it is no wonder that the Eskimos were exposed to epidemics of colds and other types of infectious sicknesses which spread very quickly through a village. The stories of what happened to many villages in Alaska following the introduction of new diseases brought by the white man, diseases to which the Eskimos had little immunity, give vivid examples of what happens when unhygienic conditions exist, like tinder in a dry forest, only waiting for the spark (see Aronson, 1940).

This is not to say that in Gambell now as contrasted to 1940 there is knowledge of how sickness is spread or of the germ theory of disease. No adequate understanding of the essentials of hygiene and sanitary practices is widespread. But there does exist a groping reaction based on the very vivid realization of the effects of sickness in the community; and though perhaps the etiology is not understood in any scientific sense, the experiential fact of sickness and its effect on mortality is altogether apparent.

Up through 1954 hospitalization was provided by the Alaska Native Service, but in 1955 this responsibility was transferred to the U.S. Public Health Service. Such hospitalization was not at all a feature of the care of the sick in 1940, although there had been a nurse for several years prior to that time. Now quite a number of people have had the experience of leaving the island for possibly several years of hospitalization (as noted in Chapter III). Some have been cured and later returned to Gambell. Others were sent outside too late.

Within the village, care of the sick is the responsibility of an Alaska Department of Health field nurse, who actually serves the two villages of Gambell and Savoonga. Ordinarily she spends half the year in each place, journeying back and forth by dog team or skin boat. When she is in one village and an emergency occurs in the other, she is contacted via radio by the teacher, who handles medical rounds in her absence. If the case is serious enough to warrant it, she returns, but most of the time treatment can be suggested by radio. Such "radio medicine" is, in fact, a characteristic feature of practice throughout native Alaska; for with the absence of sufficient trained nurses and doctors, the skills of any single person have to be multiplied by all means possible. Thus the nurse (or teacher, acting in her absence) regularly maintains medical sessions by radio with a doctor on the mainland, during which symptoms are described, treatment discussed, and advice given. Often as a result of such a conference a patient has been sent to the mainland as an emergency case.

In the village the nurse holds an important place, for she is the emissary of white medicine, one of the most highly valued aspects of mainland culture. The usual practice of daily medical rounds, clinics for pregnant women and mothers with infants, classes on various aspects of a health program, and explanations concerning proper use of many strange medicines all fill her days. There is the further task of records to be kept on illness and progress. Beyond this, when there is an epidemic in the village—influenza, measles, whooping cough—she may be called upon to go for many days with little respite from the round of visiting patients. But the service which she offers and the image of health toward which by her actions she is working have important ramifications in a village long concerned with sickness. In terms of the potentiality of immediate and direct benefits as seen by the Eskimos, the nurse, indeed, may hold a more important position than any other white person in the village.

One of the most difficult of all aspects of sickness to treat in the hospital is the homesickness and sense of estrangement of the patient who goes there, perhaps for the first time, to remain for what may be one or two years. Some excerpts from a daily diary kept for a total of thirty-five days at my request by a young man who went outside for hospitalization with a severe case of tuberculosis will help illustrate the range of his reactions to the new experience. His sentiments are not atypical of others.

July 9, 1955: I arrived here in the hospital today. I like my room and the nurses. I like my roommate, but I feel sorry we cannot talk to each other much, because he doesn't understand English.

July 10, 1955: I like today even better than yesterday. The day is a sunny one and I like the nurses better than yesterday. I like the hymns sung by the natives most. But one thing—most of the visitors don't speak English and I can't understand them. And I have to stay in on this nice day. I feel a little bad about that.

July 11, 1955: I woke up kind of lazy today. The day seemed to be longer. I was glad to write a letter to Dad and send it by Ethel going back the next day. The nurse gave me a blood test this morning. There was a little cup of some kind of oil in the breakfast. I'm afraid it will be every morning.

July 12, 1955: Today was very much like yesterday, except I got a shot and nice warm bath. I enjoyed my bath very much, but not the shot as much as I enjoyed my bath. I mailed out some letters, too.

July 14, 1955: Nothing much happened today. And I did nothing but read, write, eat and rest. The day seems kind of flat and dreary. I almost wish I could get out of the hospital.

July 15, 1955: This morning I got a shot again, and find out it is going to be twice a week. The doctor told me I have a big spot in my lung. I thought I will have to stay in the hospital for quite a while.

July 17, 1955: Today there were lots of visitors. . . . I liked the day even though I had a hard time talking to most of the visitors. Best of all, I liked the Services held in the hall, made me feel at home.

July 20, 1955: Today I was surprised by a woman who visited me and talked to me in my own language. My roommate's daughter came in to see us too. I think Sunday and Wednesday are best days of the week, because we are visited by lots of people.

July 25, 1955: This morning I wake up thinking about home and my mind goes back to the times when I was once well. Maybe that's the beginning of homesick—but something brightened me is that this afternoon a girl came in with a handful of letters for me, letters from home and other places, from relatives and friends.

August 1, 1955: The day began brightly but it is getting calm and foggy. Even though I'm trying my best not to, I'm beginning to think back of the times past, and of home. The days seem to be longer everyday. Maybe I'm going to be homesick soon; and I like my shots less every night.

Thus, for many Eskimo patients who are hospitalized in treatment of bodily illness the sense of loss of human companionship, which is so valued a thing in their village, is very deep. This is no doubt a constituent factor in the hospitalization of any patient; but it is accentuated where there is no possibility of regular visiting from home people, where the language is strange, and where the environment of regulations and strict orders is so different from that known in the village.

## Sentiments regarding Sickness and Health

Expressions of deep concern about one's health and that of other people in the village were extremely common during our year of residence. There is nothing to indicate that the year from September, 1954, to September, 1955, was unusual in this respect, since in numerous ways desire for good health and the prevention of sickness was institutionalized by many basic sentiments and practices in traditional St. Lawrence culture. Aside from its being the central concern in the curer-patient relationship, already mentioned, it was threaded throughout much other activity. For instance, whenever a child was sick, no one in his family could do any work. If they did so, it was felt that the child would become worse and eventually die from the illness. Many expressions of concern for health were found in prayers, taboos, and ritual proscriptions on certain types of activity, ranging all the way from hunting to the daily behavior of a pregnant woman.

The great corpus of Eskimo belief about the nature of the world and man's relation to the supernatural remains unchanged for most people. Thus there is relevance in the fact that concern for health was institutionalized in the traditional religion, which, in the main, sought to ensure both a steady food supply and good health through multifarious techniques and religious observances. As one informant in 1955 said, certain actions were performed so that the malevolent spirits, *tongnugaek* (which he figuratively translated as "the enemy: sickness"), would be exorcised. One of the most dramatic ritual expressions of this concern with preventing illness was found in the course of the funeral ceremony, which, as noted in the previous chapter, was still being performed in 1940 according to ancient rite, and it may be used as one illustration of the institutionalization of sentiments concerning health.

After the funeral procession had left the house with the body of the deceased, they went to the "Destroying Place," as was briefly mentioned in Chapter III. There were two of these areas, both located on the north side of the village. At such a spot, the oldest living relative of the dead person took the small vessel which had been used for bathing the corpse and directed that the next oldest living relative stand over the head of the body. Then the oldest person made a sweeping motion with the vessel, now empty, down the front side of the second oldest, going from the head to the feet. Next, he did the same thing to the back of the second oldest, who had turned around. All during this time, the second oldest relative had been holding a long strand of grass (about two feet long) which was tied to the dead person's head. After the sweeping motions were finished, the oldest relative cut off a small piece of the strand of grass and gave it to the second oldest person. Then, proceeding down the line in chronological order to the youngest family member, the oldest relative went through the same actions with each, ending finally with himself. At this point he either swept himself with the vessel or had someone else do it. He took the final piece of grass.

The Eskimos themselves have interpreted the meaning of the sweeping motion as the sweeping away of all sickness from the remaining clan members and the depositing of it in the body of the already-deceased person, so that it would be buried with him.

The powerful effects of sickness on motivation can also be seen in former patterns of ritual suicide, most of which were followed because of the desire to avoid prolonged suffering from sickness. Some people committed suicide, however, in the belief that by doing so they could take away the sickness that was infesting a loved one and he would henceforth be safe from harmful spirits.[10]

Storytelling has always been, until recently, one of the principal recreational patterns in Eskimo culture; and after the recitation of a story, the traditional custom is that the raconteur spits into the air, saying *Pfaii,* and expresses the wish for good weather on the morrow and good health to the listeners.

Such ritual attention to the prevention of sickness grew out of an empirical situation similar to that described by an elderly man in 1940 as he recalled his childhood:

When I was a little fella, we had a big family. Twelve brothers and sisters. We were very poor because we were a big family: our father had no brothers. Sometimes we ate cooked rawhide. Six brothers and sisters died; six stayed alive. [What did they die of?] Sick sick; they died of sickness. Some of colds, some of aches, some maybe of rheumatism. One, I know, of a bloody nose.

One of the younger men was asked in 1955, "What is the biggest problem in the village right now?" He answered:

Right now? Health. That's the biggest problem we're fighting right now—especially t.b. That's or biggest problem right now, t.b. [Do other people feel like that, too?] Yes, it's an outstanding problem now: health.

This statement is but a capstone to many others, not as clearly expressed or formulated.

A further example of other such data is the keen interest shown in the publications of a contemporary evangelical "faith healer" of the continental United States, a person who purports to be able to heal sickness through the mechanisms of faith. The one in question

[10] For a fuller discussion of this pattern, see Leighton and Hughes, 1955.

found a particularly receptive audience among some Sivokakmeit, although little of his message is understood other than the possibility of curing sickness, and I was questioned closely as to whether this man actually can cure.

Two further excerpts from the field notes are particularly vivid in summarizing many of the sentiments toward health and medical facilities. They are statements made by the two most prominent leaders in the village:

In the old days I would start early to talk to my boy. I would say, "You have to build up your body now. Make it able to do the work. So you could hunt, you could escape from a strong current or wind, from the ice, you know. And then you can beat the boys from the other side [Siberia]." But mostly for the hunting part—so he could be able to live up to his family. Won't be lazy. [Were people healthier in the old days?] I'm pretty sure of that. I would say they had been much healthier. Very few had t.b. I don't know the start—but on the other hand, we don't have x-rays. Only we can know the ones that spit blood. Very few. And there have been no sicknesses like we had now. Only in springtime, when we had visitors from Siberia, we catch cold. And when the trader comes. No cold. But now we had maybe twice a month. More t.b.'s.

When asked whether people were supporting the chemotherapy program, he answered emphatically in the affirmative. And when asked, "What do people think of the medical facilities—would they want a doctor here, for instance?" he replied:

Yeah, that's one thing I have been talking strong about. And having a hospital, you know, where those patients can take their bed rest while waiting for their hospitalization, away from their families right away, and yet near enough to be seen once in a while. That way I'm pretty sure the sickness can be cured faster. By staying around their families—near enough to be seeing each other once in a while. [Do people get homesick when they go away to the hospital?] Yes, they do—even they make worse. From having too much thinking about their families, you know.

A second man has this to say about sickness:

Before, when I was a boy, there's not much sickness around. We never get sick, only we get cold, cough, when the Siberians come. That's the only time we have coughing. Those people over there, they cough too much, all the time. Only once in a while some kind of plague, like that flu, or something, that swept the island here. That's what I heard from my father—everybody sick. . . . Two years ago was very bad year. And that whooping cough, too, very bad on the children. That Mike used to have lots of children; all of them died. During the whooping cough. Lots of children died in whooping cough. [Did there used to be as much t.b. before as there is now?] No. Those t.b. persons they are very careful about it; we, too, ourselves. They got sputum. Very carefully always cover it with piece of walrus hide. When they want to cough they turn around. They don't spit on the floor or ground outside. It says you wouldn't get well, if you do; if you spit every place, you wouldn't get well. [Who told them they wouldn't get well?] People; that's what the order is; I'm telling you the order of t.b. person. Instruction, or something. . . . Now, we folks, too, become careless too; became careless in burning, too, in burning and spitting. And so maybe t.b. spreading that way. . . . Everything that occurs now it's our fault. It's our own fault.

## Summary

To the picture of very widespread ill-health and death as a result of sickness (particularly among the younger age classes of the population) which has just been presented, only a few other observations need be made. In terms of health practices, there are now, paradoxically, perhaps as many unhygienic and unsanitary habits in the changed housing and clothing patterns as there have been improvements in health facilities with the advent of white influence. From houses that could be taken down and aired each year and then reconstructed on rain-washed ground to houses that are small and permanently built so that tearing them down for aeration is impossible; from clothing that was sufficiently warm for the weather to clothing that is clearly insufficient; from dietary patterns which maintained health to those which have done much to lower resistance and hasten incredible tooth decay; from strictly enforced programs of body building to general laxity in this regard—these are some of the salient aspects of change in hygiene and sanitation that have occurred in recent years. Many of these changes have happened since 1940, especially in terms of the intensity of practice of the mainland pattern.

Another aspect of the change since 1940 has been the loss of at least public faith in the traditional curer of the society, the shaman or *aliginalre*, and a devaluation of the role of this individual who brought all the weapons that man could bring to the side of the sick person. Even if the shaman were not always successful in curing the sick, at least there was a rationale for failure which was understandable and on which action could be taken to prevent future sickness. Further, the weight of religion was with the curer in alleviating the sick in a manner which is not true today.

Finally, the main effect of the hospitalization which began since 1940 has not been to lower the morbidity rates. It has been, rather, to raise hopes about cure and prevention of illness which the mainland purports to accomplish. Given the deep sentiments of the Sivokakmeit concerning the problem of sickness in their lives, such hopes about prevention and cure conceivably exert a powerful lever in their relations with the mainland.

# CHAPTER V

# Warmth and Well-Being

MAN in the arctic spends most of his waking life in work to provide his body with nourishment and protect it from the loss of heat. In this chapter, I will consider in some detail those aspects of modern Sivokak culture that have to do with the acquisition of food and subsidiary goods, with material exchange and distribution patterns, and with other subsistence institutions. As in previous chapters, in the discussion the main axes of interest will concern changes in such patterns and the sentiments which cluster around these cultural activities. The first sections deal with the native food of the island. They will be followed by discussion of other aspects of subsistence and survival patterns, both those still predominantly Eskimo and those adopted from the mainland world, such as the store.

## The Work for Food

### WALRUS HUNTING

On the basis of food tastes, the St. Lawrence Islanders could well pre-empt the name "walrus eaters," since they live astride one of the richest walrus-hunting areas in the world and for centuries that animal has been the mainstay of their diet. The purpose of the spring hunt is to lay in a supply of several hundred *tochtak*, or "meatballs," which are made of long rectangular sections of walrus hide with blubber and some meat still attached, folded over on themselves and then laced together with a thin strip cut from the same skin. These *tochtak,* weighing an average of 110 pounds each, are stored in meat cellars or meat houses for several months before use by both humans and dogs. In 1940 the St. Lawrence people said, in response to the question, "What do you like best to eat?":

Ever since the people was formed on the island we eat most walrus meat, and we like it best.

But if we got one whale, we forget about walrus meat for a while. But we never get tired of walrus meat. I think because we raised by them.

And walrus is still the favorite meat food of the Sivokakmeit, although certain parts of the bowhead whale are considered extremely tasty. Walrus is often contrasted to seal meat to illustrate its excellence, and seal is said to be "too soft," to spoil too quickly and not be amenable to preservation for as long a time as walrus. An excerpt from the field notes points up this preference:

Ivan said that when people go out to the hospital "in two or three days they want our food." They want walrus. He told me that people here don't want birds or fish—they want *walrus.* He said, "It isn't like your soft food; it is hard." I asked him if it is the Eskimo's "real food." Ivan said it is, and then said, "It's our 'bread.' "

The same sentiment is heard over and over—that *"our* food is walrus." This section will describe patterns of hunting the animal and will discuss how these methods have changed since 1940.

Fifteen years ago walruses were still hunted, by some of the men, with a modified form of the traditional hunting technique. Briefly, this meant that they still used a harpoon and line to anchor the animal to its breathing hole or to a patch of open water, but that it was then killed with a rifle. For hundreds of years the walrus hunter had stalked over the winter sea ice with his hunting bag hung lightly on his shoulders, his harpoon and coiled walrus-hide rope, his lance and ice tester, and his baleen toboggan for hauling the meat home. Having located a walrus's breathing hole, which was usually several miles out from the village, he waited for the animal to surface for air and then harpooned it in the nose and ran back some distance from the hole while letting out the line. Before the walrus, which was swimming under the ice to get away from the ivory and flint head stuck in its cheek, came to the end of the forty to fifty foot line, the hunter had jabbed the bottom of his sharp-pointed harpoon shaft down into the ice through a loop in the end of the rope. Then came the jolt when the walrus suddenly reached the end of the line. The hunter strained, bracing his body and strength against that of the walrus. Finally, however, the animal had to return to the hole for air—if it had not already pulled the line free of the hunter—and in the slack time the hunter sometimes would use his knife to gouge out two holes in the ice about a foot apart and lace the line through them and make it fast. If possible, he would tie the end of the line around an upright ice cake. He could then go to the hole and wait for the walrus to surface for air once more, when with his lance he would try to kill by wounding the animal in the neck or chest. Often the walrus would return to the water several times, wounded and its strength ebbing, before it would finally die there or be killed when it came to the hole once more for air. Sometimes, in a last attempt at survival, it would climb out onto the ice and try to kill the hunter with its tusks. But oftentimes, too, the hunter would inadvertently get a foot tangled in the walrus line and be pulled under the ice by the powerful animal. Even within the last ten to twelve years a man in Savoonga was lost this way—whence came the insistence by the old men that a hunter always wear his knife where he can quickly grab it to cut the line if he has become entangled.

With a method that is still used, the dead walrus was pulled out on the surface of the ice by a native block-and-tackle arrangement made by tying the harpoon line to one of the animal's tusks, passing it through a slit in the skin at the back of the neck, looping it around a knob cut in the ice, and once more passing it through the slit in the neck.[1] The line was then pulled from the ice, with the series of loops acting like a pulley. The hunter would cut up the animal on top of the ice, often with the help of other hunters whom he had called over after the kill. Those who came shared in his meat. The successful hunter kept the tusks and the heart, but the rest of the flesh, including the delicacy, liver, was equally divided among all who came.

[1] A drawing of such a primitive pulley device is found in Elliott, 1898, opp. p. 166.

The pattern of hunting just decribed was that practiced in the depth of winter, when the sea currents are stilled by January weather. St. Lawrence Island lies in the path of walrus migration, and in the winter many of the male walruses remain among the ice floes on the north side of the island.[2] In former years they were plentiful, and informants claimed that often a man would kill a walrus almost every good hunting day. This was not so true for seal hunting, the pattern of which has greatly changed with the introduction of the rifle, as will be shown later.

In the spring hunting season before the introduction of the rifle and outboard motor, a boat full of hunters would silently paddle to an ice floe on which a group of walruses were sleeping. Then the striker of the boat (a role explained in the following chapter) would quietly jump onto the ice and try to kill several of the sleeping animals with lances and knife before the rest slid, alarmed, off into the water. At other times walruses swimming in the open sea were harpooned and lanced if they could be approached closely enough.[3] When the animals were harpooned from the boat, inflated sealskins, called "pokes," were attached to the harpoon line in order both to impede the swimming of the animal and to help keep the carcass afloat after it died. It was finally killed with the lance.

By 1940 the spring hunting had changed considerably from this ancient method. Outboard motors were introduced as early as 1916 for the walrus-hide *angyaks* (the more commonly known term for this open, approximately 22–26 foot long boat is *umiak*, an Alaskan mainland word). The rifle had become an integral part of the hunting technology since the first contacts with whalers and commercial ships in the middle and latter part of the nineteenth century. With these two new technological devices the pattern of hunting walruses among the moving ice floes of the arctic spring became much more efficient than formerly. Now (in 1955 as well as in 1940) the boat approaches a group of sleeping walruses with the motor turning over as slowly as possible; as it circumspectly meanders among the small icebergs that fill the melting spring sea not only the striker but usually several other members of the crew

[2] For a discussion of the spatial ecology, life history, and population of the Pacific walrus which has considerable relevance to this chapter, see Fay, 1955a and 1957.

[3] See Elliott, 1898, opp. p. 163.

aim their rifles into the mass of walruses. When the animals begin to show alarm or when the boat is thought to be as close as possible without danger, the shooting begins. Usually at least one or two animals are killed, but sometimes several. An effort is made now not to kill more than four, i.e., only the number of carcasses that a boat can safely carry. Sometimes, however, it is necessary to shoot more than four in order to protect the boat and hunters; for the walruses, especially young animals two to four years old, can become angered and will sometimes try to rip the skin boat with their tusks. Swimming underwater, they approach the boat on their backs and with their tusks rip open the bottom of boats made from the hide of their own species. In the spring hunting of 1946, a boat was thus ripped open, but it was close enough to an ice floe that the crew could reach safety before the craft swamped.

Other variations of walrus hunting that were practiced in 1940 have remained essentially unchanged through 1955. For instance, winter walrus hunting now is done mostly by a crew that pulls its boat across the large, flat pans of ice and through the all-too-frequent fields of broken ice which result as the edges of huge cakes grind against each other. The boat crew looks far into the distance for the dark spots on the ice which mean a group of walruses (or sometimes only a lone walrus) sleeping. Occasionally there are open leads in the ice—a few hundred yards or possibly a mile or two. But the main bulk of winter hunting consists in sliding the boat on the firm ice; in treading lightly with it across the young, thin ice and the brash that presents a mushy, treacherous foothold; and in the only occasional motoring in open leads that thread among the floes. For this winter hunting a minimum of four crew members are needed, because the boat is heavy and the way is long, especially if walruses have been killed and a half a ton or so of meat has to be hauled four or five miles back to the village. Often a few dogs are taken on the winter hunting, and, harnessed to the bow, they are of considerable help in pulling.

If walruses are sighted on the ice, winter hunters try to approach silently on foot and shoot accurately so that the animals will be killed before they slide off into the water (see Figure 18). Walruses always stay near open water, and if the wounded animal can dive through his air hole, it will probably be carried away and lost by the strong currents under the ice. This is one of the main advantages in using the harpoon—the carcass can be hauled back to the hole even if the animal goes under the water.

All too often, however, walruses killed with rifle fire on the winter floes (and this is more common during the spring) will slip into the water and sink, irretrievably lost because no line has been placed in them. One of the most frequent criticisms by the older men of the new hunting technique is that the walrus is not first harpooned before it is killed with a rifle. They even go so far as to say that the old method of hunting with harpoon and lance was much more effective; for not only was the animal always secured with a line, but in addition several hunters could fully exploit the hunting possibilities of any given area because of the silence of the lance. Now, when high-powered rifles shatter the stillness of the ocean ice, other walruses nearby are quickly frightened off.

And so it often happens that a day's work of pulling a boat over several miles of ice is unrewarded with meat, the animals having been carried away by ocean currents. The winter season is a slack time for walrus meat. The animals are not abundant anyway, and winter boat hunting is undoubtedly the hardest work with comparatively the smallest return of the many forms of hunting done by the Sivokakmeit.

When ice and weather conditions on the sea stretching westward from the village are not right for boat hunting in the winter, men will sometimes take their dog teams over to the other side of the mountain a few miles away or go off onto the sea ice from the northern foot of the mountain to hunt the walruses which use, for breathing holes, the open leads made by changing currents. For this type of hunting, some men use a harpoon and some do not. The usual method is to try to kill the animal with a rifle and then attempt to snag it with either a harpoon or a seal hook. (The latter is a small wooden float with three sharp hooks which are attached to a cotton-string line; its primary use is in snagging the floating dead seals after they have been shot.) Hunting off the north side of the mountain, even more than off the west side, requires keen knowledge of the changes of current and tide; for if the current has changed behind a hunter several miles out on the ice, there is a good chance that he will be swept away and unable to make land. Many hunters in Sivokak-meit history have misjudged the changes of current and been marooned on an ice floe, some to return, some not. One of the first lessons the young hunter learns while out on the ice is to watch the older men, to see when they pick up their hunting bag and other gear and return to the shore ice. The current changes approximately every six hours, perhaps with a change of tide, and that which is best for hunting is the southward current, for it pushes the ice close to the land. The northward current pulls it away and leaves great stretches of open water. One quite elderly man, remembering his youth and thinking of how hunting conditions have changed, remarked:

When I was a little boy, at that time every year a man was lost. Lots drowned. Because they went far to hunt. No gun. They going far out to hunt. If they see walrus, they passed them. Sometimes lots of walrus in water, but they passed. [Because] they want to find little hole in the ice. . . . Today is an easy time. Before, a hard time; very hard time.

In summary, the principal changes in walrus-hunting techniques since 1940 seem to be as follows. ( 1 ) The method of using a harpoon at the breathing hole is rarely, if ever, practiced now. It was asserted that one or two men still use a harpoon; but this is not at all certain and it is not frequent. Even if the harpoon is used, the actual killing is done with a rifle. ( 2 ) More walruses are hunted in the wintertime by locating the animals on top of the ice and then shooting them with the rifle. As a consequence more animals sink, dead, into the water and are irretrievable. The older men specifically decry this as a waste of animals: "Rifle no good; losing too many walrus." ( 3 ) The only other changes seem to be those of quantity rather than quality—e.g., motors for the boats used in the spring hunting have more horsepower and thus require more gasoline because longer journeys are taken to find walrus. In addition, more ammunition seems to be used now. Some discussion of the monetary expenses involved in hunting will be given below, in a later section of this chapter.

## SEAL HUNTING

The Sivokakmeit hunt primarily three species of seal: the "hair seal" [4] (*Phoca hispida*), the "spotted seal" (*Phoca vitulina*), and the

---

[4] A local English term for this particular species. In other places, the animal is known, in English, as the "ringed seal." The more common vernacular term for the *Phoca vitulina* is "harbor seal," and for the *Erignathus barbatus*, "bearded seal."

"mukluk seal" [5] (*Erignathus barbatus*). To some extent, methods for hunting these animals differ because of the seasonal variations in supply of the animals. For instance, the spotted seal is primarily a summer and fall game animal, whereas both the hair seal and the mukluk seal are found from late fall through the spring. I will first describe the ancient winter-hunting techniques for these animals, since such techniques were more important than those at other seasons.

The most common hunting pattern for both the hair and the mukluk seal was that found in most other Eskimo groups—locating a seal's breathing hole in the winter sea ice, cutting the ice away from the hole just enough to allow the harpoon head to enter, standing above it quietly without moving, harpoon poised for the seal when it comes up for air, and then quickly jabbing it with the flint-bladed, ivory-headed harpoon. When the animal had to return to the hole for air, it was killed with the butt end of the harpoon, which was itself a sharpened point used primarily for testing the thickness of the ice. This type of hunting, obviously similar to the pattern of walrus hunting, was practiced throughout the winter when ice conditions permitted. The ice had to be such that the seals were forced to make their own holes; for if there were large stretches of open water made by currents breaking up the ice fields, the animals could find ample open surface for breathing and the hunter had no chance to harpoon them in a small space where he was sure of his target. Largely for this reason, probably, comparatively few seals were killed by men practicing the winter-hunting techniques in the days before the rifle. Old men now claim that hunters used to kill more walruses than seals in the harpoon-hunting days, which is very unusual for an Eskimo group. The reason may have been simply the greater abundance of walruses in this particular area; for the similarity between the methods of hunting walruses and seals on the winter ice fields is apparent, and it is unlikely that there was any difference in efficiency of the method used for one rather than the other animal.

---

[5] Because the English spelling "mukluk" is commonly used for this animal, I will not change it to accord with the phonetics I am using here. In the scheme by which I transcribe other Eskimo terms into English, it would be "maklak." The common Alaskan mainland Eskimo word for this seal is *oogruk.*

A major technological change came with the introduction of the rifle. Now the seal hunter could kill the animals seen sporting in the open leads and patches of water, which he had previously had to bypass in his attempt to locate a breathing hole. But with the one rifle shot that killed a seal came the need for the functional equivalent of the harpoon line previously used to snag the seal; for now the animal would float away with the current unless caught by some device. The seal hook was introduced—it is said from Siberia—for this purpose. It is a small, somewhat gourd-shaped piece of wood, about 8–10 inches long, with three sharp hooks projecting from the diameter at its widest. The smaller end is attached to a piece of rawhide thong 3 or 4 feet long, which is in turn attached to a cotton fish line up to 100 feet long. The device is twirled around vertically and then let fly until it alights on the water on the far side of the floating animal. The hunter pulls it toward him and in so doing snags the carcass on the hooks and brings it in. The device is also used to retrieve dead birds or, in some cases, a floating walrus—although with the latter the line can easily break.

Old men now say that, although the Sivokakmeit used to kill and eat more walruses than seals, at the present time they kill many more seals, but still prefer walrus. The rifle, therefore, made the killing of seal easier and considerably changed the hunting pattern. Previously there had been little hope of eating seal during the spring hunting season, when they would be sleeping on ice floes and could easily escape before a harpoon was put into them. Nor could they be as easily killed along the shore near *Nai'vukh puk* (the Big Lagoon), a favorite feeding spot for seals in the fall, as they can now with the rifle. The fall as well as summer feeding of seals at this spot and at certain others on the island was the basis of a second major seal hunting pattern.

A few miles from the village, over the mountain and down the slope, hunters have through the years erected a series of individual "breastworks" consisting of stones, whale ribs, sticks, and lumber. These structures are located ten or fifteen yards up from the shore line for a distance of possibly a mile up and down the beach. During the summer and particularly during the fall, hunters go to this stretch of shore very early in the morning, there to wait in their blind for seals below them to come close to the shore during their feeding. The hunters are often successful, and if they kill a seal, they bring it to shore with a seal hook. The pattern of hunting from these blinds is the same now (1955) as it was in 1940. This type of hunting continues until well into the fall, when the ocean freezes and prevents further use of the blinds. There are at least two or three other spots like this along the shore lines stretching away from the village where hunting of this nature occurs. Many people have cabins at these spots, and some families live there during several months of summer and fall in order to hunt the seals that come to that place. They also gather greens and other vegetable products, as well as shoot sea gulls and other types of birds.

Another pattern of hunting seal that has not changed appreciably since 1940 is the "modern" method of winter hunting on the ice, as contrasted to the aboriginal harpoon method. The hunter takes his position before a patch of open water, often resting his rifle on a cake of ice for surety of aim, and then waits—sometimes for several hours before he gets a shot at the elusive animal that may raise its head above the water for only two or three seconds. During that interval the hunter must spot the animal, grab his rifle, take aim, and hit the small target. Some rarely miss. The hunter will often take his team of dogs out onto the ice with him, both for transportation and for carrying home the meat that he hopes to kill. Other men take only a baleen toboggan and pull the meat home themselves (see Figure 13). Hunting of this type, out over the sea without a boat, occurs usually only off the north side of the island, as does the solitary hunt for walruses. Again, a keen knowledge of currents and weather conditions is necessary for safety of life; and the younger men are cautioned that they should not go out alone until they have been properly trained by an older, experienced man wise in the skills necessary for winter ice hunting. Most of the young men accept these cautions realistically.

The spring and fall seal hunting takes place mostly from the boat which is out looking for either walruses or seals. Animals are shot in the water or on the ice; and the boat strikers develop great skill in picking up a dead animal from the water with their uncovered hands as the boat swoops by it without stopping. If the seal is too heavy to haul into the boat (e.g., a mukluk), it is harpooned and then pulled onto an ice floe for butchering.

A subsidiary method of hunting seals which was practiced until fairly recently in certain parts of the island was that of netting. This was done on the north side during the fall for spotted seals and in areas on the southwestern side of the island where young mukluks gather in May and June. The animals were killed either with clubs or with small-bore rifles. Netting has been done much less frequently in recent years and probably will soon disappear as a hunting technique.

## WHALING

Whaling has traditionally been the chief glory of the Sivokak hunter. In it the virtues of skill, perseverance, and courage are tested to their limit. This was even more true in the days before the white man's whaling ships introduced some aspects of modern whaling technology than it is now, when boats with motors, guns with powerful bombs, and steel-headed harpoons make the killing of the sixty-ton bowhead whale a much more efficient and less dangerous operation than it was for uncounted generations.

For at least several hundred years (and probably much longer) Eskimos in the Bering Sea region have hunted whales. This is attested by archeological finds of whaling harpoon heads in the Punuk and other ancient culture sites. Throughout the region the bowhead whale (*Balaena mysticetus*) has probably always been the species most hunted, for their calving ground is the nearby Sea of Okhotsk on the other side of the Kamchatka Peninsula, and their summer migrations take them through the Bering Strait to the Beaufort, Chukchi, and Siberian Seas. The only other type of whale regularly hunted is the gray whale, or "summer whale" (*Rhachianectes glaucus*). There are native terms for several of the other principal whale species hunted, and sometimes these animals are found in the surrounding waters, although not in as large numbers as the bowhead. They are the killer whale (*Orcinus rectipinna*), the beluga (*Delphinapterus leucas*), the humpback (*Megaptera nodosa*), the finback (*Balaenoptera physalus*), the minke or piked whale (*Balaenoptera davidsoni*), and the harbor porpoise (*Phocaena phocaena*).

Whales are killed in the spring months, when they pass northward following the retreating ice floes. "Whales, he like 'em ice," as one old hunter said. The season begins in April, when the sea has opened to wide stretches of water, and the whales begin to move into the ice-studded ocean. Only rarely does a whale come into the region before April; and within two months the great bulk of whales has passed north. During the summer only an occasional gray whale, beluga, porpoise, killer, or piked whale is found.

The open skin boat, the *angyak*, was traditionally propelled both with paddles and with a sail made from a number of walrus stomachs sewn together. Following the voyage of whaling ships to this region, canvas sails replaced those made from the walrus. Aside from the introduction of somewhat different types of weapons, the general pattern of killing a whale remains the same today as it was in ancient times. The boat quietly approached the swimming, surfacing whale from the left rear side, the harpooner (or "striker") with his equipment ready. The ancient Eskimo harpoon was an ivory head tipped with a stone blade. The harpoon head was fastened to a long rawhide line of baby walrus hide, to which in turn were tied as many as three inflated sealskins ("pokes"), used for the same purpose as those in walrus hunting. The boat approached as closely as possible to the whale, and the striker threw his weapon. Others in the crew had the special job of throwing the inflated sealskins overboard and watching to see that no one got a foot tangled in the coiled rawhide line. The whale would sound in its attempt to get away from the harpoon head in its flesh, but swimming was impeded by the bouyant capacity of the large sealskin pokes, and the animal would tire quickly and have to return to the surface for air. The pokes marked the place of surfacing, where the boats (several boats hunted whales together) waited for it. In the old days stone-headed lances were used to kill the animal, and it was sometimes difficult for men equipped with only small boats and lances to kill the sixty to seventy foot long bowhead, whose tail could smash a boat and a dozen men in a moment of anger.

Often the dead whale would be butchered out on the bobbing ocean if there was too much ice between the boats and the village. This meant that as much *mangtak* (whale skin) as the boats could carry would be stripped from the carcass and then the animal left to float free. If there was not a great deal of ice between them and the village, however, the several boats attached themselves to a central line and towed the whale to shore, where cutting was more

*Figure 9.* Christmas celebration in the mission, 1954.

*Figure 10.* A typical house in 1955.

*Figure 11.* One of three families still using the seal-oil lamp in 1955 (the lamp is the container under the kettle and holds the burning seal oil).

efficient and thorough. Since the whale was towed by men using only paddles, it sometimes took a couple of days to get the carcass to the shore. Killing a whale was a festival event, but its elaborate ritualized accompaniments cannot be fully presented here.[6] Some brief descriptions of ritual events attending whaling will be found in the following chapter (pp. 261–264).

In 1955, as well as 1940, canvas sails are used rather than either walrus-stomach sails or paddles for approaching the whale. Boat motors, although taken in the boat, are not employed because the noise would frighten the whale. The slightest sound, even talking, is proscribed; and most of whaling consists in long hours of cold, silent waiting, looking for the telltale spout in the distance.

When any of the several boats hunting together sights a whale, a black flag is waved to indicate to all that absolutely no noise can be made. If the boat succeeds in fastening a harpoon line into the animal, it runs up to its masthead a sealskin poke or other article as a symbol of success, and all boats take down their sails and use their motors. In the modern day, whaling guns (introduced by white ships) are used along with the harpoon, and these guns fire a bomb into the whale's body at the same time as the harpoon head fastens a line to it.[7] This "darting gun," as it is called, which the striker uses, consists of a heavy wooden shaft about 6–8 feet long, tapered so that it is considerably thinner on one end than the other. To the smaller end is attached a steel rod culminating in a sharp harpoon head. The harpoon head is tied to the wooden shaft with a manila rope which is then tied to a walrus-hide line. Attached either to the underside of the wooden shaft or directly on the small end is the bomb gun. This is a breech-loading barrel of brass about a foot long. To load it, a cartridge is put in, then the bomb (about 8 inches long), and then packing. The gun is cocked, and the trigger release rod attached to the trigger. This rod projects out beyond the end of the brass barrel. The force of the shaft striking against the whale's body pushes the trigger release rod backward, tripping

---

[6] For discussions of whaling ceremonials in other areas see Margaret Lantis, *Alaskan Eskimo Ceremonialism.*

[7] For a most helpful article summarizing the era of commercial whaling in the North Pacific and Bering Sea areas and describing the types of equipment introduced to the Eskimos by the white whalers, see VanStone, 1958.

the mechanism. Optimal use of this instrument requires a delicate adjustment, for if the bomb explodes too near the harpoon head, it will dislodge it and the whale can pull away from the head and line.

The whaling line itself consists of a 60-foot section of manila rope, followed by a section of baby-walrus-hide line about 100 feet long. The three pokes are fastened to the walrus-hide line at approximately 50-foot intervals, the last coming at the end of the line. The bombs for this gun, bought from mainland maritime supply houses, have cost anywhere from $10 to $15 each in recent years. Sometimes only one bomb will kill a whale, but more often at least several are required. They are timed to explode a few seconds after being fired, and the force of the cartridge impels them into the whale's body, where they explode.

After the harpoon line has been anchored to the whale, all boats circle around the general area where the bobbing pokes indicate that the whale will be surfacing for air; when it does come up, the boats swoop down on it with motors roaring, and the strikers attempt to put more bombs into the animal. After it is finally dead, the job of towing it to the village remains, but this is made infinitely easier now with the 24-horsepower motors. Nonetheless, when a sixty-ton bowhead was killed in the spring of 1955, it required six hours for nine boats to tow it a distance of about five miles.

Whaling is exciting. As one young Eskimo describes it:

We made a pass. This whale was spouting; we made a pass. But the engineer had the motor speeded up too fast. And before he came up we were past it. First pass, I didn't strike it. But there were two more boats making the same pass as we were making. The second boat behind us was Johnnie's boat. The whale came up just when Johnnie's boat was alongside, and they threw their darting gun at the whale; the shell went off, and threw the darting gun back in the air. And the bomb went in the whale, and I heard the explosion—I could feel the bomb blowing up inside the whale. And I was little worried, because I wanted to get shot at it myself. The minute the bomb blow up in the whale, instead of whale getting wounded, it must have hurt him pretty bad, because he just push up that old water all over—got mad, real mad. Throw his flippers up and then down, splash —you could hear that splash. Then he was all right again, still spouting, still going strong. We were making a turn now, around, you know. Coming for the second pass. By this time, Henry's boat was making a pass. And

old Otto was striking it. It did the same thing—the bomb blow up; didn't
bother the whale at all. And we were making that second pass, coming
towards the whale, coming by the last poke. Last poke . . . second poke
. . . and the whale was still surfaced. This time I'm going to strike it for
sure . . . and the last poke. And from the last poke there's only 10 fathoms
of manila line to the whale. And we came by about 10 feet away from
the whale—10 feet, that close. And whale was still surfaced, swimming
around. Long whale—this was a big one, boy! Big one. I got ready; waited;
got ready; and you know the whale's nose where they spout, it goes down
and it drops, and up again, towards the body? I hit him right there in that
hollow, in that valley. With this big strong bomb. And my darting gun
went up in the air. And by this time we were past the whale; I turned
back and looked. And watched the whale—by the time we just passed
the whale, the bomb inside blow up. It made more sound than the first
ones, I know; it was a stronger bomb, I know. Just like slapping the boat—
that sound. And I saw that whale shook—shook up the whale. And the
whale just turned right there. Just turned up, belly up; it means he's dying.
Dead. Didn't even make any move; just stay there, dead. And all the boats
start coming towards it; and we were happy it's dead. You know, I found
out later that they been chasing this whale since 2 o'clock, and trying to
kill it—5 hours! And we kill it in only 15 minutes! Another good strike—
I was little proud again, this time!

At this point something can be said about changes in the butchering and sharing of the whale once it is brought back to shore. The
traditional pattern of cutting was based on a differential distribution
of the *mangtak*, baleen, and other valuable parts of the animal, depending on the order in which the boats involved had helped strike
the whale. The striking boat and the three or four others next
striking it, for instance, received proportionally larger shares than
did the rest. The order of striking the whale was formalized in a
series of titles. The striking boat was called *aegavungilret;* the first
boat coming to assist, *athhot;* the second assisting boat, *pInaiyoot;*
the third, *sakemagoot;* and the fourth, *ivaeloovak.* Apparently after
the fourth they were not named. Ten pieces of baleen went to the
striking boat, 8 to the first assisting boat, 6 to the second; each of the
rest usually received 4 pieces. Within the boat crew itself the spoils
tended to be divided equally.

As for the *mangtak* (an especially prized food item), each boat
was entitled to the skin in a particular circular ring around the cir-

cumference of the whale's body. The first three boats were given rings at the whale's greatest girth, and those boats which had not been as responsible for killing the animal received rings of *mangtak* of lesser diameter.

Within the last generation or so, however, this system of division began to break down. Boat crews had normally cut their own *mangtak* from the whale, the boats all lined up with their bows facing the carcass and crew members cutting as fast as they could. But it is reported that the crews having the stronger men sometimes cut from the *mangtak* belonging to other boats, and there was much bickering at the butchering of a whale. While such argument has been reported from several informants, apparently actual fighting over the spoils rarely broke out. In any case, the division of whale was traditionally primarily in terms of each boat as the basic unit.

Within the last twenty or so years[8] this system of boat shares has changed so that now the household is usually the basic unit of division, with each share being equal. This change has been attributed to two of the elderly men, each of whose boats had killed whales (which therefore "belonged" to them as far as directing the butchering was concerned). On the first such occasion the *mangtak* was placed in equal piles, and then the boat captains were directed to choose a pile; the meat was then divided equally among the crew members. On the second occasion, however, which occurred within the last four or five years apparently, the pattern of equality went one step further. Division this time was in terms of a pile for each household. The rationale for this newer pattern of division was that, under the older system, some households which contained no men able to hunt in a boat crew—such as that of a widow with young children—might not receive any, or at least very little, *mangtak*. This did happen sometimes. It was felt that with the newer pattern every household would be assured of receiving at least a part of the meat from the whale (as in Figure 12).

The pattern of division is still somewhat flexible, therefore, and choice of which type of distribution will prevail is left to the elderly man who has charge of the whale cutting. This man is sometimes the captain of the striking boat; more often he is the retired boat

[8] Smith, 1937, describes the cutting in of one whale as being done by the older system. He was the Gambell teacher for a few years in the early 1930's.

captain who is headman of the lineage or clan whose boat kills the whale. And at least one boat captain in 1955 claimed that, when he gets a whale, the division will still be in terms of boat, rather than individual household.

OTHER SUBSISTENCE PATTERNS

*Birds and egg-collecting*—Hunting birds has always been an important supplementary subsistence pattern in St. Lawrence Island culture, and the island is well provided in this respect, for countless thousands of birds of a wide variety of species nest there.[9] Although it is not on the same level of taste as walrus flesh, bird meat is relished for variety in the diet, particularly if the only meat availrble is taken from several months' storage in a meat cellar. In addition, there are times during the year when a fairly crucial reliance is placed on birds to provide a steady source of meat of some kind until the principal hunting begins. The fall, for instance, is the time to lay in a supply of many ducks and, especially, many sea gulls as insurance against poor winter hunting of walruses and seals. During the heart of winter, after all the other birds have gone southward and when the walrus and seal hunting is poor, the old squaw duck, or "saw bill," remains on the edge of the shore ice and is hunted to provide daily supplies of fresh meat.

Hunting of birds is done with a wide variety of techniques, ranging from the aboriginal method of netting to the modern use of the shotgun. Perhaps more than in any other type of hunting, the technique used varies with the season. Throughout the year, of course, adult birds are killed with a shotgun. But during the summer months auklets are caught with a wide-sweeping net as they fly near the rocks among which they nest; baby auklets are hooked out from their nests with long wire hooks; baby cormorants are gathered by hand from their nests on precipitous cliffs; adult cormorants are very carefully picked out of their nests when they are asleep; young geese are captured by hand as they run along the shore; and a type of sea gull is caught during the spring with a fishline baited by a piece of blubber. Not all these methods were used in 1954–1955,

[9] For a discussion of the bird species found on the island, the reader is referred to Olaus J. Murie, "The Birds of St. Lawrence Island, Alaska," in Geist and Rainey, 1936, pp. 359–376, and to Fay and Cade, 1959.

but they are still in the subsistence repertory of the Sivokakmeit. In addition, the eggs of cormorants and murres are gathered by the hundreds when they nest during June and July.

The greatest intensity in hunting adult fowl with shotguns occurs in the fall, when large flights of birds are migrating southward, and during the spring months of May and June, when they are returning northward. Particularly during the spring the sky is sometimes filled with a long, black swath of birds that takes two or even three minutes to pass by one point. As noted in Chapter I, various species of ducks, geese, auklets, puffins, sea gulls, cranes, loons, and other birds nest on the island.

One of the greatest changes that occurred in the aboriginal bird-hunting pattern was, of course, the introduction of the shotgun. Prior to its use, the huge flocks of birds could be hunted only with a bolas-type of weapon—several braided sinew strings weighted at the outer end with walrus teeth and the inner end coming together into a handle which the hunter used for throwing the weapon into a flight of birds. This type of device is still used by small boys for hunting.

In 1940, birds intended for preservation against later lean periods were skinned and then placed in a barrel or a sealskin poke filled with seal oil, where they sometimes were left for several months before being used. They became somewhat spoiled, or "high," as did most of the other meat stored in this aboriginal Eskimo fashion. But by 1955 the pattern of storage in seal oil had almost completely disappeared; birds now were either eviscerated and dried in the summer or frozen in the winter. The oil storage had not been used extensively in recent years, and only the stringency of the food situation during the year made a few of the older women store some birds this particular way. It was not used at all by the younger women. In fact, the general use of seal and walrus oil, which for hundreds of years had been a crucial item in Eskimo subsistence, has lost its paramount status and is rapidly declining. Not only the change to fuel oil, replacing the seal-oil lamp, but also the change in food tastes, particularly those of the young people, has dealt the crucial blow.

Since 1940, then, the actual patterns of hunting birds have changed fairly little. The shotgun was used at that time and is used now.

Some of the older methods of capturing birds had already passed from general use, such as the snare, the bolas, and a special type of net (consisting of a series of horizontal ropes from which small, open loops were hung) which was stretched across the face of a cliff where many birds were sleeping. In using this net, someone would make a noise to frighten the birds from their nests, and many became caught in the open loops when they tried to fly away from the cliff face.

One development with regard to bird hunting was quite important during the food-scarce year of 1954–1955. Having become very dependent on the use of the shotgun for bird hunting, hunters were considerably frustrated when, during the fall of 1954 and spring of 1955, the community store was depleted of shotgun shells just when the most intensive periods of bird hunting should have occurred. The store has had difficulties of like nature in recent years, but perhaps it reached its peak in 1954–1955; and its failure to provide the ammunition on which modern hunting techniques are based was particularly vital during a year when the most important forms of game had been very scarce. The store in its role as the principal funnel of white culture into the village will be discussed below.

*Fishing*—Like bird hunting, fishing has always been only a supplementary subsistence activity for the St. Lawrence people. In fact, they rely on fishing much less than do some of the other Eskimo groups who are not so well provided with walruses, seals, and whales. Nevertheless, in the past the fish life of the surrounding ocean tended to be exploited with the same combination of ingenuity and careful articulation with the changing natural world that characterized most other aspects of the economic life. Everyone agrees that much less fishing is done than was the case even in the youth of now middle-aged people. And there is certainly less done than in 1940. An excerpt from the field notes is to this point:

Caroline showed me the fish and birds which she has drying, and said that when she was young there used to be lots more. That women didn't ever get to bed sometimes during this season because the men would bring home fish which had to be skinned and hung up, and birds which also had to be prepared for the rack.

The traditional Eskimo pattern of summer activity was to leave the large settlement (Gambell, for instance) and go to a fishing camp. Many of these were on the south side of the island, located on the rivers emptying into the Big Lagoon. There the arctic char (*Salvelinus alpinus*) came during annual runs. Other salmonoid fishes occurring in the area and occasionally taken are the chum or dog salmon (*Oncorhynchus keta*), the red salmon (*Oncorhynchus nerka*), and a few silver salmon (*Oncorhynchus kisutch*). Lake herring (*Coregonus sardinella*) and grayling (*Thymallus arcticus*) are found in great numbers in the lagoon on the south side. Some of these fish are still caught by hand lines from boats off the beaches near Gambell during the summer months. Many people used to remain in their camps during September and October, not only for continued fishing, but also for seal and bird hunting. This is rarely done now.

A certain type of fish, the tomcod, is said to have washed ashore in considerable quantities almost every fall, during November. This had not happened for some years, but in November, 1954, it occurred again. Men, women, and children waited along the beach for each successive wave to throw the small fish onto the gravel, where they were gathered in pails and other containers. Some people gathered up to 75 pounds of the fish, which was eaten either raw or boiled. At times the people also pick up other animals thrown up by storms, such as mussels, clams, crabs, and a variety of tunicate which in Eskimo is called *Opa*.

A common pattern is that of fishing for sculpin through the winter ice, beginning in January or February. The fishing grounds are located about a mile from the village, in a sheltered cove at the base of the mountain. The crabbing season begins at the same time and at the same place. The methods, however, are different in some respects. For both sculpin fishing and crabbing one has to chop out a hole in the ice, which is between three and four feet thick in the middle of the winter (see Figure 17). The hole has to be kept clear of the ice that continually forms over the water, and for this purpose a small baleen scoop is used. A fish head or some other type of meat is used as a bait for crabbing, but for fishing only a spinner or bright object is attached to the line and hook. For both types of activity the line is wound longitudinally around a small stick (about a foot long) that has a loop-shaped area notched into each end for containing the line. The fishline must be continually jiggled, whereas the crabbing lines are left by themselves. A fisherman often will have two or more crab lines sunk into the water. He tests them at intervals to see whether a crab has taken the bait—and also to keep the line from freezing into the hole.

Neither crabbing nor winter sculpin fishing provides a large increment to the diet—only variety and a rare surfeit. But the activity is important, for it is something women, old men, and boys too young for the strenuous winter boat hunting can do to help provide food. Everyone can have a place in the ceaseless round of extracting sustenance from nature.

*Gathering greens, berries, and seaweeds*—As with fishing and crabbing through the winter ice, the gathering of greens, berries, and seaweeds is an activity in which the less vigorous members of the family can contribute toward the supply of food. Children often help their mother gather the plants that wash up on the beach during the fall storms or the *stlchta* [10] which, like great masses of long, wet hair, marks the farthest edge of the tide along spring beaches. Several other types of seaweeds are gathered in both the fall and the spring, and they are eaten either raw or cooked. Some of the supply gathered during fall is frozen for use in the winter.

The most important of the "greens" collected in the summer is called, in Eskimo, *noonivak*. This plant is *Rhodiola rosea* (=*Sedum roseum*), a common arctic plant widely scattered across North America, eastern Asia, and northern Europe. Its small leaves are picked during July and August and are placed in either a sealskin poke or a wooden barrel. With each day's accumulation in the barrel, a little water is poured in and the entire mass of leaves weighted down with stones. A family tries to fill two pokes or barrels for their winter use. The purpose of putting them in water is to "sour" them, making a prized food item.

[10] To my knowledge, no identification of seaweed species of St. Lawrence Island has been made, and thus I am not able to identify these particular plants any further. However, see Heller, 1953, p. 9; she lists three types of seaweeds as being common in the Alaskan area and used for food by the Eskimos. They are giant kelp, laver, and dulse—and probably these seaweeds are among those found at St. Lawrence Island and used for food. With regard to land plants, two useful articles are by Porsild, 1953 and Oswalt, 1957.

Greens are not always stored away for winter, however. They are sometimes eaten fresh, but never as the main item of the meal. They are always eaten with meat. When a barrel is permitted to freeze for winter use, a portion of the frozen mass is taken off and ground or pounded to a fine consistency and mixed with melted lard (formerly only seal and walrus oil or reindeer fat). Sometimes this mixture is refrozen and then sliced off as wanted for a meal. The roots of the same plant, *noonivak*, are gathered during the fall, after the leaves have turned brown; and these, as well as other types of roots, are also eaten with a meal of meat.

In the fall, berries and roots or tubers are gathered. The St. Lawrence people speak of small "potatoes" which formerly were taken from the storehouses of mice and other small rodents; these are probably the "Eskimo potato" (*Claytonia tuberosa*) referred to by Porsild (1953, p. 31), for this species is found over Siberia and northern Alaska and is widely used by the Chukchi and Alaskan Eskimo for food. There is also an indeterminate number of other tubers and roots that are picked in the summer or fall.

Berries are often placed in pokes or barrels and allowed to freeze in the same way as the greens. The most common of these are "salmon berries" and "black berries." These types are undoubtedly the black crowberry, or curlewberry, and the cloudberry (otherwise known as salmonberry or baked-apple). [11] In addition to some of the other berries, probably it is the bilberry, or whortleberry (*Vaccinium uliginosum*), that is also found on St. Lawrence Island, for sometimes a "blue berry" is referred to by local people. But positive identification has not been made for this.

Gathering seaweeds, greens, and berries was always primarily the woman's task, although young children and even old men too feeble to hunt helped out. But the activity has considerably declined, both from what it used to be in the memory of old people and even from the intensity of activity found in 1940. In recent summers fewer and fewer women have toiled their way to the mountainside to spend days, half-stooped over, picking the small leaves that would go into a poke or barrel for their family's winter supplement.

[11] *Empeterum nigrum* and *Rubus chamaemorus*, respectively. See Porsild, 1953, p. 21.

In the summer of 1954 very few women had done picking—fewer still of the young girls whose task it traditionally would have been. And thus in the winter of 1954–1955, the supply of the few families that did have greens left from the summer's picking was soon depleted by those coming to ask for some of the vegetable food. The families concerned gave, because greens are still very much liked by many people, even the young, and sharing of food is a fundamental sentiment. During the summer of 1955, probably prompted by the joint motivation of food scarcity as well as the liking for greens, many more women went to the mountain on the days when picking could be done. But the eventual fate of this ancient subsistence pattern seems fairly clear.

*Polar-bear hunting*—The flesh of polar bears is not important in the diet in terms of bulk, for normally only one or two bears are killed on St. Lawrence Island in a year. Nonetheless, hunting this animal is an exciting affair even in this day of high-powered rifles, and the skin of a bear is a valuable item for sale to curio shops on the mainland. In this way, the hunting of bears can contribute importantly in the work for food; for example, the skin of the only bear killed in Gambell during the winter of 1954–1955 was sold for $100.

In the days before the acquisition of rifles, polar bears were killed only with lances. The difficulties inherent in this feat were implicitly recognized in the fact that only those men who had killed either a whale or a polar bear during their life were qualified to be buried at the top of the mountain. The feat was also recognized ceremonially by special observances lasting for five days similar to those for a dead whale. During this time the head of the bear, with its mouth propped open, was placed on a wooden trencher in the most honored corner of the room—behind the seal-oil lamp —beads and charms appropriate to its sex were suspended over it, and stories were told and songs sung while all hunting ceased in honor of the soul of the animal. On the fifth day the skull was boiled to dislodge all the flesh clinging to it, and in the presence of a group of invited men and women, the leader of the extended family (or perhaps clan) would offer bits of the softened meat in sacrifice to the high god and to the spirits. The meat to the god was thrown into the air, and to the spirits (of the ancestors) into the fire. Following this rite the skull was usually placed near the graves of clan ancestors on the mountain along with other bear skulls.

The hunt itself consisted of a long march over the ice, either one or several hunters following the bear and trying to get close enough to wound and kill it with a lance. It is said that a bear has a characteristic way of turning its head to either the right or the left when looking backward and that a hunter therefore could make his approach from a relatively blind side. If possible, he tried to cut the tendons of the heel to impede the bear's movements. Sometimes, though not always, dogs apparently were used in the same way as in other Eskimo groups—to surround and harry the bear, perhaps to nip at its heels. There was a belief (which appears still to be prevalent) that a wounded bear must never be allowed to escape; it must be followed until it is killed and its soul thereby released. If this is not done, the offended spirit will cause the hunter sickness and harm.

The skills of the bear hunter demanded strength and agility and an adeptness at avoiding the swing of the crushing paw while trying to lance through to the heart. Some hunters were famed for their quickness in such darting and jumping with a lance; they were the *paenaethllk* (skilled lance men) referred to in Chapter IV as men of prowess singled out by special designation.

Today the long trailing of the bear still occurs, but the dangers of close struggle are minimized by the rifle. Nevertheless, it requires several shots to kill the animal and during that time much can happen. Although there were no reports of hunters having been killed by bears in the last generation or two, the hunting of these animals remains a dangerous activity, and the capture of a bear still is regarded as a definitive mark of a young man's becoming a "real" hunter.

Apparently the same patterns of division of meat occur with respect to a bear as with walruses and other animals. This happened at least with the one bear killed in the winter of 1955, when the captain of the boat, two of whose crew had killed the animal, apportioned the meat so that each household received a share. The skin and skull—both items of possible commercial value—remained in the captain's family and later were sold.

## FOX TRAPPING

Although the fox (*Alopex lagopus*) was a relatively insignificant animal before the coming of the white man—never being used for food, for example—since the demand for its pelt became so great, trapping has been an extremely important (though indirect) subsistence activity of the Sivokakmeit. Therefore, in this section dealing with the ethnographic aspects of St. Lawrence subsistence patterns, it seems relevant to discuss the fox-trapping complex. Later in the chapter it will be examined from the point of view of the income it brings into the village.

Trapping is acknowledged to be difficult work—taking place during the coldest part of the year out on the wind-swept tundra miles away from human habitation, where the sudden blizzards that come up often make finding one's way back to camp a matter of chance even for the most experienced. Men have been lost on the trapping trail.

The trapper's clothing differs from that of the hunter on the winter ice floe. The former is made mostly from caribou or reindeer skins, which are warmer than sealskin but not as waterproof. Particularly the boots (and sometimes leggings) are made from reindeer. In the days when reindeer were abundant on the island, inner pants and even parkas were made from fawn skin. Attired in this outfit, a trapper could endure a winter night spent out on the open trail, even if storms forced him to lie huddled among his dogs for warmth.

Trapping grounds are traditionally "owned" by individuals or groups of kinsmen, who often trap together (see Figure 20). They are "owned" in the sense that public opinion concedes trapping rights to those individuals who currently use them and continue to use them without lapse. At least in the current conception of legal norms on the island, they cannot be "sold," for, as one young man put it, they are not owned by virtue of legal papers and hence cannot be sold by the same process. If a man stops trapping in a region, any other person can begin to use it as his own.

Great respect is shown for another's trapping territory, and during the season no one intentionally ventures into the region where the traps and bait are spread out over several miles along a trail known usually only to the trapper who owns it. To bring a strange dog team into the region would leave scent traces that disturb foxes and keep them away from the bait. A man simply has no business—unless it is an emergency—entering another's trapping area; and the main traffic trails to Savoonga and the principal camps of the island bypass the trapping grounds. Formerly, a man's trapping area was also his hunting area—the geographic locus of the clans which now have moved into the village (see the following chapter). But the old geographic identifications have been weakened and, as one older man said, the trapping grounds are becoming "all mixed up."

The trapping season now extends from December to the middle of March, but long before it opens the trapper must begin his preparations for the year. He must either have his wife sew the necessary warm clothing or buy it from another needlewoman; he must make sure his dogs are in proper shape for the rugged winter work on the trails; and he must have a supply of dog harnesses, which he makes himself from mukluk skins or buys from someone else. Early in the fall or even in late summer the prospective trapper places his bait at points a fraction of a mile apart along a trail that he knows well. The bait is always a large chunk of meat—preferably rotting meat, which foxes are said particularly to like. When there was a herd on the island, reindeer carcasses were often used for this purpose, but now any decaying animal is used—walrus, seal, sea lion, or any other—and meat was taken in great quantities from the two whales caught in the spring of 1955 to be used as fox bait. The hunter's purpose in laying his bait so early is to encourage foxes to come and nibble regularly at the meat without fear of man. After the opening of the season, when the foxes have become accustomed to the bait as a steady source of food, the trapper will bury open traps in the snow.

The extent to which trappers tend their lines varies considerably, depending on the energies of the man, the weather, the distance of his line from the village, hunting conditions in Gambell, and other such factors. Those men whose lines are only a few miles from the village will usually go out every clear day to see whether they have foxes. Others, whose lines are more distant, will sometimes leave traps untended for two or three weeks while they remain in Gambell and then will spend a similar period of time at the camp, every day dog-teaming or walking the several miles of trap line. Often before the trapper can take the animal, a polar bear will have left only fragments of blood-stained white skin in the trap.

Trappers must be particularly careful not to leave any scent of humankind around the trap—for instance, they should never wear on the trail boots that have been used around the gasoline- and oil-soaked floors of the cabins, for the scent would immediately warn a fox of danger. For the same reason, the dog teams are never taken too near the bait.

If the fox is still alive when the trapper reaches the bait, it is killed by stepping on it to collapse the lungs, in order not to leave bloodstains on the white fur. Once the frozen fox is brought back to the cabin or the village, it is hung up to thaw and dry completely before being skinned. Both women and men do the skinning; and in the seasons that are particularly productive, sometimes the wives of successful trappers must stay up all night skinning a day's catch of five or six animals. The skin is stretched on a rack inside the house until dry and then is scraped and cleaned.

Trapping itself is not exclusively a man's task, although it is mostly men who do it. Near the village (and, in the older days, near the trapping camps) women and girls often set traps with the hope of getting several of the skins which (in 1955) they could sell for $15 each or trade at the store for clothing, cosmetics, or food.

THE SEASONAL CYCLE

The painstaking patterns of getting food from a small corner of the arctic have been described in some detail. Perhaps now to follow these patterns as they change from one month to the next during the year will be a helpful way of summarizing these data; for if there is one outstanding feature of Eskimo economy, it is its versatility and flexibility, its readiness to exploit to the fullest the nuances of nature.

A proper starting point might be the fall. In September picking of greens has just about finished, but berry picking begins, as well as the collection of various types of roots and tubers. This continues until the ground becomes too frozen, less than a month later. Bird hunting with guns continues—particularly for ducks and geese and sea gulls. Walruses are not found in the early fall, nor hair seal; but hunting of spotted seals continues during September and October and then dwindles off during November, when the ice comes. In the months of October and November women and children gather seaweeds of various types from the shores, washed up by the high winds and waves of the fall. In addition, sometimes tomcod are gathered. In former years there was some fishing for cod and sculpin in the fall before the ice came, but that activity has generally disappeared now.

By November many of the species of birds begin to leave the St. Lawrence area. Only the sea gulls linger for a short while before they, too, leave; and the traditional custom was to kill as many of these big birds as possible to freeze for use during the coldest part of winter, January through March. The first sea ice comes in November, and with it—usually—the walrus herds journeying southward with the edge of the ice sheet. Often, however, there is a period, between the departure of the spotted seals and birds in November and the coming of the first ice with its burden of walruses later in the month, when there is no real source of animal or bird food available. Sometimes, too, the walrus herds do not come with the ice or are too far out for hunting. At such times in former days there was famine. If there was hunting, however, it was very intense during this time, and one middle-aged man now recalls his youth in the following terms:

From the first part of the winter there was a good hunting. For seals, and walrus, and everything. They hunt much as they could. Save every part of it—blubber and meat. Pretty soon, carcasses piled up; and they just take the skin off and leave the blubber on the meat. They leave it like that; store it, never touch it. Because the current is very close in the first part of the season, the winter. The latter part of the winter when the shore ice gets heavy, the sea animals travel way out to where there is loose ice; open leads out farther. For that reason, we try to get all we can; because ahead there lies shortage of meat and oil. For that part they store everything. No, they don't store as much meat now.

Hunting of walruses, hair seals, and mukluk seals on the winter ice is then the principal activity of men from December through March. This hunting is done either from along the shore, where currents break up the ice, or out on the flat pans themselves, where a man will go with his dog team or alone, walking, or with a boat crew. Even so, the period from January through March is the worst of the year; for not only are there fewer animals, but the hunting conditions are much more dangerous and the weather is extremely severe. Often storms and bad weather last for many days at a time and permit no hunting whatsoever. It becomes a work of fair proportions to maintain a household with light, heat, and water. During this time of the winter some men are occupied with their fox-trapping line and must leave the village daily to attend their traps, or else they stay for extended periods at camps located some distance from the village. The only bird hunting during the winter is for sawbills, or old squaw ducks, which remain throughout the winter along the edge of the shore ice and are hunted by the men and boys when they are not otherwise busy. Sculpin fishing and crabbing begin in January and continue until the ice starts to break up in late May.

In March the sea commences to open once more, and there are more leads. Boat hunting is the only type possible on the ice now, and the walruses become more abundant. In April the whaling season begins, and with it a period of intensive hunting for about two months. During April and May the great bulk of food supply for the entire year must be laid away. Supplementary hunting activities during the rest of the year contribute, of course, to the nurture of the community; but without an abundant hunt during April and May food scarcity or even famine will be a possibility throughout the year. This is what happened in the spring of 1954, and it was only slightly better during 1955. It has occurred several times since 1940.

With the whaling, the killing of walruses and mukluks and hair seals goes on as well. And by late May and particularly early June, the birds are returning in great numbers. Auklets, murres, cormorants, puffins, geese, loons, and gulls all come back to their native rocks.

June sees the end of walrus and hair-seal hunting and of whaling. The main herds of walruses have passed to the north, but some of the males remain in the ice near Savoonga for part of the month. By the last days of June, however, they too have swum after the retreating ice. Only occasionally is a gray whale killed in the summer. June brings a harvest of seaweeds as well as birds, and picking some of the greens begins as well. In the latter part of the month boats travel to cliffs forty miles south of the village to gather murre and cormorant eggs by the tubful.

June is also the month for preparing the spring's catch of meat for storage in the meat cellar (*siklowaek*), or meat house. Walrus meat has already been rolled into "meatballs" (*tochtak*) and put away. Now baby walruses and mukluks are cut into strips and hung on racks to dry in the summer sun, along with orderly rows of eviscerated birds and fish. The meat dries all summer unless eaten first, and then the dried meat (*nafkoraek*) is taken down in the early fall and stored. As noted before, in 1940 much of the stored meat was placed in barrels or pokes of seal oil, but in 1955 very little was preserved in this manner. During the latter year perhaps the general scarcity of meat precluded storing very much of it, but nonetheless the pattern of preserving meat in seal oil is very clearly passing out of the culture. I will examine some of the reasons for this change later, in connection with the sentiments about using seal oil which the Eskimos have acquired by their contact with white people.

In July the picking of greens begins in earnest, and hunting spotted seals in the lagoons of the island is a principal activity of the men. Netting of auklets now starts also, and it continues for a period of only a few weeks. Duck, geese, and puffin hunting with shotguns is another subsistence activity occurring during the summer, and some netting of fish takes place. The months of July and August are essentially the same as far as subsistence activities are concerned. With the browning of the September grasses a new phase begins, and the yearly cycle once more is repeated. The seasonal activities are summarized in Table 12.

In 1940 and before, when there was a stable population living at Southwest Cape, one of their principal June-time activities was the netting of young mukluks, which gathered on the beaches at a particular point. Only occasionally do people from Gambell make that trip now. But in general, the rest of the seasonal pattern remains today the same as it has always been with regard to the native foods of the diet, although certain aspects have diminished in intensity and technological changes have altered it to some extent. For example, the eider duck snare is no longer used in the summer as it was traditionally. Fishing, however, is that aspect most changed. For possibly hundreds of years the usual summer pattern of activity was for the large winter settlements to break up into small family bands which went to their own hunting and fishing camps, where they laid in great stores of fish, hunted seals and birds, and gathered greens and roots. This, in general, was the pattern of 1940, although even

*Table 12.* Subsistence products gathered by season

| Product | Jan. | Feb. | Mar. | Apr. | May | June | July | Aug. | Sept. | Oct. | Nov. | Dec. |
|---|---|---|---|---|---|---|---|---|---|---|---|---|
| Walrus, mukluk, hair seal | x | x | x | x | x | | | | | | x | x |
| Whale | | | | x | x | | | | | | | |
| Spotted seal | | | | | | x | x | x | x | x | x | |
| Roots, greens, berries | | | | | | x | x | x | x | | | |
| Seaweeds | | | | | | x | x | x | x | x | x | |
| Fish | x | x | x | x | | x | | x | x | x | | |
| Birds | x | x | x | x | x | x | x | x | x | x | x | x |
| Eggs | | | | | | x | x | | | | | |

then the tendency was for a yearlong residence in Gambell. The schoolteacher and other government agents had specifically urged that people living in outlying camps move to Gambell permanently in order to send their children to school throughout the year as well as to be closer to medical care. In this respect, therefore, increasing dependence on the white world even at that time influenced settlement and economic patterns of the Eskimos. By 1955 the tendency had culminated in there being no permanent settlements outside the two villages of Gambell and Savoonga. Since 1940 the last remaining family had moved in from their regular home in Puwowalak, or Southwest Cape, and now their camp site is used only for a trapping and hunting location.

In this connection, some further attention should be given to the intermittent camping life, for it is still in the minds of many people an important object of sentiment formation, one that is sometimes juxtaposed, however unknowingly, against the attractions of the white world.

CAMPING AND THE OUTDOOR LIFE

Eskimo life alternates between the small, cramped spaces of an inner room filled with many people during a winter storm and the vast stretches of open tundra and sea that seem empty of all living things. Practically all the older people and many of the younger Sivokakmeit have lived for long periods of their lives in the camps and small cabins scattered along the shore lines of the island at favorite hunting or fishing sites. One of the most frequent comments in connection with their recollections of life at camp is, "How clean is the air, how clean the camp," compared to Gambell village now. People speak of the chance to eat "lots of fresh meat and greens"; and the desire to go camping in the summer is still quite strong in the village, although there is decided ambivalence about leaving Gambell for too long—Gambell, where the airplanes come in, where recreation is found, where there is excitement. Even children speak glowingly of the "fun" and opportunities for play that they can find at camp, wandering along the beach, climbing cliffs, looking for small animals and birds. Camp life involves the natural world with all its fascination and freedom of activity for children and its perspectives of emotion and recollection for adults. One man was asked whether he still likes camping, and his reply effectively summarizes many others to be heard in the village:

Yes, because I'm hunting every day. My children real happy. Because never need anything; always eat fresh meat. Seal, fish, something like that. Now my other children, they want to move to lagoon—they always ask me: "When you go down to camping again?" And I tell them, "A little later on."

This enjoyment of the outdoor life is still one of the important features of Sivokakmeit psychology:

Etta said that Dale was getting upset because she always has to stay home and take care of the children, while her mother goes green picking or her father goes hunting over the mountain.

The sentiment is not at all unusual. It is probably to be expected in a culture whose ethos is hunting and collecting from nature. A grasp of the subject of sentiments toward the hunting life is fundamental in understanding much of the Sivokakmeit system of belief, social structure, and personality.

SENTIMENTS TOWARD HUNTING

Although in the last fifteen years there have been major inroads into the basic structure of St. Lawrence economy and total culture, it remains today, as it has been for so long, a culture oriented to the killing of animals and consumption of their flesh. The role of the successful hunter is pre-eminent in the prestige hierarchy of this society. As one young man, himself a worthy and energetic hunter, said to me: "Eskimos are professionals—professional hunters." It is this role of the professional hunter—and its excitements, suspense, and freedom of activity, but also its dangers, insecurities, and frustrations—that clashes with the changing occupational requirements of life in the modern world; and in the clash is engendered much of the stressful effect of culture change.

Evidences of the orientation toward hunting are at every hand. All able-bodied males are expected to fulfill their proper role as boat-crew members, to be industrious in their solitary pursuits over the ice in search of game, and to show enterprise in gathering nature's seasonal offerings of birds and their eggs, fish, and even seaweeds. The man who fulfills this prescribed role is given high praise and prestige; he is the cynosure of approving comments. Those who fail, through whatever reason, to be industrious or even to try to adapt to the role—there are few of the latter, although not all who hunt like it—are strongly contrasted with the active hunters and are set aside from the main stream of cultural approbation. Traditionally, as noted before, the men receiving the highest esteem and honor were those who had succeeded in killing at least one whale and/or polar bear during their lifetime. To be called a "great whaler" was the highest cultural reward. As seen through the eyes of a young hunter, this cultural goal still has cogency:

And first I try to find out whose boat had this poke on the mast. It's very exciting to find out who's getting the whale! It's some excitement. That's one thing we always want to find out—who's getting the whale!

It was the great hunters who after death were buried on top of the mountain. All others were put on the lower slopes, graded somewhat in accord with their status in life (e.g., a woman tended to be lower than a hunter, although this was not always strictly followed). Even now the legitimacy of this prestige ranking in terms of burial is accepted, and there is a strong propensity to follow the pattern, among the young people as well as the old.

The attractions of the hunting life are many and perhaps are obvious. A chance of expressing individuality, of winning cultural rewards for accomplishment, of gambling, with its risk, suspense, and spontaneity; a proving of oneself the master in a dangerous situation; an opportunity to project and work out suppressed hostilities and frustrations—all these would seem to be components of the motivational complex involved in a hunting life. It is perhaps a relevant caution here that one cannot necessarily attribute motivations toward killing and the projection of antisocial impulses found in a nonhunting culture to a psychology based on the killing and consumption of flesh as a daily economic activity. In this connection, however, a word by Lantis is pertinent and is a reminder that here is an area where further research can be done—what does it mean psychologically for a man to take animal life day after day?

It appears that these people who are among the world's most effective hunters, that is, among the greatest human predators against animals, feel continuous guilt for this very effectiveness and so must enter into the myriad small rituals, must observe the tabus, load themselves down with amulets, rush to confess what seem trivial offenses, practice the magic, in order to reduce their anxiety. We who analyze hunting in terms of bird-spears, harpoon-heads, and other cultural forms forget that psychologically it is an act of aggression. [Lantis, 1953, p. 136]

She goes on to mention some of the components of the hunting moment:

When people depended solely on hunting and fishing, the physical need for food, social need for prestige of the great hunter, psychological need to satisfy an ideal of the self, the suspense, competition, excitement of the chase, fear of defectiveness of equipment at the crucial moment, fear of personal injury or death in storm and accident—all this built up a tension that was released, often, in a frenzy of attack on the caribou herd or walrus herd. The hunter must have sensed his own deep hostility against these creatures that so often eluded and frustrated him. The hunter had sound psychological reasons for fearing revenge from them. [*Ibid.*]

Whether or not one accepts this type of psychological interpretation, it points to the rich and exciting materials of Eskimo religious and ceremonial life, which were in large measure devoted to beseechment and placation of the animal world. To anyone interested in the sentiments that surround a life in which creatures conceived to be one's spiritual brethren are killed, the ceremonial and ritual cycle gives rich data indeed. In it are formalized and explicated some of the deepest social concerns of the entire group. Although in the present book the subject cannot be explored in detail, its relevance must be pointed out. Some brief examples are found in the subsequent chapter.

To return now to the Sivokakmeit. In speaking of the hunt, one young man phrased it this way: "It's hard work to cut up the animals, but it's fun to kill them." The work of hunting is, to be sure, tiring and very exhausting; but, just as surely, the excitement is intense. A man remembering when he first started to school said, "I was not completely happy, because I missed something very much —hunting, good hunting. I had learned to like it very much." At the time to which he was referring he was about nine or ten years old. Another hunter, who had spent some years away from the island, said, "I like this island. I like the outdoor life and the hunting." He later spoke of the rigorous aspects of hunting with a nonchalant laugh that long-term observers of Eskimo life have learned not to interpret as lighthearted, saying, "To live up here is to take the weather, the blizzard, the cold . . . and to break through the ice. That's the way to learn!"

A boat captain during the heart of the frozen winter, when hunting had been impossible for two weeks and food was scarce, said: "One thing white people don't understand is that we Eskimos can't grow anything. All we can do is hunt, hunt, hunt." Speaking about her husband, a woman remarked, "He is hunting most of the time, hunting, hunting, hunting. That is what he loves to do." And the husband himself, at another time, spoke with great enthusiasm of hunting for duck's eggs and for birds at his camp on the other side of the mountain.

Opinions vary among the older men as to whether the young are really learning their traditional hunting role and becoming as highly motivated for the active life as they should be. The elders say, for instance, "Look at all the young men standing around now. They should go hunt. They are lazy." Or "Arthur's boy is lazy; he never goes hunting."

But a young man himself disputed the charge. He referred to boys who return to Gambell from school on the mainland and, when asked whether the young men like to hunt now, answered:

That's one main reason they like to come back out here—hunting. They'd rather hunt. They were raised hunting, you know. Of course, it's our trade. From our childhood on up, hunting is our main trade out here.

Much of the apparent contradiction in such statements no doubt comes from inevitable generational differences in point of view and selective memory. Without question, too, there has been an actual decrease in interest and practice of the hunting life from what it was in the youth of men now old. I have mentioned before that the young men no longer exercise and strengthen their bodies for exposure to cold and fatigue. And they are becoming more and more influenced by thoughts of an occupational role very different from that of hunter—the job which pays a salary. Since 1940 this influence has increased markedly through many diverse sources, and it will be the place of a later section in the present chapter to examine these sources.

### FLUCTUATIONS IN NATIVE FOOD SUPPLY SINCE 1940

The St. Lawrence people have known starvation and real famine in their history; some, even within their lifetime. Although they are more richly supplied with animal life than most Eskimo groups, they have often felt the lean year, and concern over food and the possibility that next season will be one of starvation is deeply imbedded in the sentiments of the people. But even against this background of expected shortage, universally the Sivokakmeit now feel that with each passing season hunting is becoming much harder and less fruitful. The question is really whether this is an actual change since 1940 or whether it may be due to new standards of comparison, plus the juxtaposition of a disappointing present with a hyperbolic past.

It is said in the village that there are now fewer animals, that they are farther out, and that the weather has become so bad it permits little hunting even of these few animals. Both old men and the young observe this reputed phenomenon. An excerpt from the field notes reads:

He said that the weather is getting worse all the time—that when he was a boy it was good weather during the spring. And that the animals are fewer also than when he was young. They used to be in very close. In November, when the herds of walrus passed, you could lie in your bed and hear their grunting, they were so close. [Is hunting easier and better now?] No. Looks to me on the other side, little harder. Because animals getting wild. . . . There were many, many seal before, in the lagoon. Now, nothing. Yeah, too much shooting, too much noise, and too much smell. . . . Before, when we have no motor and not much shooting, oh, my! plenty seal, plenty seal! And walrus! And good weather! Always good weather!

These words are echoed by a young hunter: "Hunting is getting worse every year."

What evidence there is must be brought to bear on this central problem; for if it is in fact true that the established patterns of subsistence are being undercut by drastic changes in the physical environment of supply, then a powerful factor predisposing to change or readjustment has come into the picture. The possibility must of course be recognized that the perceived change may be as much a resultant of new standards of evaluation brought to the situation as an actual, objective decrease. It is highly probable that both have occurred in this situation.

The walrus herds are the center of the question about decrease in supply; and since there are some data concerning walrus population since 1940 (and before), the discussion of possible decline in game animals will be limited to that species. Some of the Eskimos say that if hunting of one animal is poor, hunting of everything will be poor that year. Although there may be some objective ecological reasons for this, at least in part the observation could also be a contemporary reflection of aboriginal religious beliefs about the relations of man to the animate world about him.

The village of Gambell, given its present size, has traditionally needed approximately 200–250 walruses per year to feed itself and its dogs. To reach this number, each hunting boat expects to kill from 30 to 40 or more walruses during the hunting season from March through the end of May. But during the spring hunting of 1955, the boats killed only between 10 and 20 walruses each (making a total village kill of 120); and during the spring of 1954, the kill was usually less than 10 (a total of 70). These figures compare with the season's total of 313 walruses that was listed in June of 1940.

This can be examined in a little more detail. In Table 13 is enumerated the number of walruses killed by one of the most successful hunting boats. Except for the entry for 1950, these are the April through June totals; the figure for 1950 is that for the entire year, from the preceding fall (and hence is higher). The record of this boat is representative in its trend of all others. In actual numbers it is probably higher than the average.

*Table 13.* Walrus-hunting record kept by one boat

| Year | No. killed |
|------|------------|
| 1950 . . . . . . . . . . | 39 |
| 1951 . . . . . . . . . . | 34 |
| 1952 . . . . . . . . . . | 37 |
| 1953 . . . . . . . . . . | 14 |
| 1954 . . . . . . . . . . | 11 |
| 1955 . . . . . . . . . . | 19 |

A table prepared by Dr. Francis H. Fay for the walrus harvest of some eighteen Alaskan Eskimo villages over the past fifteen or so years tells a similar story in terms of community totals. The figures for Gambell, extracted from the Fay table,[12] are included in the compilation in Table 14. Also included are recorded data on annual

*Table 14.* Annual walrus kill for Gambell village
(selected seasons since 1940)

| Year | Total killed |
|------|--------------|
| Average, late 1930's . . . . . | 300 |
| 1940 . . . . . . . . . | 313 |
| 1946 . . . . . . . . . | 172 |
| 1947 . . . . . . . . . | 178 |
| 1948 . . . . . . . . . | 70 * |
| 1949 . . . . . . . . . | 250 |
| 1950 . . . . . . . . . | 300 |
| 1952 . . . . . . . . . | 275 |
| 1953 . . . . . . . . . | 200 |
| 1954 . . . . . . . . . | 70 |
| 1955 . . . . . . . . . | 120 |

* This figure is an estimate. It is based on the description of 1948 as a year of food distress and the fact that 1954 was also described as a very poor hunting year. The number of walruses killed in 1954 was 70; and hence it is possible that a similar number were killed in 1948. In actual fact the number may have been less.

[12] Fay, 1955a, p. 160. I have included only those years for which there is a number given; I have also changed Fay's figures slightly in one instance to give a total of 313 for 1940, rather than for 1939, since it was the former hunting season to which the figure more properly refers.

kills for the years 1946 and 1947; estimates for 1949 and 1950 made by the Gambell teacher; and an estimated figure for 1948. Some of these data come from Alaska Native Service records and are used here with their permission; other additional figures come from Dr. Fay (1956).

It is difficult to obtain exact annual kill figures for the early 1940's. The records indicate, however, that 1946 and 1947 were only mediocre hunting years. An Alaska Native Service "Walrus Census" dated September 2, 1947, lists a total of 178 animals obtained for the current season (i.e., from early winter of the previous year through the spring) and an estimated number of 172 for the previous season (1946). Furthermore, although no specific figure is given for the number of walruses killed, the spring of 1948 was such a bad hunting season that government memoranda and records speak of a "food shortage" and of the necessity for army relief supplies to be brought in to feed the people. Apparently the entire preceding winter as well as the spring hunting season had been very poor. It is spoken of in these terms:

The adverse conditions as far as hunting is concerned have been unprecedented according to the natives. When the ice moved in in the early part of the winter it was very rough and so far out to open water that it was difficult for the people to do effective hunting.

And the teacher in Gambell, discussing the food situation, said in July of 1948:

The weather last winter played a part in the distress. According to the Weather Bureau here in Gambell the wind from the north continued for weeks keeping the ice packed to the shoreline, creating open water far out into the Bering Sea which made it impossible for the people to go out to get their walrus and seal. It was not until March and as late as May that the wind changed, moving the ice pack out, allowing the walrus and the seal to migrate in the open sea along the shoreline of St. Lawrence Island.

In the same memorandum it is said that "for several years no whales have come near the island." During the spring of 1940, five whales had been killed; and, although so large a number was very unusual, apparently only rarely had a spring hunting gone by without at least one whale being killed. Prior to the two killed in May of 1955, there had been no bowhead whales captured for two years and only one gray whale in 1953 and 1954. Thus the average number of whales killed per year from 1940 to 1955 was certainly far less than one.

Although no walrus-kill figures are available for 1951, there may also have been a food shortage in that year. In any case, the situation in the early winter look very unpromising. A teacher's letter reports the matter as of November 28 (1950):

The weather report secured from the local Weather Bureau Office stated that no ice has been seen throughout the Bering Sea as far north as Point Hope. This is an unusual condition for this time of year. At best, there will be no ice bringing walrus to this vicinity for at least three weeks. It will depend on a north wind, which has not been in evidence so far this year. Jonathan stated that he camped for one week on the north shore and got nothing. There were no sea gulls anywhere. This is an indication that there are no fish or other food available for them, as sea gulls follow the food supply. Jonathan mentioned that meat balls stored in meat cellars last spring will probably last through December. But this meat is very strong and spoiling fast. Several had brought to our attention, and again mentioned at the meeting, that this is a very hard time, especially for the pre-school children. They cannot stand the spoiled meat. It makes them sick. They refuse to eat it and lose weight. The store is well stocked with staple foods, but most families do not have sufficient money to buy enough of this food to make up for the lack of fresh meat.

The spring of 1942 was also a poor hunting season, although it was due not so much to inclement weather or lack of walruses as to the disruption caused in the Eskimos' annual cycle by the beginning of World War II. For a period of some weeks during the main hunting season the population of the village was evacuated from Gambell and moved over the mountain to live in tents and the few trappers' cabins along the north shore. This was done because of rumors of an impending landing by the Japanese (who were invading the Aleutian Islands and bombing Dutch Harbor that spring). Only the able-bodied men were left in the village, and even they could do little or no hunting, for, as members of the Alaska Territorial Guard, they spent hours patrolling the beaches and guarding the village. One informant remembers it this way:

At that time we got no food. Whole village was short food. . . . The store got no stuff, very short. We never get much food; that springtime was the war, that Japanese war. We never go out hunting. I move down to other side of the mountain. That's what kept us from getting meat enough to eat.

Thus within the last fifteen years there have been at least three major periods very short in food and several more when the hunting returns have not been up to normal needs.

REASONS FOR THE POOR HUNTING

Some of the reputed causes for bad hunting years have already been mentioned. Hunters of Gambell say that, in addition to the simple fact that there are fewer animals now, the walruses are frightened away from their traditional migration routes, which took them quite close to the village, by the smoke from petroleum-oil fires, by the bright lights showing through house windows, and by the disturbances of people, rifles, and other types of noise. Now, too, the loud roar of airplanes as they come into Gambell must help keep the walruses from swimming too close to the village. This air service, on a semimonthly regular schedule in 1954–1955, was established after 1940.

The problem of walrus abundance, their possible decline, and likely reasons for this was the subject of the study done by Dr. Francis Fay, which has been referred to above (Fay, 1955a). In the following terms he has summed up the general nature of the walrus population problem:

At the time of Bering's voyages, walruses were definitely more abundant than at present. They covered a much wider range (south to the Alaska panhandle and southern Kamchatka) and they were more frequently encountered. A conservative estimate would place their numbers at more than three times the present population. As whaling developed in the North Pacific and the demand for ivory grew, the walrus population was gradually reduced, the greatest bulk reduction apparently taking place in the mid and late nineteenth century. Ivory hunting continued into the early 1900's until the shortage of walruses, coupled with restrictive legislation, apparently rendered commerical exploitation economically unsound. The last remaining white traders, who obtained their ivory from Eskimos, were apparently put out of business by the "Walrus Act" of 1941, which effectively banned raw ivory export from the territory.

The decline of the walrus herds did not stop with the end of commercial exploitation, though it has probably diminished in rate since then. Russian estimates of the total stock in the mid-thirties were approximately 60,000 head, while present estimates place their numbers at about 40,000. The effects of this have been most noticeable in the "fringe" areas at the extremes of the walrus range and about the coastlines, while the island communities such as St. Lawrence, Diomede, and King have been relatively unaffected. This is evident from the harvest figures of the past 25 years. . . .

I believe that several things are operative in keeping game away from the village area, and oil smoke may be one of them. Certainly outboard motors have had an effect, and airplanes also frighten the animals away, though both may merely be temporary. Walruses tend to steer clear of any village—always have in modern times, at least—probably because they can hear and smell it. [1955b]

The influence of the weather on hunting, whether or not the former has changed for the worse since 1940, is decisive. I mentioned it earlier in connection with 1955 winter hunting, when for several periods of a week or two at a time no effective hunting was possible because of blowing snow and blizzard conditions. But during the main hunting months of April and May as well, the weather can sometimes prevent going after the herds that are found in the opened water. Fay has estimated that from the spring of 1952 to 1955, inclusive, there was in Gambell an average of one hunting day per 2.4 calendric days (Fay, 1955a, p. 152); he has further indicated that the ratio for any given individual boat is probably closer to one hunting day in five calendric days (Fay, 1958, p. 12). My own observations would corroborate this for the spring of 1955. There were, if anything, even fewer good days in 1955 than in previous years —and the great bulk of food for the entire year must be gathered during the two months of April and May.

Another important factor in the decline of the walrus herds has been wastage in the hunt. This comes about through loss of those animals which are killed but then sink or float away unretrieved or through the taking of animals mainly to get their tusks while the carcass is discarded. The latter occurs in some of the other Alaskan coastal villages, but not on St. Lawrence Island, where it is strongly condemned. Fay estimates on the basis of one study that only about half the animals wounded are ultimately secured and butchered (Fay, 1958, pp. 15–16). A third form of wastage occurs during the latter part of the spring hunt, when much less of the carcass is saved for use than is true earlier in the season (*ibid.*, pp. 19–20).

Regarding the question of actual decrease in the over-all Pacific walrus population, Fay points out that there has been considerable decline in the number of the animals both since the time of first contact with Europeans and in more recent years. Estimates of the total population place it at 200,000 animals in the seventeenth and eighteenth centuries and at some 40,000 to 45,000 animals at the present time (Fay, 1957, p. 437). During the period of greatest commercial exploitation by the white world (1860–1900), the over-all population was dangerously decimated, and it reached a very low point in the 1920's. Yet since that time the "population has been either stationary or slowly decreasing" (*ibid.*, p. 438). And what is more, with a walrus population of the size it presently is, wide fluctuations in number of animals harvested in any given place are likely to occur from one year to the next.

Equally important, however, for the purposes at hand is the fact that apparently the Gambell people believe that hunting has become much more difficult and unrewarding than it was even as recently as 1940. One aspect of this feeling is that there are actually fewer animals, even though St. Lawrence Island itself is still much better situated than the Alaskan coastal villages, which have lost walrus hunting entirely because of shrinkage in the range of the animal since the last century.

A second crucial development since 1940 regarding changes in subsistence patterns happened as early as 1948, and it probably had irrevocable effects: relief supplies to feed the Gambell population had to be brought in from the outside. Thus, for food, the people for the first time became significantly dependent on outside sources of supply and not on their own efforts in a traditional manner of dealing with the physical world. Relief supplies also had to be flown in several times during the winter of 1954–1955; when these came, what they consisted in, and the people's sentiments toward the parcels will be treated in more detail in the section of this chapter concerned with diet.

## THE REINDEER HERD

Yet far more serious in its consequences than the decline in walrus harvest has been the virtually total loss of the large reindeer herd that existed on the island in 1940, from the herding and annual slaughter of which the Sivokakmeit obtained meat and hides. The reindeer was not indigenous to the island; before 1900 the St. Lawrence people obtained reindeer hides from the Chukchi and from Indian Point Eskimos. The herd on St. Lawrence was introduced at the turn of the century by white authorities to help offset the serious depletion in the Eskimos' supply of maritime animals that had occurred because of the incursions of white commerce. A brief background account is in order. The story of reindeer on the island is one of slow but finally successful introduction of a new economic form that required fairly major changes in habit and motivation on the part of the Eskimo population; from this uncertain beginning came growing reliance on the flourishing herd by the people and then its sudden decimation in the years since 1940.

The introduction of the reindeer to St. Lawrence Island is described in the *Tenth Annual Report on Introduction of Domestic Reindeer into Alaska,* by Dr. Sheldon Jackson. This occurred on July 27, 1900, and Dr. Jackson's account is interesting for ethnographic purposes as well as important for its historical value; for instance, note the relevance to Chapter III of the second paragraph quoted below with its discussion of the effects of sickness:

The ship hoisted anchor and steamed for St. Lawrence Island, reaching the settlement at Gambell at 2:45 p.m. It had been in the plans of the Department [Department of the Interior] for two or three years to stock this large and important island with a herd of reindeer, but it had not been convenient to do so until the present season.

Reaching the village, we met an unexpected difficulty. The people were so discouraged by the large number of deaths that they had lost all hope and ambition, and did not care whether they secured the reindeer or not, although on several preceding seasons when we visited them they had been begging and urging that deer should be placed upon their island. The temporary discouragement was so great that none could be found who were willing to become herders. Under these circumstances, nothing could be done but abandon the project at present of placing deer upon the island. . . .

During the night, however, some of the younger men of the village who had been off hunting returned, and finding that I had decided to take the deer away, they called a meeting of the more progressive men of the village and came to me with their earnest remonstrances against

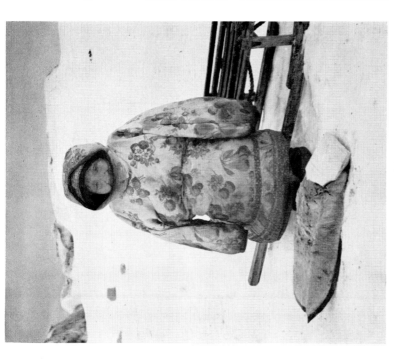

*Figure 13.* An elderly hunter with a seal killed along the shore ice, 1955.

*Figure 12.* The oldest woman in the village in 1955, born in Siberia, with her share of whale *mangtak*.

Figure 14 (left). A retired boat captain, wearing an intestine rain parka, 1955.
Figure 15 (right). A young girl of modern Sivokak.

Figure 16 (left). Typical Sivokakmeit method of carrying a child.
Figure 17 (right). Chopping a hole for fishing through the ice.

not landing the deer. Informing them that it was a question of finding a number of young men who were willing to become apprentices and learn to manage the deer, they at once offered their own sons. Consequently, on the afternoon of the 30th, twenty-nine reindeer were landed on the island to the eastward of the village. [Jackson, 1901, p. 37]

In September Captain Tuttle . . . upon his return from Point Barrow, called at Teller Station and took 45 deer from the Government herd, and after a stormy passage landed 42 on the island [St. Lawrence Island]. Two were drowned in passing through the surf and one injured and killed en route, leaving a herd of 70. [*Ibid.*, pp. 17–18]

Lapp herdsmen who were landed with the reindeer were to teach local Eskimos how to handle the animals. It was apparently a difficult transition period for a number of years, for herding required a new type of living pattern and adjustments in the occupational cycle. Many difficulties arose because of lack of knowledge concerning the habits, needs, and predispositions of these animals, and for a number of years quite a few of them died. But above all, herding required an entirely different motivational complex from that of the Eskimo hunter stalking his prey with the aim of killing it, and new patterns of subsistence at a fairly fundamental level had to be absorbed.[13] There is a similarity here between the introduction of domestic reindeer to the Eskimo and that of cattle to the Plains Indians.

In the system of herding first used, the young men spent an apprenticeship of three years with the herd, working under the guidance of older men who by now owned deer privately and had acquired a sufficient knowledge of herding techniques from their Lapp teachers. After that period, the younger man became a full-fledged herder and received his wages in deer. Then he himself could hire men to care for his own animals. Each man's deer were earmarked with a special sign, although all were herded together. During these periods of training, the apprentice could have his family with him at the herding camp, and small permanent communities centered around the care of the herd were established at various points on the island.

Although the system of ownership of the herd changed in 1923,

[13] For a discussion of this as a general difficulty in the history of reindeer herds among the Alaskan Eskimos, see Lantis, 1950 and 1952a.

the pattern of herding did not alter too radically. Through the late 1930's there were still some of these permanent herding camps where men lived with their families and took shifts watching the wandering herds. Such herding was under the direction of a "chief herder," who had complete charge of all the herd on the island and was hired for this job by the Reindeer Company (a corporation owned by the people of the island). The main duties of the herders were to protect the animals from danger and to keep them from exhausting the hillside pastures during the summer; for in the winter such relatively snow-free forage was about all they could easily obtain, since snow and often ice covers the flat ground.

The center of active interest in the reindeer herd shifted away from Gambell some ten to fifteen years after the deer were introduced. The other village on the island, Savoonga, was established in 1917 primarily as a herding camp; and that village's main economic base during the years since then has remained the reindeer herd and, secondarily, fox trapping. Its walrus hunting is not as good as Gambell's, and whaling is nonexistent. During the time when reindeer were owned by individual herders, most of these people moved to Savoonga. And when the shift in ownership patterns occurred in 1923, it was a Savoonga man who was appointed chief herder. One reason for this may have been that, at its prime, the herd roamed the central and eastern parts of the island—thus favoring Savoonga as a location for its control and herding. The reindeer camps already mentioned were also located near to and east and south of Savoonga. Perhaps for this reason there tended to be far fewer Gambell men who moved with their families to the herding camps.

Gambell people owned stock in the herd, however, and participated in the annual slaughters. For instance, teen-age boys from Gambell were hired for special herding during the fawning season (April to June), when young deer were born and had to be protected from wild dogs, foxes, polar bears, and other animals. Several men from the village did the herding under a leader, and there were weekly stints for those who wanted to work. The crew stayed with the herd, watching in twelve-hour shifts of half the men on duty and the rest sleeping. The pay was rather low—30 cents per hour—but meat was free.

From all accounts, herding was an activity the boys greatly enjoyed. One said, recalling his days as a herder:

Oh! lot of fun! [What did you like about it?] You know, when we get away from the village, we boys feel free—free to do anything! Lots of fun; have to walk from place to place, put our tents up on a little dry spot, and rest. Then the sun was shining before we spot reindeer. We boys always have little swimming when we get to the lakes. That's sure a lot of fun!

The animals were usually rounded up and slaughtered three times each year. In June, after the two months of herding during fawning season, the herds were gathered together for the killing of fawns for their hides (since fawn skin was very much prized as the warmest material for winter parkas). At the end of the summer there was a second roundup of as much of the herd as could be collected for counting, butchering, and castrating of the young bulls. This occurred in the large corral located between Gambell and Savoonga, and the majority of the people in both villages went there for the week of slaughtering to earn meat and hides by helping with the work. Finally, the herd was usually rounded up during the food-scarce fall in order to supply sufficient meat.

The roundup was an exciting affair. People from both villages went to the corral on the north side of the island, and the summer roundup and slaughter provided, in fact, the only occasion on which most of the St. Lawrence people met face to face in a common activity. The importance of the socially integrative functions of the week-long common work and play would be hard to overstate. It was there that many people had a chance to visit relatives long unseen, to meet new people, and to recall old experiences. The loss of the herd therefore had significance far beyond the decline in a steady meat supply, for no comparable social activity has arisen to take the place of the summer roundup.

*Ownership of the herd*—As noted above, in the early years the reindeer were owned by private individuals, each of whom had earned their deer by three years of apprenticeship. But in 1923 the system of ownership was changed so that the entire herd became a corporate entity, with shares owned by the Eskimos. It was formalized into the "Reindeer Commercial Company" under the policy of the Reindeer Service and was merged with the community stores of both Gambell and Savoonga to become a single institution. A teacher's annual report of some ten years later gives some of the details

concerning the formation of the Reindeer Commercial Company. . . . There were only 2 representatives from Gambell present while practically the entire male population of Savoonga attended the meeting. The assets of the newly organized company consisted of the reindeer herd and the stores. There were 60 shares of stock in the Eskimo Building and Loan Association [the name of the two stores] valued at $600.00. These were owned by three men, 2 from Gambell and 1 from Savoonga. This stock was transferred to the Reindeer Commercial Company. The first record of stockholders in the Reindeer Commercial Company is dated Nov. 25, 1925. This shows that there were issued 4,629 shares of deer stock valued at $46,290.00.

Another report, undated and unsigned but very likely written by the same teacher at the same time, implies an unfairness to Gambell:

The statement of Alfred indicates to me that the organization of the Reindeer Commercial Company was anything but fair. Gambell, which had everything to lose, had only two natives representing it, while Savoonga was represented by the entire village and the teachers. The store, which after a struggle of 13 years was becoming profitable and in a position to help Gambell, was handed as a gift to Savoonga herders and absolutely no consideration was given to the people here. If they wanted any share in the profits they must buy stock for each. The wireless equipment and light plant which was ordered for this village and paid for with store funds was delivered to Savoonga so as to be of assistance to the reindeer herders.

As the Eskimo Building and Loan Association was organized it was a cooperative organization and each customer was in effect a co-owner. It is my impression that in a co-partnership no individual co-partner can act for the others without their consent. If this is true the combining of the stores with the reindeer herd was not in accordance with legal practice, as no consent was obtained from the majority of the co-owners of the store.

Nonetheless, it was a *fait accompli*, and for about fifteen years (until 1939) the store and reindeer herd were operated as part of the same corporation.

The formal structure of the reindeer corporation consisted of a president, a manager, two secretaries, and a board of five directors (three from Savoonga and two from Gambell). These positions were elective, chosen by the stockholders of the company. The officers in turn were responsible to the official local representatives of the Bureau of Indian Affairs (the schoolteachers of the two villages), and the latter, for their part, were responsible to the General Reindeer Supervisor of the Department of the Interior. No data are available on the term of office, but it was probably four or five years.

Individuals who owned stock in the herd received a dividend of approximately 10 per cent—i.e., for each ten shares of stock they owned (which could be thought of as ten deer), they received one deer carcass at the roundup. Above and beyond that amount, if they wanted more meat, they—together with people who owned no stock—had to purchase it at the rate of anywhere from $6 to $10 per carcass. Helping at the roundup was one way to earn deer, and the pay (at 20 cents per hour) equaled the price of meat per pound. This system was described in a memorandum of 1946:

I asked . . . where they had arrived at their figures for butchering during the last five years, and he stated that they butchered dividends. I finally found out that this meant that for every 10 deer a stockholder had on the books, he was allowed to kill one deer; if a man had 200 deer on the stockbooks, he could butcher 20 deer per annum.

Such an interest rate meant, in effect, that 10 per cent of the herd was slaughtered each year. The greatest bulk of stock was owned in Savoonga, but some was held by Gambell people. And although not everyone in the village had stock, distribution of the shares was rather widespread in Gambell.

*The decline of the herd*—At some time after 1940 the herd began to decline, for reasons that are not clear or agreed upon by either the Eskimos or outside students of the problem. Nor is the exact date established. But between the year 1943 or 1944 and 1948, the herd had so catastrophically declined in numbers that people could no longer kill any of the animals for meat. Possibly (and probably) this decline occurred over a number of years, with several factors operating. One reason averred by Eskimo informants is that the animals were not herded properly; and, in fact, memoranda of 1946 say specifically that the reindeer had not been herded at all for about five years and were being allowed to run wild. An Eskimo informant, who himself had herded deer in his younger days, said:

You know, I think they starved to death. The place is over-grazed, and nobody cares for it. [Do you mean it wasn't being herded?] No, I don't think so. The herd died off gradually, but worse one year. Sometimes I found 3 or 4 deers all curled up together, dead and frozen.

Several other types of explanation are also offered, such as loss of part of the herd on drifting ice when they inadvertently wandered off onto the frozen ocean.

No more precise data concerning the demise of the herd were obtainable from Eskimo informants, doubtless in part because the event had occurred a number of years earlier and its causes were uncertain. What was obtained did, in general, agree with the statements noted above, with the further addition that several people say that a very bad ice storm covered the tundra early one fall and made it impossible for the deer to dig through to winter forage.

Data from other sources help somewhat to fill out the picture. Fay, mentioned before, spent parts of three different years on the island, and he notes that the possibility of an ice storm covering the tundra is not to be discounted. He also feels, however, that a more likely factor is range devegetation, such as that which occurred on the mainland of Alaska when the herds were allowed to increase beyond the point of optimal use of range (Fay, 1955b).

Besides range devegetation, unwise slaughter practices may have contributed to the decimation of the herd, at least in its declining years. In 1940 and for some years previous to that, the Eskimos estimated that the herd numbered 10,000 animals. That this figure may have been too high—plus concern that it might have led to herd-depleting slaughter—is indicated in the following excerpts, taken from records pertaining to the herd:

[April, 1946] It is clear that there is much watered stock [in the Reindeer Commercial Company] in the number of 10,000—supposedly the number of deer on the island. It was agreed between the Directors and ourselves that the stock should be de-watered, and the stock will have to be cut 75% in order to bring it down to the figure of 2,500 deer, which are estimated to be the total on the Island at present. This seems to be a tremendous figure, but the industry on the mainland has suffered the same losses. Using your figures of a year ago, and mine gathered on my recent trip around the island, the herd can be estimated at about 2,500 deer. I feel that this is a good estimate. You remember that we figured the annual kill should be 10% of our estimated total, which would leave 250 animals per annum to use for expenses.

Another memorandum of the same date expands on the overestimate of the herd:

I have just returned from a ten-day trip to St. Lawrence Island. From what I could gather, the 10,000 deer supposed to be on the island was an estimate on the part of the chief herder, who reported this number to . . . [the schoolteacher] each year. [The teacher] had never made a trip over the Island, and it was natural that he take the chief herder's figure. A year ago last winter, however, the stockholders elected a new chief-herder—a young man who had been with the herd all during the time the former chief herder had had charge of the stock. When this young man took over, he informed . . . [the present schoolteacher] that in his opinion there had never been 10,000 deer on the island; following the old Eskimo custom, he, the younger man, even though he was right, had not ventured to contradict the older man who had had more experience. This young man . . . wanted some Government man to check the range with him, and as a result, [the teacher], in company of the chief and four others, spent six days in a tour of the Island. These men, with . . . [the teacher], estimated the number of deer at 2,500. . . . There has not been a roundup on the island for about five years, and I instructed [the young chief herder] to have a roundup and marking and counting in July, if at all possible. . . . I asked [the chief herder] where they had arrived at their figures for butchering during the last five years, and he stated that they butchered dividends. I finally found out that this meant that for every ten deer a stockholder had on the books, he was allowed to kill one deer; if a man had 200 deer on the stock books, he could butcher 20 deer per annum. Of course, all figures were based on the total of 10,000 animals supposedly on the Island. Right there was the leak; they were butchering dividends, as they called it, on stock that had been watered 75%. This procedure has stopped. No one will get any meat unless he pays cash for it, and only when the Directors and Local Superintendent feel it is safe to sell meat in order to secure cash to buy staples for the needs of the herd in general. . . . I believe that the Island should only be allowed to have 5,000 deer at its peak. From what I could gather from natives, and from my own observation, it is evident that part of the range has been overgrazed, regardless of the deer the Island has supported in past years.

But the warnings were in vain; for in two years the herd was already being spoken of in the past tense:

[Date not available, but unquestionably 1948] This is in reply to your letter of March 5 relative to the reasons why more of the reindeer were not utilized during the recent food shortage on St. Lawrence Island. The reindeer are pretty well scattered over the island and at times may require considerable travelling to locate them. . . . [Monthly] reports show 134 deer have been killed up to and including December of this year. The allowable kill that the reindeer company has set is 240 per year which they feel is safe and will not endanger the reduction of the herd. I have written . . . [the teachers in Gambell and Savoonga] suggesting that perhaps some plan might be worked out with the reindeer company whereby it could be arranged to loan the deer to a group of two or three reliable natives on a contract basis.

[May 4, 1948] The stockholders of the reindeer company are aware that the deer are not being herded properly and were willing to make a contract between the company and [two] individuals for the care of the deer. For the past three or four years the deer have not been herded and consequently have become very wild—so wild in fact that from the reports I heard the deer had to be hunted with rifles when the company decided to butcher and that many times they were unable to get close enough to the deer to shoot them.

[From letter dated September 7, 1948, written by the Gambell school-teacher] At present the reindeer herd on St. Lawrence Island has dwindled to the point where a law was passed forbidding the killing of any reindeer for any purpose. . . . There has not been an actual count of the reindeer for some time. . . . The . . . men who made a fairly thorough investigation of the island saw a few tracks and saw a herd of deer only once. They estimated the herd at about 50 deer. They also reported that there were skeletons all over. About the most optimistic estimate from the natives is 250 on the entire island. The deer, of course, have not been herded since the law was passed against shooting them, consequently, they are very wild. And it would be very difficult to corral them at present. It would be very desirable to have reindeer meat again to help alleviate any possible food shortages similar to the serious one last year.

The estimated number of live deer on the island during 1954–1955 was from 80 to 100. By this time people are aware that the days of fawn-skin parkas and reindeer meat are gone—at least for many years. The following statement is typical of sentiments about reindeer meat, and it also illustrates the auxiliary role the herd had in Eskimo economy, for it could be used as one means of stabilizing an otherwise fluctuating food supply:

[Did people depend on the reindeer meat a lot?] A lot of people used to depend on the deer meat, especially in the fall. If we still had it we wouldn't be worrying about the shortage of meat now. We would just wait for a big herd to come in at the end of the lake . . . and then go down and shoot as many as we want. Then we would have 4 or 5 boats hauling the meat and skins across the lake to the village. We would butcher any time when the meat was scarce, especially in the fall, like this. So we've had only seal and birds in the fall since then. . . . Sometimes I crave reindeer. When I think about it I want to taste it . . . Oh my, fine!

When in 1954 the store ordered some frozen reindeer carcasses from Nunivak Island—to be brought on the fall trip of the ANS supply vessel—these were very anxiously awaited. As the carcasses were being brought ashore, many people recalled that one used to be able to buy a whole reindeer for no more than $10, whereas those then on the beach were selling for $40.

## Diet

### CHANGES SINCE 1940

The actual labor patterns involved in obtaining native foods have been described in some detail. It now remains to determine what contribution those native foods make to the total diet in relation to the white man's food eaten and to ascertain to what extent this relative balance of food type has shifted since 1940; for in an acculturation situation, the prestigeful and symbolic—not necessarily the nutritive—significance of food often dictates new patterns.

There have been several significant changes in food tastes since 1940. Traditionally, the Eskimo meal consisted only of products derived from the island and surrounding sea. It often began with "old" meat followed by a portion of sour greens and then ended with some fresh meat, all this sliced into small bite-size portions by the woman of the house as she sat at one end of the eating trencher, or *kaiyootak*. In 1940 this general commensal pattern was still followed, but for some thirty or forty years there had been various items of white man's food included in the diet, the most important of which were tea, coffee, flour, sugar, baking powder, and dried fruit. But without question the relative balance of this mainland food in the diet has shifted since 1940. Now there is consumption of more mainland food by many more of the population much more of the time. This is especially true among children and young people, as the Sivokakmeit themselves recognize:

Paul said that he likes bread fried in seal oil very much, but they never have it anymore because his kids don't like it [i.e., the seal oil].

[Do you think that people are buying more white man's food now than before?] Oh yeah, yeah. More. See, our food here getting less now. We use more whiteman food. This year we use more whiteman food. Good thing we have it, whiteman. If we haven't that, maybe some of them starve. [Which do you like best?] Just about the same now, on me. When I eat most our own food, I like whiteman. So I eat. See, we always eat half our meat, and half whiteman. Some days we eat all whiteman. [What do the young people like best?] Oh, maybe whiteman. They want most, whiteman. . . .

I asked if they are eating more white food than they used to, and Frederick said, "Oh, my yes, like it more all the time." He said that they mix the Eskimo food and the white food in all their meals. First they eat Eskimo meat and put that down and eat some kind of white people's food. I asked about their children's food preferences, and he said they don't care so much for walrus and seal. "Mostly they eat bread, oh my, they like bread."

Another important general change in the 1940 and traditional food pattern is the enormous decline in use of seal and walrus oil, such as eating it with the meal or employing it as a preservative for birds, fish, or meat. The St. Lawrence people apparently used much more of the walrus oil than seal oil, in contrast to the Alaskan mainland Eskimos. In 1940, for instance, they said, in response to the question "What part of the seal do you eat raw?":

This part muscle [back] after frozen, lay it down on rock and hammer and every bite dip in a little dish of oil, and then we bite. Sometimes without oil.

And in referring to walrus oil there is even a stronger statement:

We eat the blubber with the skin [said in reply to "Do you eat blubber?"]. You know, we cut the skin with about one inch blubber with it. Everything we eat have to have a little oil in it.

For preservation, as noted before, seal and walrus meat, birds, and fish were dried on a rack and then placed in sealskin pokes filled with seal or walrus oil and stored against the winter. One man notes the change in 1955 in these words:

Big difference now. We no more eat that good meat like before. Long time ago pack up meat for winter. Now we no more. Pack in poke or they make big walrus hide just like barrel—for pack up meat. Now we no more that way.

Seal and walrus blubber, which for centuries had given the Eskimo light, heat, and food, is often discarded out on the ice and not even brought back to the village in any quantity. A modern Gambell hunter says:

You know, blubber used to be the most valuable thing we have—use it for heat and light. Now we throw it into the ocean.

And another puts it even more cogently; some of his words have been used before in this chapter:

When I was a boy, become a hunter, we used to save every part of the animal. Mostly blubber. [Now do you throw it away?] Yeah. . . . From the first part of the winter there was good hunting. For seals, and walrus, and everything. They hunt much as they could. Save every part of it— blubber and meat. Pretty soon, carcasses piled up; just take the skin off and leave the blubber on the meat; store it, never touch it. . . . The current is very close in the first part of the winter. The latter part of the winter when the shore ice gets heavy, the sea animals travel way out where loose ice and open leads are. For that reason, people tried to get all they could; because ahead there lies shortage of meat and oil. For that part they store everything. . . . No, they don't store as much meat now. That's our fault—this hard time. Shortage of meat and oil—short on money, by trying to use lantern—kerosene and gasoline. That's our fault here. When we were using sea oil lamp, no need to have kerosene, gasoline for lamp; nothing. No stove oil. If we were doing like we did before, pretty good. . . . Plenty oil in reserve. Lots of meat. Now that's gone— hard time. Trying to use kerosene to cook with and gas lamp for light;

too much cost. Before that, very easy. Now that blubber is gone, everybody trying to use whiteman's way. It's pretty hard for the Eskimos. So that's why I say that's our fault. One seal blubber lasts a long time. Two or three lamps, a week or a week and a half—by adding other kinds of oil. And mukluk blubber last long; use the oil, and at the same time use up what's remaining of the blubber. Same way with the walrus blubber—put the blubber in a poke, and two or three pokes last long time. Use up the oil, and the remaining, eat it. [Do people eat it now?] Yeah, we eat it sometimes some of the family. . . . If I were using that blubber, I would be a rich man. I would be using some of the money for other stuff. [Why did you change?] I don't know.

I have quoted at length from this man's thoughts even though it carried us outside the narrow sphere of diet, for the context of his ideas and mode of expression are worth keeping. What he has said about heating problems will come up again.

The last of the principal changes in food patterns since 1940 lies in the ideational rather than the material realm. It is the increased awareness of being dependent on the outside world for food supplies, particularly in times of shortage. This dependence was critical during the winter of 1954–1955, for, owing to the poor hunting season of the preceding year, native food was scarce in supply. The village faced hunger or, at the extreme, actual starvation. As a result of action by various governmental agencies, relief food supplies (consisting in large part of surplus milk, cheese, lard, some canned meat, beans and other cereals) were distributed, once in the month of October, twice in December, twice in February, and once in March. As early as September, the village leaders had realized that there would be severe shortages, particularly of food for dogs, and an unprecedented hunt for sea lions was therefore organized. This meat helped somewhat in the fall feeding of dogs, but was not at all sufficient to offset the continual drain on their energy caused by hard work in the cold. In late December and January the situation was becoming much worse for both people and dogs. Hunting continued very poor, and a public meeting was organized at which it was decided that the food supply in the village was small enough to declare an emergency and ask for help from the Alaska Native Service and the Civil Defense Headquarters. During December and January over fifty dogs had died in Gambell, principally from malnutrition.

It was as a result of this public meeting that one February shipment came and later that in March. The food was evenly distributed to each household by the village Welfare Committee, acting under the authority of the village council.

This greater reliance on outside sources for emergency food—as well as staples—began during the ten years that the Civil Aeronautics Administration unit was operating, when some people had steady jobs and could get groceries and other items from Nome. One man, who was employed there for several years, now looks back longingly at the time when he could obtain groceries cheaply at the commissary; and most of the village, even if they could not directly get food through this installation, saw here an example near at hand of white patterns of food consumption, and many new foods were introduced to the Eskimos during the time the unit was in operation.

After the departure of the CAA group, the air force and army installations took on much the same significance, although neither one was as close to the village or employed as many people. But both fulfilled (and the army installation continued to do so through 1955) the role of an agency of the white mainland that could be appealed to for help in time of emergency. One young man, pointing in the direction of the army base, said to a soldier, "We won't starve while you're out there." The truth of this was shown at several critical times during the year, when surplus food was donated to the village.

In the larger scope, however, the store itself is both the focus and the symbol of the village's dependence on the outside world, and many people recognize that an irrevocable step has been taken in the direction of including some white items as "essentials" in the Eskimo diet. This came out in several ways. One man, discussing the store and how it had ordered very ineffectively that year, referred to certain essential items that must be on hand, and he listed flour, tea, sugar, baking powder, oil, and kerosene. In his somewhat pragmatic view, all other goods are superfluous and Eskimo life could go on without them. But for most other people, the store and its stock of white man's food have moved in to occupy a critically functional role in village life:

Barbara said that if it wasn't for the store, there would be a famine here now.

[Do people eat different food now from what they used to?] Yeah, lot of change. If we got none of our food, we turn to store. That pretty good —that good idea from white people.

George said he appreciates the whitemen for the food they are bringing in now—all you have to do to have food is to put in some hot water!

[Are people eating more store food now than before?] Yeah. Trying to eat from the store—even though we are hard time to get it. Too many toothaches, maybe from store. Growing too much. Store get rich; toothache occurs.

FOODS EATEN

A few reservations should be made about using the year 1954–1955 to index the fifteen-year change in diet. It was something of an unusual year by reason of the shortage of native foods and the resulting greater use of mainland relief food. Aside from this, however, the weight of evidence points to the irrevocable shift in diet since 1940, and there is probably no unduly exaggerated importance given white man's food. In some respects, in fact, there may actually have been more native foods used during this year than in the average of preceding years since 1940; for, with the store running short of food, some people gathered more greens, fished more, and made more use of native products in general than they had done during the preceding summers. Even some types of meat were eaten that are not normally consumed, such as seal feet.

Another reason for the use of more native foods by some people was the tighter credit policy of the store and the general lack of money in the village. For a number of years prior to 1955, the store had been quite free in allowing credit, and there had been no barrier imposed to the exercise of tastes for the white man's food.

These reservations having been made, the year 1954–1955 will be examined in some detail as the terminal point for this study of diet change since 1940.

*Seasonal changes*—At my request, several people kept diaries of their food consumption for a week during the months of November,

January, March, and May. Although they were not the same individuals in all cases, there were either four or five diaries for each month. Listed in these diaries were the types of food the individuals themselves and/or their families ate for each meal of the day during that week. The profiles of diet change throughout the year gathered by this method are in essential agreement with the food data from other sources, and the individuals represent a good sample of people in different acculturation situations.

In attempting to find a measure that will best summarize the mass of diet data, I have used a construction that I call the "food-meal index." This needs a few words of explanation. The "food-meal" unit is constructed on the same basis as the "man-hour" unit used in industry, for example. Thus a "food-meal" is that unit constituted by one type of food eaten at one meal. My main purpose here is not in assessing sheer bulk contributed by different types of food to the diet; there is no question that meat still constitutes the largest bulk item. Rather, I want to discover the change in the types of food eaten at different times of the year. One method, which I attempted to follow, was simply to calculate the relative proportion of meals at which a given food was taken (e.g., walrus flesh or tea), let us say at 14 per cent and 56 per cent of the total meals recorded. This says nothing about how many people ate that food or in what quantities. But it does give some indication of how often a particular food, considered only by itself in relation to a given number of meals, is consumed.

Also important is how often a specified type of food is consumed, both in relation to a given number of meals and in relation to how often other foods are also eaten. One important aspect of diet, particularly in times of change, is variety of foods. This is actually one of the most important functions of white man's food in Gambell —to give diversity and change from a steady meat diet. Many people say that when they eat their own food exclusively for a few days they want to change to white man's food, until they also tire of it and return to the native diet.

If one considers only the percentage of meals at which a single food is eaten, time is the principal dimension, and there is no accounting in the same index for the diversity of other types of food consumed. The food-meal is, therefore, one measure of the participation of a given food item in the diet, relative both to the number of times it appeared at a meal as well as to the number of times other food items also appeared in the diet. The index is constructed by

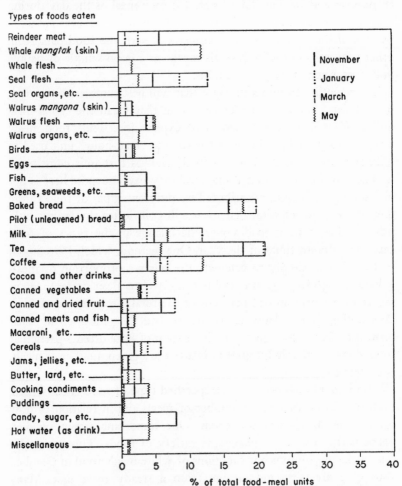

Chart 3. Food-meal profile, seasonal variation, 1954–1955.

The "food-meal" is defined as that unit constituted by one type of food eaten at one meal. For example, bread eaten three times a day yields three food-meals; bread and tea taken twice a day yields a total of four food-meals; and so on.

Total meals reported: Nov., 98; Jan., 78; March, 88; May, 115.

Total number of food-meal units: Nov., 369; Jan., 247; March, 224; May, 364.

summing up the total number of times that each food has been eaten and calculating the percentage of the total that is contributed by any given food, e.g., walrus flesh. The pattern of diet change throughout the four months of November, January, March, and May, as figured by this method, is given in Chart 3.

Several features are important in this profile. First, the consumption of reindeer meat, following the arrival of the supply ship with frozen carcasses in November, gradually decreases throughout the winter. By March the last of the hoarded meat has been brought out of storage. *Mangtak* (whale skin) is missing from the diet until the whale is killed in May, when it becomes a very significant item. Seal-flesh consumption rises as fall and winter progress and then falls proportionately in May. Consumption of walrus shows no spectacular change through these four months, and it is actually one of the greatest bulk foods of the total diet, although this is not as apparent in the table as it might be. Bird flesh is eaten during the fall and winter, declines in amount in March, and then once more comes into the diet in May (and particularly later in the summer, as will presently be shown). As for some of the rest of the foods, the steady reliance on baked bread throughout the year is very evident, as is the great consumption of tea (except for May, when there was virtually no tea whatever in the village—the store's supplies were completely gone). The use of white man's foods is quite irregular through these four months. This is due primarily to the influx of various assortments of relief goods, consisting of cereals, dried milk, lard, cheese, canned meat, and fruit. It is difficult, therefore, to discern from the chart any general pattern in the consumption of white foods at different seasons.

THE COMING OF THE SUPPLY SHIP

By the middle of June a situation was developing that presented something of an "experiment of nature"—i.e., control by empirical events of some of the pertinent variables of the situation. The store's stock of white man's food was exhausted and had been for some weeks. No relief supplies were in sight, and the annual supply vessel with its stock of store goods was only two or three weeks away. Here seemed a chance to find out several things of importance to the study of a diet in change: (1) What are the types of native foods most used when virtually no white man's foods are available? (2) What are favorite foods? (3) How much of a shift is there in diet when white man's food becomes available again, and what is the pattern of shift from the predominantly native-food diet to that in which there is at least the availability of white foods? (Whether that white food can actually be used depends upon several factors, most important of which is whether people have money to buy it.)

In this situation a survey was made of the foods eaten by some eleven households for one week during June, and a similar survey was made of foods eaten by those same households during a week in late August. The surveys were in the form of diaries kept by a literate adult of each household, and in these were recorded all the different types of foods eaten—similar to the diaries kept by the smaller sample of people at different months of the year.[14]

Although the ship arrived in the first half of July, I purposely did not make the second survey until a month had gone by and the first excitement of buying white food, after so long a deprivation, had passed. I felt that thereby a more valid indication of the relative use of white food in the diet was obtained than if I had surveyed the diet during the week or so immediately following the arrival of the ship.

The profile of diet both before the arrival of the ship and a month afterward is given in Chart 4 in terms of the same type of "food-meal" unit used before.

The most noticeable change in diet following the ship's unloading of cargo is the general shift to consumption of more white food. Moreover (and this does not show in the chart itself but was discovered in the analysis), there is considerably more variety of diet. The total number of "food-meal" units increased from 708 in June to 976 in August even though the number of meals reported on was practically the same in both cases (232 in June, 231 in August). The trend toward more use of white food and proportionately less use of native foods is evident in the chart; and of particular importance is the rise in consumption of canned fruit and vegetables

[14] The sample of the eleven households for the summer survey was selected systematically by taking every fifth household listed in the 1954 census, which consisted of fifty-four households—thus making approximately a 20 per cent sample of all households. There were no refusals to this request to keep a food diary, and the same eleven people repeated their task in August.

and canned meat, butter, and sugar. In addition, "pilot bread" (ship's biscuits) somewhat replaces the great reliance on baked bread, the staple throughout most of the year. Tea consumption is somewhat

**Types of foods eaten**

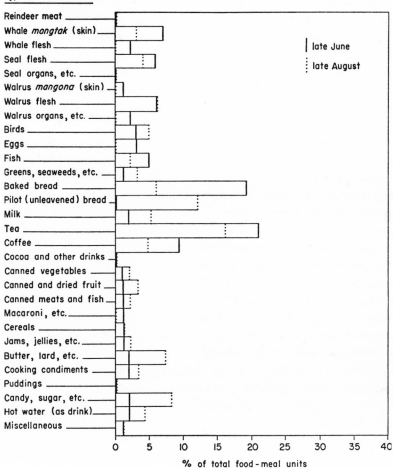

*Chart 4.* Food-meal profile, summer of 1955.

lower, but only because of the greater variety of foods contending with it in this index. The drop in consumption of *mangtak*, seal flesh, eggs, and fish is due to seasonal factors, as is the increased use of birds in the diet in August (the young cormorants are just hatching, and men climb the rocks to gather them from their nests).

Walrus flesh increases in proportion, in part because of the great decrease in consumption of *mangtak* and whale flesh, but also because people begin to bring their *tochtak* out of meat storage houses.

On the basis of this survey a decided swing is seen to relatively more use of white man's foods when they are available, even after deprived tastes have been assuaged. I am assuming, for the reasons given above, that the August survey represents the "normal" proportion in which white man's food enters into the diet in terms of variety of foods eaten—not in bulk contributed. On this assumption, there is a fair amount of different types of food contributed by the white world to the current Sivokakmeit diet.

The next question is, of course, how much this pattern has changed since 1940. Fortunately, the Leightons requested two individuals to keep a diary of all the foods they ate at every meal for a period of some eight or nine weeks. These two men, who were among the more acculturated in the village, present a diet profile that is of considerable help in delineating the change in diet reported in more qualitative terms by informants. It is interesting to compare this pattern with that for the summer of 1955, for I followed the same procedure in general to construct it, viz., I found the diet profile just before the supply ship arrived and that a few weeks after. Although there was not quite a full week of preship meals reported on in the earlier record, there are sufficient data to establish a conclusion. See Chart 5.

First of all, the arrival of the ship's supply makes relatively little difference in the total diet. The greatest changes are due to seasonal shifts in the pattern of native food (e.g., increased consumption of reindeer after the summer slaughter, decline in *mangtak* as the summer wears on, more use of birds and fish, and other similar shifts). In 1940, by contrast to 1955, consumption of baked bread increases after the store is restocked, indicating perhaps that now there is a greater favoritism for pilot bread. Tea was then, as now, the single most commonly used item of white food.

It is rather strange that the arrival of the ship seems to have made no great difference in the diet. That is, the main pattern of food consumption appears to have gone on relatively undisturbed by the white man's foods. This may very well be explained by a hypothesis advanced now by some of the Sivokakmeit themselves. In questioning why the store's supplies were short in 1955, I asked if the annual requisition had been smaller than usual. The answer from people who did the ordering was that the quantity of goods ordered was about

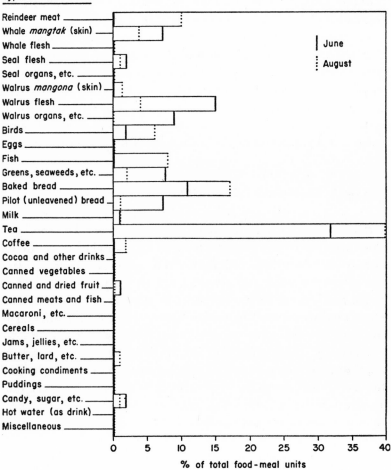

Chart 5. Food-meal profile, summer of 1940.

the same as it had been for a number of years, or perhaps even more. The principal factor making the difference was that now the old people receive old-age assistance money, some widows receive financial help from welfare agencies, and a few veterans get monthly disability checks. With that money and with other income entering the village, the store's goods are more quickly depleted now. The principal difference would seem to be that white man's food was used more sparingly in 1940. The major types of today's foods—sugar, flour, tea, coffee, canned vegetables and fruits—were found in the store then, but they were not quantitatively (and probably not qualitatively) as important in the diet as they are now.

In summary, there is evidence of a real change toward consumption of more white food than fifteen years ago. And there is particularly a shift in taste among the younger people. It is also important to look at sentiments about food, both those centering on the choice between white and native foods and those dealing with food in general; for food is still one of the most crucial nodes of social value and organization in this village based on a subsistence economy.

### SENTIMENTS CONCERNING FOOD

In 1954–1955 anxieties about food shortage were very near the surface of daily thought. The fact that such concern with food was, along with health, the principal focus of the aboriginal ritual life has already been mentioned. Suppliance to the gods of sea, air, and land was directed toward good hunting and an abundant return. In an action that is not at all uncommon in the cultures of the world, those foods that most appeal to mortal taste were saved for offering to the gods in return for good hunting: baby walrus flippers, for example, one of the greatest of Eskimo delicacies, were set aside on a special meat rack with other foods for sacrifice to the *taeganugaek* that controlled the game. Waste of food was an offense not only against man, but against the gods as well. In short, food was here, as in so much of the underfed world, a critical focus of organized social activities.

It is significant that the term which in general means "flesh" (*kamookruk*) is also applied to one's nearest kinsmen—a fusion in the linguistic form, it would appear, of two of the most important objects of sentiment formation in the Eskimo culture. Among one's kinsmen unquestioning sharing of food is a fundamental and most deeply rooted sentiment. But that generosity, particularly that in food, is a basic requisite in Eskimo life in general. One of the clans in the village is still known by a name translated as "door being kept shut always," given because some of their ancestors had once shut the house door in the face of people coming to ask for food. Hospitality is a necessary social habit and transcends kinship bonds. Typical of the many remarks in this area are these:

If anyone asks for food, we have to give it, until there is no more.
You know, our native custom is that I feed other people, too.

Although the picture is not too clear as to whether the Gambell people actually prefer white or native foods, except for some of the younger people, there does seem to be a preference for change and variety of foods taken from both the white and Eskimo larders. It is generally recognized, however, that white man's food does not have the energy content of Eskimo meat. This is phrased in various ways:

We got no food—only store food.
But when we eat whiteman food, we still hungry.
We don't like whiteman food—too soft. . . . We get tired of it. [What do people like best—*mangtak?*] No, walrus. [Do people get tired of seal and mukluk?] Yeah, but they don't get tired of walrus.
Whiteman food helps us—makes us no starve. But when we eat whiteman food, we still are hungry for our own meat. Maybe whiteman food makes us hungry. [So you ate a lot of white man's food this year?] Yeah, but we still look hungry.

Food tastes are deep-seated and resist for some time the disruptive effects of a different diet. For instance, even some of the young people who have been sent outside to hospitals for extended treatment report that one of the things they miss most is "our food," despite the fact that in the village they often disparage it:

Miss most our food, you know—meat, walrus meat, seal meat, *mangtak*, and baby walrus. Oh yes, *mukluk*. That's all, I guess.
I asked him whether the other boys in the hospital missed their native food as much as he said he did. He said yes, they did. So much, in fact, that they all used to lie awake at night and talk about their own food before they went to sleep. Some [Indian] boys talked about moose; others about fish; others about seal and walrus.

Two young women were sent to the hospital, one for a long time and the second for only a short visit. Their reactions on this point were:

Sure, I was hungry for Eskimo food when I went to the hospital. Meat. I missed this walrus meat. Liver—I missed liver, too.

[How did you like the food in the hospital?] I like it at that time. But when I was in Mt. Edgecumbe I got tired of it and wanted our own.

And a young man said, speaking about the possibility of his leaving the island someday:

I wouldn't get lonesome. The only thing I would be thinking about is old dry meat and seaweed—something like that.

It is also revealing in connection with food tastes that, when the whale was killed in May, several parents with children outside either in school or in the hospital packaged up some of the *mangtak* and mailed it to them, since for many this was the first chance in some years to have *mangtak*.

In order not to leave an impression of the exaggerated importance of Eskimo food, however, I must also mention the great quantities of soft drinks and candy that are consumed immediately after arrival of the supply ship (130 cases of soft drinks alone were drunk by the village of 300 people within a couple of weeks). Moreover, in at least one instance a man who had been several years on the mainland returned to live in Gambell but did not remain, reputedly because he had developed a strong dislike for the Eskimo diet. Further, in a remark that summarized the sentiments of far more than one young person, a girl asked my wife and me, when we were tasting *mangtak* for the first time, "Do *you* eat that stuff?" and turned up her nose.

The diet is changing, without question, but old food tastes hang on. In the meantime, however, Thanksgiving dinners will probably continue to be celebrated by the Sivokakmeit with something like the following menu of their own choosing (this was in 1954): macaroni and fish, meatballs and spaghetti, four kinds of pie, doughnuts, jello, and hot rolls. More and more other types of food will begin to supplement such items as canned milk, coffee, tea, canned fruit, pilot bread, cookies, candy bars, and tobacco. These foods were taken off the ship at Savoonga and brought a distance of 40 miles by skin boat so that people in Gambell would not have to wait a day or two longer until the ship reached their village. Circumstances like this seem a clear indication of the critical importance that some types of white food have in Sivokakmeit sentiments.

The thoughts of a 45-year-old man on changes that have come into village life may cogently end the discussion of diet. His words summarize the new patterns of consumption, in food as well as other goods, that have become part of Gambell culture since 1940:

Got lot of money in village now, because each house got some oldtimers who get pensions now. Just waiting for that money, then spend at store, then going out very fast that stuff in store. Those young people like your groceries, because got enough money. . . . Young people mostly eat some fruit, vegetables, something like that. [Don't they like Eskimo meat?] Very little. Our children, too. I watch, and they don't like it. Mostly eat some bread and some kind of fruit. . . . That white people have said, "Tomorrow, everybody will change to white-people doing." Pretty soon, some of them young people grow up and change to white people. No more use oldtimer Eskimo doing. Now every year, change. When I was little boy, old people go out hunting for seal and walrus. Now young people don't like go out hunting. Because got enough in store. Just waiting for that money from the month. Now I think young people is looking for job, not hunting. Not going out hunting. Some people I heard want to move to mainland, find some job. Me, too. I work down here in CAA, everything pretty good. I never need anything, because I got job. Every month I get some check. If I buy something in store, I don't want to go out hunting because I got enough food.

These broader subjects of money, the job, and the function of the store in the life of Gambell should now be considered. First among them will be the store, its history, structure, and operations, particularly during the last fifteen years.

## The Gambell Native Store

### HISTORY

In the fifty years since Gambell has had a store, it has been successively organized under several types of formal ownership patterns. It was originally a small entrepreneurship. Then it became a consumer's co-operative paying patronage refunds. From this pattern it changed to a stockholding corporation with shares; finally it returned to a co-operative (paying 2 per cent) and acquired membership in an Alaska-wide co-operative purchasing association. For most of the fifty years it has been the chief funnel for the influx of white man's goods into the village, although for the first three-quarters of that time small trading vessels operating out of the western coastal towns of Alaska also did a vigorous trade in fox skins, sealskins, and ivory every spring and summer. Primary focus will be on the store, however, for it has been the most important of the institutions set up on a sustained basis to bring in goods from the outside world.

In 1933 the Gambell schoolteacher summarized the early history of the store in the village, using as part of his source the diary of one of the first missionaries on the island, Dr. E. O. Campbell. One of the teacher's letters covers the salient facts of the development:

The Eskimo Building and Loan Association, which was opened for business under this name November 26, 1910 . . . was apparently the outgrowth and continuation of an agency of S. Foster Co., of San Francisco. . . . This agency was started here in 1905 . . . with Alfred, a native, as storekeeper. According to Alfred, a representative of S. Foster Co. came here and he [Alfred] believes that it was the intention of this agent to act as storekeeper here. After a conference with Dr. Campbell, it was decided that Alfred, with the assistance of Dr. Campbell, could be storekeeper. The original intention of S. Foster Co. was evidently never carried out, or was abandoned, as the following excerpt from an undated letter—probably written in 1911—from Dr. Campbell to W. O. Lopp states. "In 1907 S. Foster Co. backed out on their promise to send the supplies ordered, sending only a lot of dry goods and clothing and these in the name of Morris Marcus. On our way to St. Lawrence Island as we passed through Seattle we called on both of these firms, the Seattle Hardware Co. and Fisher Brothers. Both of these firms declared they would not credit Eskimos, but would ship up what we asked for . . . Alfred . . . to sell, if I would personally vouch for it. . . ." The store from 1905 to 1910 was then probably a private enterprise of Alfred, as he bought supplies from wholesale houses and was himself responsible for payment.

On November 1, 1910, Dr. Campbell, acting as agent for various creditors, declared Alfred bankrupt. The facts would seem to indicate that Alfred was not bankrupt but [rather that] this was merely Dr. Campbell's means of removing a competition and starting a store according to his own ideas. On November 1, 1910, Alfred had on hand stock valued at $2340.00 and $560.00 in cash, making a total of $2900, against liabilities of $2340.03. Of the $2340.03 listed, $866.74 was for a debt owed by Alfred to Dr. Campbell personally. . . . No record is available of the amounts owed to Alfred by customers here, but as much business was and still is done by credit, this must have been a large amount. Most of the credit risks here are good.

Alfred and George . . . both stated that this stock of Alfred's was the total merchandise offered for sale by the Eskimo Building and Loan Association during the winter of 1910–1911. . . . This is probably true, as the first invoices here in the name of the Eskimo Building and Loan Association are dated 1911.

A new building was constructed in 1910. . . . The building which Alfred had been using for a store remained in his possession.

While Dr. Campbell's methods were apparently questionable, the idea of a native cooperative store was excellent. [It] was cooperative, dividends being paid to each individual according to patronage.

The Eskimo Building and Loan Association was formally merged with the newly formed Reindeer Commercial Company in 1923, which has been mentioned before. Excerpts from a teacher's report written ten years later (unsigned, but probably the same teacher who wrote the above letter) indicate the following concerning the formation of the Reindeer Commercial Company:

There were only 2 representatives from Gambell present, while practically the entire male population of Savoonga attended the meeting.

The assets of the newly organized company consisted of the reindeer herd and the stores. There were 60 shares of stock in the Eskimo Building and Loan Association valued at $600.00. These were owned by three men, two from Gambell and one from Savoonga. This stock was transferred to the Reindeer Commercial Company. The first record of stockholders in the Reindeer Commercial Company is dated November 25, 1925. This shows that there were issued 4,629 shares of deer stock valued at $46,290.00. There were also $5,965.00 in cash stock which was evidently purchased by the individuals subsequent to the formation of the Reindeer Commercial Company. The stock was divided between the villages as follows: Savoonga $49,000.00; Gambell: $3,255.00.

I noted earlier that this same teacher regarded the merger of the store and the reindeer herd as being very unfair to Gambell.

In the year prior to 1940 the stores were again separated from the reindeer herd and made separate corporate entities, each retaining their share-holding pattern of ownership. This move again reflected the policy of the Bureau of Indian Affairs.

From 1939 to 1947 the store was, then, a separate corporation owned by stockholders in the village who received about an 8 per cent dividend on their shares. Each family in the village was at least represented among the stockholders, but the distribution was otherwise not very equal. The store company had a president, a hired manager, and a board of two directors.

It was in 1940, as it had been for many years, the focus of economic exchange activities in the village. It bought from local people and then sold fox furs, sealskins, ivory carvings, raw ivory, baleen, and skin sewing to the outside world through regular formal trade relations established with companies both in Alaska and in the United States. In turn it acted as the principal channel for the entering of white man's goods into native life (foods, cloth materials, oil and other fuels, tools, equipment, and hardware). In addition to its purely merchandising functions, the store owned radio equipment and an outboard motor and native skin boat to use in its operations and therefore was something of a communications center as well. Further, in the summer of 1940 it was financing the installation of a diesel electric-light plant for the entire village. Its total assets in 1940 consisted of over $71,000, and in some ways it acted as the village bank, for it was the repository of the Community Fund, a source of financial aid for needy people of the village set up by the village council and financed by a 3 per cent sales tax on all purchases from the store. And, like most country stores, it served as a purely social and visiting center.

By the end of the war years, in 1945 and 1946, most native stores throughout Alaska were in bad financial straits because of high costs, poor management, and other operations factors. Gambell was no exception. The Alaska Native Service therefore proposed an entirely new organizational plan for native stores, which would be a comprehensive consumers' co-operative system at the level of both the local store and the larger purchasing association. This was known as the Alaska Native Industries Cooperative Association. In 1947 the old store-ownership pattern was voided, and the voters of Gambell formally joined their local store with the larger association, which was intended to provide cheaper goods and better and wider service to native people throughout Alaska. As noted in one of the records pertaining to the event, "the purpose of this central association is to do the buying for the stores and to market their furs at the highest prices possible." The details of this step in Gambell's history must be traced fairly completely, for they importantly bear on Sivokakmeit sentiments toward the white world. Along with the many other confusions and insecurities attendant upon not fully understanding the operations of the Alaska Native Industries Cooperative Association (or ANICA, as it is usually abbreviated), there has been the fact that the prices Gambell people actually pay for goods in the store have increased following their membership. There are a number of reasons for this (such as a general rise in cost of materials on the market), but for the most part such factors are not clearly apprehended and the result is that an expectation of lower costs through joining ANICA has been frustrated.

As mentioned above, in 1947 the village council (by whose permission the local store was operated), speaking for the people, voted to join the new purchasing and merchandising association sponsored by the Alaska Native Service. This step involved borrowing sufficient capital from the government to purchase the old store and set it up on a co-operative basis, as one of the provisions of the ANICA charter was that, in order for the village to be a full member, the store must be a community-owned enterprise and not a stockholding corporation. Another reason for increased capital requirements was that under the new plan the entire year's order of goods had to be paid for by cash in advance of shipment. A loan of over $16,000 was therefore effected. (This loan, incidentally, was repaid in full in the summer of 1954, some six years ahead of schedule.)

A letter from the Gambell teacher to the ANS credit officer, dated in May of 1947, notes that the village had indicated its desire to join ANICA and speaks of some difficulties in operation of the previous store and of general economic conditions:

The people of Gambell have signified their desire to join the new co-operative association as a full member. I am sure that once things get organized and going here it will be well for the Gambell people, but they will have to be rigidly supervised. The store record is not an enviable one for the year 1946. The store operated the light plant with a net loss of $836.00. The forty tons of coal received were sold at cost [through a misunderstanding]. . . . Diesel oil and stove oil had been sold at a loss. . . . The thing I was attempting to do when I first came was to organize the community to operate on a business basis and avoid poor management . . . and financial losses like the store has suffered this last year. At the present time the light plant is operating at a net loss of $70.00 per month and this loss comes out of the store fund. . . . The immediate years ahead will be hard ones for the Gambell people unless some method is devised to increase the income of the villagers. Practically all of the villagers have big accounts at the store and I do not know what they will use for money. Trapping this year was poor and prices poor. It is hard to do enough carving to cover expenses of ammunition and gas for hunting and for the absolute necessities of life. I fully realize that to regulate the store as needed to keep it solvent will not be easy or popular. But strict regulation is the only way the store can handle a revolving loan. . . . I have warned them that they must determine which things are absolute necessities and which are just "wanted" items when it comes to purchasing.

The foregoing pages have presented the formal background for the functioning of the store in the village during the research year 1954–1955. Now to be examined are how the store appeared to the people of Gambell in terms of its general operation and their comprehension of this, its adequacy to supply the goods they wanted, and its general place in the social system.

GENERAL OPERATIONS

The store is directly under the management and control of the village council, which appoints the manager and the assistant manager and decides on store policies and requisitions. At times the store manager has not been a council member, but usually the post is filled by someone already holding a position on the council. The role of store manager is one of the most desired in the village because of its salary; but it imposes upon the incumbent restrictions that at times seriously interfere with other activities felt to be essential, such as hunting. It also has the common problems of bookkeeping and of making monthly store reports to be sent to the Juneau office of the ANS.

At the level of the local store, ANICA is represented by an

ANICA "director." The governing of the larger association is done by a board consisting of these directors from all member village stores. Actually this board elects an executive committee and hires a general manager and administrative staff to handle the business. The post of ANICA director is filled by local election, and the incumbent serves for a period of three years. The position carries a small financial remuneration. At present in Gambell it is filled by a person who is also a member of the village council.

The prices and policies of the store are set by the village council and the manager. With the invoices for the goods sent by ANICA there is a suggested price range, and the actual selling price for the items is placed somewhere in this range. It is on the basis of cost of the goods, service fees, insurance, transportation, and necessary operating profit that the central ANICA office sets the suggested price range. Since most of the thirty-three member stores were still obligated to the government for loans taken out when ANICA was originally founded, the margin of profit was set high enough so that payments could easily be made on the loans.

Following a general meeting of the ANICA directors in the fall of 1954, news came back to Gambell that the total assets of the Gambell store were the highest of any member store in Alaska. It was said that there was over $66,000 "in the bank." There was no knowledge, however, as to just what this meant—what bank was involved, whether this was actual cash or accumulated assets of various types, whether the Gambell store could write a check on that balance for any purpose they wished—and there were other similar evidences of lack of vital information.

The Alaska Native Service exercises guidance over the purchasing power of local stores. For instance, during the year 1954–1955, the Gambell store could not order more than approximately $35,000 worth of goods. This restriction and also the suggested selling price apparently have relation to the repayment of the loan by which the store was set up. It was said that in ordering more goods, the request would have to be cleared through the ANS credit officer. But the procedure was evidently not clearly understood, and those in the village responsible for the store's ordering fretted concerning how they might order a larger supply to prevent another year of severe shortage such as that experienced during 1954–1955.

Thus one of the points of strain during the year 1954–1955 was the apparent block put in the way of obtaining more supplies in the store. There was, on the one hand, an acknowledged fund of over $66,000 to the store's credit; but there was also an ostensible upper limit on what it could order. And there never was, to my knowledge, any realization on the part of the Gambell people that, since the original $16,000 debt was now paid, the requisition limit could be raised.

Although the Alaska Native Industries Cooperative Association was a consumers' co-operative, no patronage refunds were paid from its founding until the fall of 1954, when a check for over $5,000 was sent to Gambell. This represented a refund of 2 per cent on village purchases over the five-year period from 1947 to 1952. For a time there were proposals that the check should be used by the village council for some community necessity, such as the purchase of a new tractor. Another group maintained that it should be equally divided. In the end it was distributed among the people in amounts proportional to their patronage at the store over the five years (all purchases are recorded in a daybook and can thus be easily recounted). The refunds ranged from $19 to $198.

The store's credit policies bear some mention, since this has been a persistent problem for the management of the store throughout its history. In recent years the tautness of credit has waxed and waned, depending on the policies of the store manager and the pressures from the council, the teacher, and the ANS authorities. In the summer of 1954 it had been fairly easy to obtain credit, and several people accumulated bills of several hundred dollars. But during the fall and winter of 1955, the store's policies became much more strict, and for a time during the summer of 1955, after the annual supply vessel had come and the store was once more full of stock, no credit was given and many people had to continue in the same lack of store goods that they had endured throughout the year when the store was actually empty. In late May the store began posting a list of debtors on its bulletin board, including the amount they owed. This was done in the attempt to encourage payment.

One of the most perplexing problems for white administrators is that credit is allowed to the point of imperiling sound management; yet this apparently often happens when people enter into a monetary

*Figure 18.* Hunting walrus on the winter sea ice, 1955.

*Figure 19.* Young men cutting up a whale tongue while the elders supervise, 1955.

*Figure 20*. In a winter trapping camp, evening, 1955.

*Figure 21*. Unloading store goods from the summer supply vessel, 1955.

exchange system from a subsistence, nonmonetary economy. The store with all its operations is an area in which the old Eskimo sentiments concerning immediate sharing of food, no questions asked, clash directly with the newer requirements of a cash economy and a system that establishes a continuing financial obligation for goods bought on credit. Giving goods across the counter is, under the new system, something more than the satisfaction of an immediate want. But it is difficult for most Eskimos to understand that the store with its shelves full of food should not be freely used when people cannot hunt because of poor weather or bad health. That this may be somewhat obscurely recognized by some of the Eskimos is suggested in the following conversation recorded in the field notes:

Our custom changing, you know. We want to buy just like white, you know—anything good to eat, we want to buy. No matter we have short money.

The types of white man's goods that are funneled into the community through the store are canned vegetables and fruit, dried fruit, coffee, tea, cocoa, milk, packaged cereals and such items as macaroni and noodles, canned meats and meat mixtures, condiments, flour, sugar, butter and lard, baking powder, syrup, jam, candy, and soda pop—in other words, goods found in most stores in the States (see Figure 21). Its function as a "general store" is illustrated by the rest of the items it supplies: soaps and cleaning materials, matches, tobacco products, hardware, guns, ammunition, fuel oil, kerosene, gasoline, lubricating oil, outboard motors, and clothing. Further, although it does not normally carry such items in stock, washing machines, bedsteads, stoves, radios, and other larger pieces of furniture may be purchased through the store and brought out on the annual supply ship.

The matter of prices is of considerable concern to the people who must pay them and is a source of considerable confusion among those who must set them. As noted before, ANICA suggests a price range which is based not only on the basic cost of the goods, but also on their own service charge, insurance, transportation, and lighterage. A full price list cannot be given here, nor would it make too much sense without a concomitant discussion of consumer purchasing power. Suffice it to say that the actual "estimated selling price" is in many cases almost half again as much as the "landed cost" (i.e., wholesale price plus service charge, transportation, lighterage, and insurance charges)—and the people of Gambell know this. They feel that "those ANICA stuffs" cost much more than the store's goods used to cost before the formation of ANICA. For example, in the pre-ANICA days one could buy a hundred-pound sack of flour for $3–$4, whereas now it costs $7–$8. As another example of the general high cost of bringing in articles from the outside, an outboard motor listed in Seattle at about $350 sells in the Gambell store for approximately $550 because of all the various charges connected with getting it to Gambell and its sale through the store.

In the village itself the reasons for this comparatively higher "suggested selling price" are very unclear. Nor is there much understanding of the background of the present store and its operating policies. For instance, the field notes read:

Robert said that the store had paid off the debt on July 16. I asked what the debt had been contracted for, and he wasn't sure, but thought they were all going to improve their stores.

Much greater are the confusion and the consternation of the rest of the people who know even less of such matters:

Ted said that the people around here call the store "The Killer" because things cost so much that people can't buy them.

When we were making up that loan agreement with the government, that constitution and by-laws said it's very cheap; they thought everything was going to be very cheap—10% average. Order, then make profit. Maybe when they work it out, they thought it's going to be easy as that. But when it comes out—pretty high!

I met George in the store, and he looked over the crowds of women pushing to get to the counter, laughed a little, and said, "You can buy anything cheaper in Sears than you can get it here." I asked him why that was. He answered in one word, "ANICA." I said I thought ANICA had been formed in order to get cheaper prices. He replied, "Cheaper! Hah!"

The inability of many people to comprehend that the store is officially an expression of themselves and of their reaching out into the supply centers of the States—thereby presumably being responsive to their own needs—is summed up in a theme heard many times during the year:

"Well, they [the local store managers] are running the store—it's none of our business." He said that ANICA owns the store. I asked who owns ANICA. He said he didn't know.

This same sentiment is, interestingly enough, corroborated by the statement of one of those whose duties place him in the managing hierarchy of the store and ANICA: "For seven years the people haven't liked ANICA very well—because they don't understand."

Clearly, village sentiments are that prices are too high and they should be lowered. But in the village the way to lower them is unknown. The relation of the loan repayment in 1954 to the suggested selling price was not recognized by those in a position to make decisions about price fixing. There was, for instance, apparently no knowledge whatever of the information contained in a circular from ANICA to ANS teachers in 1948. In this memorandum, the rationale of the suggested selling price is discussed, and one of the points made is that this is a "suggested," not a mandatory, selling price. A second critically important point is summed up very clearly in the following quotation from the document: "After the loan has been repaid in full there is no doubt but what the percentage mark-up can be lowered in order to pass the saving on to the consumer." Failure of local people to comprehend these operating regulations of the institution of which they are now a part is another example, along with many others, of their increased involvement with the white world but also their lack of skills for properly adapting to it.

One aspect of the store's operations that excited the most heated negative sentiments was the shortage of supplies very early in the year 1954–1955—a year that was also very short of food because of poor hunting. A charting of the store's failures in the supply function in that twelve-month period will help clarify the situation:

September: No fruit, milk, or shotgun shells (when bird hunting was beginning).

October: This shortage continued until the supply ship arrived in the middle of the month; but the ship unloaded only part of its goods, and the shortage of shotgun shells continued through the bird season.

November: The ship finally unloaded all its cargo, but somehow the winter's supply of pilot bread had not been brought on the vessel; soon after the ship's departure, the store was out of butter, tea, white gas, lubricating oil for boat motors, and batteries. (No white gas had been ordered on this vessel; it is used for the lanterns that most people have for lighting.)

December: Orders for food to come by parcel post are being sent to Nome stores on essentials that the store is out of—tea being one of the first.

January: Another shipment from Nome arrives containing food (tea and margarine) and cigarettes. By late January the store is out of matches also.

February: Oatmeal and other cereals are low. In late February the store had to borrow ten barrels of kerosene and eight barrels of white gas from the mission to provide for the winter.

March: The store is out of toilet tissue; another air-mail shipment of goods is received from Nome consisting of tea, gum, and tobacco. (It is noted at this time by an informant that when the CAA was in the village and kerosene ran short, the store could always borrow sufficient barrels to carry them over until the supply ship came.)

April: The store is also out of puddings and sweet desserts; it distributed the last of the canned milk among the families and rationed the remaining flour; it has no tea, but orders more from Nome.

May: For six weeks in late April and May no airplane can get into the village because of the weather-bound landing strip. During this time there is no tea, coffee, lard, matches, milk, flour, salt, fuel oil, kerosene, white gas, fruit, or cocoa in the store. In late May a plane finally comes in, and tea sells at $1.81 per half pound, coffee at $2.00 per pound.

June: The store is completely out of fuel oil, and it is discovered that only relatively few barrels are coming on the supply vessel; this happened because in the ordering of oil, which took place in the winter, there were thought to be barrels of oil under the snow, but the spring melting showed that these did not actually exist. In addition to the items which the store ran out of in May, it is now out of baking powder and shotgun shells during this very busy bird-hunting month. Its remaining gasoline (for boat motors) rises in price from $34 per 55-gallon barrel (May price) to $40 a barrel.

July: The supply vessel comes, but someone has forgotten to order any flour, so none will be on hand until the return voyage of the ship in November. The store also runs out of sugar in a short time.

In the face of this record of failure in the supply function throughout the year, both the leaders and the people of the village acutely felt the pinch of shortages. In spite of the fact that there had not been as much wagework in 1954–1955 as in the two or three previous years, there was money in the village that might have been used for goods. An upper limit remained on the total quantity that could be brought into the village, a limit that appeared unbreakable.

Whether it was a matter of perception and selective recall or whether there were actually more goods ordered in years past, people now say that the store formerly did not fail them and that it used to have supplies the year round. Even in the early years of the store there were always goods. In speaking about the first manager of the co-operative store (1910 and later), an informant says:

> He used to order lots of groceries, food, and clothing. The store never run out of fruit, pilot bread, flour, and other stuff the whole year round until the ship comes.

This fact of a reliable supply through most of the year was true even in more recent years (including 1940).

In the early days of the more affluent economy since 1940, the money in the village was apparently not spent in such great spurts at the store, and the supply of goods lasted through the year. But since that time, the increased money has been ever more quickly used in the store, and its supplies become depleted in a shorter time. The volume of sales has increased, and—hence—there is a greater relative deprivation when supplies run short. One informant speaks of this increased "waste" (meaning, interestingly enough, simply increased use) of the store's goods:

> [Did the store ever run short when the CAA was here?] That time was never short. Because no waste groceries and flour—eat slow, like that.

The same observation was made by many others.

VOLUME OF BUSINESS

The increasing dependence on the store can be indexed not only by the perceptions and sentiments of the people, but also by some of the available records. In Chart 6 the monetary value of goods in the store exchanged each month for cash is averaged for the years 1948–1955 (excluding 1953, for which there were no records, and including only half a year each for 1948 and 1955). Incomplete though the records are, they are useful in helping to show the place of the store as an inlet for white goods.

The great peak in purchases from the store was reached in 1951, with only a slight drop in the following year. The source of the precipitous wealth behind the purchases was construction work for most of the men in the village. During these two years, the average monthly value of goods exchanged for cash was over $5,000. Even in the face of the regression in the last two or three years, there has been an over-all rise in the amount of goods that the store annually brings into the village.

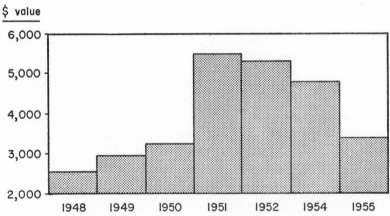

*Chart 6.* Gambell native store: goods exchanged for cash, 1948–1955 (monthly average).

In Chart 7 is traced for the same years 1948–1955 the monetary value of goods exchanged for furs or other marketable native products. This refers mainly to fox skins. For the years 1951 and 1952, when there was the most wagework, there was the least production of native products for money. The relationship between wagework and the adaptation of native economic pursuits to the acquisition of money is regularly inverse through 1948–1955. A striking confirmation of this inverse relationship between cash jobs and the gathering of marketable native products is shown by superimposing one chart over the other. (Note that the dotted line indicates only the profile of "goods exchanged for cash," not the monetary value.) This in all probability indicates that when cash work is available, the economic base shifts—and will continue to do so as, progressively, the older generation dies off.

One of the most striking findings from examining the records is the astonishing amount of monetary wealth in the village at times, given its general economic situation. Also evident in the statistical data are the fluctuations in spending power through the year and from one year to the next. Table 15, which plots the monthly distributions of goods exchanged for cash over these seven years (1948–1955), shows the generally high peaks of spending in July, when the boat comes in, and some tendency to a relative paucity of goods

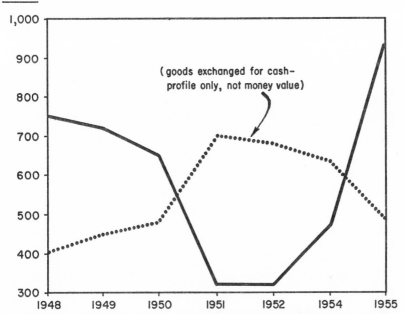

Chart 7. Gambell native store: goods exchanged for furs and other marketable native products, 1948–1955 (monthly average).

exchanged during the heart of the winter, when both supplies and income are short. It is also notable that the highest single monthly total, over $11,000, was spent in September of 1954, the month in which checks were received for a summer construction job on the Gambell airstrip. There is some purchasing from the store by army personnel and others—buying ivory carving, for instance—but this is relatively negligible in the total compared to that spent by the Eskimos. A very interesting facet which Table 15 brings out is the irregularity of spending patterns (and, very likely, of the availability of money). Supplies come, and money goes, all concentrated in a relatively short time of the year. In some years the spending patterns from one month to the next are very sporadic (1952, for instance).

*Table 15.* Value of goods exchanged for cash through the Gambell store, 1948–1955 (monthly totals)

|        | 1948 * | 1949 | 1950 | 1951 | 1952 * | 1954 * | 1955 |
|--------|--------|------|------|------|--------|--------|------|
| Jan. | $ | $1,804.73 | $1,632.02 | $2,762.52 | $3,061.41 | $4,881.99 | $8,081.76 |
| Feb. | | 1,975.46 | 2,011.62 | 2,853.87 | 3,588.47 | 2,655.33 | 2,365.90 |
| Mar. | | 2,952.55 | 1,768.69 | 3,334.40 | 3,577.03 | 2,424.45 | 4,237.29 |
| Apr. | | 2,249.68 | 2,540.36 | 3,872.93 | 4,770.64 | 4,514.08 | 4,367.93 |
| May | | 2,197.28 | 2,362.46 | 4,429.19 | 6,245.54 | 2,893.71 | 3,074.53 |
| June | 662.45 | 4,793.07 | 2,633.44 | 3,984.24 | 2,391.98 | 2,418.34 | |
| July | 6,138.54 | 3,507.14 | 8,324.42 | 8,626.36 | 11,187.62 | 7,569.76 | |
| Aug. | 2,287.51 | 4,004.99 | 4,333.47 | 10,267.77 | 6,940.05 | 4,170.39 | |
| Sept. | 1,719.89 | 2,512.12 | 3,485.27 | 6,634.06 | 6,078.83 | 11,411.82 | |
| Oct. | 2,351.48 | 3,436.36 | 3,298.07 | 9,430.49 | | | |
| Nov. | 1,793.41 | 2,701.63 | 3,635.17 | 6,334.75 | | | |
| Dec. | 2,906.07 | 3,163.86 | 3,135.66 | 4,012.41 | | | |
| Monthly average | 2,551.33 | 2,941.57 | 3,263.38 | 5,545.24 | 5,315.73 | 4,771.09 | 3,420.08 |

\* No figures are available for the missing months.

THE PLACE OF THE STORE IN THE VILLAGE

Progressively and irrevocably the store has become indispensable to the life of the village. Not only does it increasingly serve as a source for white man's goods—upon which the success of hunting depends and the villagers often rely supplementarily when that hunting fails—but it has become a marketing and outlet center for native products. Fox skins, for instance, are purchased locally for anywhere from $6 to $8 (1954–1955 price) and then sold on the Seattle market for $10 to $18. (The difference between the two prices is returned to the original owner, minus a small service charge that the store receives.) The store also buys other native products both for local sale and for export if there is a market, e.g., mukluk hides, which it can sell to the now affluent Pt. Barrow Eskimos for boot soles. It pays $1 per pound for raw ivory; from $6 to $10 each for mukluk hides; $3 for hair-seal skins; $3 or $4 for spotted-seal skins; and $30 or $40 for walrus hides (but these are rarely available in recent years).

The store has also taken over the function of a raw-material supply center for some families who have no hunters. Skin sewers, for instance, can buy the sealskins to use in sewing parkas which they then sell to army personnel or other buyers. This is a pattern of market development foreign to ancient Eskimo exchange systems. The store also is serving as the display center for some of the native goods produced, such as items of skin sewing and ivory carving. It even acts as an outlet for the rudimentary beginnings of a bakery industry: one man sells loaves of baked bread in (but not to) the store. As noted before, the store still manages and supplies the Community Fund under the direction of the village council. The same tax rate of 3 per cent on all purchases applies now as it did in 1940.

More and more the store is considered, even with its supply deficiencies, a necessary part of the Gambell economic system. The culture of 1940 is not the culture of 1954. Older skills have slipped imperceptibly from the scene with the death of the old harpoon and lance walrus hunters, so that now it would be a serious calamity for hunters if the village were completely cut off from the mainland. And taste in food has changed the orientation of want, from that which found its locus on the island to one that increasingly finds its satisfaction in the outside world. One man, for instance, spoke in these terms:

[What do you get from the store?] Mostly tea and sugar and flour. Mostly everybody want to buy that. [Fruit and candy also?] Young people like fruit. Now my children don't want to eat meat. Just mostly eat bread; bread—and your stuff, fruit and vegetables. Peas and everything. Now is different. I think little better than other life, long time ago life. That food is lot of help; something healthy. Fruit and some of that stuff—orange juice and something like that. Now I think when young people is growing up, no more hunting. Just watching the store, and looking for job.

Another man, asked about changes since the trading ships were visiting the island, replied:

Yeah, it looks different to me; I've been changed, myself. I don't look for a trade with ships now. . . . I'm looking to the store now. That's my habit, ever since I become a store director; I try to work for the store. I try to get money for the store.

Thus, whether for good or ill, people recognize that they could not now get along without the store and that they must find ways of getting its peculiar *modus operandi*, money. Irrevocable steps away from the past have been taken; whereas once meteoric iron or slate and ivory were the most necessary technological items, today some way of earning money has become uppermost in most people's minds. It is not hunting seal or walrus by itself that now characterizes the seasonal round, so much as the close articulation of hunters with the store, both in terms of their basic tools and weapons of trade and in the food itself. One man saw the Gambell store this way:

Now is different—those that make money every month [meaning pensions, welfare money, etc.] take it to store. Store gets lots of money, then orders more stuff. Then freight boat bring it here, makes lots of big piles. Then everybody goes to store—almost a dozen, twelve times a day.

As an institution, the store has therefore become increasingly more central in the village's economic structure compared to 1940. Fifteen years ago it was equally vital to the subsistence of the village, but for a more limited range of goods and as an economic outlet. Now a far greater reliance is placed on it in terms of its total operation in the economic system.

But the personnel who manage and control it are the subjects of much debate and antagonism for their policies: for their failures to comprehend how the store should be run for the benefit of the village as a whole, their failures to order necessary supplies, for their pricing, and for their sometimes unequal distribution of scarce goods. Village gossip rarely leaves them untouched; for example:

He said the store hadn't gotten any tea in on the plane today. He said, "No tea in store" . . . then said it is a "no-tea store." Then he added: "No brains!"

Another man, asked the general question whether people are unhappy with the store, replied:

No. Some people may be unhappy about the men working at the store; not the store. The management, not the store. [What's wrong with it?] Pride. Yeah, most of the men try to hold all the jobs.

The mention of jobs serves to introduce the next section, concerned with ways of making the money that has become so important in village life. In the following chapter some aspects of the social relations of the store as an institution will be considered, along with those of the council and the village generally.

## Income and the Job

### HISTORICAL BACKGROUND

In the latter half of the nineteenth century the region of the northern Pacific Ocean, the Bering Sea, and the Arctic Ocean was one of the most intensive whaling grounds of the world. The North Atlantic fishery had been effectively depleted, and new grounds were needed. Whalers turned to the Northwest, but even there the animals became fewer and fewer, being killed in numbers beyond their capacity to reproduce. Toward the end of the century, whaling ships had to go farther and farther north into the arctic ice regions in search of the bowhead whale. Some captains went beyond the bounds of caution in remaining in arctic waters to fill their oil casks. In October of 1871, for example, virtually the entire American arctic whaling fleet, thirty-three vessels, was crushed in the ice because it had stayed a few weeks too long in the arctic and the winter ice had come, as it sometimes will, unpredictably early.[15] The same thing happened in 1876 and 1888, although fewer ships were lost.

For most of the last century the bowhead was sought mainly for its oil. Although the most highly prized oil was spermaceti (from the sperm whale), which was used in high-grade candles, oil from other blubber whales was utilized for less refined illumination and lubricants. For the first two-thirds of the century, whale oil lighted the lamps of the world. But with the development of natural gas and petroleum products, the market for whale oil in its various uses began to decline, a victim of technological advance. By the end of the century the major market for oil was completely gone (a modern

[15] For a vivid personal account of this event, see Williams, 1902. See also Hohman, 1928, for an excellently written and most helpful study of the American whaling industry, especially chaps. xiii and xiv for a discussion of the rise and fall of the arctic whalers. The book contains a good annotated bibliography. On the topic of how commercial whaling in the arctic affected the Eskimos, see VanStone, 1958a.

market for it has since developed); however, there remained a demand for whalebone,[16] which was used in various manufactures because of its combination of strength and flexibility. Corset supports, other stays of various types, umbrellas, hoops, and whips were all made from this hard but flexible material. Without yet having an effective substitute, such as there was for whale oil, and with the whalebone itself becoming ever more scarce because of the decimation of the animals from which it was obtained, baleen soared in price toward the end of the century. Then, abruptly, only a few years following its peak, the market completely collapsed, again through the development of commercial substitutes.

After the middle of the nineteenth century, when the first of the American whalers arrived in Bering waters, ships stopped at many of the small Eskimo villages dotting the arctic coast to take on supplies, water, and trade goods. For centuries the Eskimo had been hunting the bowhead, mostly for its skin, meat, and blubber, but also for its baleen. The latter was used in making small hunting toboggans, cooking utensils, and other tools of a native economy. In the whaling ships, particularly toward the end of the century, the Eskimos soon found a ready market for extra baleen, which before that time had been only a relatively subsidiary product of the whale hunt. The value of whalebone, in Eskimo eyes, quickly jumped completely out of proportion to its uses. Around the turn of the century, for instance, the Sivokakmeit were receiving $3.50 a pound for baleen—and from one whale there would be several hundred pounds. Hohman notes that "in 1897 the average price of whalebone at San Francisco was $4.00 per pound" (1928, p. 307), and at another date the price apparently went as high as $7.00 a pound. It was truly, as one informant said, "black gold"; and an elderly man now living in the village remembers buying a wooden whaleboat entirely equipped with oars, sail, harpoon gun, lines, and bombs for only six large pieces of baleen.

But the whaling men bought more than baleen in their commerce with the island. Not only the whalers but also exploring, trading,

---

[16] Or "baleen." These are the flexible blades or plates which descend from the palate of the whale. Fine fibers along the edges form a straining apparatus, entangling the minute sea life upon which the whale feeds and at the same time allowing the water to escape from the mouth. See Beddard, 1900, pp. 83–84.

and other vessels of the commercial world visited the island and bought ready-made sealskin parkas, pants, boots, and mittens for winter wear. Traders also wanted raw sealskins and raw ivory, and it was largely through the ruthless hunting of walrus and other maritime mammals by white men themselves that the large herds began to be seriously decimated in the latter years of the nineteenth century (see Fay, 1957); this caused Dr. Sheldon Jackson to urge and finally accomplish the introduction of Siberian reindeer into the Alaskan Eskimo economy. The beginnings of the St. Lawrence Island herd have already been discussed.

From Gambell, but more from villages on the Siberian shore across the Bering Sea, the whaling ships also recruited hands for their summer cruises in the Beaufort and Chukchi Seas. There were a couple of winters, too, when whaling men lived in the village and went out in their wooden boats with an Eskimo crew during the regular spring hunting season of the Sivokakmeit.[17] For such labor, trade goods and other products were received—guns and ammunition, knives, tools, cloth, and some food.

During the late ninteenth century, small commercial vessels began to ply the shores of the northern oceans in considerable numbers. One of their chief purposes was to get arctic fox skins (*Alopex lagopus*). This small white animal, which had no real value in the native economy, was another of the products of their habitat that interested the white men to such an extent that egregiously high prices were paid for it. Another skin greatly wanted was that of the extremely rare blue fox.

In the 1890's, then, the peak in the search for baleen was reached. Thereafter fewer and fewer vessels left the ports of California and Massachusetts bound for the Bering whaling ground, since it was very unprofitable to equip a vessel to hunt for baleen, and this with an uncertain chance of success. But at this time fox skins were beginning to bring from $7 to $8 each; and from then on, it was fox, not baleen, that was the most valuable of the autochthonous products of the island. The market for baleen did not drop off immediately, however, for in the early 1920's the St. Lawrence people were said to be still receiving $1 a pound for it. But by the 1930's the demand completely disappeared.

[17] This practice is also discussed by VanStone (1958a).

The market for fox skins, on the other hand, grew steadily from the beginning of the twentieth century. There were years, to be sure, when the fox trapping was poor—the weather too stormy, the animals fewer and more wary of traps. Nonetheless, there was sufficient wealth in the village during the first third of the century that several of the boat captains could buy wooden whaleboats costing anywhere from $600 to $1,000 each from whaling ships.

During the decade of the 1920's, the world market for arctic fox skins reached its highest point in history. In the peak year, 1929, one large fur-buying company was paying an average price of $63.13 per white pelt for Gambell fox skins (Steffen, 1958)—and a good trapper could catch a hundred or more white foxes each season. But it was the rarer blue fox that made trapping a really lucrative occupation, because during this same decade these skins sold for $150, $200, or even $250 each. Such returns induced several of the Sivokakmeit to take up trapping as their main occupation— forsaking more of the hunting life than would be usual for an Eskimo. Gambell people still speak of several of the older men who were thought of as "great trappers," rather than "hunters." They would spend most of the year in isolated camps scattered around the island, having their families with them and coming into Gambell only for supplies and short periods of hunting. A teacher's report of the early 1920's speaks vividly (and perhaps somewhat unsympathetically) of the wealth in the village at that time. Without doubt she overestimates monetary wealth, but her perceptions are quite interesting:

With the exception of four families in Gambell, all of whom have wealthy relatives, there is no person who is not far more prosperous than any mere school teacher I ever saw. They have their living with little expense to them in labor, sacrifice, or money. They all have houses, skins, more guns than the most enthusiastic white hunter ever thinks of accumulating; ammunition, stores of white man's food which they hoard like squirrels and pretend to be always in want of; boats, which cost them a thousand dollars each, white man's clothes, phonographs, fine pipes—everything they want—and more actual cash than they know what to do with. No white man knows or ever will know how much money they have. From little dabs of things the faster white man would not bother with, they accumulate thousands every year. The traders beat them and pay them too little for their produce but the trader lives the complicated life of the outside and makes far less out of his ill gotten gain than they from the small prices he pays them. Men who would be called young outside are worth in goods and money from five to twenty-five thousand dollars.

Her estimates of income are based, probably, somewhat more on envy than on observation. In any case, trapping was an extremely rewarding occupation during the 1920's, and there are several men who caught more than one blue fox during a trapping season that was equally successful in terms of white pelts. With blue foxes selling for $200 a pelt and with a hundred or more white skins bringing $30 to $40 each, a small-size fortune could be amassed by a man willing to take the bitter January and February winds that sweep the length of a frozen tundra trap line.

In the years before 1940 there were only a few ways other than trapping to make money. The principal means was through sale of carved ivory to the outside. St. Lawrence Island carvers had long been known for the high quality of their work, and each piece was distinctively marked as having come from St. Lawrence Island—a practice rarely occurring with the carving of other groups.

Trading of bulk raw ivory was stopped by government regulations in 1941, although it had declined some years before that. As mentioned above, raw sealskins were sold to the small trading ships that plied the coasts and brought the outside world to many an isolated Eskimo family living in a hunting and trapping camp on the edge of the arctic nowhere. Herding the reindeer and helping in the annual slaughter paid 20 cents or 30 cents an hour, but this was usually taken in deer meat rather than cash. Most people, including women and girls, helped carry goods to the store when the annual supply vessel disgorged upon the beach; and one man had a regular business of manufacturing sleds that sold for anywhere from $35 to $50. Occasionally also money could be earned by transporting the nurse or teacher from one village to the other. But these were about the only prominent means of making money during the two or three decades prior to 1940.

PATTERNS OF INCOME IN 1940

During the decade of the 1930's notions about earning money were the inherited notions of elders—trapping foxes and carving ivory for trade—and the objects of trade were better and more abundant tools for hunting and store supplies for supplementary food. Ivory carving was important as a source of income, but fox trapping was without doubt the principal means of earning money, and most of the village men and boys did at least some trapping during the season, which lasted from December through March. At that time many would move out to their camps, there to remain during most of the winter months. Some would take their families with them and then return to Gambell in time for the April and May hunting season.

The ivory carving was done for the tourists that came to Alaska —a few to Nome but many to the southern Alaskan centers of Anchorage, Seward, and the towns of the Inland Passage. The carved pieces were sent out by the store and merchandised through an agency of the Alaska Native Service. It is said that in many cases higher prices were paid for the ivory in the 1930's than are being received at the present time for much of what is carved. Although this may be true of some items, the prices received now for at least one type of carved piece—the "bird rookery"—are rather high, these objects representing a "showpiece" for the carver. Similarly expensive single pieces of carving were the cribbage boards, which often had small animals carved upon them or were decorated with etchings of hunting and other Eskimo scenes.

Skin sewing was also done for the tourist trade, but not at all in the quantity of today's production by the women and girls of the village.

Helping to herd the reindeer at spring fawning time was one way in which young men earned money, as they had done in earlier years, and unloading the ship was another, an activity in which girls as well could participate. After earning money as laborers for archeological studies done in the late 1920's and 1930's, the Eskimos themselves began to dig for "specimens" at various of the many abandoned villages on the island—at Punuk, at Kukulik, at Kitngeepalok, and at the three or four sites between Gambell village and the mountain lying behind it.

In 1940 there were very few "jobs" in the village. The missionary, nurse, or teacher hired occasional domestics and handy men for small jobs, but this was not at all on a large scale. The role of mail carrier had been instituted in 1936 to cart the accumulation of a year's mail from the summer ship which brought it along with groceries, outboard motors, and clothing. One of the two jobs of any significance and permanence in the village was that of storekeeper, which even in 1940 was a full-time occupation (with some days taken out for hunting during the spring). But perhaps the most important job by virtue of its long-term establishment and prestige was that of janitor in the school. One man had held this position for many years. He not only did the janitorial work in the building but also some teaching, particularly of the young children who did not yet understand English.

A form of income not really coming from any particular job consisted of the dividends received from stock held in the native store. This has already been discussed. For some of the largest stockholders, it provided an annual $200 or $300.

INCOME SINCE 1940

The main wealth of the Sivokakmeit has come in other ways since 1940, although fox trapping and ivory carving still continue. Indeed, in looking back over the past 50–75 years, one can trace some important qualitative steps in the patterns of economic relationship with the mainland, and one of crucial importance has occurred only since 1940.

The early prosperity of the Sivokakmeit was founded on the whims of fashion and taste of the mainland. Since this was based on products which had no utility in the native economy (or, in the case of baleen, relatively little), the Eskimos rode the successive waves of an optimal producer's market first in baleen and then, when the value of that product was declining, in fox skins. The market for the latter is still extremely important in the economy of the island; but by comparison with its former value, it has considerably declined. In terms of the relative amount of wealth the people receive for their primary raw material (by contrast, for instance, with the 1920's, when not only the absolute amount of money paid for a pelt was much higher, but also costs of white man's goods were lower), it would seem as if the Sivokakmeit are actually poorer now than they ever were before. Their primary raw material is steadily decreasing in income power, and they have no other product with which to replace it. The only economic activity that brings at all the same type of "big money," as they say, is the ephemeral construction work that has come to the island during the last decade. As will be presently brought out, this shift involves more than a mere change of the raw material that is being offered for sale to the white world. It implicates entirely new patterns of activity, skills, and living arrangements and brings in its wake changed conceptions and sentiments about money, its value, and its function.

*Fox trapping*—This activity has continued to be very important in the native monetary economy, even though there have been significant annual fluctuations both in the number of pelts collected and in the prices they brought on the Seattle or St. Louis fur market. During the war years, for instance, prices were relatively high—up to $35 each—whereas in the years since then the price has dropped to about half or less of that figure. In the winter of 1954–1955 a white pelt of first quality brought from $15 to $18, depending on size. This meant that the trapper himself received about three-quarters of that amount after the store's service charge and that of the fur exchange had been taken out. The winter of 1954–1955 was an average or less than average trapping season, with the highest number of foxes taken by one man being fifty-two. The previous year had been much better, with the highest number caught being seventy-nine. The mean catch for the very active trapper is now about fifty per year. In the other village of the island, Savoonga, men are much more dependent on trapping as a source of livelihood, and they generally take about twice as many foxes as the Gambell trappers.

Since the end of the war ANS teachers have prepared an "Annual Statistical Report" on economic activities of their village. Excerpts from the reports available for Gambell show some of the fluctuations in income from trapping that were mentioned above. Although the data are grouped under the rubric "raw furs and hides" (which presumably includes sealskins), the great bulk of the hides sold in this category was certainly fox skins. The total value of the raw furs sold by natives is plotted in Chart 8.[18]

[18] There are no reports for the years 1943, 1944, and 1953. Although presumably reports were made, I could not locate them in the files, nor does the central office have copies.

The most obvious feature of the graph is the precipitous drop in the value of skins shortly after the war. Also shown is a recent apparent rise, at least during the year of this study. But during the last eight years, there has not been as much money coming into the village from the sale of raw furs as there was at the end of the war. The figures from the statistical reports are corroborated by data obtained from one of the principal fur buyers for the St. Lawrence Island pelts. The average price per pelt during the three years from 1943 to 1946 was slightly over $20. In 1946 and 1947 the price was down to $10; and from 1949 to 1954, the average price paid was only some $7.77 (Steffen, 1958).

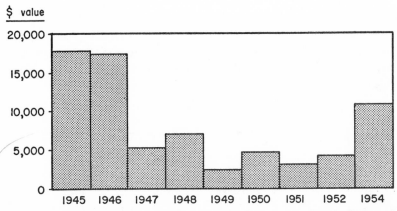

*Chart 8.* Gambell village: income derived from sale of raw furs and hides, 1945–1954. (Source: Annual Statistical Reports.)

*Native crafts: carving and sewing*—The carving of a wide variety of objects from walrus ivory—small animals and birds, letter openers, pickle forks, butter knives, cribbage boards, buttons, toothpick holders, and similar gewgaws—has markedly increased since 1940, at least in quantity if not quality. This has been very largely due to the ready market for such trinkets in the CAA establishment, the air force base, and the army base, as well as to the greatly increased ship traffic to the island since 1940. The crews invariably wander into the village and pick up souvenir ivory. The great majority of men and older boys (and even some women) do carving; and for the old men past the age of hunting this is a useful, full-time occupation. One such man pointed with pride to his radio, washing

machine, and oil stove, saying, "Come from ivory." Prices vary
considerably, but some elaborately carved and shaped cribbage
boards have sold for more than $100. Even at this, prices of St.
Lawrence ivory are generally cheaper than those on the mainland,
where the tourist trade is much more intense. The St. Lawrence
carvers, however, have been steadily increasing their prices as the
demands of the market continue, and even augment, with military
turnover. One progressive man, looking to the mass production of
an item that is in demand, has applied an electric lathe to certain
shaping and polishing phases in making a cribbage board; and when
he has enough raw ivory, he claims that he can carve $125 worth of
cribbage boards a day. Raw ivory is not always available, however,
for when the hunting season fails, not only meat is short, but also
the tusks that provide the basis for this industry. Because of scarcity,
in fact, during the research year raw ivory jumped in price in the
store from $1 to $2 a pound before the major spring hunting began.

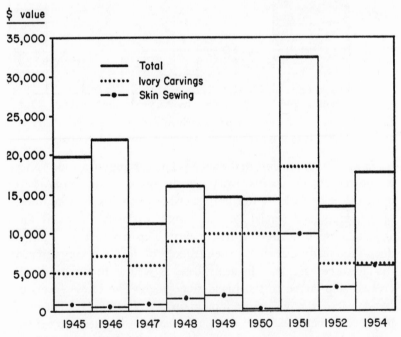

*Chart 9.* Gambell village: total income from native products, 1945–1954.
(Source: Annual Statistical Reports.)

Dependence on an active local market for the sale of ivory products began with the air force installation in the late 1940's. The personnel bought a great amount of ivory carving, and annual sales markedly increased (see Chart 9). The same tendency continued with the army camp, and many carvers have preferred to sell their work to the soldiers rather than place it for sale through the store. The payment usually is much quicker, and the price is often somewhat higher. In placing the piece for sale through the store, an initial payment is made to the carver and any difference between that and the sale price is later given to the carver in the form of a "rebate" —in the same way that fox skins are handled.

But there is another aspect of the trade relations with the military. This involves social relationships and will be more fully examined in the next chapter. Some difficulties have arisen, through the years, between the village and the soldiers—violations of visiting regulations, price disputes, and similar types of disturbance—and at times all contact between the two has been cut off temporarily, with intimations that a permanent curtailment of visiting might be imposed if relations did not improve. Such a possibility caused considerable anxiety among many of the carvers, who felt that they would suffer a severe economic loss if such a ban were effected.[19] The situation persisted for at least three or four years prior to 1955, and the issues are clearly presented in the following excerpt, taken from the field notes:

Ernest said that he has heard that the council is going to "stop" army personnel from coming into the village. He said he doesn't like this, because if they "stop" the army, "then our money stop, too."

The sewing of skin clothing (parkas, jackets, boots, mittens) and other skin items, such as wall hangings, dolls, and toys, has also greatly increased with the influx of troops having money to spend. Formerly, of course, skin sewing was given over only to utilitarian ends—the production of a watertight seam in boots or pants, for instance. Young girls six or seven years old were expected to begin learning this activity so vitally important to the native economy. But in some cases skin sewing has now been so oriented to the

[19] A study of their reactions now that the army base has been closed would be very helpful. See Chapter VIII.

pursuit of money that an accomplished needlewoman does not have time to sew clothing for her hunters, who must still go out in the winter weather. She turns her time, rather, to sewing fancy and decorated parkas for soldiers, which sell for $60, $75, or perhaps more. Even a few young girls turn out skin balls or Eskimo "yo-yo's" for the white trade. It can be seen, in fact, that some rudimentary forms of specialization are beginning to occur in this, as well as in ivory carving, since certain women are noted for their skin boots or slippers and others for their jackets and parkas.

In addition to the sewing and the carving of ivory, the sale of drawings is an important form of income for a selected few. Painting or drawing on whitened sealskin is done by several, and etching of animals and natural scenes on ivory is quite common. In 1940 only one woman considered herself an "artist," although a few others did drawings. Now, however, many people decorate their ivory with etchings.

In Chart 9, which is also based on the Annual Statistical Reports for Gambell, are plotted the rise and fall of ivory sales, skin sewing, and the combined total of net income from native products (which therefore includes the sale of raw hides, given separately in Chart 8). The sharp drop after 1945 and 1946 in the total income is due to the great decrease in raw-hide sales. The rise in purchase by military personnel of native arts and crafts and the general trend toward increased sales volume of these goods since that time (with the exception of ivory sales for 1952) can be seen in this chart.

*Construction and maintenance work*—Nothing has been so important in setting the current notions about making money as the service, maintenance, and construction work on the island since 1940. The Sivokakmeit had their first introduction to large-scale construction labor when the present school building was built in 1939. It is difficult to be more exact, but apparently most of the village men were employed in the common labor, carpentry, and painting in connection with the building. Carpentry had always been one of the technological skills highly valued in the culture (used for building wind-tight houses, boats, and similar construction), and several men still are considered to be experts.

They received their next chance for mass employment in 1943, when the CAA establishment was built. In this instance, their employment really began with the unloading of the ships which brought the building supplies; and, for the greater part of the workers, it ended when the buildings and a sod airstrip were finished later that year. Many men were left richer by more than a thousand dollars each from this job. As one Sivokakme put it, speaking about the construction of the school building, it was "the first time we see that big money in the village"; and then about the CAA construction he remarked, "Then make lots of money. That's bigger than the school house."

Throughout the ten-year stay of the CAA and the Weather Bureau, at least one Eskimo from the village was continuously hired on a full-time basis as the "station laborer." Odd maintenance jobs and small repairs of various types also required the occasional employing of others in this period.

It was the women and girls, however, who were most affected through their contact with the CAA, for many were employed in the homes of white families to help with the housecleaning, cooking, and baby care. For them it was a daily exposure to the white way of life, and they were eager pupils. According to the field notes, one woman thus remembers her experience:

When I asked if she had ever worked for the CAA, she said that she did for a while; she said she liked the work, it was easy. Washing with a machine, ironing, it was easy—and cooking too.

Often the Eskimos were included in some of the recreational events of the white families, such as parties and dances. And the white people visited in the homes of the villagers, often in search of ivory carvings to buy.

The influence of the CAA extended beyond its stay in Gambell, however, for on several occasions when a white family was transferred back to the mainland they took an Eskimo girl with them to continue in the role of household helper. For these girls, this was the first experience of living on the mainland and seeing, on a large scale, the culture which they had seen in but microcosm in the few white houses near the edge of their village. This chance to work on the mainland left deep imprints on all the girls who went outside, and some who returned to the village express dissatisfactions all the more vehemently by comparison with their life working for a white family.

The CAA establishment's operations overlapped for a couple of years the first of the military construction, which began in 1949 or 1950. Actually, there were few jobs for the Eskimos in the military base—none in the construction itself and only relatively few in the maintenance of it. The same is true of the army base, a year or two later. At the present time, however, one important source of income provided by the local base is in the stacking and draining of fuel-oil barrels. This provides either fuel oil or money for the man who does the work. But on the whole the military bases have been important to the economic life of the village mainly for their purchase of native arts and crafts.

The work which consolidated the positive quality of many Sivokakmeit sentiments toward the white world, and made it in many ways irreversible, was the construction of a large military establishment at a distant end of the island, which occurred during the summers of 1951 and 1952. Thirty-three Gambell men went there to work during the first summer, and probably about the same number during 1952. The pay, at $2.75 and more per hour, plus the usual time and a half for overtime and double time for Sundays (and often work went on fourteen or sixteen hours a day, seven days a week), made a profound and lasting impression on the Gambell workers. More than one man made two or three thousand dollars in the short space of a few weeks, and this was indeed, in their phrase, "big money":

Yeah, this was the first time I'd made that much money—just like gathering money from the beach.

Yeah, some people—all people—go down to work at East Cape. And 2 or 3 weeks stay over there, and make lots of money, and full wallet. Everybody happy.

Much of the work was common labor, but there was a chance for the Eskimos to show their talents and skills, too. It was with considerable pride in his own group that one young man related some of his experiences on the job:

Most of the Eskimo workers were common laborers. Those white people down there thought Eskimos were dumb—don't know nothing. Just good as shovel operator. I was a shovel operator. One time we took some of the carvings to where our foreman and superintendents were. We get in and our boss ask us if we don't know nothing, like he heard. They always thought that was the first time we seen tractors. It *was* the first time we saw cranes. I told my boss I can drive tractors. He turned: "What! You, an Eskimo can drive tractors?" I showed him my driver's license—government driver license. I showed it to him, and he said, "I don't believe you." He said "I'm going to test you." So we got one of those D-8's [large caterpillar tractors] over there; course I hadn't drive it yet. We go back, and we talk, and the boys said, "Come on, Dave, you show them white people what Eskimos can do." . . . [Speaking of two young men,] both of them were operating compressors and cement mixers, things like that. Look at Bert, he didn't got to school; but it seems right now that he knows how to handle all kinds of motors—just from experience. . . . They thought we were dumb. But they found we were dependable and hard working.

From 1952 to 1954 there were no such jobs for the men of the village, although their tastes had by then been whetted by the Northeast Cape experience. During the 1954 summer, however, a metal airstrip was laid on the Gambell gravel, and many of the village men were employed for a period of a few weeks working on that. The pay was not at all as sizable as what they had received two and three summers before, but nonetheless it was welcomed. The combined experiences of working at the Cape and on the Gambell airstrip seem to have left most men in a state of expectation, and many were the rumors during the spring of 1955 that in the summer of that year there would be some type of construction work. Indeed, a list of those men willing to work during the summer was drawn up in the spring, and 44 men and older boys (out of approximately 80 males in the age range from 16–60) signed to the effect that they would like summer jobs. The skills they listed for themselves ranged from common laborer to carpenter, painter, caterpillar-tractor driver, and diesel and gasoline motor mechanic. But no such construction work materialized during the summer of 1955.

*The established "jobs" of the village*—By contrast with 1940, there are now more permanently established "jobs" in the village

—regular positions paying a salary. The teacher's assistant and janitor still remains the most highly prized, paying as it does over $3,000 a year. But there is also the job of postmaster, which is almost as lucrative. This position was established in 1946, before which time the mail had always been handled by the schoolteacher. The position of mail carrier still remains in the hands of the man who held it in 1940; and the same individual also holds the jobs of Department of Public Welfare representative and Alaska Airlines representative, which are both new since 1940. All three of these particular jobs, however, are active only irregularly.

The positions of store manager and his assistant are much the same as they were fifteen years ago, but a new post in connection with the management of the store was created by the ANICA (director, discussed before). It is very significant for patterns of social relationships in the village that the jobs of postmaster, teacher's assistant, store manager, and ANICA director, the highest-paying jobs in the village, are all held by members of one clan.

There are a few other jobs in the village. A marriage commissioner now dispenses licenses, for which a small fee is paid. This post was created in 1948. For taking care of the natural consequences of the marriage commissioner's work, several women in the village serve as midwives, receiving a fee of $2.50 for each delivery they attend. This particular occupational speciality was also found in ancient Eskimo culture. Another source of income is that from providing dog-team transportation for the nurse or visiting white people, the same as in 1940. The final type of job in the village, which was present in 1940 and in which a few people are now employed, is that of woman helper or male handy man for the missionary, teacher, and other white people in the village.

Another source of monetary compensation which is important for many in the village is that from membership in the local National Guard unit. This, of course, did not exist in 1940. The size of the group varied between about fifteen and twenty men during 1954–1955, and one of the reasons for enlistment was the monthly check received, even though it was relatively small.

*Irregular sources of income in the village*—The selling of specimens (archeological artifacts such as arrow and lance points, harpoon heads, scrapers, other ivory remains) is an activity in which even small children can participate. Sometimes on a warm summer day, an entire family of mother, father, and little diggers will go out to the ancient site of Seklowaghyaget or Ievogiyoq (see map in Collins, 1937, p. 32) to dredge up what the archeologists have left behind. In addition, skins of the comparatively few polar bears killed during a winter are quickly sold, either to soldiers on the island or to the curio shops on the mainland. As noted before, one bear was killed by Gambell hunters during the winter of 1954, and its skin sold for about $100. The sale of sealskins or walrus skins for money or for trade to the store has also been mentioned.

Helping to unload the supply vessel now pays $1.25 per hour and always gives some extra cash to most men and boys of the village. The women and girls can no longer assist in this work, another change from 1940. But a few carry on one of their specialized and still vitally important jobs—splitting the female walrus hide which is used for covering the boats and formerly was used also as a house roof, walls, and insulation. They receive a few dollars for each job. None of the young girls is now learning the skills of her ancestors in this delicate and fatiguing task. The women also sew the skin cover to the boat frame when the covering has to be changed, and for this they receive payment. Few of the women have sufficient skill to do this properly, and it is said that this, too, is becoming a lost art. Sleds, dogs, harnesses, and other tools of the native economy are sold from Eskimo to Eskimo (a good lead dog selling, for example, for $35); but this is not an important regular form of income for anyone. Nor is the sale of meatballs or skins widespread, although it forms part of the exchange pattern among the Eskimos themselves.

The beginnings of occupational specialization can be seen both in behavior and in aspiration. One man is the village dentist, having taken over the practice and tools of the self-taught person who filled the post in 1940. Another, as said elsewhere in this chapter, bakes bread. But in addition to these men, several have expressed ideas about starting businesses in the village through which they might have a steady income. Setting up another general store, for instance, is a fairly popular notion. But also the idea of a coffee shop, a beauty parlor, a recreational hall, a movie house, and even maintaining a waiting room for the airlines' passengers who come to the village have all been mentioned as ways to make money.

*Unearned income: welfare and other types of checks*—Since 1940 there has been a precipitous increase in the amount of welfare and compensative income. This usually takes the form of the monthly check in the mail, which brings money to those who are sick, widowed, or too old to work or those who find themselves without husbandly support for an illegitimate child.

Of the several types of income of this nature, one of the most important is the unemployment insurance benefits on which men who worked on the Northeast Cape construction and the 1954 Gambell airstrip could draw when that employment ended. Discovering this source of income came as a pleasant and unexpected surprise to the Sivokakmeit, and it provided some extra income for part of the winter months after those operations were finished.

At least three or four army veterans receive sizable monthly disability checks, and people who now return to the village for a period of posthospital convalescence from tuberculosis treatment receive a small monthly stipend for a stipulated period of time, during which they are not supposed to do any active work.

The most important form of this type of "unearned" income for the village as a whole is provided by the Department of Public Welfare of Alaska. This service, which gives monthly financial aid to those qualified in several categories (the most important being general relief, old-age assistance, and aid to dependent children), has increased markedly through the years since 1940. Whether this increase is a result of an increased need or an increased awareness of benefits available is an important question. Public welfare authorities responsible for St. Lawrence feel that the latter is true. My own observations would corroborate that conclusion, for there have always been Gambell people in situations that would be defined by modern terms as "welfare cases"—even in 1940.

Very important in interpreting the increased use of welfare and other types of financial assistance is the fact that the receipt of money often has a meaning different from the one intended by those offering it. Although the old-age assistance is not an old-age pension, it is interpreted as that: simply becoming old is thought sufficient justification for receiving the monthly check, whereas the welfare service is intended only for those old people who have no familial or other support. Likewise, the widow's allowance and the temporary assistance given to a family when the husband is sick or disabled have begun to be considered perhaps more as a "way to make money" than as temporary financial assistance. Considered against a background of no income or little income, the welfare checks are greatly prized, ranging in amount up to $75 or more a month for some individuals. They handsomely supplement what can be earned from ivory carving for some of the old men of the village. As one man said regarding the aid to dependent children (which is often given to widows having families to rear):

Today every widow have to get right away pension so she don't have to go anymore hunting. She got money by herself. She going better than when she got husband; when she become a widow, that is a better way, because she got a pension. That means she don't go hunting anymore.

The extent of dependence in the village upon unearned income has increased considerably since 1940. As estimated in the Annual Statistical Reports for the years from 1945, part of the picture can be seen in Table 16. This picture of increased use of welfare and

*Table 16*. Estimated annual unearned income for Gambell, 1945–1954

| | |
|---|---|
| 1945 . . . . . . . . . | $ 1,020 |
| 1946 . . . . . . . . . | 3,960 |
| 1947 . . . . . . . . . | 3,229 |
| 1948 . . . . . . . . . | 9,118 |
| 1949 . . . . . . . . . | 8,282 |
| 1950 . . . . . . . . . | 10,618 |
| 1951 . . . . . . . . . | 14,105 |
| 1952 . . . . . . . . . | 10,947 |
| 1954 . . . . . . . . . | 12,175 |

similar funds is confirmed by examination of the records of the Nome Welfare Office.[20] The first applications for welfare assistance of any kind to come from Gambell are dated 1944. There were 3 applications that year, and then the case load picked up to the extent of 2 new applications in 1945, 3 in 1946, 3 in 1947, none in

[20] I wish to thank Mrs. Clara R. Salisbury, head of the office, and Miss Beatrice Miller for their kindness in making the above data available.

1948, 5 in 1949, 8 in 1950, 1 in 1951, 3 in 1952, 1 in 1953, and 4 in 1954, making a total of 33 applications. In December of 1954 there were 8 people receiving dependent-children assistance, averaging $60.50 per month. In addition, the office records showed 5 other cases closed for various reasons, all of them taken out since 1940. Seventeen people were receiving old-age assistance in December of 1954, at the rate of $46.87 per month. Five cases of this category had been closed, all of them by death of the recipient, and they also had all been started since 1940.

*Average yearly income since 1940*—At this point it is relevant to broaden the presentation and discuss average yearly income for the village since 1940. Informants questioned about it agreed that most households earn from about $600 to $1,000 per year. A few of the more industrious families earn over $1,000; but without the assistance of high-paying construction jobs or without holding one of the salaried positions in the village, not much more than that can be made. Annual living costs, on the other hand, are said to be from about $1,500 to $2,000 a year. This depends a good deal on taste, to be sure, and spending patterns will be discussed below. But the

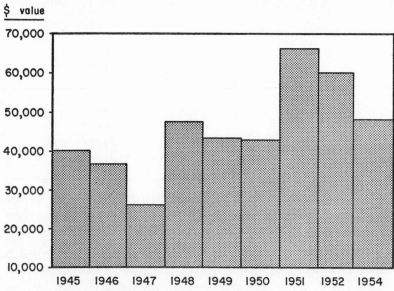

*Chart 10.* Gambell village: total individual income (native products and all other income), 1945–1954. (Source: Annual Statistical Reports.)

most important feature brought out in considering these matters is that there is a gap between how much families make and what they say they need or at least would like to have.

Once again it is the Annual Statistical Report for Gambell which provides some indication of fluctuations in income. Chart 10 plots the total individual income (including income from all sources—

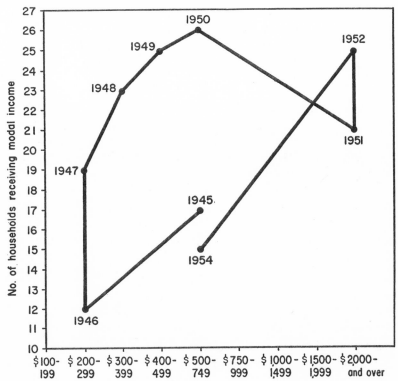

Chart *11*. Gambell village: estimated modal household annual income, 1945–1954. (Source: Annual Statistical Reports.)

native products as well as wages and welfare checks) for native residents of the village over the years covered by available reports. One of the most striking features of the graph is the rise in total village income to over $66,000 in 1951 and $60,000 in 1952, the years of the Northeast Cape construction, and then the decline to about the general level that seems to have prevailed before that time. The year 1947 was, however, a disastrous one, with total village income being only slightly over $26,000. Within the space of four years, therefore, village income practically tripled. There is strong evidence to suggest that such rapid change was not without its harmful long-range effects.

The distribution of individual family incomes in the village for the same period can also be presented. The Annual Statistical Report contains a breakdown of income by number of families in specified income classes; see Chart 11. Notable in that graph are the somewhat abrupt rise and fall of modal income by families, from the relative height of the postwar year (1945) to the low of 1946 and 1947; then the steady and slow increase until 1950; a dramatic flood of wealth into the village in 1951 and 1952, when 25 out of the 50 or so families made over $2,000; and, finally, the return to the more usual distribution in 1954. Within the space of four years (1947–1951), then, the modal income for families jumped from less than $300 per year to $2,000 or more, and from one of those years to the next it quadrupled (1950–1951).[21]

Some of the potentially detrimental effects of this situation, especially for someone moving to the mainland and having to adjust to a cash and job economic context, are unrealistic notions about money and prices, about how easily it can be made, and about the obligatory nature of a loan. Concern has begun to be centered not only on the acquisition of money, but also on its function as a standard against which other aspects of life are weighed. Most notable in the latter respect is the contrasting of the whole way of life in the village to what is conceived to exist elsewhere, and the main point of comparison is money.

*Sentiments toward money and the job*—A man who has seen the sun rise on a Gambell with no white men's houses in it says, "cost lot of money to living now," and another states, "I sometimes think of the hard life we have here—how expensive everything is." An old man, regarding his granddaughter's schooling, comments, "They

[21] These figures on income are estimated by the teacher and are not based on an actual survey of households. The instructions on the form which the teacher uses to complete the Annual Statistical Report say specifically, "Do not attempt to make any special surveys in preparing this form, but give your conscientious estimate as to the probable amount." In view of the fact that other data corroborate the general picture shown here—such as the store sales—this graph of income rise and fall can probably be accepted as reasonably valid.

learn everything—make money." As in the last quotation, young and old alike feel this necessity for money:

He said . . . that the young people now think that with education they can get jobs and make money.

I said that maybe the boys were thinking too much instead of building their bodies. Floyd said yes, they are—they are thinking about how to make money.

You know, some people here don't think—all they think about is making money. But we got to eat, too.

You see, if a woman make a split hide, she charge $5. Just little bit before—mostly nothing. Now, they charge for everything. Everything— even a little something. If they go get water, they charge. Now, young fellow wants money.

The young people themselves echo these sentiments about money:

The main reason they go there [mainland] now is hospitalization, and a little bit of work. The younger folks, they've heard about working there —big money. They want to go to other places than Nome. Wherever they can find big money.

Ann said vehemently that she wanted to get away from Gambell and make some money; there is no way to make any money around here. "I'm going to save my money for the plane fare to Nome."

A man was speaking of help that he had received from others in building his house and I asked, "Did you pay them?" He said no; people around here like to help like that. I asked, "Without pay?" He said yes, then added, "But some want pay now; they like money."

One man who failed to take a salaried job offered him in the village said, "I refused . . . because I love hunting at that time. Mostly for the sport. That's where I made a mistake! Instead of making money, I try to go hunting. After a few years I find out about my mistake—when I need some things."

An older man replies in terms of money to the question, "Do you think people would be happier on the mainland?"

Yeah, they want to be happier. They want to find job, make money. That make happy. Because they never need anything.

Further excerpts from the field notes are given here because of the crucial importance of sentiments about "a job" in the problem of relations to the mainland:

Raymond said to me again (as he had once before) that he has "thought hard" about getting a job someplace else and moving away from the island. "I'm sure my children will be on the mainland someplace—someplace where they can get doctors and nurses and transportation."

A man who had worked for the CAA said, "Because I got enough money, I got enough food from the commissary. At that time I'm almost living like white people. Every week my wife go down and buy something at commissary. Bring full sled, some food. Every week. Living just like white people. I never go out hunting, and just keep job."

He said that sometime—"I don't know when"—this village "will be like you," with people having jobs instead of hunting. "No more boats hunting—maybe mining, or something." I asked if many people now want to move away from the island. He said he thinks so; he thinks that boat hunting is getting less every year and that this will make people move away to look for jobs.

Stephen said that he might have to move away from St. Lawrence if the hunting didn't get any better than it was last year. . . . He thought he might have to go to southeastern Alaska, where he could perhaps find a job in a cannery.

Some of the young people thought it would be a good thing if the survey people started a mine, because it would give them jobs. When I asked if there had been any changes in the way people make money, the reply was: "Yes, I think so; I think there's a big change in that. Because when a boy is able to work, you know, like 16, he just looks for a job."

The young people have this to say:

Where there's a good-paying job, that's where I'll go.
[Is anybody thinking of leaving to get a job on the mainland?] Yeah, some boys may think about that, because it's getting pretty hard to live here, while the prices are getting pretty high.
[Would you like to go back to the mainland?] Yeah, if I get out of a job I may go to mainland and look for a job. But I like it here more than anywhere, probably—with a job. Without a job it's pretty hard to live.

Two young men agree in their evaluation of money-making as a life pattern:

Try to get a job, you know, and save some money. I'll think about that. The best thing to do, you know: try to get a job.
[Did you like the job?] Oh, yes! That time I learned about things. I made a mistake, trying to hunt. I find that making money is more important than anything else.

Such conceptions of the job as an answer to all ills and something that gives maximum security have been engendered by the brief and very pleasant contact that the Sivokakmeit have had with jobs, particularly the well-paid ¦construction work. But also very important in this respect has been the experience of some of the young people who have actually moved to the mainland, some going for schooling and then later finding work and others having been taken by CAA families or missionaries. By 1954 more than a score of young people, many of them girls, had had some extended experience working in the white world. Their impressions and evaluations filtered back to Gambell, there to be involved in the massive task of changing a culture through the modest beginnings of interpersonal influence. Men, too, have worked in Nome and at other points on the mainland, and most of them would like to return there.

*Spending patterns*—Through the years 1940–1955 there has been a great deal of what can only be called "impulse buying." This does not refer to the washing machines and other items of equipment that came in with the village's electric plant during the 1940's or to the considerable necessary expenses for hunting supplies. More and more the prestige value of an item (of what value is a woman's girdle in this parka-covered group?) and its immediate, short-range appeal are the criteria of choice. For instance, during the food shortage in the winter of 1954–1955, candy bars and tobacco practically always constituted at least half of the cargo of emergency food that the store ordered by airplane from Nome; and cases of fruit (coming by air freight with postage at 25 cents per pound) were ordered by several families, although the ship's supplies were to come a month and a half later. As one man said:

> But now Eskimos, when we have about $50 or $100, we try to buy all that item at the store, you know—we want to have a good eat for 2 or 3 days, and then all is gone. Rather than buying something that lasts a couple months.

The desire for new, white man's style of clothing, especially for children, is a widespread culture pattern. On Christmas and the Fourth of July, holidays that are important to the Gambell people, many sport a new outfit (see Figure 9). There is much money spent for clothing, especially through the large mail-order houses, but often a particular article is the wrong size, so that it soon wears out or is discarded. In addition, the cheapness of items is one of the most important factors considered in buying—but the cheaper clothing does not have the quality of long wear.

Other items purchased are radios, watches and clocks, toys (the store's order of expensive Christmas toys was very quickly sold out), toy pistol caps for the children at exorbitant prices, and rabbit and calf skins that have to be imported from the mainland United States. The rabbit skins are usually used only for the women's parka hood, but some of the younger girls now make entire jackets from them. Costing up to $2.50 each and requiring from ten to twelve for a parka, they are much less warm than any native skins available. The calf skins are used for decorating other skin sewing. Many of the women and young girls also have a great desire for cosmetics or "face powders" as they are called. Even young girls five or six years old are seen with lips reddened, following the example set by their older sisters.

One of the most detrimental of the spending patterns now, given the financial situation of the village, is the practice of gambling, which some of the young men who were in the army or National Guard brought back with them. This was a problem for a few families during the year 1954–1955, and scarce money and valuable items changed hands.

It is not true, as one might be led to believe, that the Sivokakmeit are improvident and do not save against the future. Laying in supplies for the winter months was always one of the most deeply ingrained of cultural precepts. But putting away several dozen frozen sea gulls is different from accumulating bits of paper and metal, and with money the meaning of "saving" seems to have changed. Probably both because of the pressing demands for goods of all types and because of different and much enlarged wants, money tends now not to last very long in the hands of the consumer. (One might contrast this, incidentally, with the investment in store stocks by some of the successful trappers in the late 1920's.)

Especially during the days of affluence, when there was work on the CAA construction and at Northeast Cape, much spending took place (as can be seen in part in Chart 6 showing store sales for the period of the Northeast Cape construction). The man who was a storekeeper at the time says of the work on the CAA buildings:

Yeah, big money. I think some of them earn $1,000. [How did they spend it?] Food and ammunition, oil; they order motor and they buy lumber— built new houses. Yeah, through the store. When they get bigger money, they used to order motor and lumber, washing machine, and some other things. When they get bigger money, they used to order any kind they want.

The spending sprees in the store following the receipt of its annual supplies (in which, for example, canned chickens sold for $2.50 each) cause even one perceptive Sivokakmeit to say, as recorded in the field notes:

"This village is moving toward civilization pretty slowly. . . . There are lots of things we have to learn yet." He quoted as examples how people buy things in the store. He said that as soon as the store gets in an order of dry goods, people rush over there and buy it all out. "What do they do with the other clothes they have? . . . I don't know—throw them away maybe. . . . We Eskimos are getting careless now." He said that they are throwing away the blubber from the seals they get—things are different now from what they were long ago when people didn't have money.

Another echoes the same theme: "probably the store will be out of everything when some fellows bring in foxes soon."

In the years before 1940, the former store manager recalls that people spent most of their money for ammunition, tea, tobacco, bread, white man's clothing, and guns. But since that year, two new and costly items have been added to the slate of expenses. For one thing, people with gasoline-driven generators producing electricity must spend a considerable amount of money servicing them. At present there are three in the village, each of which serves several families. During the years when the town furnished electricity, all houses had been wired for lights, and the electricity bill became another form of spending for the whole village. It did not last many years, however; the town was forced out of the power business when most people failed to pay their bills. The heating and cooking bill is the other principal item since 1940 that takes a great part of the income of practically all people. This will be discussed in the next section.

Hunting expenses have considerably increased since 1940. Not only are the boat motors of a larger horsepower, thereby requiring more fuel, but guns, ammunition, and gasoline are more expensive, and the distances traveled for hunting are longer. In fact, probably the greatest single category of spending is that for hunting: during a period of a few weeks in the spring, from $200 to $400 will be spent for each boat (and this does not include labor). The outboard motors themselves cost from $300 to $500 if a new one is needed for the season (and they receive rough treatment in the ice floes). The more than half of all the boat captains whom I questioned about their hunting expenses said that they use from 5 to 8 barrels of gasoline during the spring hunting, and these barrels sell for about $30 each. In addition, there is lubricating oil for the motor, which cost $1 per gallon during 1954–1955, and one gallon is needed for every 5 gallons of gasoline used. Sometimes one entire 55-gallon drum of gasoline is used in only two days of hunting. Ammunition is also expensive. Whale bombs cost $10 each (and the whale killed in the spring of 1955 required from 10 to 15 bombs), and prices for the various calibers of ammunition used range from $3 to $5 per box. Each boat shot up between $100 and $200 worth of ammunition just for the spring hunt. As an example of the expenses that were all too frequent during the spring of 1955 (and 1954 as well), one captain noted with some discouragement that on a particular occasion he had used 25 gallons of gasoline, which he calculated cost him $19, and much ammunition, bringing the total cost for the day's hunt to $42. The day's kill in game was only three baby mukluk seals. Sometimes an expensive day such as this goes by and no animals whatever are killed. Fay, reporting on a series of 50 trips which he made with Gambell hunters, estimates the average cost of hunting, aside from labor, at $19.00 per walrus (Fay, 1958, p. 25).

## Housing and Clothing

Something further will now be said about housing and clothing, which were discussed in Chapter III with respect to their relevance in the subject of health. The particular concern now is the relation of housing and clothing to man's needs for conserving his body heat. A considerable amount of descriptive data pertinent to this topic has already been given and will not be repeated. Rather, a summary of the most important points will be made, together with additional comments that have particular relevance in the broader interest of the discussion, i.e., relation of the group to the white mainland.

It will be recalled that in 1940 houses were of lumber, even as now. But then there were both winter and summer houses, the winter house being very well adapted to the climate, with insulation of walrus skin and small-size quarters that could easily be heated with seal-oil lamps. The summer house was generally larger, and in it were found those items of white culture which were to become in much greater quantity a part of the only house of 1954: tables, beds, chairs, stoves, and other assorted pieces of furniture.

The 1940 houses were the end result of a long development of Sivokakmeit dwellings which began, as far as archeological evidence indicates, with the semisubterranean pitlike house, the *ningloo* proper, constructed of sod, stones, and driftwood. This was gradually replaced by the *mangtagaek*, which was introduced from the Siberian shore about 200 years ago, according to Collins (1937, p. 261). The *mangtagaek* was a driftwood and walrus-skin house ideally adapted to the needs of winter warmth and summer ventilation, for each spring it was torn down and the housing site aired while the family lived in a tent. The white-style lumber houses began to be built about 1900, after the first missionary had come and established himself on the island. This style of house received an important impetus during the plush 1920's, when fox skins handsomely paid for the expensive lumber that had to be brought in, and a few people even built two-story houses. The trend toward white-style lumber houses was marked by the disappearance of the last remaining permanent winter house of walrus hide, the *mangtagaek*, in 1940. From then on the pattern was irrevocable—more and more white-type exteriors and especially more white furnishings inside the house if these could be afforded. Then occurred, first, the days of CAA construction and, secondly, the 1951 and 1952 construction, when such things as linoleum flooring, new stoves, washing machines, sewing machines, and so forth were bought.

With this new equipment have come, to a very few people, new conceptions of house usage and the reluctant realization that some of these items are not really adapted to the Sivokakmeit pattern of living. One woman's husband expressed his wife's feeling in this respect, saying, "You know, she is telling you that it is very hard to keep house clean the way we live." In this statement there is perhaps just as much self-criticism as comment on living conditions. A more concrete example of the incongruence of new patterns to Sivokakmeit life is in the plight of some people who have to attempt to cook on oil heaters which are simply not constructed for cooking. But the costly investment of $100 or so has been made in the heater, and more money cannot be spent for a cooking stove as well.

The central change in housing since 1940, therefore, bears on the problem of preventing heat loss. In 1940 the modal form of heating, especially for the winter house, was the seal-oil lamp. This has now changed, and the Gambell people themselves recognize that the newer-style houses are not as warm as the old and that through the discarding of blubber they have given up a valuable economic item. They say, for example, on the matter of the old skin houses:

> Sure—that's warmer, you know. Because it's somewhat like a thermos bottle. Like living in a jug.
> If I had enough money, I would build a house like that for winter.
> Sometimes we think of building one just for ourselves, because it costs so much to keep a big house like ours warm during the winter.

Of the change from using seal oil for heating, there are wistful second thoughts. Older men say:

> Long time ago save the blubber, cut it up and save for fuel. I don't know why the women don't like to use it! Maybe too much work!

And speaking of another change from 1940, when a great deal of driftwood used to be gathered for heating, a man commented:

> The Eskimos are getting lazy; they are burning oil and coal instead of coming along the shore as they used to and gathering this good wood. When I was younger I did that many times, filled a boat every good day.

Some of the younger people recognize the value of the old way, as in this comment by one young man speaking of his boyhood:

> We had a seal-oil lamp, where we'd get light from, and cook our food with, and get the heat from too. It never cost us for fuel, light, and heat.

But the more common reaction of young people is recorded during the time that the store was out of fuel oil. "Well, girls, shall I get out my old Eskimo lamps?" a mother asked her daughters. And the girls made faces and said, "No! They smell too bad." Yet at the same time they recognize that a good part of their income goes for fuel oil.

Only the most perceptive of the Sivokakmeit see the plight that change brings in its wake. Rare indeed is the person who can phrase as clearly as this man his sentiments regarding cultural change (some of these have been given previously):

That's our fault—this hard time. Shortage of meat and oil—short on money, by trying to use lantern—kerosene and gasoline. That's our fault here. When we were using seal-oil lamp, no need to have kerosene, gasoline for lamp; nothing. No stove oil. If we were doing like before, inside that sleeping compartment were 4 or 5 lamps. Pretty good. Plenty oil in the reserve. Lots of meat. Now that's gone and we have hard time. Trying to use kerosene to cook with and gas lamp for light: too much cost. Before that, very easy, Now that blubber is gone, everybody trying to use whiteman's way. It's pretty hard for the Eskimos. So that's why I say that's our fault.

The same theme—that of recognizing the value of things now discarded but nonetheless being reluctant to use the old after the new has been sampled—is seen also in the principal changes in clothing since 1940. The white man's style of clothing was used fifteen years ago, but it was most frequently worn only in the summer months and by the younger men. The majority of the old men still wore traditional skin pants and parkas even in the summer. The women were then, even as they are now, more conservative in matters of dress, although the young girls were wearing woolen stockings, dresses, and other mainland items.

Native clothing before the coming of the white man had always been of skin. Sealskins predominated, although reindeer hides traded from the Siberian shore were very valuable, especially for the winter trapping costume. Following the introduction of Gambell's own reindeer herd, fawn-skin and doeskin clothing became very common. One of the warmest winter-hunting outfits for men comprised reindeer and sealskin socks worn inside sealskin boots (or reindeer boots for trapping); inner pants of reindeer and outer pants of sealskin; a fawn-skin parka covered by a waterproof intestine parka (as in Figure 14) in turn covered by a canvas garment of similar construction. The women's costume generally resembled the men's, with a "jumper" taking the place of the pants. (Some variations occurred in terms of season, decoration, and special clothing for ceremonials.)

There are several important changes since 1940. First, intestine parkas (made from either mukluk or walrus intestine) have practically disappeared from the hunting wardrobe. These were exceedingly effective in blocking the wind and keeping out the rain, and in 1940 they were quite common. Another change is the decline in use of bird-skin parkas, which were extremely warm. The parka, pants, and socks of reindeer mentioned in the previous paragraph have disappeared, and they have been replaced with white man's materials such as alpaca or sheepskin (see, for example, Figure 9). This clothing is decidedly inferior, even for Eskimos having a measure of inurement to cold. The only sealskin parkas worn for hunting during the research year were worn by white men. Sealskin boots have given way to rubber boots much of the time, although the sealskins are still used for the winter hunting and trapping.

There is, in summary, a great increase in the use of white man's clothing on all age levels, but particularly among the younger generation. As noted previously, army-style clothing is especially popular with the young men. See Figure 19 for an example of the contrast in clothing styles worn by those fifty years old and over and those in their twenties and thirties.

Many Sivokakmeit themselves recognize that their contemporary clothing is not as warm as what they used to wear. One young man, rubbing his hands together in the canvas gloves he was wearing and trying to warm them after have pulled a seal out of the icy March ocean, said: "We don't wear the right kind of clothes." A woman agrees in these terms: "The blanket parkas that women wear now don't keep them as warm as the older skin parkas." And a young hunter, speaking of the change in clothing that the younger generation has made, says:

And they don't dress right anymore. . . . A lot of them don't wear any more reindeer parkas. Course a lot of them would still wear a reindeer parkie but they think it's clumsy. And they freeze in these alpaca parkies. They try to use these alpaca parkies for substitute for reindeer parkie, or sealskin. And they're just like cloth—wind just goes through them. But some of them wears this intestine parkie between the snowshirt and the parkie—to keep the wind out. A lot of them don't have it now. A lot of them will say it smells; some of them will say it tears easy and they try to use these water repellent and windbreaker cloth for parkie, which never come close to this intestine parkie. This nylon stuff, windbreaker cloth, never comes close.

A comment by one of the older generation is a good summary:

Yeah, people buying more clothes, especially for the school children. Those that have some money to buy. All winter now they're using rubber boots and shoe packs [a type of boot]—even 18–25 year old boys and girls, they don't use Eskimo boots now. And pretty soon, we, too, won't use them—if we buy big enough boots for winter. But traveling from here to Savoonga and trapping, Eskimo boots better for any kind weather, hot or cold. And our alpaca coats—we used to have deerskin and bird parkas; now no more, except Duncan, Rudolph, Clinton, and Jonathan. We're using all alpaca-lined parkas; not very warm. We should use either walrus or mukluk intestine, bleached, between our alpaca and snow-parka—to keep out the wind.

In many diverse and subtle ways the utilitarian aspect of clothing has given way to its prestigeful qualities. This is especially true for most of the clothing worn by girls. Light jackets and slacks, rubber boots, head scarves, and wool gloves form their costume for much of the year (along with other ways of adorning the body acquired from the mainland, such as using cosmetics and cutting their long black hair in order to use home permanents). Costume jewelry from the white world is popular, even among very young girls, and the ancient Eskimo women's decoration of beads laced throughout the long strands of braided hair is disappearing.

One further aspect of the change in clothing patterns since 1940 was briefly noted before: many of the girls are not learning to sew the skins from which the only feasible winter-hunting clothing can be made. One man sees the latter development in these terms:

No—now the girls don't want to sew. You watch now in town. [Do they make boots?] No, no. Now is changed. Just wear overshoes. Before, make skin boots, mittens, raincoat, skin pants. Not now. I see just curly hair; just walking around in town.

## Transportation and Communication

Some of the most significant and far-reaching changes in the Sivokakmeit pattern of life since 1940 have been those in transportation and communication contact with the mainland. The 1940 Gambell people had inherited from their fathers the old Eskimo means of transport and travel and knew through their own experience of the white world's ships and airplanes. As noted before in this chapter, whaling ships, traders, coast guard vessels, and supply ships had been stopping at the village for about 80 years. Airplanes, in 1940, were still a very rare sight, and the first airplane to come to the island had flown around foggy Mt. Chibukak only three or four years before. In all, there had been very few airplane flights to the island.

Some modifications of the ancient Eskimo sled and boat occurred before 1940. The single-man skin boat, the kayak, had apparently passed from the culture some time ago.[22] The open boat, the *angyak*, had gradually come to be modeled after the wooden boats that captains had acquired from the whaling ships during the early years of the century. The whaleboats follow a much truer course under sail than do the lighter *angyaks*, but there are disadvantages to their use. If staved in by a sharp piece of ice, they cannot as easily be repaired out on the ocean as the walrus-hide boat. The latter can be hauled out on the ice and sewn up with a piece of skin. In addition, the wooden boats are much heavier, requiring a larger crew to haul them. For a number of years, however, their advantages for the spring whaling hunt outnumbered their disadvantages—they provided more safety, larger carrying capacity, easier manageability, and more accurate sailing control—and in 1940 most of the spring whaling was done in the wooden whaleboats.

The aboriginal style of the *angyak* was one of a flat-bottomed, ribbed boat with no prominent keel. When taken out on the winter ice pans during the January through March hunting, small sleds were taken along for carrying the boat over the smooth ice so that the hide would not scrape along and wear away. But gradually the design of the aboriginal *angyak* was changed and a keel was added —probably for easier maneuverability—and the sleds were dispensed with, because now the keel itself held the skin away from the rough ice. In 1940 there were still a few boats of the older, flat-bottom style, but by 1954 none existed.

Even in 1940, outboard motors had been used for more than

[22] However, Elliott (1898, opp. p. 163) includes a drawing of the St. Lawrence Eskimo hunting walruses from kayaks.

twenty years. A teacher's note in the 1916 records marks the first use of outboard motors on the island; Mr. Dupertius says:

Evinrude demonstration given on the lake. Worked fine. Everyone much interested. Had a walrus chase with it on the ocean. Got two walruses and brought them in with the Evinrude working like a charm.

And in his own words an elderly Eskimo now remembers motors replacing paddle and muscle:

One of the teachers he came and he think about motors. I don't remember what year. He ordered 2 motors for the store. I was store manager that time. The Evinrude, single cylinder. I think 2½ horsepower. He thinks it would be very cheap, buying some motor oil, or gasoline. That Jonathan's father bought one; I bought one myself. We started with 2 motors. [Did they make quite a difference in hunting?] Yes, most people talk about those 2 motors, too much noise, and when run boat this way [in path of smoke], they smell gas, and he thinks "not so good."
[Did the noise of the motor frighten the animals?] They think it might, but one time when we got out hunting, we use paddle, go off to the mukluk on top the ice. Pretty hard to get near them. Before shot them, go down. . . . Then I told them: "Someone said if we go after anything like walrus, mukluks, anything on top the ice, let the motor run, and go after them. Try to hide every crew man except the 2 men in front. Just put every crew man low down in the boat." We tried it this way, with the motor; because we didn't get any mukluks without motor, with the paddle. Keep steady the boat. Not go this way or this way [zig-zag]. Then an old man said, "That motor too much noise; maybe we can't get it." But the mukluks put head up and he watch; he looking for other way. Some times turn his head toward us, but turn other way too. Then we near enough to shoot, and we kill it. Then we learn! We use the motor. Then come home, my uncle told other man, "We not scared those mukluk." [Did other people start to use motors then?] Yes, afterwards they all Johnson motors; mostly use Johnson motors, first. [Before that was there only paddling and sailing?] Yes, paddling and sailing. Even when get a whale—paddling and towing. [Has the motor made a lot of difference?] Yes, he go out quicker and come home quicker too. Help a lot. He like to go faster. But expensive for running the engine.

Since 1940, the use of the wooden whaleboats has almost completely disappeared. Outboard motors, on the other hand, have increased in their horsepower. Fifteen years ago only the largest engines were 25 horsepower, and there were only one or two in the village. The standard size was 12½ or 15 horsepower. Now the usual motor is 25 horsepower, and there are even some motors of 35 horsepower. With the increased horsepower comes increased gasoline consumption, and the implications of this for greater dependence on the mainland have already been discussed.

The dog sled is everywhere part of the Eskimo cultural inventory. On St. Lawrence Island until apparently the middle 1920's the sled was a low-slung, narrow arrangement with front runners looping back on themselves and without any back stanchions or side supports. This is a type commonly found in northeastern Siberia. The driver sat at the rear of the sled and with a whip guided his dogs —which were probably fastened "Nome style," i.e., in parallel traces. But in the late 1920's, apparently, this sled pattern was changed by the introduction of the stanchioned sled with side supports. Thereafter the old sled completely disappeared, and from 1940 the newer type of sled has been used. In this respect, therefore, no change in Eskimo transport patterns has occurred, and still, during the heart of the winter, it is the dog sled with rime-coated driver that is the only dependable means of travel in bad weather.

But massive changes have occurred in other forms of transport. Much increased ship travel is only one aspect. More important has been the regularizing of airplane travel to the island. Beginning with the CAA in 1942, which built a sod airstrip on the edge of the village and used this for year-round supply trips, the sight of a large two-engined transport plane winging its way around the north point has become commonplace. Many types of aircraft have come to the village in these troubled years of war and its aftermath. Military airplanes were among the first, with the Gambell children going down to the lake to watch amphibious craft landing on the water or, later in the year, to see the airplanes heavy with equipment come in on the frozen surface of the lake when the airfield was drifted with snow. The coming of airplanes is an uncommon enough happening so that many people still go down to the airstrip.

The airplane has dramatically worked itself into the complex of white man's medical facilities as well, for many times seriously ill people have been flown outside for treatment. Mail is now brought in by plane throughout the winter months, whereas in 1940 there was only the summer vessel, which brought an entire year's accumulation. In 1954–1955, regular mail and 'commercial passenger service on a biweekly basis was established for the island, and there were other planes landing each month for the army. It was discussed above how food supplies were brought in by mail and air freight on many occasions throughout the year when the store was depleted of vital and wanted goods. Perhaps a good index of the functional importance which connection to the mainland by air travel has assumed in the present culture was the anxiety attending the enforced isolation of the island during April and May, when the airstrip was snowed over and could not be kept free long enough for airplanes to land.

Radio contact with the mainland was regularly maintained in 1940, and since then it, too, has increased in volume and usage, especially with the advent of air service. A commercial telegraph is maintained through the government facilities, and now, with many more people outside in school or hospital, this is used much more than it was fifteen years ago. Home radios were absent in 1940, but are now common in the village.

Eskimo thinking has begun to adjust itself to the realities of airplane flights to the island, and there has been more travel to and from the mainland since 1940. At that time only very few people had traveled to the white man's world. Now, as noted in Chapter III, quite a number have done so. The main impediment is the $85 one-way ticket to Nome. People go to the hospital and to school. Some few have taken jobs, the presagers of many more likely to go; and the airplane has become, for some, a symbol of much else the white man has done to the island. One ancient shaman, with what appeared to be a mixture of facetiousness and animism, exclaimed about the wonderful "big bird" as he watched an airplane succeed in landing safely during a blizzard in the middle of January.

Some of the younger men are not so awed, however, that they do not attempt to bring to the island more of the white man's paraphernalia. For about fifteen years there has been a caterpillar tractor in the village, owned either by the school or by the store. But during the CAA occupation there were other types of vehicles traveling the gravel: snow jeeps, tractors, and all the various models of vehicles with tires. With the influx of military vehicles of the air force and army, many new possibilities are being presented to young Gambell men. Some of those who have been to Nome and seen pickup trucks driving over the muddy streets envision that one day this will happen in Gambell, and they speak of saving money to buy such a truck.

## Summary

This chapter has brought out the astonishing diversity and ingenuity of subsistence activities by which traditionally the Eskimos dealt with a harsh environment. Not only knowledge and skills, but also tools and habit patterns appropriate to the changing nuances of seasons and weather were developed in great detail. Marine animals, fish, birds, and plant life of the rocky slopes were all studied for their every vulnerability of life patterning, spawning, nesting, or blooming in order that they might be exploited to the needs of man. There was, throughout the culture, an emphasis on industry and zeal in the subsistence activities in which all must share, even the small.

In these pages is seen also the story of change. At first it was trading with the white world objects taken from the environment known to the Eskimos: fox skins, baleen, and sealskins. More recently, it has been skin sewing and ivory carving. But now there has begun a shift in the very conception of how to use the environment for feeding and clothing oneself. No longer is it only the cyclical extraction of the products of nature that is thought of as the basis of livelihood. Rather, it is some sort of secondary, manipulative activity in which something is done *to* the environment (as construction work) or some service in a position based on needs engendered by a more complicated social system (e.g., postmaster or storekeeper) that is conceived to be the way to earn one's living.

This latter inclination seems to have many of its roots in the vicissitudinous returns that are a feature of the Eskimo life under aboriginal conditions. The weather, the season, the hunt cannot be predicted. One can only hope for good weather and work toward the successful hunt. But the hoping and the working do not in any way guarantee a full meat cache; and one of the strongest of the underlying themes in discussions about wanting a white man's job is that the latter is thought to be "steady."

Yet at the same time, even though there has been some exposure to the white man's job and its earmark, the salary, there has not come for most people the security which they had thought automatically attends a job. Work has been intermittent and only occasional; and when it did come, wages soared out of all anticipation, only to vanish the next year. But the return was not to the same equilibrium, for new tastes and ideas about life had been encouraged by the brief contact with the job. A residue of want has been left which, up to now, is unsatisfied. The St. Lawrence people had known money before in their history, for it was money which they had received from trading a portion of their physical environment for the white man's products. Now, however, it is their ideas of life which they have exchanged for his products.

In the latter connection may be noted some of the implications of the economic changes that have occurred in Gambell with respect to certain basic sentiments and habits of thought, especially those relating to initiative and self-decision, which traditionally were prime requisites for the Eskimo hunter. In the early days of contact with the white world the changes brought about in subsistence habits by the introduction of reindeer herding and fox trapping were substantial, but the same virtues of independence of thought and decision prevailed in the new cultural complex as in that of hunting. Later, however, employment in construction jobs on the island posed a different problem of adaptation. Here the goal was much more sharply and narrowly defined and the procedures for the task clearly outlined. It was only a question of learning the procedures appropriate to the goal, and such techniques involved mainly mechanical and manual dexterity, for which the Eskimos have long been famous.

Today, with the possibility of moving to the mainland in search of jobs being seriously considered by some of the men, a wholly different range of problems of adaptation is created. On the one hand, a good deal of initiative is required on the part of individuals to effect such a move. That the Eskimos are capable of such initiative and decision when necessary is quite clear. But the context of decision in this case is of a wholly different order and much more complicated than that of hunting or any of the other activities which they have known on the island. When they move to the mainland they are moving into a situation of relative lack of knowledge of the many factors making for success or failure in the venture. In general they are poorly equipped in terms of both intellectual skills (i.e., formal education) and appropriate sentiments required for successfully adapting to such a move.

With regard to yet another feature of subsistence patterns, the reversion, since 1940, to more use of skin boats as compared to wooden whaleboats is interesting in that it suggests that the trend toward acceptance of the mainland culture is not completely irreversible or adamant in the face of rational considerations, even though many instances of nonrational behavior relative to the mainland may be cited. It will be interesting to see whether and under what conditions there might be other reversion to native items formerly used but discarded as a result of contact with the mainland, such as the utilization of skin clothing or seal oil for heat. If times get too difficult, one might expect something of this—at least until the older generation disappears—given the adaptive ingenuities of the Eskimos.

Nevertheless, since the year 1940, the primary base line for examining sociocultural change in Gambell, the story has been that of an originally well-provided and economically fairly secure Eskimo village which underwent a series of fluctuations and deprivations in its economy (the loss of the reindeer herd being most important) and was in rapid sequence subjected to sustained exposure to the white man's standards of housing, clothing, food, and recreation. This culminated in two brief years of buying large quantities of mainland goods, only to be left with no prospect of renewing the source of wealth. The uncertainties about what tomorrow will bring now apply not only to the weather and the ice, which the people have known from an Eskimo past. They are found also in the white world of money and the job. And there has not been, in either world in the last few years, any prospect of stability and reliability in the satisfaction of wants. The response to such uncertainty is not now, as it was for so long, the nighttime singing of the shaman to divine the cause of the breaking of nature. It is rather a reaching out for the newly conceived means of control of weather and the world—money. Money and mainland opportunity.

# CHAPTER VI

# The Texture of Social Life

MAN is unique among animals in the extent to which he is himself a significant object in the environment of his fellows. Indeed, a preponderant part of the cultural processes of a group consists in the detailed inculcation into the young of rules for behaving toward other people in a wide variety of social positions and circumstances. In this chapter the social organization of the Sivokakmeit will be examined, as well as the salient changes that have affected those patterns over the past fifteen years. The first sections will treat aspects of the social organization which are today, as for countless centuries, the heart of the socioculture: the kinship system and solidary groups based on kinship principles. Following this will be a discussion of social forms adopted from the mainland, such as the village council, school, National Guard unit, and church organization. Finally, several other formal associations which have been organized in Gambell since 1940 must also be briefly discussed as further instances of the progressive articulation of this group with the mainland.

## The Kinship System

Of the infinite number of relatives that any individual has by genetic connection, only a comparative few are segregated out by the culture and given formal recognition as "kinsmen." This is true not only of the Eskimos, but of all human groups. It is a "cultural universal." Murdock has reckoned that, outside nuclear family bonds, there are 33 separable potential categories of genetically related people who are "secondary relatives" (immediate relatives of one's own nuclear family; for example, ego's son's wife and their children or ego's wife's brother and so on) and 151 "tertiary relatives" (similarly related to one's secondary relatives). With this calculation he stops, pointing out the unending logical ramifications. In no culture are all or even most of these potential kinship categories picked out and used for the structuring of human relations. The result is that an elaborate pattern of choice and selection exists in which particular types of persons are designated from among these many "potential" kinsmen. They are people toward whom an individual, by virtue of his birth in this network, is expected to act in definable ways and from whom he similarly expects to receive predictable treatment, whether this be material and emotional support, joking and disparaging comments, or patterns of avoidance. The kinship system of a group represents the culturally transmitted set of such reciprocal expectancies.

But it is also important here to note that such a system is a different abstraction from that which segregates out definable, namable social groups based on a kinship or other criterion. Examples of the latter are such groups as the community, family, or clan. The kinship system does not of itself create such groups; it merely sets up wideranging networks of social relationships in which every individual can be taken as the center of reference. All persons occupy multiple roles in many networks simultaneously—brother, son, father, husband, grandson, cousin, brother-in-law, and so forth (Murdock, 1949, p. 92).

In other words, there are people to whom an individual is related who are not in his kinship "group" (if such groups exist in his socioculture); and, to people of his kinship group, an individual may be related in several of the definable types of kinship relations linking a mass of human beings. So both conceptions must be dealt with here: (1) the abstract system of relationships which, through linguistic terminology and patterns of expected behavior, links an individual to only a limited number of the people to whom he is genetically related and (2) the separate, delimitable social groups whose defining characteristics are based on kinship principles.

## KINSHIP TERMINOLOGY

One element of the behavior linking two people in a kinship network is the linguistic term (or terms) by which they refer to each other as a result of their relationship. Murdock has noted that all groups have at least some special terms for use between kinsmen and that in most societies these terms rather than personal names are used in social intercourse between the two people involved (1949, p. 97).

The basic pattern of Sivokakmeit terminology and depiction of those kinship positions that are chosen for special emphasis by being given a distinctive term can best be communicated by means of a chart. In Chart 12 each number refers to a distinctive kin term. When the same numeral designates relatives in different kinship positions, ego uses that one term for all people in those positions (see, for example, the several empirically different positions for which the English term "grandfather" would be used). In the key to Chart 12 the Eskimo terms for various types of relatives are given.

Several features of this kinship system are of considerable interest, particularly with reference to other Eskimo systems. The Sivokakmeit, for example, depart from what has been called the "normal" Eskimo type of social structure (Murdock, 1949, pp. 223, 227) in that they have a different cousin terminology and unilinear kin groups. Murdock says on this point, mentioning the principal criterion on which his "Eskimo type" of terminology is based, that ego's father's sister's daughter and mother's brother's daughter are referred to by the term that is used for ego's parallel cousins; they are, however, differentiated from his sisters. Further, usually (but not always) there is only one term covering father's sister's daughter and mother's brother's daughter (*ibid.*, p. 223).

In the St. Lawrence data, the terms for father's sister's daughter and mother's brother's daughter (*ilowaek*) are not the same as the terms for parallel cousins (*ataligoon* for father's brother's daughter and *aeganaligoon* for mother's sister's daughter). To be sure, cross-cousins are differentiated from sisters, but, on the other hand, the

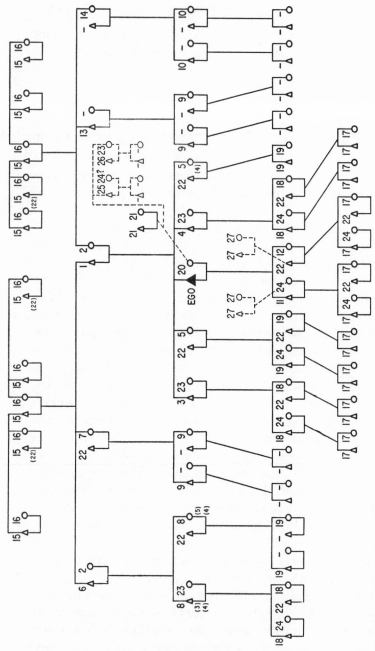

*Chart 12.* Sivokakmeit basic kinship system (male ego). Numerals refer to the kin term ego uses for the relative. Numbers in parentheses are alternative terms, equivalent in their social significance. Where no special term exists, a dash is used. (See key on opposite page.)

## Key to kinship terms (male ego*)

| Eskimo term | English term |
| --- | --- |
| 1. *aeta* | father |
| 2. *naegaka* (sometimes *nae*) | mother |
| 3. *anlngaeka* | older brother † |
| 4. *oyuowaek* | younger brother or younger sister |
| 5. *naiyuk* | older sister or younger sister |
| 6. *ataeta* | father's brother |
| 7. *aesuk* | father's sister |
| 8. *ataligoon* | father's brother's child |
| 9. *ilowaek* | father's sister's child or mother's brother's child |
| 10. *aeganaligoon* | mother's sister's child |
| 11. *Iganak* | son ‡ |
| 12. *paenei* | daughter |
| 13. *angak* | mother's brother |
| 14. *anaena* | mother's sister |
| 15. *aepa* | father's father or mother's father |
| 16. *nlngyuoei* | father's mother or mother's mother |
| 17. *thtowaek* | grandchild |
| 18. *kangiyak* | brother's child |
| 19. *oyugo* | sister's child |
| 20. *noolelk* | wife |
| 21. *sakei* | wife's parent |
| 22. *nlngae* | son-in-law (i.e., generally "man who marries into the family") |
| 23. *agi* | brother's wife or wife's sister (reciprocal; i.e., for a female ego this is husband's brother or sister's husband) |
| 24. *okaek* | daughter-in-law (i.e., generally "woman who marries into the family") |
| 25. *sakeraek* | wife's brother |
| 26. *noolingkaelootkothreit* | wife's sister's husband |
| 27. *noo∂lk* | parent of spouse of son or daughter (reciprocal between the two sets of parents) |

* Most of these terms are the same if ego is female, but a few differences exist. Data are incomplete on this point, but it seems that some of these distinctive terms are: *kowaek*, for older brother; *aekaek*, for older sister; *kochka*, for older brother or younger brother; *nowhaek*, for brother's child; *owi*, for husband; *ngoroongeraek*, for husband's brother's wife; and *sakeraek* (or a variant, *sakaech*), for husband's sister. Further work should be done in this regard.

† *Angligoon* is a general term for sibling—any age, either sex—and also is frequently generalized to include *ataligoon*.

‡ Ego calls his son *Iganak* before the son's marriage; but after marriage he is apparently called *nIngochtak*. Any of ego's children are also apparently called *aevaekotak* before marriage (reciprocal is *angaiyokaek*). I do not know whether there is a special term for other children after their marriage.

term for paternal parallel cousins is often used interchangeably with that for sister (*naiyuk*), whereas the term for maternal parallel cousins is never used that way.

Murdock also sets up eleven types of "social organization," using not only kinship terminology but also rule of descent, residence pattern, types of kin groups present, marriage rules, marriage type, and type of household (*ibid.*, pp. 225–226). In several major respects the Sivokakmeit data are contrary to the "Eskimo type of social organization"; for this, by Murdock's definition, is based on the existence of "Eskimo" cousin terms and absence of unilinear exogamous kinship units. It is further characterized

by monogamy, independent nuclear families, lineal terms for aunts and nieces, the bilateral extension of incest taboos, and the frequent presence of such bilateral kin groups as kindreds and demes, though these may often be unreported. [*Ibid.*, p. 227]

Although several of these features will be discussed at greater length shortly, at this point the St. Lawrence patterns will be compared with this generalized Eskimo model as a background to the ensuing discussion. As noted above, the Sivokakmeit do not have the Eskimo cousin terminology (having, rather, the "Iroquois" pattern), and unilinear kin groups do exist. (The latter, however, are not necessarily exogamous.) It is true that monogamy is the prevailing form of marriage, but on the other hand residence is matri-patrilocal, not neolocal. Lineal terms for aunts exist only partially, and not at all for nieces as the primary term. There is apparently asymmetry in the extension of incest taboos, although data on this point are not too clear. Yet, finally, there is, in agreement with the list of criteria, a bilateral kin group similar to the kindred reported here.

In most critical respects, therefore, the Sivokakmeit pattern of kinship and social organization does not conform to that formulated by Murdock. It should also be noted here that other commentators on the kinship organization of the Eskimos, such as Spier a generation ago (1925, p. 79) and Driver and Massey more recently (1957), similarly depict a type from which the St. Lawrence Island system significantly departs. Driver and Massey, for example, do not even take a position on the question of which type of clan (patrilineal or matrilineal) may be found among the Alaskan and Siberian Eskimos; for they have already classed these peoples as having bilateral descent, in which case clans by definition are impossible (*ibid.*, p. 413).

Giddings (1952), however, has recently noted, in agreement with Lantis (1946), that the kinship organization of the Nunivak Island Eskimos does not correspond to this general type discussed by Murdock and Spier (nor, therefore, would it correspond to the type accepted by Driver and Massey). The systems of some other Alaskan groups which he knows are also different. It appears, therefore, that the pattern which Murdock chose as the prototype for the Eskimos is valid only for the Eastern and Central groups. In Alaska, where approximately half the entire Eskimo population lives and where there is considerably more cultural complexity and heterogeneity, there appear to be somewhat different patterns of kinship and social organization.[1]

The St. Lawrence kinship system is characterized most prominently by the equation of father's brother's children with ego's own primary siblings. Although there is a distinctive term for these parallel cousins (*ataligoon*), frequently the sibling terms themselves are used; and as will presently be shown, the behavior expected of ego toward his *ataligoon* is the support and loyalty expected toward his primary siblings.

Another feature of the system is its tendency toward generational classificatory terms. This is seen particularly at the grandparental and the grandchild levels and with regard to affinal relatives. For example, the general term for a man married to one of ego's female relatives is *nlngae*, no matter what generation. The term means something like "one who works for that woman." Similarly, the term for daughter-in-law (*okaek*) is generally used to refer to inmarrying females in generations succeeding ego.

The pervasive lack of kin terms for children of ego's crosscousins (*ilowaek*), as well as the lack of them for children of ego's maternal parallel cousins (*aeganaligoon*), contrasts sharply with the

[1] A brief discussion of the St. Lawrence Island kinship system and social organization can be found in my paper "An Eskimo Deviant from the 'Eskimo Type' of Social Organization," *American Anthropologist*, LX (1958), 1140–1147.

numerous terms which exist for children descended in the line of male relatives—another indication of the relatively greater importance of the paternal line in this culture.

Perhaps the most widespread principle on which the entire kinship system is constructed is that of the equivalence of brothers. This comes out in several ways, in addition to the greater development of terminology for the male line. The similarity between the term for father (*aeta*) and father's brother (*ataeta*) attests this, as does the term for father's brother's children (*ataligoon*), which is said to mean "from one father." Furthermore, father's brother's wife is called by a term which is derived from that for mother (*nae*) and which is often used as the term for direct address to mother. Ego's *nae* is expected to act in the capacity of mother, and ego, that of son to father's brother's wife.

The term for ego's mother's sister (*anaena*) is likewise similar to that for mother, and she is often equated with ego's mother and acts in much the same capacity. But the equivalence of sisters appears to stop at this point and is not further extended as is the solidarity of the male line. *Anaena*'s husband, for instance, does not act in a role similar to that of ego's father's brother. He is quite outside the system of inmost relations.

KINSHIP BEHAVIOR

With many of the kin terms are associated distinctive patterns of behavior expected between relatives. Kinship terms are not generally used in direct discourse between people—personal names or affectionate "nicknames" being used instead—but nonetheless they function as signals governing alternative patterns of behavior between people standing in particular relationships. Some of the most important and clear-cut interpersonal behavior patterns must be mentioned here, but a full inventory of role relationships will not be attempted. Besides, not all kinship roles are culturally defined to the same extent; some are only minimally structured in terms of expected and proscribed behavior. It should be added that what is described below is the general pattern, perhaps the "ideal culture pattern," which is met in varying degrees of practice, but which nevertheless must be adhered to in most instances. Changes that are coming into the system of relationships will follow later in the chapter. There are also, apparently, a few slight differences in expected behavior among some of the clan divisions of the village, but the typical pattern is presented here.

A general term for someone to whom an individual is related in any sense is *ilaekwaek*. The Eskimo translate it as "relative," but they go on to make an important distinction—in English—between people to whom they are "related" and people who are their "relatives." In this latter more refined sense its use brings up the matter of kin groups, which will be discussed after examination of the behavior patterns expected among people who are "related" in the general scheme of kinship relationships.

*Brother and brother*—The unlimited sharing of goods, mutual help, and unstinting loyalty expected of brothers is the cornerstone of the ongoing social system. As one young Sivokakmeit himself sees this:

In our ways the brothers were supposed to live together, help each other and share everything they have and get, and teach their children to do the same things in every way.

This relationship, though of the greatest solidarity, has overtones of emotional restraint and interpersonal reserve. A quality of what the Eskimos translate as "shyness" or "shame"—probably a better translation is "respect" or "dignified reserve"—pervades interaction between brothers. The respect is especially heightened in the case of a younger brother interacting with his older brother (his *anIngaeka*). As one man puts it, in referring to his older brother, "always I at attention for him." No note of joking or frivolity can creep into the conversation between brothers:

We talk plainly, nicely, and try to be kind. Try not to make them sorry and unhappy. Try to make them happy and talk to them very plainly.

Apparently at times this respect takes on aspects of the typical avoidance relationship, at least in some of the patrilineages, where it is said that if two adult brothers are alone together in the same room they should not look directly at each other when they talk. If a third person is with them in the room, however, they can freely carry on a conversation. Such inhibitions with a brother are not found among children, but they are gradually learned as the young child grows into awareness.

*Brother and sister*—As with ego's relationship to his brother, mutual help, abundant support, and heightened respect are characteristic of his relations with his sister. Conversation is inhibited and circumscribed. No harsh words should be spoken, and an effort is made to be extremely kind. Between a brother and sister, in addition, there is even more of an emphasis on respect and avoidance of frivolous or sex-laden topics than with siblings of the same sex. A man, for instance, should not be alone in the same room with his sister—but if he is, there is "great shame" (extreme respect) involved in the situation. When the context is that of the entire family group, however, all the children can join in the light banter and good-humored interaction that occurs.

*Sister and sister*—As commonly found, this relationship is one of mutual support and affection, with considerably less development of restraint behavior between the two individuals than is true of that between brothers. Still, however, the element of respect exists here, and there is none of the indiscriminate joking that is found, for example, with one's cross-cousin, an *ilowaek* (to be described later).

*Father and son*—Ego is "humble, always humble to the father," as one man puts it. Not only is there the theme of unstinting support and care for both parents during their life, but also the element of "shyness," of respect and utter obedience to one's father, is never relaxed, even though ego may be an adult in his prime of life:

As long as the children are under the control of the Dad, they can be scolded at will by him. . . . There is no age limit. It's not like the 21 age limit, when the person becomes an adult. He may be 30 years old in the Eskimo way.

Even after a man has retired from the active hunting life (anywhere from 50 to 65 years old), he still is consulted by his sons as to when to go hunting, the care of the boat and other equipment, decisions as to the apportionment of goods, and so on. It is primarily from his father that a boy learns the exacting skills of ice hunting, bird netting, fox trapping, and the multiple other technical roles that are those of the Sivokakmeit male. And, with such a relationship of unequals, there is the frequent concomitant of mutually respectful and restrained behavior.

*Mother and son*—With this relationship, which crosses sex lines, there is even a greater emphasis on mutual respect and circumspection than is true of the father-son situation. In the local English idiom, the son is "bashful" before his mother as well as his father. But the deference in this case is tempered by its extremely warm emotional context. As an elderly man says, "To an Eskimo, the mother is most important of all."

*Mother and daughter*—The commonality of sex between mother and daughter fosters less restrained behavior than is found between a boy and his mother. The girl is expected to be very helpful to the mother in the latter's role of managing the household, taking care of younger children, helping to provide the woman's share of food, such as greens, and so on. The mother's role expectations from the child's point of view are outlined in the following passage, in which a woman is speaking of life with her grandmother, by whom she had been adopted as a daughter:

She is just like a mother to me, she very good. Used to be real mother to me. She used to make my clothings. And saved the best of things for me— food, cookies, bread, chewing gum, candies. I felt very bad when she died.

But the girl, on her part, is expected to be "bashful" and obedient to her mother, although elements of humor and pleasantry can come into the relationship.

*Father and daughter*—With the father the girl is to show the utmost respect and circumspection in behavior. The father has complete authority over her activities; and as a contemporary father says, the daughter is "humble; very much obey the father." A woman, remembering her relationship to a father-surrogate, her grandfather, speaks of the authoritarian quality in a father-daughter relationship:

He used to rule me while I was with him. I used to do everything what he said to me. But when I get married, he don't have to rule me any more. He leave all these to my husband, as I become my husband's and no more my father's.

*Husband and wife*—As indicated in the preceding quotation, the husband-wife relationship echoes the authoritarianism of the father-daughter combination. A woman is said to "belong" to her husband, and upon marriage she loses in a real sense her clan affiliation by virtue of birth and joins that of her husband. For the first few years of their married life, a man and his wife are "shy" in each other's presence, and in some of the patriclans they do not use personal names in direct conversation. Often it is not until several children are born that personal names come into their conversation. Until that time contrived affectionate pseudonyms are used between the two. Although the husband publicly has complete charge of the household and his wife and her activities, in the quiet of an inner sleeping room the woman, according to her personality, can exert considerable influence over the man's decisions. Light humor and joking of a mild sort are permissible, but never the deliberate disrespect that is characteristic of the *ilowaek* relationship. Based as it is on the economic complementarity of man and woman in this culture—in which a man has to have a wife if he is to be a successful hunter—the relationship at times is one of considerable support, affection, and respect. The woman, too, has a sphere in which she has complete charge. The game animals and all other food that a man brings into the house are turned over to her, and it is she who decides whether and to whom to distribute meat. The husband has no voice in the matter; and if a man were to go to another house and ask a woman for meat, he would be refused even though his wife would be given some if she were to go. One man says, speaking even of store foods:

When I bring it home, everything I bought belong to my wife. If some woman ask her for flour, little sugar, she give it to her. Yes, even meat. Just put it in house, and wife take care of everything.

Another area in which the woman of the house holds an absolutely pre-eminent position is her relationship to a daughter-in-law.

*Son-in-law or daughter-in-law and parents-in-law*—The relationship of either a son- or daughter-in-law to his parents-in-law has, as put by local informants, "a *lot* of shame." The respect and restraint behavior in this case are heightened and magnified much more than with any other pair of relationships, except perhaps the relations between the two sets of parents of the married couple. With the in-marrying girl the restraint is perhaps at its extreme, for since residence is ultimately patrilocal, the patterns of expected behavior extend throughout the lifetime of both parties. Although the girl can speak somewhat freely with her mother-in-law—there is no element of "avoidance" in this relation, only extreme respect— she is under the complete authority of the mother-in-law as long as she lives in the same household. The daughter-in-law, the *okaek*, is expected to do a large share of the household work:

That *okaek*, lot of work. In the fixing and in the house. Yeah, lots of work, and fixing things and waiting for me and what I say.

And a woman herself was concerned that she do right in this respect:

Elsie said that she has t.b. according to a recent x-ray report and did not want to be a burden to Michael's mother. She said that she feels very ashamed to have her mother-in-law working for her when she should be working for Michael's mother.

Another young girl in such a situation echoes these observations:

Edith said that Eskimos aren't like white people, that when a girl is living with her husband's parents she has to do everything they say and she has to ask them about what she can do.

With her husband's father, the *okaek* shows extreme respect behavior and in some instances avoidance patterns. "He's like a king, a great man to her," as one man said; and she should not speak to him unless he calls for her. She is extremely attentive to him and helpful and tries to anticipate his wants, as in this passage:

In olden days, those father-in-laws are something like a big honored man to the daughter-in-law, but anyway they are kind to each other. But the girls don't do much talk to them like the rest of the families talk with them. They always ashamed to say anything to them. I always kind of embarrassed to stay close to Clyde when I moved to them and couldn't even speak to him often, although sometimes I speak to him. In my mind I thought like this: Maybe Clyde thought that I am against him just because I don't talk much to him at all; but he knows that daughter-in-law should be like this to father-in-laws in those days. [How about now?] No, not embarrassed with him like I was before, but little bit, still little bit.

And a father-in-law himself tells how his son's wife should treat him:

Daughter-in-law very humble. Sit closely—we don't do that. And I can't stay with her just alone. But it's all right if a meal or something like working. Then to stay with me is all right. Should be bashful and ashamed when together.

The same man says in regard to his wife's parents:

I can't do anything wrong way. Very very danger if some kind of wrong word. Very shameful that, to father-in-law and mother-in-law. Both man and woman. I tell my father-in-law very plain words; very quiet and true. Not fooling. [Your wife acts the same way to your parents?] Oh yeah, yeah. Just like she is better than her real mother, her mother-in-law. [And her father-in-law?] Just like very holy, yeah, very holy.

With his father-in-law a man shows very respectful behavior, but the sameness of sex renders something more of an open relationship possible. The fact that the man lives in the household of his father-in-law to be only a short time relieves some of the pressures of the long-term respectful relationship to which the in-marrying bride is subjected. The marriage pattern includes at least a year of "groom work," during which the young man lives in his fiancée's household and during which he must show extreme respect and avoidance behavior toward his mother-in-law. If the two are in the same room together alone, they cannot look at each other and do not speak directly to each other. At all times conversation between them is extremely strained and is usually carried on through a third person. These contingencies on behavior probably continue after the young man has returned, with his wife, to live with his own parents.

*Father's brother and brother's child*—Following again the principle of the equivalence of brothers, ego treats his father's brother (*ataeta*) much the same as his father—with respect and considerable assistance. Ego is "kind and humble, just like to father," and *ataeta* reciprocates this behavior; he is "supposed to treat me—*kangiyak*—like a father would." The wife of father's brother, who is called by the term equivalent to that for mother (*nae*), is likewise expected to act in the supportive and indulgent role of mother to ego. She "acts the same way as a real mother," by giving clothing, food, and other goods to ego, and he finds the "two houses all the same." There is, however, with both the *ataeta* and his wife, the same sort of respectful behavior that is expected toward one's real parents.

*Father's sister and brother's child*—Ego's relations with his *aesuk* are quite open and free. She makes clothing for him and gives him gifts. There is very little restraint in their behavior and conversation —little of the "shame" that is involved in so many other relationships. Ego is "never shame to her," and there is "not much difference between us—we can talk and even visit." *Aesuk*'s husband, *nIngae*, is not an important figure for ego. His role is much like that of son-in-law—socially very reticent—and the same term is used.

*Mother's sister and sister's child*—Another warm, motherly figure for ego is found in his mother's sister, his *anaena*, and there is the same respect behavior. She is similar in role to *ataeta*'s wife, but for her husband there is no term or expected behavior, as was mentioned before.

*Mother's brother and sister's child*—This relationship is less structured than those that have been discussed thus far. Apparently the same respect and humility prevail, but they are quite muted in intensity, as is the reciprocal help on the part of *angak* to ego. Relationship bonds with *angak* verge on being tenuous; for, unless he is of the same patriclan as ego, he is not of ego's father's people and hence is of considerably less importance in terms of reciprocal relations. *Angak*'s wife is not designated by any specific term, and no pattern of expected behavior governs ego's interaction with his mother's brother's wife.

*Father's brother's children and ego*—The relations among *ataligoon* are in theory indistinguishable from those among first-order siblings. "My father's brother's son is like my brother"; "all same, like my own brothers, same thing"—these are the precepts that guide behavior between two individuals standing in this relationship. In many instances, they refer to each other with sibling terms rather than cousin terms; and the same prohibitions against intimate and jesting behavior prevail here as with real sibling behavior. Again, much greater emphasis on the male than the female line of descent is shown here, and through the principle of brother equivalence there can be individuals who, genetically speaking, are related only in a third or fourth order to ego; but he will refer to them as his "brothers" or "sisters," and their children will be his *kangiyak*, his brother's children, because the parents are distant *ataligoon*. It is true that with such distance the closeness of the tie somewhat diminishes; but in theory and in much practice this extension of sibling support and affection is very wide.

*Mother's sister's children and ego*—Ego's *aeganaligoon* are not as close to him as are his *ataligoon*. One reason is that very often they are of a different patriclan. There is, nonetheless, an element of mutual support and sharing in this relationship, as well as, apparently, some avoidance relations similar to those between siblings. But in no case is it a relationship as close as that found among *ataligoon*.

*Father's sister's children or mother's brother's children and ego*— Only in relations among cross-cousins are there patterns of behavior radically different from the usual restraint and respect behavior that seem characteristic, in differing degrees, of many other relationships. The *ilowaek* are expected to play jokes on each other, to insult, to fool and deceive, and to humiliate each other. This is especially done in a public place, where the laughter of the audience can resoundly reinforce the *ilowaek*'s jibes and taunts. The two parties involved are not supposed to get angry from such exchanges; rather, they should be inspired to even greater wit in the contest.[2] There are many sexual references in such interchanges, both between male *ilowaek* and between a man and his female *ilowaek*. Taunts about sleeping with an *ilowaek*'s wife or references to sexual activities and so on are very common in this relationship. But another feature is that frequently *ilowaek* are dancing partners. Two men, for instance, together perform a comic dance, or they may put on a mock fight for the audience. Moreover, in days past, a particular ceremony was held only between two *ilowaek*, in which each man, with chosen relatives, would exchange gifts in the context of dances, songs, and stories.

There is some indication that the full development of joking occurs only between *ilowaek* who are somewhat distantly related, not among the first-order cross-cousins. Sometimes, outside the joking behavior, mutual help and sharing occur in this relationship as in so

---

[2] One cannot help comparing this structured kinship relationship to the famous *nith* contests found among the Central and Eastern Eskimos, in which two disputants to a quarrel sing songs before an audience intended to embarrass and insult their opponent so drastically that the approbation of the audience wins the case for the wittier of the two.

many others. But joking behavior on so extensive a basis and with so deliberately disparaging aspect does not occur in any other relationship. A child is taught early who his *ilowaek* are and how he can treat them; if he begins to tease someone outside this relationship, parents will say, "Don't tease him—he isn't your cousin [*ilowaek*]."

*Grandparents and grandchild*—Another relationship of extreme affection and support is found between grandparents and grandchildren. Aside from the fact that very frequently a child will be given to a grandparent to raise as the latter's own, the bonds that unite individuals in this relationship are very warm and affectionate. It is not untinged with respect behavior; but this has little of the "shy" quality so common in other respectful behavior, and good-natured interaction can occur. There is no "joking" in the *ilowaek* sense, but neither is there the "shame" in the sense of avoidance patterns. The emphasis is on the mutual helpfulness and kindliness of both parties.

*Ego's affinal relatives*—The most important of ego's affinal relatives have already been mentioned, and brief mention can be made of the remaining relations. Rules for behavior toward these relatives help provide some insight into pervasive cultural sentiments. The relations between a son-in-law and his parents-in-law, which have been discussed, are the basis for the behavior expected of any in-marrying man: much restraint, helpfulness, and respectful demeanor. Likewise, any in-marrying woman aside from daughter-in-law (such as the wife of a male grandchild) is expected to fill the role of *okaek*, i.e., act with utmost helpfulness and submission. With the parents of the spouse of one's child—the parents of ego's son's wife or those of his daughter's husband—there is again a relationship of extreme respect. It is a "very holy way, should be very important word to us; we keeping together very humble." This is especially true if the girl has had a boy child. Then the father of the young groom is particularly humble and respectful to the father of the girl

because in his mind—doesn't say it out loud—he is very, very thankful to us. That's the way we do. Because he is glad to get boys.

Similarly, with the siblings of ego's wife, there is again this pervasive injunction to "humble," "holy" behavior which is, no doubt, the familiar restraint and circumspection on a somewhat lessened scale compared to that for one's parents-in-law.

With reference to the wives of one's brothers (*agi*) the avoidance patterns are again stressed to a considerable degree. Ego is "very shameful, shame to her."

> She can't say anything to him. She is afraid of him. She never say anything to him. Oh, my brother too, very bashful to her [i.e., my wife].

The relationship between a man and his brother's wife is apparently of much the same order of avoidance as that between a father-in-law and daughter-in-law, but perhaps less stringent.[3]

One general observation possible at this point is that the bulk of kinship behavior partakes, in varying measure, of respect behavior. In some cases this is maximized so that emotional and almost physical avoidance is prescribed. In other cases this dimension is manifested only in respectful speech and quiet, attentive demeanor. Hence there seems to be a good deal of "holding oneself in" with respect to most relatives, a considerable proliferation of relationships where generosity, kindness, thoughtfulness, and selflessness are expected of an individual.

Against this background stands the sharply contrasting *ilowaek* relationship, in which one is allowed, even expected, to act in a quite different manner toward the relative. He is to insult, to jibe, to fool, to humiliate—and he wins cultural approbation for such behavior. The development of this joking behavior may be interpreted as a displacement mechanism for the release of many suppressed feelings about kinsmen that cannot come out in other ways. The joking relationship is a subject of some interest in anthropological literature. It is, as Radcliffe-Brown puts it, a relationship of "permitted disrespect" and is the source of hypotheses concerning functional sociopsychological interrelationships in a group. Radcliffe-Brown sees it, for instance, as the other alternative mode of behavior arising from problems of divergence of interest among people who are

---

[3] A hypothesis concerning the functional aspects of such avoidance behavior can be developed out of an examination of the close and highly interdependent living between brothers—usually even in the same household—and the continuing necessity to place all sorts of obstacles in the way of arguments and disputes that might arise. The injunction to avoid any sort of intimate interaction with one's brother's wife could easily prevent jealousies arising between the two brothers.

related and who might otherwise come into conflict (the first mode of behavior is that of respect and avoidance).[4] In the present case, however, its function as a patterned and legitimate way to express pent-up and displaced antagonisms would seem more prominent.

### SENTIMENTS ABOUT KINSMEN

As might be expected, sentiments about one's closest relatives are very warm and supportive, even within the framework of behavioral restrictions that surrounds some relationships.[5] There is considerable cultural exaltation of the family as a base, and the reactions of people to long periods of separation from their parents and siblings cogently illustrate the psychological reality of the cultural value. The question whether people in the mainland hospital get homesick brought this typical reply: "Yes, they do. Even they make worse from having too much thinking about their families." And a young boy, who was offered a chance to go to school on the mainland after having been released from the hospital, decided against it, mainly because "we want to see our folks, you know! We want to go back home first."

Traditionally, wealth and the good things in life were to a large extent measured in terms of human relationships—a large family, especially of boys:

An Eskimo likes a big family because when boys and girls grow up, he's like a millionaire. Girls go down to pick greens, then boys go out hunting and get some meat and bring it home—lots of meat. Never need anything whole year; every year good luck, because big family. Lots of children.

An old, weather-beaten man remembers his father teaching him to hunt and in an eloquent passage recalls the poignancy of loss upon his father's death:

My father was boss. Even if he didn't hunt, he brought something home, meat, and divided it. And after I'm maybe 10 years old, I try to hunt bird

[4] See Radcliffe-Brown, 1952, chap. iv.
[5] There are some indications that in the witchcraft complex, which formerly existed in this group, those who were often first accused of witchery were one's relatives. This was not always the case, however—old people were very frequently the witches. But the pattern is mentioned to indicate that there is another possible dimension to sentiments about one's kinsmen, a dimension which cannot be examined here. The most striking feature of the sentiment pattern is, nevertheless, the strength of its positive qualities.

myself. He with me, my father. I no go alone. He teach me how to get bird with a net. I study. Miss most of time, but sometimes get 2, sometimes 5 birds. And my father speak: "I'm glad. I sit down and I teach you. By and by no more hunting for me. Thank you very much, my son." He speak like this all the time. He sit down behind me when I hunt. I waiting for bird. If little too far, he says, "No, too far." If close, "You try 'em." Sometimes if I get bird, he kiss me, my father. He speak all time, "You learn, by and by. When you learn, I sit down in the house, and you hunting for everything. Maybe sometimes you even get smoking tobacco for me." I tell him, "I promise big pile, by and by; big pile smoking tobacco." When I big enough, I get everything—I learn to strike seal with harpoon. My father no more hunt. I feed him. I think me 18 years old, he sleep. In October he die. Evening he die. They want to put clothes on him. I'm crying, crying. I thought no dead; he sleep, I think he sleep. And no tell me that he died. No, I don't know; they say, "He sleep now, be careful, you." By and by I clear up; maybe try to put clothes on him, but hard time—getting stiff. All joints. I grab him; I touch—cold. No breathe. That time I find out he died. I think one week I no eat something—hurting. They want to put in grave. I like to help, but nobody call me that time. Maybe they afraid I'm worse again, lonesome. More worse, lonesome. No like show it outside. They try to hide what place they put grave. Suppose I know it, I go look all time, maybe every day. They hide it. I stay in house. . . . When I'm big enough, I found his grave on top the mountain. I go look—dead, bones, that's all. I believe that time no more father. I thought visit someplace, no die. That time I learn when I go to grave. I see bones already white, some gone. I believe he died.

Other statements illustrate different aspects of sentiments toward relatives:

The same summer my second brother was born. . . . He added more joy to my life. It was very good for me to have one more brother to play with and take care of. He seemed more dear to me because he was the youngest brother I had.

[And on asking people for meat or other goods] Yes, she mostly go to relations. She would feel a little shamed to go to a not relation. Mostly even when little she try to ask father's or mother's relations.

## Kinship Groups

The Sivokakmeit themselves make a distinction between people who are "related" to ego and those who are considered his "relatives." The difference appears to mean that the first are those individuals who are uniquely tied to ego through the widespread net of kinship behavior just described, whereas the second term refers to those people who are, with ego, members of a definable and separable group. The ensuing discussion will therefore deal with the rule of descent; the names and structure of the corporate descent groups; the principal features of the groups in terms of cultural characteristics and functions in the social system; changes in the kinship system; and marriage and residence rules as these relate to the groups. At various points lesser social groups empirically based on kinship principles, such as the boat crew, will be mentioned. A last consideration will be a discussion of changes in the kinship system since 1940. The importance of such changes as have occurred cannot be seen except against this background of the functional matrix of kinship organization.

RULE OF DESCENT

Although certain types of ties to an individual's mother's kinsmen are culturally recognized, a man takes his primary and immutable social identity from his father. Descent, in other words, is patrilineal. With but one qualification, all people are considered as belonging to their father's descent group, not only in a social sense but also in a spiritual sense; for every individual is the reincarnation of a now-deceased member of that group. The qualification referred to is that of women who marry outside the group into which they were born. Upon her marriage, a woman in most regards loses her original social identity unless her husband is of the same group, and she is said to "belong to her husband" and his people. She is spoken of only as having "come from" the other group, not as still being a member of it—except in the transcendental sense that her name-soul irrevocably belongs to the host of spiritual essences which is the group. This is apparently the only vestige of her original identity that she retains. Her change of group is shown here:

Leila belongs to me now. When we take our wife, we call her just like *ilakwa* [i.e., "relative"]. We bring from her father, and her father give to us and she never belongs to her father anymore.

The descent pattern is again illustrated in the case of a woman whose husband dies. If she remarries outside the group into which she first married, her children remain with her former husband's people and they never lose their birthright—"the people think the children should be with their close relatives." This injunction apparently promotes the practice of the levirate, for it is said to be preferable that the woman remarry either one of her husband's brothers or his *ataligoon* (which is socially equivalent). Moore, in fact, notes that in 1912 the levirate was practiced: "After the death of a married man, his brother is expected to marry the widow and care for the family" (1923, p. 267).

The emphasis on the male principle of descent is seen also in the present circumstance of two of the descent groups in Gambell, which are said to have died out because the only surviving representatives are females whose husbands are of different groups. Thus the children of these women will not inherit their mother's original social identity, and the two groups in question are effectively defunct. The greater social valuation given a male child in many contexts of the culture besides the one of descent affiliation is also stated here:

In the Eskimo way, a boy is best. People like boys, because they help a lot, hunting and other things. It is hard to make a boy up here—girls are easy to make.

A limited number of descent groups exist. They are known by definite names; share distinctive subcultures in terms of slight dialectic and vocabulary differences and, especially, religious and ceremonial patterns; have unique social histories; exhibit pervasive patterns of cohesion; and are recognized by all participants in the common culture as distinctive sociopolitical groups. Every individual in Gambell clearly belongs to one or another of these groups —in the case of an adult woman, that of her husband; in the case of a man, that of his father.

This does not mean that the ties with one's mother's group are socially unrecognized if she was born into a group different from that of one's father or that a woman who married out of her natal group thereby completely forsakes her consanguineal kinsmen. An informant put the balance nicely: "The Eskimo custom is that relationship is from the father—mostly." The qualification contained in this statement refers to such practices oriented toward the mother's group as preferential sharing of meat and other goods between two descent groups linked by a common marriage. It is sometimes said that a woman marrying into a different descent group thereby becomes something of a "peacemaker" between the two groups, and patterns of amity and generosity should follow the bonding by a marriage. Although this may not actually prove to be the case, it is nonetheless a definite social tie involving patterns of expectation between the kinsmen of both spouses. The children of the woman, in particular, will show deference and respect behavior to the older people of their mother's group and will—ideally —act in a helpful and kindly manner to all their mother's descent-group relatives. They will, of course, act in a similar manner to relatives on their father's side; but in addition to this general injunction to treat both sets of relatives respectfully, they are bound inseparably to their patrilineal male relatives by the insoluble bonds of socially defined descent involving widespread patterns of support and self-sacrifice for those relatives.

It is also important to note another aspect of the exaltation of the male principle: although one has female relatives in one's descent group, the stable core of the group consists of the related males who will never lose their social identity through out-marriage. This point will come out again in the discussion below, when analysis of an individual's most intimate culturally prescribed social environment is undertaken—the environment of his hunting companions, his loyal supporters in time of need, in other words, clansmen of his own generation. Moreover, by virtue of the social equivalence of brothers and the fact that a male takes his descent from his father, all the male relatives of one's descent group are in effect considered "brother" in some degree. If they are not actually first-order *ataligoon* (children of father's brother), then they are children of father's *father's* brother's male descendants and are linked into the male net of relationships. In any case, the end result is a group of clansmen modeled on the sibling relation.

## THE DESCENT GROUPS

I have chosen to call the descent groups "patriclans," following Murdock's definition of the term as a group of unilinear descended kinsmen who share a common residential alignment (Murdock,

1949, pp. 65–66).[6] Interestingly enough, the English term which the Eskimos themselves often use for referring to these social groups is "tribe," no doubt a designation they picked up from white men in the early days. There is, however, some justification for this term, and if it would not lead to further confusions it might actually be more appropriate to continue its usage here instead of calling the descent groups "clans." One of the main distinguishing features of each descent group is that its ancestors originally came from a particular geographic place, either on St. Lawrence Island itself or in Siberia. In general, Eskimo bands all the way from Alaska to Greenland are commonly called local "tribes," having somewhat distinctive subcultural traits and organization. Many names they use for themselves, moreover, are translated as "people from —— place," for example, Nuniwagamiut, "people belonging to *nuniwach* (Nunivak Island)." The Sivokakmeit, likewise, tend to label their descent groups as being groups of people whose ancestors originally came from different coves and camping places of the island.

In view of this social and cultural history, it may be that we see in Gambell village a newer structuring of social organization superimposed upon an originally pan-Eskimo base. Prior to probably several hundred years ago, the only people living in what is now the village of Gambell were the "Sivokakmeit"—i.e., "people belonging to Sivokak." It is said that now there is only one "real" Sivokakme living on the island. At present in the village are found people belonging to several other clans, the ancestors of which were living, some hundreds of years back, in various other small camp sites on the island. There is no evidence to indicate that such small villages were anything but homogeneous in terms of descent-group and social affiliation. But with immigration from Siberia about 200 years ago, a new group of kinsmen came to live in Sivokak. It is also likely that for many years other local groups from St. Lawrence itself

[6] Several reasons dictate the choice of "patriclan" rather than "patrilineage" or "patrisib." Although it is said that each descent group can trace its origin from one man, this is apparently not always the case, and genealogically I have some doubt in regard to the groups for which a single man is given as the progenitor. Moreover, the "clan" rather than the "sib" designation is preferable because people of the same descent group do, actually, tend to clump together in neighborhoods in the village. In general, boundaries can be drawn around the living places of each patriclan.

had begun to move to the site of Gambell, and the contemporary social heterogeneity began. At any rate, it is quite clear that such moves have been made in the past 80 years, until now, in the 1950's, there are no more such distinctive local villages—which were in reality holistic descent groups. In this manner there could develop a new pattern of social organization through the coming together in close physical proximity of social groups which previously had been kept separate.

These conjectures are pertinent to the interpretation one can make of the clans and clan activities which will be discussed, and they add some insight into the characteristics of these social groupings. It may very well be that some of the apparent divergence of the Sivokakmeit kinship system from the Murdockian typology is to be explained on the basis of this geographic accumulation of what were originally small, bilaterally descending local "tribal" groups in which an individual nevertheless thought of himself first as a member of his father's "tribe." And now, in the context of Gambell village, with its collection of competing descent groups, the emphasis has shifted in such a way that the higher priority is given to one's "tribal" affiliation and identification rather than to the more diffuse kindred affiliation, which was more important in the local group. Under the latter situation the tribal identification was taken for granted and was not brought into focus through the daily juxtaposition of different groups, as happens now.

In Gambell at present there are three patriclans of major importance in terms of power and numbers. They are the Puwowalagameit ("people belonging to Puwowalak," a former village site on the southwestern corner of the island); Meruchtameit ("people belonging to Meruchta," a site a few miles east of present-day Gambell); and Aimaramka (a Siberian group, with a name given them by the Chukchi meaning, reputedly, something like "never afraid, any one of them"). The suffix *ramka* is said to mean "belonging to" or "related to" in Chukchi—it is similar to the suffix *meit* (or *miut* in the Alaskan mainland tongues)—and since it is often used by the Sivokakmeit themselves in referring to the local descent groups, it will be used interchangeably with "patriclan."

There are also several smaller *ramka* in the village at the present time. Within the past half century others have died out completely.

Those which have surviving male members, however, are the Naeskaegomeit ("people belonging to Naeskaek"), Ualeit ("people living at the north end"—of Gambell), AmIchtowaet, Aemagago-meit, Avaetmeit, Laelkaegameit, and OongwaezIgameit. The last three groups are families which have immigrated from the nearby Siberian coast in the last thirty or forty years.

It is important to recognize that for most of the *ramka,* especially the larger groups, the name given above is actually something of a blanket term that unites subgroups which also have more particular names for themselves. Within the context of Gambell village, the group Puwowalagameit, for instance, is a clearly bounded unit. But distinctive subgroups are recognized within that larger whole by the Puwowalagameit themselves, and in a historical context these sub-groups take on identities of their own. Union with other subgroups in the larger whole called Puwowalagameit is done for political purposes as well as by reason of cultural similarities. Thus a given individual might be Puwowalagameit, but his subgroup affiliation (which also derives from a local camping-place name) would be Nokaegomeit; another Puwowalagame might also be Poongugame, descended from people of the Punuk Islands, who are said to have been the original "Puwowalagameit." Similarly, a Meruchtame might also be, in a more refined social identification, a Nangoopae-gaegome (named from a camping site located very near Meruchta). But for all practical purposes in Gambell village life, the people of Nokaek and the descendants of campers on Punuk Island think of themselves as one, as do the people of Meruchta and Nangoopaegaek, although they recognize differences of some degree between them-selves. In no case, however, would a Poongugame, for instance, feel he was as close to an Aimaramkut (person belonging to Aimaramka clan) as he is to a Nokaegome. It is a question of relative identity, but certain clear and irrevocable lines can be drawn. The Aimaramka likewise have subgroups within themselves, but there is no need to go into them at this point.

## FUNCTIONS OF THE PATRICLAN

What does it mean to be a member of a particular *ramka* in Gambell? It means a great deal, if one can judge from both objective analyses and informants' perceptions: "They claim to treat each other as a family—as one whole family." A young man speaking about his grandmother says:

And then she used to take me to Kovik's family for to know that they are of our tribe. That's the main thing in Eskimo custom—that you know your relatives, your tribe, ever since as far as you can remember. They want you to remember who your relatives are, my grandmother told me that.

Other people likewise remark that their mothers and grandmothers taught them early in life to know their relatives, taking them to visit and impressing on them the importance of having clansmen. One of the most widespread sentiments pertaining to one's kinsmen was pointed out by one Sivokakmeit: "he said that if your own tribe didn't help you, you couldn't expect help from any other tribe."

*Sharing of food and material goods*—The most common and perduring feature of *ramka* function is that of credit union. The fundamental sentiment on which the social solidarity of the clan rests is the unstinting sharing of meat and other foods, material equipment, and social well-being. Although meat is given freely to anyone who asks for it, it is one's clansmen who receive the most bounty and to whom one makes preferential distribution, especially in times of famine and scarcity.

We give first to our relative, if we kill some whale or walrus. And if not much food, we call just our relatives to come and we give some meat.

For help and assistance given a relative a man does not expect payment, but he will anticipate receiving immediate compensation of some kind for helping a nonrelative. For the job of sewing a walrus-hide cover onto a boat, for instance, the captain must immediately pay a woman who is a nonrelative, but with a clanswoman he will pay her at some later date by a gift of meat or a useful article from the hunt. (Incidentally, in this connection it is said that the boat-owner asks his own sisters or other clanswomen to do the sewing—not the wives of his kinsmen; this may be related to the religious sentiments and practices formerly surrounding contact with the boat.)

From a clansman or an individual related to ego in his kindred (a kinship group discussed below), a man knows that sometime in the future he in turn will require assistance for which he will give no immediate monetary or material payment. Thus the prevailing standard is one of unequivocal sharing of goods and services on the implicit assumption that a balance will be worked out over time:

That's like if I own 3 or 4 motors, and one of my relatives needs one, I just give him one. That way we help each other. In one *ramka;* among relatives. [What about outside the *ramka?*] No; not much. Mostly they pay for them outside the *ramka.*

A hint of the way this spontaneous assistance may be changing is indicated in this excerpt from the field notes:

You know, most people say, "He's not your relative; why do you help him?" I think that is wrong. What Dad used to tell me about was help anybody, anybody you see, whoever he is. Not just your relatives.

Thus the sharing of worldly wealth is done without being asked. It is expected that it will be done, and the onus of justifying why it is not done immediately and without reservation rests on the individual and is not given the sanction of cultural norms. Stinginess is a general social evil here, but it is all the more heinous if practiced on one's clansmen.

Other aspects of the sharing are found in the fact that upon marriage it is from one's clansmen that gifts are solicited, first by the father of the groom to give to the girl's parents and then later by the girl's parents to offer to the boy's parents when the marriage is consummated. At the same time, the gifts which are received by each group are distributed to clansmen.[7] In former days, on this matter of obligatory gifts, it was one's clansmen and relatives who paid the shaman for attempting to cure a sick person. The items were much the same as those given as marriage gifts: skins, skin ropes, tools, weapons, and so forth.

*Hunting companions*—Boat crews are almost always made up only of clansmen, although sometimes a nonclansman is a regular member of the crew. When this happens, however, it is for idio-

---

[7] An interesting situation develops when the marriage is clan-endogamous. Then, of course, it is very largely the same individuals who both give and receive the same gifts. What apparently happens is that a redistribution of valuable economic goods held by clan members takes place through the accumulation of gifts and the subsequent free choice from among the items.

syncratic reasons, and there is no general cultural pattern which makes it expectable as the structure of the crew. Occasionally, too, an outsider will hunt in a boat on a particular day if the crew is shorthanded. But the cadre of the crew consists of men of one clan.

Cultural sentiments have long supported this arrangement. It is said that in days past the old people strongly urged that a man hunt only with his relatives, because if the boat got into trouble out on the ice a nonclansman would be less prone to help a man out of difficulty. In a situation of danger on the floes, the tightness of the brother and *ataligoon* tie might be a threat to the safety of an individual who was outside those bonds.

The boats and their crews are often referred to by their *ramka* names. It will be said, for instance, that "Puwowalagameit is out hunting today" or that "Aimaramka just got home." The individual captain and his crew (and he is usually the owner of the boat) are thus sometimes submerged in the exaltation of the clan.

If there are more than one boat and crew from one patriclan, the several boats tend to hunt together and help each other on the ice. A group of boats composed of clansmen is called by a special term, *aelraekothreit*. These boats "hunt with each other and help each other; they stay close." The hunting union among boats of a clan was more pronounced in the past than it is now, however. It was remarked by several that "this is changed now—now all boats, no matter what *ramka*, help each other." No doubt some loosening of the clan bonds has occurred in this, the most fundamental venture of clansmen, even as the bonds have loosened in other respects.

When a whale is killed, it is said to "belong to" the particular clan whose boats were the first to strike it. The elderly men of that *ramka* are the supervisors of the cutting in and distribution of meat and skin. Their word is law.

At this point it is appropriate to discuss the boat crew in somewhat more detail than has been done thus far; for it is one of the most crucial economic as well as social institutions in the entire culture and is firmly rooted in the kinship system.

*Social structure of the boat crew*—The boat crew is probably one of the most ancient of Sivokak institutions and in its general outlines has resisted all sorts of pressures to change. Modifications have been made in the equipment used for hunting, but they have been absorbed into the pre-existing social pattern. This pattern was based on the bonds of loyalty which existed among several close relatives and over which was imposed a scheme of technical-role relationships and a chain of authority and command.

In the days before outboard motors were used, seven or eight men were required for paddling a boat. This crew was collectively known as a *yoopenroot*. Apparently the individual crew member was known as *angwaechta* or, simply, *yook*—"man." Strong men as paddlers were much in demand, and it is said that sometimes captains had to go outside the bonds of kinship to find sufficient men for their crew—despite the injunctions against having an outsider in the crew. But now, with motors, only four or five men are required for the cadre of the crew, and, in general, this number can be found in one's own patriclan. Nevertheless there are times when more crewmen are desired:

But still kind of short, if only 4 men. Danger then if too much ice or too many walrus. If we have enough men, if many walrus on ice or we in among walrus, not much danger that way. Every man got own job: some of them paddling; some try to start motor; some try to fill tank, some of them watching the walrus by gun. So still we looking to have enough men.

There are at least seven positions which are clearly discriminated in the crew, each with separate technical duties and each fitting into a niche in the authority structure. At the apex is the boat captain, the *angyaellk*. He is usually but not always the principal owner of the boat. If age or sickness prevent his taking the boat out, he will delegate authority to a son or brother. A man does not in general become a boat captain until he is in his late thirties or forties, and until that time he clearly acknowledges that he is a novice, learning from his father or from the boat captain the techniques needed in the position he is one day to fill. The skills required of the captain are numerous and command great admiration. Knowledge of the ways of animals is only the beginning. Much more crucial is a keen knowledge of weather and ice conditions. In past years, also, the captain had to know a great many of the proper ritual and ceremonial details for establishing the optimum relationship with the souls of the animals he and his crew would kill. A man in his middle forties told me that he is beginning to take over the captaincy of the boat from . . . his father. His father said that he is getting old and that Ernest had better begin learning some of the skills—and apparently this extends over several years. Ernest said that when they go out over the ice, for instance, the older captains will put the young one in charge and let him bring the boat home, and then not say anything unless the younger one gets the boat into too much trouble. Ernest said that "they think experience is the best teacher."

The *angyaellk* has complete authority over the crew and the pattern of the hunt, and he is responsible for the boat and its care. He decides when the weather is safe for hunting, when the crew members will arise and prepare themselves, where they will hunt, when they will return, and how the meat will be divided. There is no more important and prestigeful group in all of Gambell than then ten or twelve boat captains (even with the inroads into the prestige patterns that are made by the white man's "job" with its steady income); for the *angyaellk* is

always ready with everything—all the boat stuff. This is captain's job. If harpoon doesn't work anymore, captain fix it. And gun, sometime he works himself on every gun; he cleans it and oils it. Everything ready in the boat, that is captains's job. Except they don't touch, anymore, the motor . . . he the boss. He always watch the directions, where to go. And he watch the time, and which way they going by compass.

The *angyaellk* usually takes care of buying all the ammunition, gasoline, and other equipment his boat and crew members use during the hunt. Yet he does not necessarily take a proportionally larger share of the meat or ivory tusks because of his greater investment. In most boats equality governs the division. The captain's principal return is in terms of greater prestige, and this is considerable.

The striker is only slightly below the captain in authority and prestige. The *angyaellk* is in the stern of the boat, with a hand on the rudder (see Diagram 1). The striker, *sivooyachta*, on the other hand, stands in the bow. He is the first mate, the second in command of the boat, and normally is the man who succeeds the captain upon the latter's retirement or incapacity. His is the job of spotting the game and then of taking the first shots at it and, in the case of whales, of sinking the harpoon line into the animal. He is usually the best marksman of the crew and is given the first chance to shoot. Only after he has shot, or in conjunction with him, can other crewmen try to hit the seals or walruses. Many years of training and practice go into producing a skilled *sivooyachta*, and not all who try succeed. It is not unusual for a middle-aged man to be the striker for his crew. One captain says:

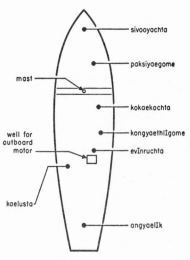

*Diagram 1.* Position of boat-crew members during a whale hunt.

I like for striker mostly those with good mind, good understand to think about what rope, or harpoon, or rifle gun, or how to shoot. To me, I like to use that boy.

Now beside school, we have to train the young people how to shoot and how to strike. He have to learn; because still we hunt and eat from out there [motioning toward the sea]. If that striker never learn, he don't kill not a one. He don't know how to strike. [Does he learn by going out hunting?] Yeah. And at home, too, we teach it. So they learn when gone out there. [Is it the striker who becomes captain?] Yeah. But even when pretty much learn young man, no matter if become man, still keep in front as striker. Boys don't much understand. Just a few years back I'm quit from striker. Many years I was striker. . . . But when a good mind in those young boys, just like Neal, I train him now. And whaling, too. Yeah, I always teach him.

Sitting behind the striker in the boat is the third man in the authority structure, the *paksiyaegome*. It is he who usually moves up to the striker's role, after having been an apprentice for a few years. But his principal jobs, aside from the continual watch for game, are in caring for the first of the inflated sealskin pokes on the walrus and whale lines. The *paksiyaegome* inflates them, makes sure that they are fast to the line and that the line is not tangled, and then at the proper moment, when the striker has put his harpoon into the walrus or whale, throws the poke overboard.

The man sitting behind the *paksiyaegome* in the boat [8] is called the *kokaekochta*, and his principal duties are to look after the second sealskin poke in the same way as the *paksiyaegome* handles the first. This technical role is called into play only when the boat is whaling, for on the walrus line just the one poke is used. When the boat is walrus or seal hunting, the *kokaekochta* is merely another rifleman.

In whaling, when three pokes are used, the third is inflated and thrown overboard by the next man in the boat going from bow to stern, the *kongyaethllgome*. Except when occupied with the pokes, this man (with the *kokaekochta* and the *paksiyaegome*) is always looking for game, and in the middle of a group of animals he helps with the shooting.

Sometimes the role of the *kongyaethllgome* is filled by the apprentice hunter, the *kaelusta*, who usually sits behind the four people mentioned above. He is the beginner, the neophyte, the learner, and his main duties are to bail or pump the water from the boat, help mix gasoline and oil for the motor, and do other sorts of unspecialized but useful tasks. Sitting near the stern of the boat, he can listen to what the captain tells him and receive instruction in his future trade. Often retired captains go along on the hunt, and they, too, sit in the stern, and from them also the *kaelusta* learns.

The *kaelusta* is to keep his eyes and ears open and learn as much

[8] A special term was used by a couple of informants to designate the man who was said to be next to the *paksiyaegome* and who fires the shoulder gun into the whale. He was called the *bomechta*, but I do not know whether this term is generally enough used to include it here as a separate role. Very likely firing the shoulder gun is part of the striker's job, for some of the other informants did not recognize the term.

as he can about hunting, after he has first prepared himself psychologically for this activity:

Mostly when pretty young boy, not old enough to go out in springtime in boat, we try to train them, teaching them. Then that's the way they learn. They can learn by themselves—just have strong mind, keep quiet. . . . You know, out in the sea, kind of danger. We try to teach good mind, strong mind; never be scared right away.

In this job of teaching the *kaelusta,* all boat members contribute when they have pertinent points to make.

Many times the *kaelusta* moves from his original position to the role of "engineer," whose task is to maintain the motor. The *evlnruchta,* a job which came into existence with the adoption of outboard motors, is the technically trained expert of the crew who fits into the authority structure in various spots, depending on other factors than his technical training. In some cases an older man runs the motor, but many times it is one of the younger men who has been more interested in mechanics and has devoted time to tinkering with and working over the motor. The fact that the place of the *evlnruchta* in the chain of command is not at all well defined— whereas each of the other positions is very sharply placed— probably also attests its recent development.

In Diagram 1 is indicated the seating pattern of the boat crew when the whaling line is being thrown out. The engineer— *evlnruchta*—does not, however, operate in that capacity during the actual whaling, for the motor is not used at that time. The individual who acts as engineer might well be filling the role of *kongyaethllgome* during this time. In the diagram the *evlnruchta* is shown in his usual position when the motor is being used.

*Social support*—In this society lacking a judicial system and a cultural tradition of legalistic procedure, disputes in former times were settled mainly by the threat or exercise of brute strength. Such a settlement usually involved one's kinsmen. Although many quarrels were stopped by the caution of old men on both sides, at times they had to be decided by a wrestling match between the disputants or some of their clansmen. Sometimes, too, there was bloodshed. In such a situation the strength and number of one's clansmen were very important. The political union of two subgroups which go to make up the clan Meruchtameit has already been mentioned. In the face of trouble, these two subgroups were as one, providing an illustration of the commonest basis of social control: "Meruchtameit, with us, no fight. He watch. Somebody trouble him, we together."

*Religious and ceremonial patterns*—Only brief attention can be given here to St. Lawrence Island ceremonialism. Nevertheless, a few examples of the major ceremonials will be presented in order to convey some idea of the manner in which kinship and religion interweave.

One of the most crucial functions of the *ramka* has now passed from the culture—the observance of the unique rites for hunting success and bodily well-being. The religion of the St. Lawrence Island Eskimos was in reality the various religions of the different clans; for every *ramka* had its own esoteric lore, beliefs, proscriptions, and ritual patterns which—except for the obviously public features —were secret and passed down in the male line. A boat captain sang his hunting songs softly, for instance, so that his daughter (who might marry outside the clan) would not overhear them and later teach them to her husband for his successful hunting. The stories that were told and the mythological rationale for ritual tended to be unique to each group and unknown to the others; taboos which pertained to members of one clan were often not applicable to the rest. There were, of course, gross similarities in many patterns of observance, as in the most important hunting rite, the boat captain's ceremony, which each clan held just prior to the spring hunt. But in specific manifestations there were usually some differences.

The major rituals of hunting centered on the whale and polar bear. Ceremonies celebrating the killing of the polar bear have been described earlier (see pp. 123–124). It is surprising that there were no principal rituals oriented toward either the walrus or the seal —nothing resembling the great Bladder Festivals of the west-central Alaskan villages, for example, during which the bladders of all sea mammals killed during the year were ceremonially returned to the sea.[9]

[9] Lantis, 1947, pp. 53 ff. Lantis states that on St. Lawrence Island the bearded seal (mukluk) was included with the whale and polar bear among the animals ritually honored (p. 51). I could find little evidence for this, though it may have been true.

The main ritual event of the winter on St. Lawrence Island occurred anywhere from February through April, when each of the hunting boats conducted a ceremony in preparation for whaling. This was called the *chkwaek* (apparently meaning "the sacrifice"), and its details were traditional for each patriclan with its one or several hunting boats. The ceremony was held only at the time of the full moon, and it was customary that no two boats could conduct the ritual on the same day. This is perhaps the main reason that it required from February through April for all the clans to conduct this first launching for the whaling season.

Preparations for the ceremony were begun long in advance. Throughout the previous spring and summer, greens from the mountain had been collected and sorted in a special place; reindeer fat (procured from Siberia in the days before the St. Lawrence herd) was similarly set aside; tobacco traded from the Russians made up part of the sacrificial foods; and a final item usually was fish of some kind. All these foods were considered extremely holy and were placed in sealskin pokes on a meat rack, out of the reach of children and dogs.

When later in the winter the day of the ceremony finally arrived, the boat captain, his wife, his striker, and sometimes the rest of the crew took all the foods down from the meat rack and, working on several wooden platters, molded them into long low mounds, in the form of a "pudding," as Lantis calls it. These were placed in the center of the room in the boat captain's house and covered with a walrus skin. Over the foods were hung the captain's hunting gear —such as his special visor, worn only on the hunt and symbolic of his status as well as presumably possessing an inherent power. The captain's bag of special hunting charms was also hung over the foods; this was a small sealskin container in which were placed various bits of flesh or organs from animals that the captain had killed—whale, polar bear, walrus, or sometimes even a sea gull if there had been something unusual about its killing. The captain and the rest of the group then sat around these foods singing and praying through the night.

Long before sunrise all the participants went down to the shore, carrying the trays of food with them. There they lowered the boat into the water, all the crew got into the craft, and they paddled out a short distance from the shore, where they once more uttered prayers. They then returned to the shore to await the coming of sunrise. At the breaking of dawn, the sacrifice of food began. The captain took a small portion from each platter, broke this into small bits, and threw these into the air, into the sea, and onto the land. As he did so, he recited prayers asking for a good and successful hunt during the coming season.

Following the sacrificing of ritual foods, the crew ate what was left on the platters. Anything remaining after that was distributed to other people in the village.

If a boat was successful in killing a whale, a different sort of ceremony occurred. First, out on the water before the animal was towed back to land, the captain, raising his special paddle (another mark of status and, like the visor, embodying supernatural power), shouted "Ho-ho-ho-ho." Then his boat circled the whale in a set pattern, stopping at the front and at the back once again while the captain shouted in the same way. The purpose of such shouting was to inform Aepa, the all-powerful, Supreme God, that the whale had been captured and to thank him. Before towing the animal to the shore, the captain cut four small pieces of flesh from the tips of the tail and flukes and threw them back into the sea. This was again a mark of sacrifice to Aepa [10] and to the spirits. During the towing to the shore the captain twice shouted in his distinctive way.

With the animal finally tied up to the shore, the cutting in began. While this was occurring, women of the captain's clan gathered to sing in front of his house, with the captain's wife wearing a special costume for the occasion. She also decorated her head with a band of white reindeer hair, the meaning of which is unknown.

From the cutting in of the whale, several pieces were saved: bits of the tip of the tail, the mid-section of the tail, and small portions of the flukes, eyes, and nose. Immediately after the cutting in was completed, the boat crew (along with the entire clan of the boat which had killed the whale) went to the captain's house, in front of which all these various parts of the animal were spread out on the ground in a form suggestive of the whale's body. A fire was built in front of the animal's nose, and then the captain's wife brought

[10] Note that this is the same term used to designate the person who in English would be called "grandfather"; see pp. 230–231.

a pail of water containing small pieces of whale meat and *noonivak*. She offered a part of the water and *noonivak* to the whale—symbolically putting some into its mouth. Next she threw portions of the whale meat into the fire (in an act of feeding the ancestors). After this all the family walked around the parts of the whale and then on top of them.

Finally, all the pieces were taken into the captain's house and hung up over the fire for five days, while songs were chanted and stories told. No hunting was possible during this time, similar to the prohibition on hunting following the killing of a polar bear. At the end of the period, most of the parts of the animal were distributed among the clan relatives and eaten. The parts not eaten were the mid-section of the tail, which was saved for a ceremony during the coming summer, and the eyeball of the whale, from which was made a black substance used for painting special designs on the captain's paddle and on the bow of the boat.[11]

In July another type of ceremony occurred in which the entire clan participated. At this time the group went to the mountain to a special shrine or altar known to and used by them only. Some of these altars were located near the graves of ancestors. The family took with them special sacrificial foods, including the tailpiece of a whale if one had been killed during the spring, and baby walrus flippers, a delicacy which was considered proper food for the spirits of the ancestors. At the altar site, a fire was built and small bits of the sacrificial foods were thrown into it by the eldest member of the clan, who spoke first to Aepa and then to the spirits of the ancestors as he tossed the food into the fire. His prayers took a form such as, "I am feeding you; thank you for the meat we have received. Please send more. Send us health," and so on. Following this feeding, the eldest member of the family took a strand of grass and, passing it over each family member, "brushed" away all sickness into the fire. Occasionally all the sickness was brushed on to a dog, which was subsequently killed; or at times an implement, such as a cup, was the object of containment, and this was then broken. The formal

---

[11] The ceremony described here is different in some details from that described by Lantis (1947, pp. 49–50). Her data were from field notes of Henry P. Collins. The differences may be due as much to clan differences as to differential recording of data.

ritual was now over; the participants ate any food that remained and then returned to the village.

A relatively nonreligious ceremony might be mentioned which also implicates the clansmen of the participants. The *magalook* or *Iveiyak* ceremony was held between two *ilowaek* cousins and their clan kinsmen. The major feature involved a ceremonial exchange of gifts which began in a song contest between the two principals. One *ilowaek* would sing a song asking his cousin for certain gifts of a valuable nature. The cousin would respond with a song, similarly artistic and creative, in which he would also ask for gifts. Then there occurred a symbolic warfare between the clansmen of the two principals, who performed a ritual dance with lances and simulated the wounding of opponents. After this the gifts, including platters of meat, were exchanged by the wives of the two male *ilowaek*, the principals of the ceremony.[12]

*Leadership and authority*—The system of the clans provides a considerable degree of orientation and control of social life. Elders of the clan have always held a particularly crucial role in the leadership structure, for not only are they respected by virtue of the general aura surrounding age, but also they are traditionally the keepers of the esoteric and religious lore of the patriclan. There is always one individual who is the acknowledged leader of the group, and in some of the clans it can be either a man or a woman. Always, however, it is the oldest living member. Many of the functions of this clan leader are referred to in these excerpts from the field notes:

You see, Eskimo this way. Oldest is boss for everything. Nobody miss: if boss die, another fellow he pick up.

Eskimo always ask first our oldest one, when we do something.

Yes, I in charge of it [the cutting in of a whale]. Yes, I boss for all my relatives. They let them be boss who are the oldest.

It is the oldest member of the patriclan, usually in consultation with other elder statesmen, who advises on such decisions as the right choice of marriage partner for a young person; the proper

[12] For further brief descriptions of St. Lawrence Island ceremonialism and of rituals in fairly closely related Eskimo groups, see Lantis, 1947. See also my translation of I. K. Voblov's description of Eskimo rituals on the Siberian coast (Hughes, 1959). None of these sources, however, can be considered complete in presenting St. Lawrence Island ceremonialism.

behavior for young people; the placing of orphaned children for adoption in a clansman's home; the settling of family or marital disputes; the division of material goods; and the like.

With respect to one aspect of the former religious system—the naming of the newborn—the elders remain crucially important. It is they who make the choice of the Eskimo name that the newborn baby of the clan shall bear. St. Lawrence belief gave to the individual multiple souls or spiritual essences, one of which was his "name-soul." This is a pan-Eskimo culture trait, and, in common with other Eskimo groups, on St. Lawrence Island this name-soul is immortal.[13] After death it hovers around in the universe waiting to be reincarnated in a newborn infant. The clan is thereby eternal, consisting of a series of name-souls, some of which are presently in a corporeal phase, some of which are not. The eldest of the patriclan knows the catalogue of clan names, or souls, and he consults them to see if any wish to return to earthly existence through the infant. The elder supposedly has direct access to the spiritual world for this operation. If a soul is agreeable to reincarnation, the elder informs the child's father, and the infant is named accordingly. Since the name is a soul, only one living individual in each tribe bears that name at any one time:

I asked him if the name of a person who is still alive would be given to a newborn baby. Joseph looked up, surprised, and said, "No!—Because he's still living!"

In addition, however, a living individual is not really just himself, the "me" of the present day in this time and place: he is also the salient personality characteristics of all the people he *was*. This comes out in many ways:

You see, my name not mine.
My father's name is in Savoonga now.
My brother Dick is in Mike's son—his name is my brother.

And some intimation of a psychological function can be seen:

Just like a son come back, just like that. If my mother and my sister, if somebody call a baby by their name, I am very proud and I am very glad. Just like alive again.

[13] For a very stimulating article on this subject, see Carpenter, 1954.

And somehow we like that woman's name, you know. Maybe when they're lost, good person like that, we want her back if only by name. Somehow we feel better.

There exists a practice of preferential treatment accorded to a baby who bears the name of a close relative. A series of "pseudo-kinship" relations is established upon this basis, in which a widow may refer to a newborn baby in the village as "my husband" and give him special gifts and personal attention. About a woman and her grandson, for instance, "Frances said that he is her husband." And a newborn baby was named after a young girl who had died a few years previously; the mother of the girl "made a lot of baby clothes for Phyllis and comes down and takes care of the baby a lot, too." This contrived kinship relation is recognized by other people in the village, and often the two individuals are referred to in terms of their supernaturally rather than genetically or socially derived kinship relation, no matter how incongruous it may be in terms of age or sex.

*Wife-exchange partnership*—One practice of considerable ethnographic interest can be mentioned here as another example (along with the pseudo-kinship relations established when an individual bears the name-soul of a relative) of the transference of kinship patterns and behavior to other situations. Its mention here also bears on the subject of interclan relations.

Many Eskimo groups have institutionalized "brother" or partner relationships between two men for mutual help, protection, and advantage. One aspect of such a special brother relation includes the practice of exchanging wives. The exchanging is done not only for functional utility (as when a man's wife is pregnant or sick and is unable to accompany her husband on the trail to do the woman's share of the work), but also for sexual gratification.

Such a relationship existed in the old days on St. Lawrence Island, and one's wife-exchange partner was called a *nangsaegaek*. It was always arranged by the two men, and the women had no formal voice in the matter. Never did it obtain between real brothers or clansmen (recall the avoidance behavior between a man and his brother's wife). It was characteristically a relationship existing between two men of different *ramka*, and any single individual might have two or more *nangsaegaek* partners concurrently.

Behavior between the two partners, aside from the sexual communism, was modeled after that between brothers, with considerable emphasis on sharing goods and giving unstinted help. Such a relationship would seem to be functionally effective in allaying somewhat the deep-rooted antagonisms and conflict between the different *ramka* which were so easily aroused in the normal course of social life. The *nangsaegaek* loyalties and bonds of sentiment linking two men of different *ramka* would tend to dampen, along with the ties an individual might have through his idiosyncratic kindred relationships, what might otherwise be an unchecked *ramka* solidarity.

On St. Lawrence Island, in apparent contrast to many other Eskimo groups, this wife-exchange pattern was always formally sanctioned through a special ceremony which involved various aspects of the religious system. This ceremony, called the *kaezivae*, implicated the closest kinsmen (and their wives) of each *nangsaegaek* partner, and the various sections of the total rite extended over a period of several days.[14] Prominent in it were dancing between the men and the women guests, and in the inner sleeping room where the dances were held, these couples circled a seal-oil lamp. The men of one *ramka* danced in this fashion with the women of the *nangsaegaek* partner's *ramka*. At some points during the ceremony, every woman exchanged a platter of food or other gifts with the woman who had danced with her husband. On the last day of the ceremony, all the men and women who had danced together had sexual relations with each other. With the ending of the ceremony the special relationship between the two main principals was sealed and, unless changed for some reason, held during their lifetime. The children born to the woman were considered the children of her husband, even though it might be fairly obvious that they were the progeny of the *nangsaegaek*. At least one of the prominent motivations for a man to take on a *nangsaegaek* would be the desire to have children if his wife had been barren for some time—it was felt that perhaps the change would produce a male heir (and it often did). There is some indication that a special sibling type of relationship prevailed

[14] For a description of a rite by this name practiced on the Siberian shore among the Asiatic Eskimos, see Voblov, 1952, pp. 333–334; English translation, Hughes, 1959. Voblov's account, however, makes no reference to exchange of sexual privileges between the partners and their wives.

between the male children of the two *nangsaegaek*, as well as the expectation that they, too, would someday establish such a relationship with each other.

Even by 1940 the formal celebration of the *nangsaegaek* relationship had passed from the culture. For probably twenty years or so no *kaezivae* had been held, although the *nangsaegaek* relation on a more covert level was maintained by some. In 1954, it remains only a memory of a past cultural practice, one the mention of which is usually draped with overt expressions of shame derived in large part from the white man's religion. But its functioning in the corpus of clan and kinship relations in the old days gives some further insight into the dynamics of social control and social balance of the Sivokakmeit before the advent of the white man.

### THE LINEAGE AND KINDRED

The patriclan does not exhaust all possibilities in Gambell for social groupings based on kinship. Indeed, especially within the larger clans, there are subdivisions corresponding to what are usually knows as "lineages." This has been intimated before, when I mentioned that a given individual might be located in the clan system by two or even more names, one analogous to a genus identification and the other similar to the species or subspecies designation. Thus, there seems to be some development of a lineage type of social unit, although it operates completely under the aegis of the superordinate clan structure and for many purposes is submerged within it. For intraclan power alignments, therefore, the line of kinsmen directly descending from an ancestor, and presided over by the oldest male in that group of lineal descendants, operates as something of a distinctive social unit. However, all the lineages of a patriclan are linked by at least the primary *ataligoon* relationship.

Perhaps the clearest instance of lineage development is found in the Puwowalagameit, where three such lineages seem to be the core of the larger clan unit, with two additional lineages of lesser pedigree attached in a political and cultural sense. In some cases of naming within this clan, it is the oldest man of the lineage who would choose the name, although if he did not know of an appropriate name for a newborn infant he would consult the oldest of another lineage within the Puwowalagameit. In no case would the matter go beyond the Puwowalagameit. The Meruchtameit likewise have a development of such lineages, and the Aimaramka also recognize intraclan differences which are important for some purposes.

It was noted in a previous section that the oldest member of the clan is the leader and spokesman for the entire group. Actually, this individual operates only as something like the chairman of a board, which itself is composed of the leaders of the lineages, each speaking for his own extended family. It is this group of elder statesmen who are the ultimate decision makers in determining clan policy and custom.

But beyond the more obvious and public features of social life which are the patriclans and lineages, there is yet another kinship group which is more amorphous and ill-defined and which is not publicly segregatable in the manner of clan groupings. This is the kindred. The Sivokakmeit term for it seems to be *kamukrakothreit* and is translated freely as "one's closest relatives." I have remarked before that the root of this word comes from that applied to meat, to flesh; and this term is used in the present context to mean "of the same flesh." The *kamukrakothreit* is a unit within the clan and usually even within the lineage; and the particular personnel composing various *kamukrakothreit* are never the same except for siblings. In some senses even siblings have slightly different relatives of this order. It therefore seems advisable to call the unit, technically, a "kindred," again following Murdock (1949, p. 60), even though it appears to be a particular variation of a kindred organization.[15]

The conception and use of the term *kamukrakothreit* are possessed of much less clarity than is true of *ramka* for patriclan. There seems to be agreement among the Sivokakmeit on a general sense in which the term is used; various shades of divergence of reference exist, but these seem to culminate again in agreement upon a fairly specific referent for the concept. The general use upon which everyone agrees for the term *kamukrakothreit* is that it means one's very closest relatives:

[15] There are some qualifications to Murdock's definition to be entered—such as the relatively greater emphasis on the patrilineal aspect in one's *kamukrakothreit*, although here, as is not the case in one's clan affiliation, bilateral kinsmen are often included.

People of the same flesh, same blood.
Means something like "blood relation."
Very close, *kamukrakothreit.*
Real close relatives.
We call them *kamukrakothreit.* Because very near relation, more close from *ilakwaek.*

Used in this general sense, the referent usually includes one's wife and children, one's parents and their siblings, one's cousins, and often one's grandparents and grandchildren. In this usage it is narrower than clan relations. But it is important to stress that there is not universal agreement on the relatives covered when the reference is this more inclusive mode.

There is, however, a narrower conception to the dimension of "the closest relative." This is based on a generational principle and includes only ego's near cousins: his primary *ataligoon, aeganaligoon,* and *ilowaek.* But an even further distinction seems universally to be made at this level, and the "real" *kamukrakothreit* are said to be only one's siblings and *ataligoon,* i.e., one's generational clansmen related through the father:

Old people say: "Stay with your *ataligoon.* You have to stay with your *ataligoon* all your life. And you have to go hunting with your *ataligoon.* This is your own *kamukrak.*"
Something like brother and sisters.
Very close, *kamukrak.* My father's brother's son; very close. They call us brothers. Same name: *kamukrak.* [What about *ataligoon?*] *Ataligoon*—yes. [Is your father in your *kamukrak?*] No. [Your mother?] No. [Sisters?] Yeah, real sisters. [Wife?] No. I think *kamukrak* means real brothers, real together.

The functions of this more narrowly defined *kamukrakothreit* are those of ego's most intimate and supportive social environment. It was said before that boat crews are traditionally composed only of clansmen. It can now be pointed out further that one's close hunting companions, who are the mainstays of the boat crew, are not only clansmen; most of them are also likely to be clansmen of one's own generation, one's *ataligoon,* or *kamukrakothreit:* "Yes, should be those *kamukrakothreit* going in one boat." But also in other situations: "*Kamukrakothreit,* never trouble between them at all.

Never. If something happen between them, we trying to straighten up right away."

Hence there are concentric spheres of social identity and affiliation encircling an individual, beginning with his inner *kamukrakothreit* of siblings and *ataligoon;* including next perhaps his *aeganaligoon* and *ilowaek* and perhaps in this same order his lineal relatives; thence moving to his clansmen in general; proceeding then to those individuals who may not have been included in his patriclan but to whom ego has mutual obligations deriving from the sanctions of the kinship system; and finally coming to the residual category of the Sivokakme, the fellow villager.

## Changes in the Kinship System

In any discussion of change it is easy to lose sight of the permanence existing in the midst of that change. This is the case regarding some of the patterns of behavior which are culturally defined as appropriate between kinsmen. The problem of shifts in Sivokak kinship and social organization can best be put in perspective by providing in brief form a background of the stabilities in traditional kinship behavior.

In terms of the paired interactions between kinsmen, much yet remains of the inherited culture. Patterns of behavior expected between *ilowaek, ataligoon,* and *aeganaligoon,* for example, are still strongly held, as also are those respectful attitudes and actions found between a husband or wife and the parents of one's spouse. In a few cases the strains on the daughters-in-law are quite evident; but the behavior conforms even if the sentiments do not. Although change is beginning, older brothers are still looked up to by younger siblings; *ataligoon,* fathers, and uncles are the objects of esteem and affection; and mutual sobriety and generally respectful behavior pervades the interaction between siblings, except in a few cases, about which villagers talk, where the expected relationship is being obviously subverted. The warmth and affection characteristic of grandparent-grandchild relations will perhaps never change. Husband-wife interaction seems in no way significantly different from that expected in the past. Throughout all village life, the clan bond, that most intimate in-group, is still obviously very strong.

The major changes that have come into the system seem to be

those pertaining more to differences in generational status than to intragenerational role positions. They seem, further, to be focused more on generalized categories of kinsmen, such as "the old people," than on a particular set of ego's dyadic relationships. Difficulties in the interpersonal relations between specific individuals have begun to occur—representing changes from traditionally expected behavior —and cases can be cited; nonetheless, when change has come and when objections to the network of kinship behavior are voiced, they are manifested much more in terms of ego's generalized relationships than his particular set of relatives, and none of these particular relationships has yet been sufficiently subverted so that it has really changed the culture pattern.

For example, to the dismay of the older people, both young girls and young boys are beginning to disregard their parents' and relatives' wishes in many things. In a few cases they openly rebel.

I think most of the children's obedience to the parents is low now; very low. Only the people who are hanging onto their father's order are still obeying the parents. Some don't anymore. The children are too independent now. I understand the change, that condition, is gotten from the mainland. Most of the boy or girl that has been student in Mt. Edgecumbe have too much of experience. And they always influence others to do the same. [Does it make the parents unhappy that the children don't listen to them?] Right. And I'm pretty sure that the older people are afraid to speak out anymore like they do before, because of not knowing whether they will go against the new law of the white people. And that's one main reason why the parents are afraid to speak to their children. They're afraid to say anything against, even though they saw them making mistakes.

The sense of hesitancy and diffidence about taking action even though one feels himself to be right is almost diagnostic of the acculturation situation—this sense of straddling two moral codes.

Others speak also of the changes that are occurring with regard to the formerly pre-eminent place of old people in the society:

Duncan said that now there is a change in the village. Now Clyde's sons and daughters, for example, try to rule over him—"Wrong way! Wrong way!"

[Does it make the old people unhappy that the young people are changing now?] Oh yes. Yeah. Myself, if they change, I feel bad about it.

[Have there been changes in the way relatives treat each other?] Oh there is some change, I think. These young peoples don't obey much their parents, and just don't care about relatives in their mind. They just don't care.

[Are the young people learning the rights ways to treat their relatives now?] Ernest said . . . that they are being forgotten now. He said, "In 10 or 20 years from now these things will be forgotten entirely."

I asked if the people now respect the old people and ask them for their opinions. Johnny answered, "Not many." He said that they ask the council now about things.

And fathers speak of the new ways in which their children are beginning to behave toward them.

[How should a boy treat his father?] Humble, always humble to the father. But sometimes my older boys try to tell me exactly right things to do. He give me strong words sometime. Try to explain to me. If I don't know something really, he try to explain to me. [Has this changed from the old way?] Oh yeah, always we do that; but now kind of different. Because the children been to school now; English. Then when I try to turn back to old way, those young boys feel a little bad about old way. Some of them now pretty changed. Some of them go over the parents. Just like he thought he learn better than father does with new way.

Like before army, air force came out. . . . The women and girls were easier to tell, and listen more to their parents, minding their parents more than they are now.

A man in his middle years succinctly phrases this aspect of social change:

[How did the old people say to treat your relatives?] They teach us, when man older than we and we do something wrong, just don't say any word. Just do what he says. And if he is just like my age, if we done something wrong, just talk to him. Or if old man ask something that isn't right, don't say words back to him; just fear him. Don't laugh about him. Old man or old woman. [Does this still happen now?] Mine is doing that way. Most try to do that way. But seems to us different now. [How?] Changed, different. Older man, if he say, "Don't break that thing," young fellow say, "No matter, I break." He talk back that way. Before that when man say that to him, didn't say anything; just shut their mouth. Because their father teach that way. But now most of them doesn't do that way. [Is there a lot of talk like this now?] Most of them, what I hear; what I hear and see. They different now.

With regard to one of the traditional clan functions, that of giving an individual his social and supernatural identity through a proper name, there have also been changes. Some evidence exists that a name, even in former times, might be applied to a person who was not a clan member—this in apparent contradiction to what I said earlier about the clan as a host of spiritual essences. But it was noted that people of another clan might request that they be allowed to use the name of a loved one for a newborn infant of their clan and that sometimes the proprietary clan consented to the naming.[16]

In any case, at present names are being "stolen" (in the local phrase) by clans who do not properly have a right to their use. This was mentioned on several different occasions, for example:

Frederick says that some people in Savoonga have taken an Aimaramkut name without asking—"It's just like stealing."

It is apparently not easy to stamp out completely the religious overtones of the naming process. Even though the ostensible conversion to Christianity has been an accomplished fact for some years, the sentiments which clustered around the proprietary naming patterns for each clan are still strong.

With time, however, even these will change. One man, in fact, predicts that the practice of giving each child an Eskimo name will soon die out, and this may very well prove true in a few years. With young people moving to the mainland and being effectively isolated from older clansmen, it is easy to see how the practice could die out, especially now that it is formally cut off from its religious roots and supernatural justification.

Yet there is a more positive side to the breakdown of clan loyalties. Some people feel that now, when one's unstinting allegiance to kinsmen is being muted, by that very development more diffuse loyalties to the entire village are replacing those former bonds. Some say, for example:

[16] I am a little hesitant about accepting this evidence, for I think there may be hidden qualifications to the naming on which I have no information, such as the name being used only as a nickname and not really being the name-soul. One would expect that a name-soul, with an immutable identity belonging to one particular clan, could not so easily be metamorphosed.

All over, everybody is acting like close relations. In the past only they go by relationship. But now no matter either alien, or stranger, he's a relation.

Although this statement no doubt represents an overgeneralization, in view of the great amount of objective data on the significance of clan divisions in village life, it is nonetheless interesting as a perception of the transition from one type of ordering social relationships—for example, that which has been called the "folk society"—to a more universal pattern.

But some other features are likewise beginning to cloud the situation. Money, so important in relation to the white world, is entering into the kinship system as well as much of the rest of village life. Some people now hesitate between the impulse to give an object or goods freely to their kinsman, "in the Eskimo way," and the thought that they should directly receive money or something else in exchange for it "in the white man's way." This incipient trend toward the rationalization of economic dealings and individual acquisition may very well continue, in view of the village's current situation of limited economic potential and persistently increasing pressure from the mainland economic system. If so, it represents one of the most severe threats to the stability of the clans, in which the unhesitating sharing of one's goods is fundamentally important.

## Marriage and the Rule of Residence

The old cultural regime in regard to marriage, which was still generally prevailing in 1940 and by which all marriages were still being formalized, prescribed no particular restrictions upon choice of one's spouse other than that he should not marry a "close" kinsman. Which relatives were thus proscribed was not always clear, but it is said that one could not marry nearer than one's "first" cousin. This no doubt always included *ataligoon*, and apparently there were some clan differences with regard to whether *ilowaek* and *aegangaligoon* were also included in the proscription. No particular rule of clan endogamy or exogamy prevailed, and a spouse might come from any patriclan.

The choice of wife was always made by the parents of the young boy in consultation with the elders of their clan. The boy's father discussed with them the relative merits of his son's marriage with particular young girls of the village; if a tentative choice seemed to them best, overtures were made to the girl's parents, who, in turn, discussed the matter with the old people of their clan if the proposed marriage was exogamous.

Occasionally infant betrothal was practiced. Two sets of parents, wishing to cement bonds of friendship, would promise their children in marriage when they later became of marriageable age. Often the two children themselves would play and associate with each other quite unaware of their future relationship, until the time, during early adolescence, when they were told of their engagement. They then assumed the behavior appropriate to two people who are to be married. That is, they became shy and embarrassed in each other's presence.

When the parents of both young people had decided on the marriage, the young man began a period of groom work. Even if the two young people had been affianced as infants, this first step in the marriage process did not begin until the late years of adolescence. It was signaled by the boy's relatives, who took a sledful of gifts to the girl's house, which were then distributed by the girl's father to his clansmen. In his prospective parents-in-law's house the young man performed all types of labor. At first he lived with his own parents and worked only during the daytime, doing such jobs as carrying water and helping in other household tasks. But his primary obligation was to help in the boat crew of his father-in-law. He was the *nIngae*, whose role relationships have already been discussed. He was the man who "is working for that woman" and who must show utmost respect and obedience to his prospective affinal relatives. As one man now recalls, "I worked very hard for my wife. . . . It is easy now." Sometimes restraint was difficult, and not all marriages that were contracted reached consummation. From all accounts, it was a fairly common happening that a man would begin working for a woman and then the engagement would be broken off for some reason, either because he was lazy and did not please the girl's parents or because they found him uncongenial for some other reason. It was apparently not unusual for a person to have been engaged several times.

Frequently the period of groom work lasted several years, particularly if the girl's father was overly exploitive. Such men were recognized as having overstepped the bounds of cultural allowance in using their son-in-law's free labor. The usual period was for two or, at the most, three years. At some point during the period of groom work, the boy moved into the girl's house, and then his every activity and effort were given over to helping her family. During this time the young couple had had no sexual relations. But after two or three years of groom work, the parents on both sides discussed whether the time was right for the final consummation of the marriage through sexual union. If they so decided, an older relative of the boy (usually his father's brother, his *ataeta*) told him to begin sexual advances toward the girl. She was also told of what was to happen, and in the crowded sleeping room the union occurred. It was proper that at first the girl make some show of resistance, but this was usually only a token refusal.

In some cases, however, the boy and girl did not really care for each other, and it was a long time before they became adjusted to living together harmoniously. Even today the arbitrary choice of spouse by one's parents is remembered by some people with great misgivings:

Finally I heard he was engaged to Margaret. She used to hate him a lot, but their parents forced them to marry each other, and Margaret used to fight him. But later on they get acquainted to each other.

I think their parents forced them to get married. That is worst thing—they didn't get along much.

In the old days sometimes a bride would cry because she hadn't chosen her husband and she didn't want to leave her family.

It's very bad to married to the person whom we don't like when we have a steady boy friend; it hurts a lot. I would tell my father, but I am afraid to tell him that I don't want to married Hector; I was afraid that he wouldn't let me do my own idea. That was the olden days, the parents or grandparents have to fix us up with whom they want, not our choice.

Shortly after the marriage was sexually consummated, the young couple returned to live in the boy's house. The rule of residence in this culture was "matri-patrilocal," in Murdock's sense; i.e., permanent residence with the boy's family following a period of living in the girl's home. The return journey duplicated the first presentation of gifts from the boy's family to that of the girl when the young man had started his groom labor. The procession apparently always occurred at night, and the girl's father and uncle pushed a sled loaded with skins, ropes, rifles, ammunition, food, or other gifts. They were followed by the girl's aunts and mother, walking behind. The gifts were all collected from the kinsmen of the girl's father and then distributed among the clanmates of the boy's father. A woman married in the old way describes the journey to the home of her husband:

Then after two years of marriage with Hector, they took me to Clyde's place. Just before Hector and I moved to Clyde's, Arthur gathered up some stuff, three or four mukluk skins, some shot gun, saw, axe, drills, hammers, nails, and all kinds of stuffs. Including gunny sack of flour. Afterwards, few days later, the time comes to move to Clyde's house. Then four or five people including myself walked up to Clyde's house. We step into the front room; they put all the stuff in the front room too. Then Adah [a close relative of the bride, a clanswoman] asked me to step on each of these stuffs, step on each of them that came along with me. Afterwards she took me outdoors and had me walk around Clyde's house. Then we came in to the inner room. Then I am become completely Clyde's family—one of his family. That is the way every daughter-in-law treated when they come to their father-in-law home, became one of their family. To step on the things it means so that they won't cover us up, that is what Adah said, so that this stuffs won't cover us up. I didn't understand completely about that, seems to me it's so we wouldn't be sick.

Other than this incipient ceremonialism, there was no special rite marking the change of social status. No formal marriage ceremonies existed, and, with time and living together, the couple became socially recognized as man and wife.

CHANGES IN THE MARRIAGE PATTERN

Several important features of the marriage pattern have changed since 1940. Perhaps the most far-reaching in its implications is the tendency for the young people now to choose their own spouses. Something of this existed in 1940, apparently, but today it is the modal pattern of marital choice. The young people choose each other and then inform their respective parents, who make the necessary arrangements. As one woman phrases it:

When two young people like each other, they have a right to marry: that's the new idea that has come to this island.

But a comment by another young woman indicates that the pattern is still in transition and that there is tugging and pulling with the older cultural directives regarding the parents' choosing of their children's spouse:

[When you and Reynold got married, who decided?] We did. Then Clinton talked to my daddy about it. It was pretty hard trying to get married. Clinton wanted somebody else for Reynold's wife, and my parents wanted somebody else. So we had to fight for each other. Mostly now the kids decide for themselves.

The boy's father just referred to comments himself on changing marriage patterns:

Maybe young people they learn from white people. . . . Girls and boys, talk together, and see if they want. Before they ask parents, they decide for themselves. Long time ago, father ask the girl's parents if he has wife for his boy. Then, I don't know, sometimes 3, 4 years work for that girl and for his father-in-law. Then when come together, the father-in-law sent the boy to his home and ask those boy's parents to bring the girl home. [Which way is best, old or new?] Pretty hard to tell. We see some of these doing that new way now, sometime not happy together.

If the parents of the young people still remain adamant after the latter have declared their intentions, the young lovers will sometimes take their case to the village council for its help in pressing their suit.

The note of doubt about the wisdom of the newer custom of free choice by the young people is echoed in the following passage, in which the thoughts of one of the most important leaders of the village are brought out on the subject of changing social patterns:

One thing I'm blaming the white people's way is about these marriages. In the past the parents make an agreement to their children. This agreement is not to be changed. And they talk to their children, what their plan was. They told them to take this boy or girl. So even though the couple themselves don't like the idea, by obeying their parents they get together. And for short time, they have little trouble, you know, joining. But after a short time, everything works out okay. No fuss. And now the young people just decide for themselves. But I can see there is more trouble to the couple. More trouble than before. [Divorces?] Divorces, yeah. . . . [Now do people go to the marriage commissioner for the license?] Yeah, have to get license. But to me that marriage license doesn't help much. Because I understand the young couple bears in their minds there is a divorcement ahead of them if something happens. That way they bring more trouble to their parents. [Before, in old way, were there divorces?] Well, not much as we have now. Unless the woman is badly treated. The parents of the woman have right to just take her away. Because that was the promise made when they had the agreement.

Thus the choice of one's husband or wife is a social pattern now in the throes of acculturative change. A particular cleavage is noted between the older and the younger generation with respect to the cultural legitimacy of the old pattern and its purported greater wisdom in human relations.

Another salient change in the pattern of marriage is the innovation of a marriage commissioner, a post now filled by an Eskimo, whose duty it is to issue licenses and keep records of marriages, births, and deaths. He is also empowered to perform the ceremony. The marriage commissioner had been functioning in the village for approximately five or six years prior to 1955, and all marriages now must be sanctioned by the obtaining of a license. When the role was first created in the village, all then-existing marriages were *ipso facto* legalized.

Aside from the obtaining of a license, the rest of the pattern of engagement and marriage shows other earmarks of an institution in the process of transition. It is now left to personal choice whether the young people sleep together before or after they obtain their marriage license, and the procuring of the license may be done either before the young man begins his period of groom labor or sometime before the couple returns to the boy's house. The pattern has not yet stabilized. The groom-work requirement is retained in the present culture, although it is considerably shorter than it used to be. Now the young man works only six months or, at most, a year. But it is a custom at least nominally supported even by some of the young men who have been most exposed to mainland ideas.

There is a big change in marriage now. As you know, a long time ago—not even a long time ago; it just changed a few years ago—parents used to pick a lady for their son. Parents just pick a girl for their son that they think the boy likes, and the parents go over to the girl's parents. And even if the girl don't like the boy, well, their parents say "yes," and the girl just have to. All this marriage, just by force. And after 10 years of hard labor for the poor guy, they get to like each other. Right now the boy and the girl choose who they like—just like the white people do. I got married in 1948. [Did you make your own choice?] Yes, first guy. People thinks that's no good. Me and Viola fight for our married right. Her parents hate her for getting married to me, for she was getting married to the boy they don't like. But we fall in love, and we got married after big talk. I was first boy, and Viola the first girl, to go hand-in-hand around the village; people don't like that. They thought we were crazy. We just got marriage commissioner first time in 1948. There was about 200 people attending marriage ceremony. We came in, father bringing in daughter, and I was escorted. We get wedding gifts, first time, just like Christmas. I still work one year for my wife, though, after the ceremony. It's still a village law right now; a man has to work, even though it's a love marriage. A boy has to work one year for his father-in-law. [Do you think that's a good thing?] It's a village law; they thought that's still good. That's part of the custom they want to keep. At least a person has to work a year.

And another agrees and describes the type of work he did for his father-in-law:

Same kind of work I was doing, except all the things I catch and all the things I kill, like foxes or seals, goes to them instead of to me. And I was living there. . . . Then I believe it was April sometime we moved out. [Do you think it is a good thing to work like that for your father-in-law?] Yeah, it's a good thing—after all, you figure how much a man and woman puts in for their daughter to raise up until she's 18, you know; and they deserve that, just a year's working from their son-in-law. I think it's a pretty good idea, and we should keep it up, at least here—in this custom. It's a lot of hard work for a man and a woman to raise up a child.

Another young Sivokakme, however, expresses some doubts about the future of this custom:

Yes, they still keep that custom, Eskimo way of getting married. But the only thing changed getting married is the boy and girl has to love first. That's the only thing changed. The rest is still just the same— have to work for their father-in-law. Because that makes very good for the Eskimos. I don't know, they may stop that soon, in the future. Because sometimes a lot of trouble for some young man. Next generation may stop it.

As indicated in one of the quotations, there is often a Christian wedding ceremony that formally signalizes the change of status. Until the last year, the ceremony was held in the school; but now the custom of church weddings in the village has begun. The ceremony, however, does not invariably precede either the groom work or the sexual union. Most of the current marriage ceremonies are modeled with varying degrees of paraphernalia on the white mainland culture, with minister, gifts, and guests.

Divorce is now much more difficult to accomplish than it was under the old cultural regime, when it was effected simply by the gradual social recognition of separation. Now, when the marriage has been legalized by a license, it must also be legally broken by a divorce decree that passes through the courts, and considerable money is necessary for lawyer's fees and other costs. The village council has no power to grant divorces, although it attempts to settle domestic problems that are brought before it and will try to reconcile quarreling parties to prevent a costly divorce.

As in the past, there is still a tendency for the levirate to operate. There are several cases of this in the village, and it was remarked by one person

that usually, if there isn't too great an age difference, a man's widow will be married by his unmarried brother. Nathan said that it is good this way—everything is taken care of, the kids, house, and everything.

A point of far greater implications for the social life of the village is that some of its young girls are undergoing serious reappraisals of the woman's role and of the type of men they want to marry. Already half a dozen girls have married white men rather than Eskimo boys from their own village, and in all cases they have migrated to the mainland. Those who remain behind have not forgotten the example which was set, and they have received daily encouragement for their changing reference norms through contact with the soldiers of the nearby army camp. The fact that the girls reject their parents' wishes is a cause of considerable concern. Yet this rejection is likely to increase with coming years, when the influence of the old people and older cultural conceptions steadily dwindle under the joint impact of continued contacts with the white world and the passing into history of traditional cultural sentiments through death of the people who have manifested and maintained those sentiments. Speaking of one of the young girls who married a white man, an informant says:

I know that Marian used to tell me that she would never get married to an Eskimo boy. I think she didn't want to marry an Eskimo because she would have very hard working, as the people around here, some of them, have their wives do hard work all the time. She said that the white people treat their wives much better than the Eskimo boys treat their wives.

And an older man also speaks to the same point:

Yes, they want to marry soldiers. Pretty hard to hold back, but we try to hold them back ourselves, when they love those army boys.

In a small village the depletion of even a few potential marriage partners can have serious demographic as well as cultural effects. In this case it will no doubt be an additional spur to emigration by the young men.[17]

## Social Control

The Eskimos provide one of the favorite ethnographic examples of a society in which it is said there is "no government." Actually, social control and regulation occur, as indeed they must to some degree in any viable society; but it is true that no specified social structures exist which embody group law and have a monopoly over the legitimate use of physical force. Social control is accomplished by actuation of diffuse sentiments in most Eskimo groups, senti-

[17] Some of the Central Eskimo groups traditionally met the problem of a relative scarcity of women by the practice of polyandry. This would obviously be impossible now in the case of Gambell.

ments which are translated into behavior by the impromptu social support given by kinsmen. Illustrative of this lack of obvious political structures is the statement by Moore, describing the Sivokakmeit in 1912:

In all matters of community government, the old men, "strong men," sorcerers, and boat captains have much influence, but little positive authority. The St. Lawrence Islander's habits of life are regulated by the unwritten laws of custom and tradition which he seldom contravenes, except to obey the stronger laws of necessity and self-preservation. But, should he choose at any time to be a law unto himself, there are none with authority to command that he do otherwise; however, in extreme cases, if his actions are considered inimical to the better interests of the community, the influential men of the island decide what action will be taken and, willing or unwilling, he must accede to their demands. But it is seldom necessary to resort to strenuous punishments. [1923, p. 341]

Such was, in broad outline, the sociopolitical structure of St. Lawrence culture until a generation ago. Having no formal government, the Sivokakmeit relied, first, on the advice and sage cautions of the elders of the various clans to settle disputes and, secondly, on the coercion or threat of violence inherent in the strength and numbers of the various *ramka*. Other factors that entered into a decision were the prestige and power of the shamans and the strength of the athletic man who, in hand-to-hand wrestling, validated his legal claim by a physical victory.

With such unstructured ways of settling disputes, there was, understandably, considerable argumentation and violence. At times during the early years of the American occupation of the island, captains of coast guard vessels acted as judges of disputes. They also acted as bailiff, if there was need to transport anyone to a Nome jail, but such occurrences were relatively rare.

THE VILLAGE COUNCIL

The beginnings of a formal social institution dedicated to the governing of the village can be traced to about 1925. The teacher at that time notes in an annual report:

The village has no centralized authority. Have discussed the idea of a village council. . . . They seem impressed but have not acted on

the suggestion. I settle their small disputes to the best of my ability.
. . . Any serious trouble . . . would be referred to the Captain of
*Bear* [coast guard cutter], although nothing during the year warranted
this action.

Recollections of one of the elderly men today embody this
transition from the old patterns of government to the new forms
adopted from the white mainland:

Before, that time, we have no council. The old people try to straighten
things. Just like a council; yeah, try to straighten. Now, it turned to white
people rule, the council.

The new governing organization in the village, the village council,
was tried on a tentative basis for a year, being composed of a mayor
and five councilmen with the schoolteacher as advisor. Its main
duties in the early years, even as now, were to "care for the general
welfare of the community," and it was thought so successful in
this task that people voted to continue it after the first trial year.
Indicative of its concerns in those early years are these extracts
from minutes:

If a young man and his wife are living together and their parents try
to separate them . . . they shall go to the village council before separating. If one side did wrong he shall pay a fine according to how much
wrong he did.

Each trapper to have a sign to show where his bait and traps are.
No person will go close to that sign. Fox may smell his tracks and
stay away. Anyone who does go near another man's bait or traps shall
pay a fine of 2 dollars. If a fox is eating bait or near that bait,
no one should shoot the fox except the man who put the bait out.
But shoot any fox seen unless it is eating another man's bait. If a
dog spoils any bait the owner of the dog will be told to watch the
dog. If the same dog is seen near any bait again it will be shot.

If any dog bites a person or child, the owner shall keep that dog
tied. If the dog bites the second time the owner shall pay a fine of
1 dollar for each tooth hole bit in the skin.

Council wants every boat to have a chance to have a share in
whaling. So the 2nd, 3rd, 4th, and 5th boats to strike will get shares
instead of 2nd, 3rd, 4th, and 5th boats that get to the whale. But if
first boat kills the whale, then the 4 boats getting here first will get
a share.

And a few years later the council

decided that no boat was to kill walrus for ivory only. Limit 4 walrus a trip. Ivory taken in violation will be taken by council and sold, proceeds to be used for poor people.

[The council] decide punishment for 4 men who violated recent ruling against killing walrus for ivory only [ivory was confiscated and turned over to store].

The council decide that Ernest must take his whole family to his camp. Because anybody who left some of his family is losing their time in coming to see them. It is hard for Ernest when he leave the old man, no one will support his children. His children who are school age will come to school when they come back from trapping.

Thus the first council grew out of an idea proposed by the local teacher. Some ten years later, however, local village councils were officially given authorization by the United States Congress, and the charter under which the present council is operating is specifically authorized in the Indian Reorganization Act (the Wheeler-Howard Act of 1934, made applicable to Alaska in 1936).

The present village council is composed of eight members: a president, vice-president, secretary, treasurer, and four regular members. The officers are elected every three years, and the four standing members every four years. Elections occur in late March and follow a public meeting in which the nominations for officers are made. Only native Eskimos over 21 years old and living in Gambell are qualified to vote or hold office. No restriction is made concerning sex, although the general Eskimo sentiment about the place of women relegates them to a minor or insignificant role in this organization as in so much of the rest of public life. Meetings of the council are regularly held once a month, with special meetings called whenever necessary to consider a problem. Public meetings occur several times during the year.

*Scope of the council's operations*—The council is given almost unlimited areas of legitimate authority. It appears to be a concrescence of institutionalized power for enforcing a multitude of quite diverse social norms. Acting upon the broad directives contained in the constitution and bylaws, the council legislates and judges in matters pertaining to the health and bodily welfare of the people, marriage and family relations, economic problems of the entire village, social welfare, recreation, and crime. It is also the political voice of the village in dealing with out-groups. Something of the scope of matters that come to its attention can be seen in these illustrative extracts from minutes of meetings over the past few years, recorded in the graphic English of its secretaries:

HEALTH

The council discussed the settlement of the new dentist. . . . The council decided to pay Matthew from the Community Fund and the rate will be according to the same reduced amount which was filed last year.

[There was] a complaint that most of the village people object to dogs being shot at night, because of many dangers. Also, wounded dogs have been seen running about the village, spreading blood and germs. After discussion, the Council passed the following regulations: (1) All working dogs must be tied to avoid being shot. (2) No dogs are to be shot at night, because someone might be walking nearby and be injured. (3) Do not leave a wounded dog. Follow it until it is killed. (4) Target shooting must not be done from the door of the houses, lest someone might be walking along the shore or the skin boats might be shot through and cause trouble.

MARRIAGE

Business transacted: Another new engagement of couple was brought up to settle. One party had been forced to engage for marriage against her choice. The council conferred with the forcers and settled up the matters.

The council worked the matter all over again about marrying a couple which is difficult to settle. One party is not in age and the other party was in age. Fathers of both parties were called to appear before the council and suggested to talk over the matter between themselves. The matter has been a long one to discuss, about three hours.

ECONOMY

This meeting was called to regulate the time the store should be opened. . . . It was public opinion that regular store hours should be established. No one gave any suggestion when the store should be open and when it should close. But all agreed that the store manager should not work over eight hours a day.

The council discussed subject of setting a fair and regular charge for transportation on dog team or by boat between Gambell and

Savoonga. In the future, the price will be $15.00 plus $5.00 if for only óne way. The round trip will be $30.00 if the passenger can return within one week. If this time limit is passed, the charge will be $40.00 for the round trip.

A telegram from Juneau concerning fur prices was read to the Council by the secretary. . . . The council decided to pay $6.00 for No. 1 white fox skins, $4.00 for No. 2. No. 3 will not be accepted at the store. The council decided to give advance credit to trappers, not to exceed $30.00 to those at camp, and ⅔ of that amount to those who trap from town.

Announce the situation of light plant, as the lights plant was stopped first of March in account of unpaid light bills. The people discussed about it, and nothing seems settle any.

Shooting game such as sea animals or birds unless the killer should give them to the widows or orphans or sick people [is prohibited].

Report: The hunters used 45 gallons of gasoline and 5 gallons of zerolene to hunt whale. The total charges including tax is $29.65. The council voted to pay for this amount from the Community Fund of Gambell.

Business transacted pertains to Reindeer resources. There was some complaint about it, the result is that Savoonga directors had decided to let Gambell people have ten per cent of the reindeer to be butchered next summer and the rest was to go to Savoonga. This is to be discussed by the council so that it may be worked out on some basis so that the two villages may have the same amount of meat.

SOCIAL WELFARE

A girl recorded by former nurse, who is in pregnant, has to be inquire privately by two of the council directly to herself and parents. This case is to be investigate by whom it has been created.

The teacher bring up about school lunches and inquire of the council to have the council take a choice of an elderly woman for helper in cooking the lunches. The council have discussion and choose four women to help in the cooking, each one week by alternatively.

Business transacted: A half case of oranges was sent by the former teacher to be distributed to the sick people. The council divided it among them accordingly. Another business came up pertaining to lunches furnished by the store and the directors of the store wanted to know to whom it should be charged. The council discussed over it and decided to have paid part from the Community Fund and part by the store.

Another matter discussed pertains to the Community Fund to be distributed for relief work. The council decided to let every family have $15.00 in merchandise and this is carried.

RECREATION

The councils discussed about Thanksgiving dinner and appoint the cooks, servers, and the helpers. . . . The elders of the Church offered the Church auditorium for place to be used for dinner; but the councils decided to hold the dinner in the two school rooms as it will be more convenient. The payment will be made from the Community Fund as soon as the work is over. Estimated amount will be used for the groceries is $100.00 from the same fund.

Plans were made for the annual Community Thanksgiving dinner. All agreed to follow the usual plans: (1) The cooks will be hired. (2) School Girls will serve. (3) Water will be brought from the lake. (4) All groceries will be purchased from the Gambell Native Store and will be charged to the Community Fund.

The Council agreed to have the Christmas program and the distribution of gifts on December 22. . . . This will give the trappers a chance to visit their trap line.

SOCIAL REGULATION AND ADJUDICATION

A written notice of warning to the people of Gambell was received . . . about suspicious matters between the people of Gambell and the CAA. In cooperation the council asked for notification when anything happens and will help in investigating. The council will take prompt action when there is proof. The council thought the things missing too big in quantity. They decided to post a notice as follows: No visitors or hiking around CAA is allowed unless invited or business or emergencies.

The next problem discussed concerning Edward, who owed Benjamin's Store [in Nome] some money. This was the last notice given. Edward was questioned by the council to determine whether he really owed the sum. Edward admitted that he did and asked the council to lend him some money from the Community Fund to repay the debt. The council could not do so, as there is no money left in the Community Fund. Edward has no money either. The council decided to write a letter to Benjamin's asking him to give Edward another chance to pay this bill, so much according to how much he is earning, and the Council will collect from him. We, the council, are sorry that we did not know of Edward's debt before he reached the last chance. We would have helped him to pay sooner. One of the councilmen gave $5.00 to help Edward start paying.

Frederick was asked to present his problem to the council. Frederick told the council that hunters camping too near the "Big Lagoon" may scare the seals away and requests the council to prohibit hunters from camping in that area. The council voted against his proposal because it would be impossible to enforce such a rule.

CORPORATE CONTRACTS AND RELATIONS WITH OUT-GROUPS

Lawson read the rules and regulations to the people. The rules and regulations were made by the Gambell Native Council and was agreed on by the officer in charge of the military post in Gambell. The council asked the people of Gambell and the military personnel to observe the rules and regulations. The majority of the people were satisfied with the reading.

A CAA technician stationed at Gambell was present. He states that the CAA desires permission from the Gambell Native Council to remove the Lake Troutman pumphouse and boiler equipment providing the CAA turns over the village of Gambell, the pipeline, well, pump and building foundation and further providing that the CAA construct a frame shed over the pump. He states further that effective immediately with the signing of this agreement the Village of Gambell has authority to rehabilitate this water system to the needs of the village providing that no part of the boiler equipment or piping is disturbed.

In this survey of council operations it is of much interest to mark the points at which one can see the society passing from, to put it simply, a "folk" socioculture to one which shares certain features common to institutions of an industrial-urban socioculture; from a "society of status" to one of contract; and from a *Gemeinschaft* to *Gesellschaft* type of organization. It is now the council rather than the system of patriclans which, more and more, is performing the functions of general health and welfare, regulating marriage and family matters, exercising social control, and punishing offenders against cultural sentiments. Clearly Gambell is still in a state of transition in which only the rudiments of the "universalistic" mode of social relationships are found (Parsons, 1951); and the preponderant bulk of social influence and welfare still derives from the viability of clan groupings. But the beginnings are here in the sense, for example, that it does not ostensibly matter whether an individual is Puwowalagameit or Aimaramka; he is equal before village law.

These excerpts from the minutes contain references to two aspects of council organization which need further discussion. The Welfare Committee is (in the 1955 council) a subsidiary organization composed of five members appointed from among the candidates defeated in the general election to the council. The five members include a chairman and a secretary to record decisions and activities. The Welfare Committee's main duties appear to be those of a tactical arm of the council: ringing the bell signifying the curfew hour, after which all children and unmarried girls must be in their homes for the night; making all necessary arrangements for movies, native dances, and other types of public recreation; distributing food and welfare gifts equally among all houses; arranging for and doing much of the work for the Christmas and Thanksgiving programs; bringing people before the council who are quarreling or arguing over some matter; enforcing the curfew regulations concerning the military camp to ensure that the soldiers leave the village in the evening; and making coffins for the dead whose families cannot afford to buy them. But in addition to these tasks, the Welfare Committee chairman summed up his duties thus:

We're like ears. We walk around and if there is anything we see that isn't too good, we report it to the council.

Prior to 1954, there had been a Welfare Committee for some twenty-five years or so, and although it had been organized on a different basis and there was almost no turnover in membership, its duties had been much the same.

The Community Fund, also mentioned in the council minutes, is the financial source for many community projects. It is a fund administered and controlled by the council. A 3 per cent sales tax on all goods sold through the store builds the fund, and its monies go to provide some public entertainment, expenses for the community Thanksgiving dinner, village hunting expenses in times of duress, the payment of dental and midwife bills for all villagers, and necessary welfare to needy families. As an indication of its fluctuating size, it should be noted that from April of one year to March of the next, the amount of money in the fund increased from $1.60 to

$1,618.00 So great a range may not have been typical of all recent years.

*Changes*—In broad outline, the role of the council in the village has not greatly changed since 1940. Its scope of activity is as wide now as it was then, and it is still perhaps the most effective single regulative and integrative institution in the village. It was in 1940, and continues to be, a benevolent autocracy which had the power to regulate in matters of economics, petty crime, family relations, and recreation. The duties of the 1954 council, as seen by its president, are

all over whole town making rules and regulations, like that for better living. And now the store is included, since it was organized as ANICA.

In some areas, such as economics, the council has even more jurisdiction now than it did fifteen years ago. When, in 1947, the village—through its council—voted to liquidate the assets of the older incorporated store and join the newly created co-operative purchasing agency (ANICA), it thereby assumed direct control of an institution which before had been only implicitly and diffusely controlled by the village. In 1954, too, the council was persistently concerned with alleviating the food scarcity and had to act, in the capacity of village spokesman, to acquire relief and emergency supplies from various governmental agencies of the mainland. It did not have this problem in 1940. On the other hand, one of the 1940 council's economic concerns, the reindeer herd, is no longer a problem of management for the 1954 council, since the herd no longer exists. But the disappearance of that food resource has brought on many more problems than those simply of management and regulation.

The council has always had a strong voice in the village's economic matters. What is new in 1955 is that there is now a different context in which the council functions in the village: more dissension about its interference, more hostile sentiments about its members, more open rebellion. One might trace much of this difference to the changes in the magnitude of problems with which it must deal now, problems which it did not have in 1940. Not only have there been many more difficult situations since that year, many of them unprecedented, but they have been of a far more threatening nature. The discussion here will concern the three main areas in which those problems have arisen and in which the council, as the most articulate spokesman for village policy and village reaction, has acted: (1) the problem of relations with the people of the Civil Aeronautics Administration station and other government agencies, (2) that of relations with the military establishments that have moved near the village during the past fifteen years, and (3) the continually exacerbated problem of providing recreation that is satisfactory to both the standards of the old people and the tastes of the young.

Even in 1940 responsible people of the village knew that they must come to terms with the changes inherent in contact with the white world. They had done this for a number of years, but some even looked to the future with its problems. For instance, with wisdom extending far beyond his small arctic island the village leader at that time suggested that one of the cardinal principles of interaction with the mainland culture should be gradualism. This is the present leader's recollection:

Of course I don't know much about it myself. I heard one of the coast guard came in and two boys complained to the commander about these marriages; and then the commander of the coast guard started to talk to the councils. Everything was going to be changed right there. But the mayor of Gambell asked the commander whether it would be all right to go very slow, go into that very slow. Maybe change one thing at a time. When old people get used to that change, then change another one. That's what his request was. So the commander himself leave it up to him. Whatever seems good, do so. The mayor . . . thinks that if there is a sudden change, there's going to be a big trouble with the old people.

Note that in this instance the council still had the authority to decide which path of change to follow. The decision was in their hands, and the pressures were only such as they themselves created. Since 1940 there has apparently been a continual increase in the dimensions of problems coming from contact with the white world, and as a consequence the council's real power to control the flow of events decreased. The council now has some to assume much more the role of the regulator and ameliorator after the event, rather than in any sense the controller of the event. (This might be said to en-capsulate the entire sociocultural situation of Gambell now as compared to 1940.)

*Civil Aeronautics Administration*—The CAA station was the first of two major waves of culture contact that have come into Gambell since 1940. Of the two, this was much the more benign. Compared with the military bases which came later, the CAA base formed a situation in which the impinging group was not so large as to over-whelm the local culture. There was also something of an egalitarian and mutually respectful relationship between the two groups. Rela-tions were quite amicable and friendly throughout the stay of the white people, and there was mutual assistance and sharing of some cultural aspects on both sides. Further, the two groups were not in competition with each other, and—this is very important—changes could come about slowly and gradually, being based on slow learn-ing and imitation rather than on a sudden adjustment made necessary by stringent circumstances. Perhaps the most important single feature of this culture-contact situation was the fact that the white world was represented by several *families*, whose daily normal routines presented a realistic model of life in the donor group. Such a setup cushioned the effects of interaction much more than is pos-sible in the usual culture-contact situation. There were, of course, dysfunctional effects coming from association with the CAA people (such as overly heightened expectations about the white world); but, given the fact that culture contact must occur in the modern world, this sort of a reference group seems much less disruptive than the military or other types of models which are common. Some details of the actual CAA operation on the island can now be ex-amined.

The council has jurisdiction over the land surrounding the village, and it was from them that CAA officials had to acquire the ten-year lease covering ground for the combined CAA and Weather Bureau base. In the summer of 1943 ships disgorged lumber and other build-ing materials on the beaches and hired many of the Sivokakmeit as laborers in the construction work. Then came the people who were to occupy the new white houses:

As soon as they finished those houses, some young couples and single men came on the airplanes, as they already fixed the landing strip out of the sand and ground. These are what they call the first Weather Bureau. They keep checking weather always. It's very new to all of us, what was happening in those days. White people increasing too. The airplanes coming in and out often. [Did the people like that?] They like it. We feel happier to see more white people coming into this island.

This note of a new world in birth was to be emphasized throughout the ten years of occupation of the site. One informant's reactions to the model of white man's living provided in the new houses is recorded thus:

Right after when everything was finished down the CAA, the . . . boy who is over all these workers invited everybody in this village by families to come and see these houses. See every place what it looks like. They were furnished with everything. It was such a new building, seems to me, and everything looks neat and clean. There are some sinks with water coming on and the faucets, hot and cold. There are some refrigerators, with the electric lights on. It looks something like in the Statesides, when it is finished. Just like a home in the States. We praised them houses.

Not only were some of the material aspects of the white man's way of life seen in the actual homes of white men, but aspects of his social life were likewise learned. Villagers were invited to parties in the white houses, several native marriages were sponsored by the white people, complete with the mainland wedding paraphernalia, and friendships with white people were built up:

Right after seeing those houses, about a week later, the owner of those houses came, the first "weather bureaus." As soon as they settled everything down there, I think late in the summer, they started inviting them young people around here for parties. Sometimes they have native dance down there, sometimes white people dances.

The white man's style of dancing was not always acceptable to some of the older native people in the village or to the white missionary, but the amicability which reigned between village and white people during this period was not marred by any long-continued differences. White children went to the Gambell native school, their parents visited in the native homes, and some learned of the Eskimo's difficult life by joining the hunting crews out on the ice. In all, they are warmly remembered:

CAA very fine. Yeah, very good, very helpful people. They turn their eyes this way, toward the village, and their ears. Because maybe they can act. [How?] If we need something, we can call up for help. [Food?] Food and call a plane, and do something. Use their power if need be—power unit. [Did the village get a lot of things from them?] Yeah, most of them very nice; all of them.

The white people bought ivory and skin sewing from villagers. They often helped with their automotive equipment when some special need developed in the village (e.g., pulling the boats up from the beach). Their pipeline from the lake supplied water to the village as well as to their own site. Their physical and emotional support was given when a death or tragedy struck the Eskimo village. In these and many other ways they associated with the Sivokakmeit.

Perhaps the most portentous effects of their stay are only now being felt—in the new ideas for living that, sometimes deliberately, sometimes unwittingly, were transmitted to the younger Eskimos. Both men and women worked at the site, but it was especially the girls, working every day in the homes, who were learning a pattern of life which they would have little chance of satisfying with their own cultural alternatives. And not only were their tasks new to them, but the money they earned was an effective symbol of this newer life:

[How much did those girls get per month?] $13, $15, $18, some $30 and especially $20. Washing clothes, iron them, mend them, clean the whole house, clean the toilet rooms, baking bread for them. [Did you like the work?] Most of the time I enjoyed it, yes, interesting. Sure, I got lots of friends down there, that is the way I learned to make little dresses and jeans. That mechanic's wife she help me. When I make the little things she let me order some materials so I make them little things for the store. I used an electric sewing machine down there. Also I used to make some loaves for the air force boys down at the CAA houses. [Did you learn anything new?] I think every day when I worked down there, I learned something new which I didn't know before. They used mangle iron and electric polisher in the kitchen, and I learned them. I didn't much be with them for parties; just sometimes. They invited me often for the party, but I didn't go often.

The men, similarly, had a chance to learn how to manage and repair many tools and pieces of equipment that were new to them, how to build new structures and make use of new types of materials. In some instances it was their first chance to work with tractors and other automotive equipment.

For a few of the young girls this experience with a new way did not stop when the CAA left the island in 1953. Several went to the mainland to continue their jobs of baby-sitting and housekeeping for the white families whom they had grown to know on the island. Thus the white occupation had a lasting effect on some of the younger people. Although there were elements of unreality in the picture which young Eskimos acquired of the way (they thought) all white people live, nonetheless the picture was accurate in its broad outlines, and it was acquired slowly and gradually, built in a context of friendly and tolerant human relations.

For the village council few problems of a serious nature were posed during this time. Brief flurries over the white-style dances did not disrupt the amicable working relationship which the village —and its council—had with the white community during these ten years of acculturation.

*The military*—If the history of relations between the village and the CAA group was one of comparative peace and mutual trust, quite otherwise has been that with the military establishments which have encamped on its outskirts in recent years. There were two of these, of different branches of the military services. The first came to the island in 1948, remaining until 1952; the second arrived during the latter year and was there through 1955, the year of the research study.[18]

The army camp on the outskirts of the village engendered many

---

[18] There were some American soldiers stationed in the village during the war, from 1942 to 1945, but these were few and their relations with the village such that no significant sociocultural changes coming from their occupation appear evident. The main discussion of the influence of the military in Gambell's recent history will therefore be confined to the two military camps, both of which have contained a significant number of people and have created continuing problems of adjustment for the council and the village. It should also be noted that since the end of this study, 1955, the military base has been discontinued.

of the same problems common to an army camp on the edge of any town anywhere. A group of closely confined, single men, subject to discipline by an authoritarian control structure; a considerable degree of compulsion and coercion in their being on the island; much transience in the population; a rupture of bonds with their usual moral community—these are the main features of the situation. In addition to these common elements, there is the isolation of an arctic outpost with its attendant personality strains. And the entire problem of intergroup relations is exacerbated in this instance by cultural differences between meanings and standards of expectation and evaluation of the two groups. Perhaps all these factors go a long way in explaining many of the conflicts of interest that have developed between the village and the military in the last six years. Such conflicts that have existed show, by contrast, how relatively benign were the conditions under which cultural contact was taking place when there was only the CAA establishment in the sociocultural environment.

To the people of the village, the military camps have represented many things. One of the most important of these has been the opulence and wasteful abundance of the white world. In the beginning of the camps, relations were fairly friendly between village and military, and some of the Eskimos were invited to parties and entertainments. They describe their experiences in such terms as these:

When we gotten there our friend came out to meet us, and he took us into the mess room. They got very big-sized mess room. Then one of friends took us to PX, everybody was invited to PX. Those our friends buy us something, chocolate drinks, candy bars. . . . They bought us everything what we want to eat from the PX. They played music for us down there; they give us different kind of soft drinks.

In the beginning, the hours of the day during which the military could visit in the village were almost unlimited. Later, after some disagreeable incidents, curfew hours were instituted. But in the beginning,

no curfew at all; they stay as long as they want to until midnight or after midnight. . . . They often bring us some candy bars, beef in cans, pork and gravy, some apples and oranges.

One of the recurring problems to come in with the soldiers was that of liquor. For some forty years, at least, one of the most strongly supported village laws had been a prohibition against drinking by any native and even against bringing alcoholic beverages to the island. Much of the basis for this legal norm is said to come from bitter memories of the Great Starvation in 1878. But with soldiers has come liquor, and, as a consequence, progressively increasing breeches in the village liquor law, especially by some of the young people. The village council has had to step into the situation more than once to impose fines on or otherwise punish village members for procuring beer and selling it to young people, both boys and girls. Moreover, the example of drunkenness set by soldiers is not easily forgotten as an illustration of one aspect of the white man's way of life:

Those first air force boys were welcomed to the villagers around here. Everytime when they done wrong around here, when they come to the village pretty drunk, they restricted them for one week.

And a more recent example of the same behavior:

They do not have trouble at all, when they first getting down here. But last summer when those drunk G.I.'s came down to the village late at night, that is why they made their curfew very short.

Throughout the years that a military post was near the village this issue arose periodically. Characteristically, after each outbreak the council tightened the curfew and severely restricted the hours during which the military were allowed in the village for visiting and buying ivory or skin sewing. In some cases they were banned altogether for a few days. Although sometimes it was unequivocally stated by the council that the ban might be permanent or at least in effect for a long time, it was soon quietly broken and disappeared after a few days—a happening which the villagers themselves came to predict. The pressures from wanting ivory sales and other benefits were apparently too much.

In one case of a broken liquor law which happened during the summer of 1955, the council's principal move in handling the violation was to turn it over to the U.S. marshal on the mainland. This action cogently brought out a tendency that could be seen in many of its other decisions during the year—that of leaning on an outside authority for guidance and direction in matters over which it nominally has control.

Another continual problem is that of sexual relations between the young women of the village and the soldiers, a problem which is in no way ameliorated by the sentiments and behavior of the girls themselves.[19] The council attempts to prevent the unhappinesses which come through this interaction:

> The council had told the girls that they would cut out even the curfew hours for the soldiers to come into the village unless the girls quit fooling around "with the armies." The council had told the girls that these boys would only "push you down low and then leave."

One of the girls admits that "they catch my mind, some of those G.I.'s." Still others echo the same sentiment:

> They said that Rose told him that no matter whether she marries a white man or not, she will *not* marry an Eskimo.

Some of the army officers themselves complain that "if the Eskimo men can't control their women, we can't control our men—and that's 80 per cent of the problem, right there." This is in many ways a justifiable complaint. The older Eskimo men reflect on some of the reasons their daughters are attracted to the soldiers:

> Colin said that some girls want to marry soldiers because they think that the boys are rich and will give them many things, but he said that it is pretty hard for a marriage when the girl doesn't know white people's ways.

And the same informant goes on to say:

> Yes, they want to marry soldiers. Pretty hard, but we try to hold them back when they love those army boys. We says to our girls, "You can't marry that boy, because he is in job; he soldier boy, he can't marry right away, so you can't be married to him." We told them, "You have to go school first, have to learn white people doing, then

---

[19] The displeasure of the council and villagers over the girls' sexual promiscuity with the soldiers should not be interpreted as general conservatism in such matters. Their resistance seems to arise more from the social circumstances under which the relationships occur, such as the fact that they are a defiance of the old people.

you have easy way to marry white people. But if you don't go to school, pretty hard to marry with the white people."

But not all daughters listen:

She hates to have Eskimo home work, she hates that, I think. Hauling meat from the shore to the meat houses. The worst jobs for the woman are scraping the blubber from the mukluk skins and cutting the meat to dry out on the racks. She hates that, I think. She wants to get married to white people. [How did she get that idea about white people?] She used to go around with G.I.'s here on the island, and one of them supposed to marry her, but that guy didn't keep his promise. She learned a lesson, but she didn't mind it. That G.I. promised her that he will come back and marry her and take her back to the States. But he broke promise, and when he got outside he wrote to her and told her that he got too many girls friends that he keep a secret from her during his stay on this island. But she still wanted to marry a white man anyway.

And she did marry a white man. For others, however, the only legacy of ill-advised trysts with soldiers has been an illegitimate child.

This topic cannot be left without mentioning some positive aspects of the interaction between the camp and the village. The military has contributed much to the economic well-being of Gambell. In addition to the ready market for sales of ivory and skin sewing, which has been discussed earlier, the military camp at times has lent movies for village recreation. It has also been a channel through which the villagers could get candy and other luxury items (as articles in exchange for ivory) when their store was empty; military transportation has many times been used to take an ill person to a mainland hospital; considerable fuel oil for heating homes is obtained by draining scrapped army barrels; the army dump provides many articles which are the discards of a modern military institution but are useful in the Eskimo way of life, such as scrap lumber; and most important of all have been the emergency and relief food supplies which, in significant quantities, have been periodic contributions to the village in times of poor hunting. In fact, such has been the picture of abundance displayed by the military camps, and so frequent their generosity, that sentiments of expectation and dependence upon them for needed items have become widespread and common throughout the village. These are reiterated despite much of the other controversy that attends village-military relations:

We sure do appreciate the army.

Then he went on to say that the people in town like "the armies. They always talk kind to us, say kind things."

That lot of help, air force, because all the carved ivory sold to air force. Air force boys pay cash.

[Is the army a good thing for the village?] People over there very nice, all of them. But the only thing I don't like is they can't do much for us. They're under orders, they go by the orders.

For the most part such positive sentiments are not reciprocated by the soldiers (except, such as they may be, by men who associate with the Eskimo girls), but there are times when the military needs the Eskimos, too. Several men have been lost in blizzards during winter operations, and in such cases it is only the local Sivokakmeit who can safely go out in the blinding snow and bring them back. Although the relationship is steadily becoming more and more that of a unilateral dependence—of the Eskimos upon the military—there are still occasions when only an Eskimo with his ancient cultural knowledge can cope with the severities of the geographic situation common to both groups.

Thus the soldiers on the Gambell gravel spit have presented models for acculturation very different from those of the CAA families, a different sort of white reference group; and the entire situation in which culture contact is being carried out is one of increased pressure and much more severe demands upon the restraining cultural structure of Eskimo society. The young people, particularly the girls, are being drawn by what they envision as a far easier and happier life with a white husband. Only a few have found that. Most have found only transient infatuations. The effects of this second wave of models for acculturation have already become quite evident to some of the Sivokakmeit. But it is a double-edged influence. The discouragements arising from broken norms are countered by the benefits of emergency food and some hope of help in time of need.

*Recreation*—Before the coming of the white man, the Sivokakmeit had several modes of recreation. Impromptu games of making funny faces or noises in order to elicit laughter, busying oneself with string figures, and storytelling were all prominent means of entertainment. Especially important, however, were singing and dancing. There were two distinct varieties of the song and dance complex: (1) the "nighttime singing" (*ilaegaek*), which was the pattern of song and supplication performed by the shaman during a seance, and (2) the "daytime singing" (*aetok*), a secular form done purely for enjoyment and good fellowship. For the men, dances were vigorous, muscular sequences; for the women and girls, they were sedate and graceful with the body moving only from above the hips and the arms and hands waving in gesture to the tempo of the song. The songs, each of which was "owned" by a particular individual (in the sense that the words and melody had come to him through a spiritual transaction), could commemorate an event or praise the simplest intuition. A man might sing of his happiness at his son's hunting success or of his deep feelings upon glimpsing the village as he returned from a trap line. One man "said that the happy songs are just like a joke—they are sung to make people laugh and be happy."

In 1940, the singing and dancing, the storytelling, the making of string figures and funny faces were all part of the recreational complex. There were other features also, however, which had been adopted from the white world. Magazines and, to a limited extent, books had come into the village. Card playing was popular, and there was some mainland music—e.g., guitar music and "cowboy songs." In the 1920's one enterprising teacher had imported a series of band instruments for his school classes, and these were the nucleus of the Gambell village band during the 1930's, an institution which apparently enjoyed a few years of popularity and then died away. Occasional parties, sponsored by the village council, were held in the school for the young people, and there were infrequent movies which also were shown under the auspices of the council. (See Figure 8 for a celebration held on July 4 and sponsored by the council.) From all indications, there was little dissatisfaction with the modes of recreational life then enjoyed by the village. The young people, in particular, seemed content in their adjustment to village life.

But by 1955 the picture had profoundly changed. The white man's style of ballroom dancing (called here "Stateside dancing") was learned by some of the young people when they went outside to the mainland for high school. Others learned it at the military camps, and a few at the CAA parties. The council has pre-empted jurisdiction over this aspect of social life (i.e., recreation) as over so many others; and during most of the years since 1940 no Stateside dances were allowed in the village, although more and more of the younger people were learning how to dance in this manner. But a break came during 1953, when the schoolteacher, contravening the established practice, permitted and encouraged Stateside dancing as a recreational pattern in the schoolhouse. According to the accounts, many dancing parties were held during that winter in the school and they were extremely popular, particularly among those young people who had returned to the village from two or three years of high school in southeastern Alaska.

The way of acculturation is seldom smooth, however, and in this case the Stateside dancing was once again prohibited with the coming of a new council and the departure of the teacher in the summer of 1954. What remained, during 1954–1955, was a void— the memory of the last year, when there had been dances, and the keen feeling that little has been done to replace them. This issue was one which, during the entire year, raised persistent and widespread discontent among the Sivokakmeit, most particularly among the young people, who are not learning their native Eskimo dancing and now have no outlet for their newly acquired habits and tastes for the white man's dances. They wonder and remark:

Why won't they let us have Stateside dancing?
Ever since they started having white people's dancing before, that is what the young people around here like.

One girl who had been to high school on the mainland

said that down at Mt. Edgecumbe they used to have parties in the living room of the girls' dormitory and they were able to invite boys. She told me about how much fun it was to go away to school and to live with the girls in the dorm after she got used to it. She said that she had gone with fellows from both Mt. Edgecumbe and Sitka— nobody watched them down there, and nobody talked about them [the girls]. "Now we have to sneak around with our boy friends." She said she sure hopes there will be a party tomorrow night because there isn't anything to do around here.

Some parties were held in the schoolhouse during 1954–1955 in an effort to fill the void in recreation that was felt by all in the village. But, as comes out clearly in these expressed sentiments, they only partially met the need. A young man remarked, half facetiously:

If we were running the village, there would be dances and recreation all the time—a bar in that end of town and a whore house in this end.

Another note refers to a conversation with the same person:

I talked for a few minutes to Alfred. He said that he is going to Savoonga tomorrow. I asked why. He said he is "just going." He wants to be down there on Saturday night for the dance. I asked, "Stateside dancing?" and he said yes. I asked him, "Who sponsors it— the school?" He answered yes, the school, the council, and missionary. Then he said quite vehemently, "What the young people around here are crying for is recreation—any kind." I asked if they would like games, even if they didn't have dancing. He said, *"Anything!"*—a person "can go haywire without anything to do around here." And then he added that "all we get is Eskimo dancing."

As mentioned above, the background for this Stateside dancing was laid through contacts with the military. One woman recalls

that the women of the village used to go out there to dances and that quite a few of the people (males included) used to go there for the air force parties.

During the winter of 1953–1954, the dancing parties might extend into the early morning hours. These parties are described by one of the participants in the following terms:

Margaret noted that they used to have Stateside dancing and that they were very good parties, but now with the new president it has all stopped. She said now the council is against everything. I asked her why, and she replied she guessed that some of the old people think that the young people get into trouble. She went on, "You know, the first time there was dancing was at the New Year's party, which lasted until morning," and she and Ted were the only ones who knew how to dance, and they taught all the others.

And one of the other girls proffers:

I do think it was a good idea. All the girls like it. Most of the girls went, and some grown women did; you know, that is where they learned, most girls. Yes, married and unmarried girls went.

Some movies were shown irregularly throughout the year, and all were heavily attended. Both the school and the church sponsored them (but they were of different types). The showing of movies, like the Stateside dancing, reached its peak during the spring of 1954, when (through the generosity of the local military base) there were several shown each week in the school. Prior to that time the usual pattern had been one each week; but it is said that during the height of this period there was a movie every day. The pattern did not continue. Like the dancing, it was abruptly cut off during the spring, and from a situation of plenty the Gambell people went to one of absence of recreational activities. This harsh and sudden change is perhaps one of the factors behind the strong and determined sentiments about recreation that were expressed the following winter.

Of the forms of recreation found in the 1940 culture, all have continued to the present. Native dancing and singing are still performed (although to a decidedly lesser degree); storytelling, mimicry, and string games and a host of other games of an individual nature are still enjoyed. Important forms of home recreation are looking at and reading magazines and books and playing cards, checkers, and some other games of the latter type. Radio as entertainment is now widespread, particularly listening to the one station on the mainland which broadcasts the "western" or "hillbilly" type of popular music. In line with this, some of the young people own and play guitars and sing popular songs of that type which they have learned.

These forms of recreation do not pose problems for the council. Others, however, likewise learned since 1940, raise issues which the council must face. The white man's style of dancing has already been mentioned. Gambling, as noted before, is done to a considerable extent by some of the young men, especially those who have taken up this form of recreation while in the army or the National Guard. During the research year it was noted that several individuals suffered rather severe financial losses as a result. Although gambling is formally prohibited by village law, the council was not able to stop the practice. Some games of chance have been known in Sivokak culture for a long time—at least as long as the contact with whaling ships. But in 1940 this pattern was not at all prominent in the culture, although it might have occurred occasionally.

Drinking had been known in the Eskimo society in earlier years, but in 1940 was not a problem. The importation and imbibing of liquor were strictly prohibited by village law, and by all accounts there were strong social sanctions supporting this legal norm. But, as brought out in the discussion concerning relations with the military camps, by 1955 the problem had become one of the most difficult for the council to manage. It was one of the several knife edges of the outer mainland society that was cutting into the social system and cleaving old and young.

A cause of the undesirable behavior is revealed in sentiments about the lack of recreation expressed in these words:

That's what the young folks need here—recreation.

Alfred said that the most important thing now is to provide some recreation for the young people. He said that the young people are "like being trapped." They don't have anything to do.

What all the young people need most is recreation—every young people. Even some older folks. [What kind of recreation?] Dancing. That's the recreation they're looking for. Stateside. Schottishes, polkas, and waltzes. There's only a few of us that can jitterbug. [Did you do this last year?] Yeah, all the time, three times a week. . . . I can tell you why people don't like dancing. The old folks thought this would make divorces, jealousies among married couples. Which I doubt very much would happen—because it didn't happen. . . . As far as young folks are concerned, of course they've got the same ideas as I have. They like the church parties, sure, but I still think they'd like to have other kinds of recreation like I mentioned: Stateside dancing. . . . All the young folks up here like dancing. You would see, if I put a sign up on the board, "There will be Stateside dancing on Saturday night," if you would go out and watch from some place, you would see everybody going in. The news would go around like everything: "Dancing tonight." [When was the last dance?] June 30th. That's the last dance—lasted all night. . . . Schottishes, square dances, and polkas, I guess they don't care much [i.e., the council doesn't mind too much]. What they don't like are the waltzes. Those "love-making" dances. They thought, that guy is making a date with somebody else's wife, you know, with slow music. I'm pretty sure next year it will open. [Did any old person think the dancing was a good thing?] I tell you one point I hear from old folks: they thought dancing is pretty good deal. The answer to that is why? because it keeps their daughters indoors and keeps them out of G.I.'s. See, there were no G.I.'s allowed in dancing at all. [Are there any other types of recreation here?] Yes, they like to have that basketball—and those indoor games. Right now they need any kind of recreation, at least once a week.

*Sentiments concerning the council*—That positively oriented sentiments toward the council existed in 1954–1955 is unquestioned; but the great bulk of expressions of sentiment regarding this village organization were decidedly negative. The dissatisfactions arose over many issues. Aside from its policies on recreation, one of the most important was the reported monopolization of official council positions by only one clan, the Aimaramka (half the members were of that *ramka*), and there were many accusations of favoritism shown in policy and economic dealings.

Then I asked him, "Do people like the council?" He said, "No." Then he added, "Four men, one *ramka*, no good. One man from one *ramka*, good."

One informant, pointing up reputed partiality in legal matters, mentioned that in former days a dispute was settled by the outcome of wrestling matches between the strongest men of the disputing clans.

But now they don't do that; now they just call a council meeting in the school and call the guy over there.

He then went on to decry the fact that most of the power in the council is concentrated in one *ramka*.

For other people the existence of the curfew which restricts the military visiting hours in the village is something held against the council and the Welfare Committee:

It's not fair for them committees to put the curfew on. Many of us don't like it.

I get mad at them Welfare Committee sometimes. [Why?] They watch too much. . . . They should watch themselves too. They make mistakes, too.

There are other negative sentiments about purported dogmatism and inactivity of the council in the face of important problems:

You can't tell that president anything.
You know those councils—they won't act. Neither did the last one.

On the occasion of "Joe E. Brown Day," a special village holiday occurring in March,[20] there was no celebration in 1955, which prompted the following outburst by one woman:

Those stupid councils, committees, and presidents—they let it go by for the first time.

But to what extent have sentiments toward the council changed since 1940? Apparently a good deal. Its dominant leader of that date, and for some years before, is still remembered with warm affection:

In 1940, when Dr. Leighton was here, Gambell good living place. Just like brother, everybody. That Atook [the president], good man. Friendly everybody—white man, Eskimo. Everybody.

Another agrees that he was a "very good president" who tried to make the whole village "like brothers." The same informant, pointing to the hundreds of rusting oil drums lying strewn over the Gambell landscape now, contrasts it with the neatness of Gambell years ago when Mr. Atook was president. He recalls that each spring the village president conducted a campaign to get people to clean up their yards and the entire village of the refuse which accumulates in the layers of snow and which, with the coming of the summer sun, piles up on the gravel and grass. Prizes and public prestige were accorded those whose grounds were the cleanest.

One woman mentions the recreation which the president and the council sponsored:

Every week young people and adults used to have parties at the church before the schoolhouse builded. Every week they had parties, big ones; even adults came, and so everybody was happy very often.

[20] This is a holiday which has come into the Sivokak social calendar since 1940. It was started as a yearly commemoration of a visit by Joe E. Brown, the entertainer, who, during the war, was forced to spend a few days on St. Lawrence when his airplane, on a flight in the region, was grounded there by bad weather. His entertaining of the Gambell people, while waiting for departure, was so memorable as to become a village holiday every March 18. In 1955 this day was recognized by the receipt of a telegram of well-wishing from Mr. Brown to the people of Gambell in appreciation of their hospitality.

And a somewhat longer passage gives some indication of the scope of Mr. Atook's activities and the esteem in which he was held:

He was a very happy man. . . . Besides he is full of fun, too. He leading the people around here very well while he was the president. He used to let the 4th of July last for days and days, and other games next days, as he knows more of the old-timer games. When he was president of this village, he invited many people from Savoonga and celebrated 4th. Every night after games he let people see the movies, in the evening. I think he even invited those cutter crewmen, for celebrating 4th of July. I remember when the *Northland* came, they watching the games too. One time I remember those boys are jitterbugs at the front of the school. They brought their electric phonographs and their different kinds of musical instruments, too. One time they had a band at the school porch, those cutter crewmen. There was all kinds of instruments they brought in. Everybody likes him, Atook. He entertains everybody who visited here. He even entertains the people from Siberia, the ones that had lost out of the storm, from Indian Point, and he used to invite them to show every evening until they left back to Indian Point. Everytime when the bomber planes used to come in wintertime [during the early years of the war], Atook used to hire the boys or council men to put the signs down the lake so they can land on the right place on the very smooth place. But he got a rheumatism. One time he was sick so badly of his rheumatism. I used to give him something to eat. Finally one of the bomber planes when they came here took him away to Juneau but he died out there, even though he was taken very good care out there at the hospital. We felt so sorry to hear that he was died. Atook used to have the people around here to clean their yard every summer right after the snow is melted. Yes, I think it was very better councils then. They entertains every stranger people from outside when they visited here. Those new ones, some are kind of mean. The old council wasn't that way, and the new one often find fault now, because most of them are young boys. . . . It didn't used to be that way. The old one didn't punish not so bad. . . . They used to have open parties every week. Even schoolteacher used to invite every young adults for parties.. That was in the days of Atook's being president of this village. There was less trouble. The young people around here are getting tired because of no parties. Those schoolteachers wait on the council now-a-days, and even though they want to make the young people happy, still they wait on the council and don't go over them, what they say. [Was there anybody against Atook?] No, and the schoolteachers used to invite about twice or three times in one month to come the people all around the schoolhouse to listen to the electric phonograph; they take out the big phonograph and play some music, during time Atook was the president. He really tried to make everybody happy.

A final instance of the council's concern for its people was in sending emergency food supplies to Southwest Cape, on the other side of the island, during the winter when a family had been snow-bound for some weeks and was very short of food. The council did this more than once, but one such occasion is vividly related by one of the Southwest Cape people, himself a small boy at the time. He described the arrival of the loaded sleds and of the men whom he had never before seen and then said:

They were the councilmen of the village, and they had heard about our hard time, and they organized and bought things from the store and brought them to us. After they had gone, I asked my parents who these men were. And I learned they were the councils. I thought they were very good men, and I found out what the councils were for the first time.

Whether, in these current years of stress, the council can recapture the note of high promise it inspired in this boy appears debatable. Its environment is now much widened with problems and difficulties thrust upon it with the coming of many more white men to the island.

## *The School*

The school has long been one of the central institutions of the village. Along with the mission, it has provided a certain model of the white world and has contributed to social integration in village life for over fifty years. Since the early history of the school and that of the mission are intertwined—the missionary was also the government teacher in those days—the discussion of the salient features of the school will deal with the later years, after they were formally separated. Separation took place at some point during the decade 1910–1920.

In 1894 a Presbyterian missionary, the Reverend Vene C. Gambell, and his wife came to the Eskimo village on St. Lawrence Island then known as Sivokak and built the first really permanent white-style dwellings in the village.[21] The mission he constructed still stands today and is used as the combined sanctuary and missionary's apartment. Although Mr. Gambell and his family were drowned four years later when they were returning to the island from a vacation, other missionary-teachers soon came to continue the work he began. The influence of one of these men in particular was notable in the early history of the island's contacts with the mainland. Dr. Edgar O. Campbell, a medical missionary, lived in Gambell for some ten years. His influence in the formation of Gambell's co-operative store has been discussed earlier. But his guidance was felt in other areas as well (besides health, for which his medical training was invaluable): the older generation of men now in Gambell village speak good English, in most cases better than many younger men. Dr. Campbell's thorough instruction is given credit for this lasting effect. Some of the teachers who followed him were not so successful.

Throughout the first thirty years of this century a teacher was usually stationed in Gambell, and, less often, a regular missionary. But by about 1930, rarely did a year go by without having a regular teacher. In the two teaching posts on the island, Savoonga and Gambell, a few teachers stayed on for several years, but others were less attracted and quickly departed when their original commitment of one year was fulfilled.

Throughout the 1920's and 1930's the school curriculum included the standard subjects taught in the American classroom: geography, arithmetic, history, reading, writing, spelling, and the rest. For Gambell, too, there were classes in cooking and in sewing (both cloth materials and the sewing of skins) and classes in ivory carving for the boys. Local women and men skilled in their particular crafts taught the latter two ancient arts to the young people.

The academic subjects and craft training mentioned above were broadly, then, the pattern of formal school instruction in 1940. One

[21] Apparently a small cabin or two had been constructed in the preceding decade by whalers who stopped in the village for only the whaling season. Some data indicate that this occurred—but the long-range effect was negligible, and the dwellings soon disappeared, as did the white men who had lived in them. For an interesting account of the Gambells' first experiences on the island, see their posthumously published piece, Gambell, 1900.

of the several extracurricular activities of the students was publishing a small hectographed newspaper containing many items of local interest, such as the annual animal kill, social happenings, births, and so forth. It served as a dispenser of information as well as a recorder of historical events, and through work on this paper some of the young people, particularly the girls, learned typing and other skills valuable in interchange with the white world. The paper is no longer published.

Mention of the school newspaper points up one of the most important aspects of the school in Gambell throughout its entire history. It has already been noted that in traditional Sivokakmeit culture there was no communal village house, no *kazgii* such as those found in practically all Alaskan coastal villages. In the absence of such a communal house in which recreational events were held, in which public affairs were discussed and village political decisions made, in which the young were tutored in the ways of their ancestors, the school has appeared to fulfill some of these social functions.[22] The school would therefore seem to have been one of the positive contributions of the white world to village solidarity, for in the school in 1940 were held parties, occasional movies and native dances, council meetings, and public gatherings of the entire village. There was also, of course, the inculcation of the knowledge and skills needed for life in this newly expanding environment. The schoolhouse served in addition as a communications center for contacts with the mainland, for in it was located the radio transmitting and receiving set owned by the native store. The new school built in 1939 had laundry tubs and machines which were for village use. Furthermore, in 1940 the official post office was located in a schoolroom and the schoolteacher served as postmaster. (In 1946 a separate building was set aside for this purpose, and the new job of postmaster came into the village occupational structure.)

In connection with formal education activities sponsored by the American teachers, it should also be mentioned that during the early 1930's, under the aegis of one of the teachers who had training in

---

[22] In one other area, ritual and ceremonialism, the school now of course has no legitimate jurisdiction, and the mission has taken over this fraction of the complex of behavior formerly carried on in the *kazgii*.

and a bent for mechanics, several large machine tools were brought to Gambell. Even in 1940 the "village machine shop" was a center where many of the men and boys could familiarize themselves with lathes and other sorts of machine equipment. Just how valuable this knowledge was in light of the limited need for such elaborate equipment in the village is another question, but it was a step in the right direction. In 1955, however, the machines stand unused and idle, deteriorating in the machine shop, which is itself falling into disrepair. As reasons for the neglect, present-day Sivokakmeit say that through use the machines gradually broke down and, after the departure of the teacher who had first brought them in, there was no one in the village who knew enough about machine equipment to repair them.

The role of the teacher in Gambell village is not strictly defined, particularly with respect to that of the missionary. In most instances it has been the force of personality and individual conviction which defined it. For many years, for instance, either the missionary and the teacher were the same individual, or there was no missionary and the incumbent teacher might offer Christian services and instruction. But in other cases, the teacher dissociated himself from religious instruction. In recent years, the line between church and state has become more clear, and this poses something of a problem in teacher-missionary relations in the village power structure. The pattern seems to be worked out anew with each change of personnel in these respective roles.[23]

The teacher and the council have a formally supportive relationship. Although for many years the teacher has acted as the unofficial "adviser" to the council, his formal position is only that of government representative on the island and he is not supposed to dictate the council's actions. He interprets and clarifies mainland rules and regulations and points out the consequences of lines of action deliberated by the council. The council, on their part, submits copies of minutes of its meetings for the government files, kept by the teacher. In addition, since 1947 the council has had to bring

[23] For an article discussing the general problem of relations among white people who occupy various roles in isolated arctic communities, see Dunning, 1959.

the store's transactions to the teacher's attention, by reason of membership in the government-sponsored organization, ANICA. It is to the teacher that the council goes if they need to contact a U.S. marshall; for the teacher, as the official representative of the Alaska Native Service, is their link to the centers of political power and police authority on the mainland.

The situation of the school in 1940 may be briefly summarized as follows. For many years it had been teaching those symbolic skills of the white world which were of use in the pattern of mainland contact then current. Arithmetic and the English language were the most important of these skills. The young people of the village could receive eight years of such instruction, and none went outside to the mainland for further education. What they learned prepared them to face the then current conditions of contact. But the school also served in other ways. It was a real community center for recreation, public meetings, and laundry and health facilities, and in these functions, as well as in its central purpose of educating the young, village sentiments strongly supported it.

THE SCHOOL IN 1955

The young people have begun to leave. This statement, more than any other, points to the most erosive change in the educational institutions of the village. It is true that other things have also changed and that in some ways the school is even more of a community center now than before. For example, the school serves a hot lunch each day to the children. The cooking for this is done by local mothers who voluntarily take their turn. In the school also all weddings were held until 1955, when they began to be held in the church, and each December there is an elaborate Christmas program which follows a month after the public Thanksgiving meal, likewise held in the school. The Christmas program features a widespread exchange of gifts. Continuing in its former functions, the school is the place where movies are held during the year, and many of the public native dances are given there, as well as the parties by the teacher. On the other hand, the school's laundry and shower rooms are no longer used, and the dispensary is now located in the nurse's quarters.

But in terms of the most critical of the changes in the school, principal attention must be given to the emigration of the young to the mainland for higher education. In the effects of that lies the future of the village.

Education of itself has become of high value in Sivokakmeit culture, among both the young and the old. One young man remembers his first thoughts about attending school, after having lived in an isolated camp all his life, and reiterates the value of education in his new cultural situation:

Another thing I wanted was to learn how to read and write. Mostly, how to talk English. But I had to have some school to learn any of these, and there was no school of any kind in our camp. We would have to get our schooling in the village, and I wasn't sure I wanted to be in the village. I was used to camp life. I didn't want to be with too many strange people, even my own age. Besides, I didn't know if I would like it in school. But if I wanted to learn, I must have some schooling; and my parents wanted me to learn, too, because they know themselves it's real hard if we don't learn those three: reading, writing, and speaking English.

A village leader advises his son:

"You should have your education. Full. So you could get a job to earn money for your future family." That's the only thing I can say to him: education.

On another occasion the same man remarked that "the young people now think that with education they can get jobs and make money." The sentiments of an older man are recorded as follows in the field notes:

He said that he sees that the young people are going to school and learning things, learning skills with which to get a job. I asked if he meant Mt. Edgecumbe. He said, "No, at this school too" [in the village]. He said that sometime—"I don't know when"—this village "will be like you," with people having jobs instead of hunting. "No more boat hunting; maybe mining or something. Or people may move away from the island to look for jobs."

But the remarks of some of the young people themselves are even more revealing as instances of the fundamental reorientation which has come about in the culture. Education is not now being sought as an ancillary tool used by an Eskimo in coping with the white world; it has become a goal which will transform that Eskimo existence itself into something which it has not been heretofore. The strength of this new desire for schooling is seen in the following excerpts:

He said that he certainly missed his chance by not . . . going to school.
She wished she had gone to school when she had the chance.
He said that he wants to go out to school, but his father needs him at home.
She liked school very much and was especially interested in home economics. She said vehemently that she wants to get away from Gambell and make some money.
"But the big mistake I made was to go hunting so much. I have to quit school to go hunting."
He said a couple of times that he wishes he had more education. He won't make this mistake with the children—this is the reason he is already putting away money for their education.

Two of the older men comment on some of the effects they think will come from the increased education of the young. One is optimistic about what this will do for the village; the other sees the ultimate disappearance of the village through emigration to the mainland in search of work:

[Do the older people want to leave for the mainland?] No, we never hear the older people say that. Just young people. [Because they've been to the Mt. Edgecumbe school?] First move down to school outside, then job out there, and stay out there. I think most people do like that. Looking for job; don't want to go out hunting.
[What has been the biggest change since Dr. Leighton was here?] Maybe school. Maybe Mt. Edgecumbe school. Maybe when schoolboys come back, council maybe change, by and by. And storekeeper change. And post office change, with the schoolboys—everything change, maybe.

In each case, the village, through the education of the young, is seen to undergo profound change.

For many of the young people the motivation to go or return to school springs as much from the entirely new and different pattern of behavior open to them there—in contrast with the village and its restrictive norms based on kinship, age, and social position—as from a desire for learning. There is in the outside world an enhancement of individual choice and an exaltation of personal desire to an extent never dreamed of in their native village. This comes out both in the sentiments expressed by the young people themselves about life on the mainland when they attend school and in the sentiments expressed by the older villagers on the same subject. In many respects, the latter have fears about the moral damage being done to their youth even while economic advantage is being acquired.

Gambell's school offers instruction through eight grades. Although relatively few of the young people finish the curriculum (and of those who finish, there are more girls than boys), enough have been completing it in the last fifteen years so that they are qualified for Indian Bureau high schools on the mainland. The first Gambell person to go to the mainland went, in 1941, to the high school for western Alaska located near Nome. After the war, when a naval base in southeastern Alaska was turned over to the ANS for development into a school, the Mt. Edgecumbe high school at Sitka began accepting students. In short order there were some young people from Gambell. By March of 1955 there were eight currently attending the high school and another thirteen young people of the village who had attended. Many spent two or even three or four years away from home.[24]

As of 1955, one person from Gambell had gone on to higher education; she had received college training in the mainland United States and was employed on the ANS teaching staff in interior Alaska. There were rumors that one or two other young people were planning to continue with their education after leaving the high school.

But it is not just the government high schools which compete for the chance to educate the Gambell young people. In the first years after the war a religious denomination, the Seventh-Day Adventists, sponsored several youths, mostly girls, at their own high school on the Alaskan mainland, and one of these girls even spent some time in the state of Washington attending a religious college.

More than a score of the young people have been away from their village and their relatives and friends for a year or more. During this time they received instruction in many things new to them. But they also were exposed to contending beliefs and practices and

[24] It happened rather frequently that a young person would leave Gambell to attend a high school, but when he received a physical examination prior to entering school, he was found to have tuberculosis and was hospitalized for a year or two before being able to start school.

to people of cultures different from their own. They found many new types of recreation and stimulating new freedom to enjoy things forbidden at home. At the same time they also knew periods of loneliness when a face from home or the sound of their distinctive Sivokakmeit language would have been very welcome. What most of them found and what few indeed could verbalize was a new path of life, a new set of meanings, of goals, of priorities in behavior. They found the need for and utility of money, seemingly the bedrock of the mainland world. Only a few of them realized that they were being educated not for life in the village from which they had come, but for life on the mainland, away from relatives, friends, and cultural context, that context which is yet a constituent part of their personalities.

Caught thus between two cultural systems, some of the young people disappoint their elders by their behavior. They are cut off from their most significant moral community, and the $200 one-way airplane fare puts an insuperable obstacle in the way of their coming home each summer to renew ties with their native culture. Usually finding work in the fish canneries or some other industry of southeastern Alaska, they further compound, by that work experience, the acculturative influences to which they have been persistently exposed during the entire winter. Most of the young people, in fact, are not able to return home until they graduate from the high school, usually from two to four years after they enter. And this occurs during some of the most important of their formative years. The consequences, in terms of deviant behavior, of this effective insulation from their native culture and native social roles are often quite disruptive when the young people return to the village, as some have done.

One of the elderly men, in the context of discussing the drinking and gambling that was occurring in the village, mentioned that young people learn this when they go outside to school. He sagely commented: "The bad things they learn quick; the good things come slow."

The theme of the independence and self-assertiveness of the young is also repeatedly mentioned:

The children are too independent now. That condition is gotten from the mainland. Most of the boy or girl that has been student in Mt. Edgecumbe have too much of experience. And they always influence others to do the same.

Two of the younger leaders see the effects of the mainland schooling in the following ways:

And this school business—look at all the young people going to school at Mt. Edgecumbe. That has changed since Dr. Leighton in 1940. [What sort of effects does this have in the village?] The way most of us people think right now, this going to school is going to change everything. Soon those young men and women that goes to school at Mt. Edgecumbe will get a job and come out here with a job. [Will they get a job in the village?] Most of them right now are trying to get experience in one trade in school. [What trades do they teach?] The boys are learning bookkeeping and post-office work. And some of them are learning diesel and mechanics. The girls themselves are learning to be cooks and nurses. That's one thing they go to school for—to learn little bit of medical work. . . . That is a pretty good idea. [Are most of the old people happy about the schooling?] Most of the older people don't think it's good yet—they think they go outside to school and learn to drink.

Before the kids started going to school to Mt. Edgecumbe, they were good children. If you tell them to go, they would mind, you know; but after they go to school a year or two, when they come home, they became different person. Yeah, they became different person altogether. They think they get pretty smart, after being out in school. And they call the people on the island "dumb people." And they want to be tops. When someone tells them something, they tell them to "go to hell." That's one trouble that they invite to themselves. People on the island aren't dumb. When people leave the island for a year and watch civilizations somewhere, they think they're smart, and come home. They get stuck up and everything. They think that the people they left, their own people, are little people now. They think they're wise and smart. . . . They get away with things outside. When they get home, they think they can get away with things. But everyone's talking about it. That's one change; a big change. I don't know if going out to schooling is doing any good for the children. . . . I always think that if the kids go to school from here, they should let them go ahead and finish college—work their way through college, or something. And then release them to come home; they would be different people. To me, if the kids are halfway educated, he is a worse person than he would be before he got to school—much worse. Halfway-educated person always think they're smart, you know. It'll make them a lot of trouble—sticking their necks too far out, something like that. Without learning warning from experience and from older people. Like I say, working with older people, you can learn a lot of things, things you can't get in school.

The latter statement epitomizes the divisions found in many parts of the world between the young who leave for the larger society outside and the old folks who remain behind. Yet the acuity of this young man's perceptions about the effects of a partial exposure to education is very striking.

So the problem continues. The young are being educated away from their native culture. But they are not fully prepared in many vital respects for life on the mainland. And then many return to their village and find there social rules and cultural meanings now become strange to them.

## The Church

The Reverend Vene C. Gambell and Dr. Edgar O. Campbell, particularly the latter, established the first foothold of Christianity on the island. Dr. Campbell was in Sivokak from 1901 to 1911, and during this time many people were converted to the new religion. Some of his work, his problems, and his inspirations may be seen in the following extract from his diary (taken from notes recorded by the Leightons in 1940). He records in the entry for February 26, 1904:

Sixty-seven at service, an unusually large attendance, the average being 50–55. Glad to see the girls and young women. Had a good talk with some young men after service, then Alfred came in to share with me his trouble; his family do not care to listen when he tries to talk about God. His cousin . . . told him he should not change his religion, for soon Dr. Campbell would leave and go back to America, then he would have no one to teach him. After showing him some passages in his Bible, which he had left with me last week to mark for him, and praying with him, he seemed much happier and thanked me most heartily. He said there were so many hard words in the Bible, he could not understand what he read. I told him he was improving rapidly, and he would soon learn and that Jesus would help him. Now I should like to recall and record some of the recent incidents that have caused us to rejoice, and renew our prayer, increase our faith and works. One Thursday night after Bible class, Floyd came into our sitting room and burst out crying because he said he did not want to go to hell. Last week he came to me crying because others persecuted him on account of his inquiries about Jesus' way and the questions about rites and ceremonies now practiced by the people here. He said he had gone off behind the deer shed and prayed. Benjamin told me once last year when they could not find the deer herd they prayed and soon found them. Alfred said he was very tired the other day as he was returning from hunting, dragging a seal on the rough ice, so he asked Jesus to help him and he soon came to some young ice, quite smooth, so the pulling was easy. And when he got home he did not give the seal water as the heathen do. His mother and wife asked him why, and he told them he was going to try the other way. . . . Helen's face was a picture of soul hunger, as we talked together. . . . She said she did not understand the Jesus way and when I went to see her little sick daughter, she tried to get her co-wife's baby boy to perform for me by marching, while she sang "Trusting in the Lord Thy God, Onward Go, Onward Go." Cora said she wanted to learn but was bashful about coming to the services because there were so few women and so many men.

After Dr. Campbell left in 1911, there was a series of missionaries, of whom none stayed for very long. Many of the Gambell people converted in the earlier time returned to their native religion. By the 1920's only one or two men were still practicing and believing Christians. As noted earlier, a few of the teachers offered instruction in the Bible and in Christian subjects during the years when there was no missionary stationed in Gambell. But their work did little to prevent the wholesale return to the ancient religion of the island with its close attentiveness to the animal world.

During the early 1930's, however, a general return to the Presbyterian denomination began to appear. It was centered first in a few men, who banded together into a prayer group and requested a missionary to come to their island once again. In the early years of that decade the missionary came, Miss Ann Bannan, and she remained for ten years in the village. It was she who was the Christian representative in 1940, when the village was about evenly split between those who professed and practiced Presbyterianism and those who adhered to the *chkwaek* (the boat captain's ceremony), the *aliginalre* (the shaman who cured the sick and predicted the future), and the multifold customs of showing hospitality and respect to the animals one must slay in order to live, all of which were parts of the Sivokakmeit religious system.

In 1940 the church offered a variety of services comparable to the standard denominational program on the mainland. The regular Sunday worship was supplemented by various Sunday-school classes, and prayer meetings and sessions of women's and men's groups were held during the week. (In the church service itself men and women were segregated in their seating. It is important to note this in 1940, because by 1955 the pattern has been broken down and families sit together.)

Many of the Eskimo adherents were probably still much committed to native systems of religious belief, for they had changed back and forth a number of times in their formal affiliation. But they took a considerable part in the church activity. There was a board of elders, for instance, and a group of deacons and trustees. In addition, a few people were sufficiently versed in the Bible and things Christian that they led services when no missionary was in the village. Relations between the Christians and those who still adhered to Eskimo religion were not strained, according to available information. The village was so tightly bound by the profound ties of kinship reciprocity and the rest of the environing common culture that this religious aberration did not seriously disrupt village integration.[25]

## THE CHURCH IN 1955

By 1955 the most important change in the religious institution has been that of the virtually complete conversion of the village to Presbyterianism. There is some evidence that this occurred in the summer of 1941; attendance records of that year note an abrupt and startling rise occurring in August, from an average weekly attendance of 108 to an average of 175 for the remaining months of the year. In addition, it was said that a minister on a special trip to the island baptized many of the people at one time and then left. The information seemed to indicate that this happened during the sojourn of Miss Bannan (who left in 1942), but, characteristically, Sivokak informants could not give an exact date. Now only two men

[25] For instance, although a few of the Christians objected to the native dancing, the greater part of them still enjoyed it and saw nothing unchristian in it; so the recreational life went on relatively undisturbed by the religious conversions. It is true, however, that the missionaries had been responsible for stopping the ancient Eskimo pattern of dancing with practically no clothes on.

do not profess Christianity, far too few to celebrate a boat captain's ceremony or the ritual following the killing of a whale.

The church organization remains much the same as in 1940. Since that year there have been three different missionaries filling the post, and this service was continuous except for the years 1950–1952, when the Eskimo elders themselves had to manage the church and its activities. As for lay organization, the board of elders consists of six individuals (an election in 1955 placed two women on the board, the first time women have served), and there are six deacons and deaconesses (equally divided between men and women) and six trustees (all men). These posts are filled by congregational election. In addition, there are officers (president, vice-president, secretary) of a women's society and a youth and young people's organization. A final group in the church organization are the ushers, each of whom serves for two months during the year.

The formal activities of the mission are modeled after the Presbyterian church of the white mainland.[26] The Sunday worship service with its invocation, responsive readings, scriptures, hymns, sermon (which is translated into the Eskimo language), prayers, offerings, and communion; the Sunday-school classes; the Wednesday evening prayer meeting; the Thursday afternoon women's prayer circle; the various men's prayer circles; the adult and the junior choirs; the reading room containing religious and other types of magazines—all these features are patterned after the mainland Presbyterian church. Another example of this dependence on the outside for behavior models is seen in the "youth camp" which was held during the summer of 1953 at one of the camping sites on the island. Quite a few young people attended the week of religious devotions and instructions.

Highlights of the year's religious calendar are the Thanksgiving,

---

[26] This is not the place to discuss aspects of Christian belief and how it has interpenetrated the more basic Eskimo religious system. In many individuals it has apparently established itself very deeply; in others, it is more insulated, existing side by side with practices stemming from a more ancient mode of coping with the problems of existence, problems for which the Christian theology neither offers explicit statement nor yet specifically condemns. This entire subject of religious belief systems and ceremonialism deserves a separate treatment, and the church will here be examined only in terms of its institutional aspects, except where illustrations of belief come in tangentially.

Christmas, and Easter services. The Christmas program has always been of great importance in Sivokak, for both its religious and its general recreational value. There has usually been a tableau or program of some nature, followed by gift exchange among all the families and the receipt of a Christmas bag of toys and clothing given by the mission. Everyone wears their best apparel, and often this is new clothing. The young men, in particular, now wear National Guard or army uniforms for this special occasion (a strikingly clear symbolic indication of affiliation with mainland power and prestige). Many people send mail orders out weeks in advance to have a new dress or suit for their child (see Figure 9). In general it would seem that the Christmas program, with its special sacred and ritual character plus the exchange of gifts, is a functional analogue to some of the aboriginal religious ceremonials, in which one of the central features was the exchange of gifts.

What Christmas meant to a young boy growing up in an Eskimo camp during the years from 1940 to 1955 is vividly described in the following passage:

When I first know the Christmas I was about 3. It didn't mean anything else to me than receiving good things, and it comes once a year, and you can guess it was a happy time. I wished that it comes more than once a year. David and I often shared our toys that we get at Christmas, and our sisters shared theirs. What a good time we had for a while. Sometime after this they showed me where the Christmas is on the calendar. When I wanted some toys, candy, and popcorn I counted the months or days before Christmas, and if it is far away it made me cry and wish the days would go faster; and I would then forget about it when some excitement happened. When I remember the Christmas again I counted the days again. Boy! It was only a few days away. And my father and my older cousins or one of the uncles would get ready to make a trip to the village. If the weather became stormy a few days before, it made me sad again. And when it's good my father and his brothers brought a box of good things for each family and, besides, the box from the mission. Things they get by trading fox furs from the store. I believe it's the happiest time of every year I get until now. It brings me happiness one way or the other.

In another passage the same young man describes his sentiments concerning the Christmas program in the mission:

The next day it was December 25th. I and Dad talk to my teacher if he wish let me go back to camp. He said that he wished to keep me in school long but will let me go if I want to go badly. I do. Dad says we will go but I'll have to come back for the boxes of things I get and the box from the mission, which we were to get that evening. There was Christmas service in the church. The church was very beautifully decorated. There was program too but entirely different from the school program. I was in a singing group and had a verse to read with the other Sunday-school children. I feel very much like I did in the school program but I was little better. There was nativity scene acted by some adult people. I don't understand what that means much, but I know it have very deep meaning and it was very strange but very beautiful to me. I thought that those that were acting it were very important persons chosen for the scene, and if I ever grow up I'll be actor for the nativity too. The choir sound real good indeed. I thought there were no songs so good as those carols. All was over too soon. It passed so quickly. The packages were passed around; after the packages came the mission boxes. The boxes I always longed for before. I learned how we get it from our church but still don't know where they come from. This was all fun, but not so much as I have in the school program, but I thought it was far more beautiful and I feel happier too in some way that my words can't tell.

Practically all the village comes to the Christmas and Easter services. As many as 250 people crowd themselves into the church sanctuary for these events. At the regular Sunday services throughout the year considerably fewer attend.

Average weekly attendance at church during 1954 was 125 people,[27] but this fluctuated from month to month, ranging from 93 to 158. Much of this variation is caused by summer trips to camps and time spent away from the village on other subsistence activities. As an instance of the general pattern of fluctuation in church attendance occurring since the apogee of 1941, the average weekly attendance

Table 17. Average weekly attendance at church, 1950–1954

| Year | Attendance |
|------|-----------|
| 1950 . . . . . . . | 116 |
| 1951 . . . . . . . | 79 |
| 1952 . . . . . . . | 92 |
| 1953 . . . . . . . | 98 |
| 1954 . . . . . . . | 125 |

[27] These figures on church attendance are supplied through the kindness of the Reverend Lowell Campbell, Presbyterian missionary in Gambell during the time of the study.

figures for the past five years are given in Table 17. Unfortunately, no figures are available for the years 1941–1950.

How deeply the epidemic of measles in 1953 struck is shown to some extent in the monthly attendance figures for that year (recall Chapter IV). During September the weekly average was 114, and in October it climbed to 142. But in November, with the widespread sickness, the average weekly church attendance was only 46 people.

Some of the other activities of the church are also interesting insofar as they give an idea of the scope with which it enters people's lives in Gambell. For the year 1954, for instance, the average attendance at midweek prayer meeting was 88; that at the junior Sunday school, 62; at the adult Sunday school, 80; at the youth and young adults' meetings, 30. Although there is an overlap in these figures in the sense that some people attend multiple meetings, the figures help illustrate the extent to which the church serves as an organizing center for much of the village life.

The mission has caused dissensions and is the object of some negative sentiments now. But it, the school, and the village council have been the major village-wide integrative institutions in the history of the Sivokakmeit. That these institutions have failed in many respects to dislodge the power conflicts among the various clans is perhaps understandable, in view of the strength of the kinship bond in this society; what is remarkable is the extent to which they have succeeded in injecting themselves into the ongoing social system. This observation complements that of the previous section, in which the school was discussed as a partial functional equivalent to the *kazgii* on the mainland—the community house, the religious arena, the meeting hall.

At the same time, however, it must be noted that, in the fifteen-year time span which is the center of interest here, the curve of religious participation as indexed by attendance has risen precipitously and then fallen almost to its former level. Whereas in 1936 the average weekly attendance was 93 and in 1939 it was 83, in 1951 it was only 79 and by 1954 had risen to 125. But in the meantime, in the last months of 1941 and the first quarter of 1942, the attendance rose to the astonishing figure of 172 weekly. The abrupt rise may have been the immediate result of the mass conversion mentioned before; it may also have been one effect of World War II and the Japanese invasion of the Aleutian Islands in the spring of 1942. In any case, there soon followed a gradual leveling off to an average attendance slightly higher than had prevailed before. Nonetheless, despite this absence of a marked increase in attendance at the church, the Christian influence has decidedly prevailed, and the aboriginal religion is no longer a potent influence in the public life of the village.

Aside from its religious functions, the church's mundane activities are important from the point of view of village acculturation. Thus it attempts to fill some of the recreational needs by sponsoring a "social hour" each week during which movies or photographic slides are shown; it has sponsored such events as a craft fair and bake sales; in recent years it has given a layette of white-style baby clothes to each newborn infant; in former years clothing from the mission boxes were given freely to needy people (now, however, it is sold at an annual rummage sale); and, finally, cooking classes have recently been offered under the sponsorship of the mission. Both the mission and the school are extremely important in the sentiments of the Sivokakmeit as models of that land of abundance which is the white world, and the fact that both of them are thought to be profusely supplied with the materials of life by an unseen outside agency contributes much to fostering this impression of wealth.

Something of the power relations existing between the mission and the school has already been indicated. At the present time each recognizes the other's legitimate sphere of authority and attempts to work with, rather than against, the other. This has not always characterized the relations between church and state, however. As is noted below, the relatively sharper distinction that is now drawn arises from interaction between some of the teachers and missionaries in years since 1940.

The mission is important in the power structure of the village. During the recent difficulties with the military posts, the mission has been an influential means of liaison between the camps and the village. Because of his position as a responsible official of the village, the missionary has been able to represent certain village points of view to the military commanders and, in turn, to interpret certain of the military actions to the village council and the villagers. The mission and the council are formally separate organizations, of course, but in so small a village power connections obviously exist between the two bodies. The overlapping of particular individuals in different roles—"interlocking directorships"—exists here with regard to at least one leader who is both a church elder and a council member. In addition, the mission board is free at any time to attend council meetings and bring mutual problems to its attention. On some occasions, competition for power comes up between the elders of the church and the town council. In a couple of instances in recent years issues have arisen on which the elders felt that they had a presumptive voice in a particular matter and have expressed it, sometimes disagreeing with the council. Such problems as drinking, white-style dancing, and even the showing of movies and holding of native dances are issues on which the elders have spoken. In the case of the first two they are in agreement with the council, but there is discord on the latter.

In their part in governing behavior, the elders and other officers of the church can bring to bear on cases of moral turpitude the sanctions of congregational censure and ostracism. This happens for persistent failure to attend services or for consistent immoral or otherwise "unchristian" behavior. At times during the year a list was posted on the church bulletin board indicating those of the congregation who were being eliminated from the church rolls for various such reasons. (There was, incidentally, no striking evidence to indicate that such public exposure was very effective.)

In general, the mission is strongly supported on most issues by the village. The questions of religious conversion are no longer vital, and the mission has established itself firmly in the power and cultural structure of the village. The important feature of the situation now is that it is being assessed on grounds other than those strictly religious. And on these grounds, negative sentiments of diverse types were aroused during the research year. On the problem of recreation for the young people, for instance, it shared in the blame directed toward the council, although it was not as much implicated as was the council in the lack of recreational facilities, particularly white-style dancing, in the village. This is perhaps one of the reasons lying behind the relatively low intensity of support for the mission by the young people as compared to that given by the older Sivokakmeit.

Perhaps more than any other issue during the year, the question of food shortage and the part played by the mission in this problem prompted the most negative sentiments. Although contributions to village welfare were made and encouraged by the mission during the year (for example, it paid for some of the ammunition used in an emergency communal sea-lion hunt during the early fall, when the shortage of meat was imminent), rumors persistently arose about the obstacles being put by mission influences in the path of obtaining emergency help. Such rumors led to the exasperated comment by one man that the mission's "business is religion—that's all!" Further, the newer policies of more strict mission allotment of supplies were compared to the relatively freer distribution which had been practiced under Miss Bannan and others for so many years; and the newer policies are found wanting. By many people the mission is felt to be "stingy" with regard to food and clothing in time of need, and this contradicts what is still one of the most fundamental of Sivokakmeit sentiments.

## THE SEVENTH-DAY ADVENTISTS

Until the last ten years Gambell was not bothered by the conflicts of the differing religious ideologies of the white mainland. Although a few King Island Catholic Eskimos lived on the island for a year or two during the late 1920's, they had no lasting influence, and for the Sivokakmeit the white man's religion effectively was Presbyterianism. During the late 1940's a situation developed in which the Gambell people somewhat painfully found that numerous fine distinctions exist in the white world and that making a decision simply to change from Eskimo religion is not enough. Now one must also decide which type of white man's religion is most true—for all have announced themselves as the only true faith. The effects of this development have been to leave a minority group somewhat isolated socially in Gambell.

The Seventh-Day Adventists denomination acquired an entry into Gambell through the schoolteachers who, themselves of that faith, taught religious classes to some of the young people, particularly girls, during the early 1940's. Their teachings were so effective that more than a dozen girls renounced their Presbyterian faith and declared themselves Seventh-Day Adventists. Some adults in the village were also converted; and in a couple of years the small Seventh-Day Adventist religious community placed a request for a missionary to come and serve them. During the summers of 1947, 1948, and 1949 missionaries of that denomination came to the island, lived in tents, and baptized and administered to their converts. When the missionaries first came, they wanted to construct a church in the village, but the council did not allow this. Its deliberations regarding the matter are contained in the following minutes:

September 1, 1947: A letter from superintendent of S.D.A. is read by the secretary, who request to put up a church at the village of Gambell beside the present church. The council discussed over them and decided to reject it according to their regulation which said, "It is not permissible to put up any kind of building by the outsiders." The council decided to write back to him. Later a letter was written and prepared to mail it.

There is strong evidence that the council was not unaware of the Presbyterian mission's view on the subject.

The Seventh-Day Adventist missionaries were sufficiently effective to induce several young people to leave the island for attendance at denominational high schools or for work in one of their hospitals on the Alaskan mainland. But the congregation in the village did not swell beyond a few families, even though an active religious and social program was offered to both young and old. Since the denomination had no permanent minister in the village, the congregation began to dwindle. For several years prior to 1955 there was no personal contact between the remnants of the congregation and a missionary of that faith, and many of the former members have "backslid," as people said, to their Presbyterian faith. The few remaining are religiously isolated, the inheritors of the white man's religious factionalism. (In a few cases the religious division had even split families.) The coming and the going of this denomination have left scars—although these, with the passage of recent years, have become more and more hidden in the midst of the many others that have been made in the village since 1940. Now this religious issue is probably one of the relatively less important questions in dividing segments of the village from one another:

[Are any people in the village against the Seventh-Day Adventists?] They used to fight them very often, but not now. They hated them, they treated them just like an alien, but every time when those persons need help, Seventh-Day Adventists willingly help them; in so doing they became friendly.

One cannot help comparing this situation with that of 1940, when the only division was a muted one between native Eskimo and converted Eskimo and religious strife was at a minimum. With the white man's religious solace came also his religious enmities.[28]

## Other Institutions

There are other areas in which the social relationships of the Sivokakmeit have been altered since 1940, and these can be briefly noted. They constitute further indications of the ways in which Gambell is becoming inextricably linked with the white mainland.

One of the most important of these has been the military experiences of the Gambell people themselves—a slightly different, though related, matter from that of the influences of the military bases on village life. Gambell experienced the war between Japan and the United States in two ways. On the one hand, nine or ten of the village young men went into the army, one even getting as far away from St. Lawrence Island as Okinawa; and in the village itself there was a local home guard unit similar to other units formed all over Alaska. The Alaska Territorial Guard comprised all the able-bodied men of the village, and its duties were to patrol and guard the village. Particularly during the first year of the war (1942), when there was a very real threat of invasion by the Japanese, the ATG was most active. As noted previously, in May of that year the entire village was evacuated to the other side of the mountain because of a supposed impending invasion, and for about a month the ATG members guarded the village while their families lived in tents and the few hunting cabins located some miles away. Members of the unit had uniforms, consisting of distinctive shoulder patches which identified them as militia members, and rifles and ammunition were provided. The schoolteacher was the officer in command of the unit. It was through service in this group that many of the younger men learned their first military drill, which they were to repeat in the organization set up after the ATG was disbanded at the end of the war. The later organization was the National Guard.

[28] Correspondence with people in Gambell since 1955 indicates that the Seventh-Day Adventists have now acquired a building to use as a church. The long-range effects of this step toward revitalization of the sect should be of interest.

There is a National Guard unit in Gambell, and another platoon of the Guard is located in Savoonga. The two make up the St. Lawrence Island company. The strength of the Gambell platoon ranges between 10 and 20 men, and all clans in the village are represented in the membership. There is no grouping of leadership and control in the hands of any particular clan or extended family group. Motivation for joining the Guard comes from several sources, ranging from the small income for the several meetings a month to the prestige felt from affiliation with so powerful a segment of the white world. Membership in the unit has not been very stable. Several of the young men of the village have belonged to it at one time, but, upon a further physical examination, have been rejected because of tuberculosis. (It might be mentioned in this connection that several of the Gambell men who were called by Selective Service during the war were rejected for physical reasons and that 4 others who were accepted were later hospitalized for several years each, 3 of them because of tuberculosis which subsequently developed, or at least was later detected. For these, of course, the debilitation has meant that they receive a monthly disability check from the government.)

Membership in the National Guard continues a line of influence begun with participation in the armed forces during the war, which was one of the most potent suasions for culture change among the young men. Indications of this can easily be seen in village life, the most obvious of which is the wearing of National Guard and army-type clothing. Another involves language patterns. One of the really effective pressures toward culture change that has come about through belonging to the Guard is the requirement that all meetings and operations be carried on in the English language. Orders, books, and instructional materials are all printed in English, and the standing order is that oral use of English is also mandatory. For some of the younger men, who have not attained a fluency in English through their schooling, this mode of acculturation seems to be a very important one.

In the annual encampments of the Guard, which in recent years have been held on the mainland of Alaska, many of the young Sivokakmeit have had their first chance to see the mainland culture. At the same time, these encampments provide another instance of the interruption by the white culture of the traditional seasonal round of autochthonous Eskimo culture, as the following excerpt illustrates. One man said about the encampments:

Little bit bother me, that encampment. I'm pretty poor National Guard! I want to go down to camp early, down to my own camp. I just waiting for September 1st—after encampment over there in Nome, then I move down to my place!

But the orders establishing dates for the encampment are inexorable, not being concerned with the coming of seals or the harvest of birds from the cliffs.

For a few of the Sivokakmeit, membership in the National Guard has meant even further travels. Several have been sent out to technical schools, either in the mainland of Alaska or even further south in the United States. Such extended visits have further strengthened their knowledge of and influence by the white world, in which they have already had some experience through membership in the local National Guard unit.

Another organization which has arisen in the village because of the progressively closer dependence of Gambell on the white world with its problems is the civil defense organization and its closely linked subsidiary, the ground observer corps (sponsored by the air force).[29] The civil defense organization came into being in the summer of 1954 and has a director, an assistant director, and four committeemen, all appointed officers. Although the director and assistant director were clan relatives, the others on the committee came from several different clans. The main duties of the organization are to organize the village for defense purposes, and in line with this an evacuation plan has been drawn up under which the village would act in the event of war. Earlier it was noted that the civil defense director helped in obtaining relief food supplies for the village in the winter of 1954–1955, when the dogs were dying and people were short of food. During the year the ground observer corps had a voluntary membership of approximately 50 men, drawn from the entire village. Each took his turn manning the observation tower and scanning the foggy skies for aircraft.

The Alaska Native Brotherhood and an affiliated complementary organization, the Alaska Native Sisterhood, are both found in Gam-

[29] The corps has since been abolished.

bell, although neither is very active. The Native Brotherhood is an Alaska-wide organization of Indians and Eskimos instituted for social and political purposes (see Fey, 1955). In Gambell, there were few indications of its viability or activities, and it is probably existent in name only. The Alaska Native Sisterhood, on the other hand, has a slate of officers (president, vice-president, secretary), with members drawn from several clans, and is responsible for arranging the cooks who provide the lunches for school children. It also has occasional social teas for its members. In all, however, it is not a crucial village organization, having really few active members and limited functions.

One or two other indications of the incorporation of mainland activities and interests into the Gambell social system can be only briefly mentioned here. Gambell people vote in territorial (now state and national) elections; and for this operation there are three election commissioners, appointed officers whose function is to supervise the voting and counting of ballots. The post office, as noted above, came into separate existence in 1946. Finally, the Public Welfare Office has a representative in Gambell whose duty it is to investigate cases of announced need and report on them to his Nome headquarters, which acts on the applications. More than a score of cases receive monthly checks for one purpose or another. The intrusion of welfare agencies into Gambell is another change since 1940, although as noted before it is a change not so much in facilities as in the perception and use of existing facilities. Many more people have begun to make application for one purpose or another, a part, perhaps, of their increased probing of the larger environment provided by much widened perceptions and awareness of the white world.

## Summary

One pervasive theme runs through the preceding discussion of changes in Sivokakmeit social organization. This need be brought out but briefly by way of summary here, since it will be discussed at greater length in the next chapter.

The progressive adoption of institutional forms from the white mainland has been noted, along with a growing dependence on that outside world for models of social behavior. It is not simply a dependence on the mainland for material things, as was brought out in the preceding chapter. It is an increasing psychocultural dependence. This had its beginnings prior to 1940, with the introduction of the village council as a sociopolitical integrative institution. In addition, the store, the mission, and the school were alien institutions which had been established in village life. However, all four—council, store, mission, and school—fitted into the general scheme of social relationships without drastically altering it. They all tended to be appendices to a still basically Eskimo social system.

Since 1940, however, the long-range effects of all these alien institutions has been much more felt, and others have also entered the scene. The formal conversion of the entire village to Christianity, for example; the army units and the military experience of the young men; the going away to high school on the mainland; the increased direct interpersonal contact with white people, in the village and even within the home—all these have worked to bring about a looking to the mainland rather than to Sivokakmeit elders and the cultural past as models for behavior in the present day.

Another facet of the wave of change, and this will with time no doubt basically reshape the nature of the social system in Gambell, is the seemingly inexorable movement away from primarily a kinship basis for social relationships to one in which more widely applicable criteria are brought to bear in structuring the interpersonal behavior. This can be seen not only in the operation of the village council and the mission, but also in the rise in the number of voluntary associations in the village—the ground observer corps, the National Guard, the Alaska Native Sisterhood, and the like. But it can be seen most cogently in changes in the kinship system itself, particularly the rebellion of young people and the dampening of patriclan loyalties in favor of the generalized social category, "fellow Gambell villager." Even the distinction between "Eskimo" and "white," heretofore of some ethnocentric importance in relations with the outside, is threatened by these widespread avenues of cultural attrition.

It is true that the kinship system and patterns of behavior found in the patriclans are still very strong. But the old order is being steadily fractionated and the social alignments characteristic of 1940 are being undermined at their base—the youth whose role it is to perpetuate received cultural forms. Sketched in today's uneasy sentiments of the old people about the way the young are behaving are new sets of standards and goals, those which order the interpersonal relationships and institutions in that world outside the bounds of the island.

# CHAPTER VII

# The Xenophiles

SOCIOCULTURAL data have been presented which bear on the matter of change in patterns of behavior and thought in Gambell village over the fifteen-year period from 1940 to 1955. Such data were gathered, systematized, and discussed with a view to answering particular questions—what are the main features of the changes and what factors brought them about?

In Chapter II, reference was made to studies done in small, village-level human groups concerning the effects of technological change, and a descriptive generalization drawn by Leighton and Smith from several of those accounts was noted (see p. 30). For the most part, this descriptive generalization applies equally well to the story of recent sociocultural change in Gambell village, and it will be helpful here to restate the four parts of their generalization, together with instances of its applicability.[1]

The first pattern which they noted was a

trend away from an economic system that was primarily self-contained and independent, toward a cash economy with dependence on a larger social group such as the state or the nation.

[1] For a report on another Eskimo village in the modern world which has been affected by many of the same types of influences and has responded in many ways similar to Gambell, see VanStone, 1958b.

*339*

It is very clear that such a trend has occurred in Gambell between 1940 and 1955. Not only is it seen in the lessened use of native methods of hunting and indigenous artifacts—food, clothing, housing. It is also shown in the far greater dependence, both in practice and in aspiration toward practice, on jobs and the acquisition of cash income at the same time that the hunting complex is being threatened through frustrated expectations and the imposition of new standards of adequacy. The newly formed use of welfare assistance and other forms of "unearned income" also illustrates the change. Perhaps the most cogent evidence for the greater material dependence on the mainland is found in the marked increase in the store's inventory and sales over the fifteen years. Although the Gambell people are still largely self-dependent for food, their reliance on the mainland for other supplies has greatly increased. Even with their relative self-subsistence, however, dependence on the outside world in matters of food and survival was dramatically illustrated several times during the period, when relief supplies were flown in from the mainland to assist the famine-stricken population.

The second pattern found was a

similar shift in governmental and political affairs from relative local autonomy to dependence on higher authority in the larger social group.

Shifts of this type can be seen on both a general and a particular level. In terms of change in the form of specific institutions, e.g., that of marriage and the family, norms have changed from those of inherited tradition to those dictated by legal traditions of the mainland. Now, by contrast with 1940, a formal license to wed must be obtained and divorce must be legally accomplished. Again, reference to outside standards is being made. The same shift can be seen in the fact that Gambell people have now begun to vote in mainland elections and are subject to tax laws in a manner which was not at all true of 1940.

World War II was responsible for the beginning of a greater political dependence of Gambell on the mainland and a relative loss of the autonomy that had prevailed for so long a time prior to that. First the coming of soldiers to the village, then the Civil Aeronautics and Weather Bureau establishments, and finally the air force and the army bases—these all brought with them many more problems for the village council to solve and a need for negotiation between the council and outside centers of political power. Moreover, the types and numbers of problems with which the council had to deal during this time manifoldly increased, and the kinds of considerations brought to bear on the decisions reached were not limited, as they had been before, to those relevant only to Gambell as an Eskimo village on an isolated island. Now there were as well problems of national security and governmental procedure which at times were decisive influences on the course of action that the council could choose.

The matter of governmental and political control is part of the broad problem of self-management and autonomous control of one's actions. Such control implies and necessitates a knowledge of conditions relevant to action. In the fifteen years under study here, there has been a decrease in the amount of knowledge which local people have of the many factors of importance to them. There may also have been an increase in the extent to which white people are consulted for advice and guidance in the making of decisions; at least there are considerably more items needing explanation now. This can be seen, for example, in matters relating to the managing of the store and in completing requisitions and interpreting bureaucratic directives. Other examples are found in the filling out of income tax papers, welfare applications, and orders to mail-order houses; in clarification of the meaning of governmental circulars; and even in the performance of many local operations and the solving of problems of the village council itself. The last was succinctly illustrated by two cases within a year's time (happening in 1954–1955), on both of which the council called in the United States marshal, the first time in many years that this appeal to outside authority had occurred. In each case, the reason advanced by local people for calling in the marshal was that he would make the decisions that had to be made. It was noted, for instance, that "she thought the marshal is coming out here to straighten it out." A young woman said, "I would call the marshal and have him come out to the village and pick up those people and have him talk to them." And a man on the council itself said that the marshal "will tell us what to do." This tendency to renunciation of self-government and decision making is perhaps in the long run one of the most crucial indicators of dependence on the mainland.

There has also been evidence for the third pattern discussed by Leighton and Smith—

changes in values, ideologies, and social usages which, although they constitute a break with the traditional and are increasingly influenced by outside forces, are not altogether in harmony with the economic and governmental trends noted above, or consistent with each other within a given community.

It is generally this type of change which forms the most important focus of the present chapter and will be discussed at length shortly —i.e., a change in the system of belief with relation to the mainland and including a change in the definition of self.

The fourth pattern noted by Leighton and Smith is

progressive secularization of life, with an increasingly sharp line drawn between religious and other human activities such as work, governing, and recreation.

Here it will be mentioned only that this, too, has occurred in the present case. The relevant discussion will be found in the following chapter (pp. 380–381).

Although the descriptive generalization which Leighton and Smith have discussed holds true equally for Gambell village and for the several villages mentioned in their article, there is a further note that can be added with respect to the pattern of change in this Eskimo village which perhaps was not so true elsewhere. This is the marked inconstancy, instability, and lack of predictability in some of the most important need areas of the phenomenal world of the Sivokakmeit over the fifteen years. Beginning with birth and death; extending through sickness and its treatment; through the proceeds of the hunt, of wagework, of fox trapping, of monetary income from other means; through interpersonal relations with the soldiers and airmen stationed nearby; through community regulations with respect to outsiders; through types of recreation to be allowed in the village—in none of these areas was there a relatively dependable or predictable recurrence of processes during the period under study. All were in flux to some extent, and some were in extreme change, as illustrated by the sudden coming of sickness and epidemics to the village. It was not so much the fact that sicknesses came—for these are considered man's lot—but the unforewarned time of their coming. The stresses which are induced by this basic instability of many types of experience enter into the discussion of changes in the system of belief in the present chapter.

As noted above, it is the third pattern which Leighton and Smith discuss, that of changes in values, ideologies, and beliefs, with which I am most directly concerned in this chapter. More particularly, of crucial importance have been changes in the sentiments and values relating the Sivokakmeit to the mainland of Alaska. Such a change as this has had and will continue to have profound effects on the nature of St. Lawrence Island Eskimo society as well as personality; for it has involved a shift in *self-definition*. To put it simply, in 1940 Gambell was still an Eskimo village living according to fundamentally Eskimo life modes and sustaining sentiments and values derived from an Eskimo cultural past, not being seriously buffeted by contradictory or alternative ways of life. The people were Sivokakmeit, and without reservation they accepted such a definition of themselves. It was true that they were aware of the fact of being American citizens, but this affiliation did not enter into the personality in anything more than a very peripheral way. Furthermore, the white world was clearly accepted in 1940; for more than 80 years it had been a source of technological and material items desired in this Eskimo socioculture. But it was, by and large, merely used as a source of supplies which entered into what was basically an Eskimo social and cultural system.

At the same time, a satisfied ethnocentrism seemed to prevail in the village. This was manifested not only in the clearly expressed sentiments of people which were oriented toward support of their way of life, but also in extremely pervasive patterns of cohesion both in the kinship groups and in the actions of the village council, which directed village activities along a wide front and overwhelmingly received village support (see Hughes, 1953, chap. xi). The village as an object of sentiment formation is illustrated in the following excerpt from the 1940 field notes, and this statement sums up the modal orientation and quality of sentiments toward the mainland which are found in the 1940 notes. In it is brought out very clearly the acceptance of outsiders on a basis of "assimilation" to oneself, rather than of "projection" to the outsider's standards (Barnett, 1953; also Berreman, 1955):

You know, I think because the village is so small, people had to be acquainted from their ancestors, so we the children are almost like friends together. Then when I grow up to be a man I have in mind I would be friends to anyone whoever I met. So only feelings I have when a foreigner comes around and asks me to do something for him, I would call him as friend.

The relationship of the mainland to the island in 1940 was therefore an assimilated and contributory one. Influences of the white world were worked into what was basically an Eskimo cultural context. This was as much true of the tenuously embraced Christian religion, the village council, and the school—new idea systems that had been accepted—as it was of the material artifacts that were employed in the hunt or used in the home.

In the present day, however, the emphasis on being Eskimos has begun to pale, and personal identification is increasingly drawn toward the prevailing alternative model—that of the white man of the mainland, the citizen of the United States who has a steady job, owns a house full of furniture and electrical gadgets, drives an automobile or pickup truck, belongs to a Christian church, votes in elections, and is accepted by white people as an equal. One can say, therefore, simplifying matters only slightly, that in 1940 the fundamental "reference group" or reference culture of the Sivokakmeit was their own tradition which had maintained itself as a distinct cultural system and absorbed only very circumscribed aspects of mainland culture. But by 1955 the dominant culture, that from which critical standards for many areas of life are being derived and by which behavior is judged, is that of the mainland world of the white man. This acceptance of what was formerly an alien tradition has involved a redefinition of the situation such that mainland criteria are felt to be appropriate for use by the Gambell people in judging themselves.

A critical aspect of that redefinition has been a new and enlarged conception of personal identity, a pervasive shift in the entire context of comparison. It is as if the "figure" and "ground" have completely shifted, with the mainland now serving as the ground against which Eskimo belief and practice have to be fitted and in many cases changed. The nature of the change that has occurred can be further briefly summarized by saying that now there tends to be an apotheosis of the mainland, with its standards and criteria of choice increasingly coming to displace those of traditional Sivokak culture. The mainland has changed, that is to say, from being a contributing, utilitarian culture to being the dominant reference culture for the Gambell people (see Hughes, 1957a, 1958b).

It is useful in tracing this shift to employ some of the concepts and propositions developed in connection with the "reference group theory" of recent sociopsychological and sociological literature. It may be noted in this respect, however, that the concept of "reference group" seems to be, in many ways, a new application of the concept of culture (see Hughes, 1957a); for the important thing about reference group hypotheses and conceptions centers not on the groups per se or on any aspect of societal structure, but solely on the group as carrier or exemplifier of particular norms, orientations, and definitions of the situation. In fact, the tendency in the literature is away from use of the term "group," and one sees such terms as "reference norm" or "standard" used instead (Merton, 1957). However that may be, insofar as the questions asked in "reference group theory" concern the particular criteria of choice by which a person is judging his or other people's behavior in a specific instance—that is to say, the *appropriate and relevant* standards of evaluation in a particular situation—they take us into the heart of the change that has occurred in Gambell in the past fifteen years.

The profile of the white world that is drawn by sentiments toward it now represent it as being characterized by power, material abundance, skill, cleverness, health, cleanliness, long life, enjoyment, excitement, individual freedom, and, above all, stability and security. To share in these, which are conceived to be the good things of life, is now becoming the dominant motivational concern for most Sivokakmeit, especially but by no means exclusively the young people. If this means leaving the island, they are prepared to do so. Thus one of the most able leaders of the village, an active and skilled hunter who at the same time has mastered as well as anyone in the village a number of the necessary social techniques of the mainland, remarks:

What makes the people want to move away is only the reason of the hunting situation. It is getting very, very scarce—the hunting. Even though there might be more animals than we thought of, the weather is getting worse and worse, every year. Yeah, actually harder; much harder. I'm pretty sure most of the parents like myself want to rather move, where there can be more better life, you see, for their children especially. Of course, I'm using my own idea. I don't mean to get rich or get lot of money; no, not that. I mean to have my children's better future life.

The central theme in this cluster of sentiments toward the white world might be characterized by the phrase "a psychology of the bright new world." Another writer two generations ago put it a bit differently, but his concept was the same: "a revolution of rising expectations." The motivational and perceptual complex here is probably very similar to that often held by immigrants to the United States during the last century and in its fundamental elements is also very likely to be crucial in the massive social movements which today are convulsing former colonial worlds in Africa, South America, and Asia.[2] It is a change in men's minds, as much as—or much more than—a change in their "objective" conditions of life.

Such a profound change in self-definition with regard to the mainland as has begun to occur in Sivokak therefore demands at least an attempt at explanation. How did such change come about? What factors in the life situation might be involved? Why did it happen in the last fifteen years and not before?

## A Proposition

In his case study of one of the relocation camps into which civilians of Japanese descent from the west coast of the United States were placed during World War II, Leighton suggests a number of "principles" governing human behavior (1946, pt. II). These principles are, in effect, broad hypotheses. Pointing out that they were derived both from the particular case study of individuals and groups under stress and from propositions and ideas suggested in social science literature, the author notes that these should be further extended, modified, revised, or rejected through application to other masses of empirical data. Such research might be a highly structured

[2] In this connection, note the recent book by Hadley Cantril, *The Politics of Despair.*

operation which takes place within a small scope in order to contribute evidence for or against accepting these broad, general propositions. Or it might be research focused at the same level of "first approximation" in propositions governing human behavior, as is this report concerning the St. Lawrence Island Eskimo.

One of the principles that Leighton discusses bears directly on the problem at hand—that of a changing complex of sentiments, or "system of belief." The phrase "system of belief" is used to refer to a constellation or configuration of sentiments centered on a particular object or class of objects, held by most members of a group, and generally resistant to change (although under some conditions they can be altered). Because there are many sentiments and ideas secondarily related to the fundamental sentiments or values of a group and dependent upon these root notions by either logical implication or some symbolic or metaphorical tie, the entire cluster is called a "system of belief" to emphasize its interconnected qualities.[3] One way of looking at the core of what many anthropologists call "culture" is to see it as the several most crucial systems of belief of a society, relating to subsistence, family life and kinship, religious organization, political structure, and so forth. Linton would probably call these "cultural orientations" (1936, chap. xxv).

In discussing systems of belief, Leighton states:

The things which alter the systems of belief that people hold are:
a. Observation of fact and reasoned thinking.
b. Contact with other systems of belief.
c. All types of stress.
d. New opportunities for achieving security and satisfying aspirations. [1946, p. 314]

There are several ways in which the shift in sentiments toward the white world may be considered a shift in a system of belief. First, insofar as one of the most general functions of the culture of any group is to define the relation of that group to out-groups and to place the outside world on a scale of acceptability and worthiness with respect to one's own group, a shift in sentiments about the mainland

---

[3] A "system of belief" is formally defined by Leighton as "those sentiments which are socially shared and relatively resistant to change, but including, interconnected with and shading into a wide variety of other sentiments, complex and simple" (1946, p. 386).

represents such a shift in an important sector of culture or system of belief.

Secondly, it is a constellation of sentiments which has changed, not just a few of them. Accepting some fundamentally new points of view toward the white mainland has resulted in accepting many others which follow in train upon that first breakthrough. An example of this is the acceptance of the money standard, which almost necessarily means wanting a steady job, and this in turn implies emigration from the island to the mainland where jobs are to be found.[4]

There is an even more important reason to consider that there has been change in the system of belief about the white world. In the minds of many Sivokakmeit, the boundaries of the "in-group" have merged with those of what was formerly the "out-group" of 1940. This factor of permeability of boundary of the cultural system is generally regarded as a critical area in defining the process of acculturation (see Social Science Research Council Seminar, 1954).

In terms of these considerations the proposition mentioned above is applicable and relevant to the St. Lawrence materials. Indeed, the four sets of conditions assumed to be involved in changing a given system of belief have, in fact, borne down upon Gambell since 1940. One may therefore assume that the St. Lawrence Island materials offer corroborative evidence toward accepting the general principle, if certain modifications suggested by the data are taken into account.

The proposition will now be examined in more detail, with each aspect given attention separately.

OBSERVATION OF FACT AND REASONED THINKING

The first category of process which it is asserted will change a system of belief has to do with man's capacity for assessing the worth of one object, one process, and one situation over another. This is to say nothing of the nature of the premises—whether based on momentary goals or persistent and long-range ends, for instance. In some areas of life more than others in Gambell the cognitive process

---

[4] Sentiments constituting a system of belief are roughly equivalent in their function and their systemic qualities to Parsons' "ultimate value-attitudes" (Parsons, 1949) and Kluckhohn's "value-orientations" (Kluckhohn, 1951).

suggested here has occurred in the last fifteen years, even as it has occurred with penetrating insight in Eskimo culture for several thousand years. In a utilitarian sense of the optimization of means-ends behavioral sequences, there has been much in the empirical situation since 1940 which would provide incentive for change based on reason. In technology, for instance, there is little question that the greater efficiency of outboard motors (over paddling), of rifles and ammunition (over harpoons and lances), of steel carpentry tools (over ivory or slate) is seen to make life easier. It is not only in the tools of the chase but also in other things—such as heating one's house with fuel oil, wearing white man's ready-made clothing, eating his canned and preserved food, traveling on his aircraft to the mainland, taking his medicines and being cured in his hospitals—that the observation of greater efficiency or ease of use of the mainland culture exhibits itself. This appears in fact to be a major trend reversed in only rare instances.

But the latter do occur, and they should be noted. For example, as remarked previously, in 1940 there was far greater use than now of the wooden whaleboats originally acquired from whaling ships some years ago. The wooden boats are more seaworthy than the walrus-hide covered *angyak*, but they are heavier—requiring a larger crew—and more easily damaged in the ice floes. At the present time they are rarely used for hunting, the stated reason being that they are now considered much less efficient for the general hunting and transportation needs of the people.

A further note must be added from the outsider's point of view. Although the mainland culture is more efficient and in a real sense unquestionably makes life easier in many ways, it is often a false measure of efficiency. Only occasionally is this recognized by the St. Lawrence people themselves. They may say, for instance, that they are lazy now, throwing away seal blubber that might heat a house and using instead the expensive fuel oil which must be imported, or that they realize they are colder when wearing cloth-fabric clothing in the village or out on the hunt, but that it takes more work to prepare skin clothing and to care for it properly. In other matters they are perhaps not so cognizant of the long-range effects of choosing the easier alternative. This is particularly true in diet, which with its general lack of balance is seriously contributing to undermining resistance to the many diseases people are exposed to in these days of greater contact with the mainland.

One might also note in passing that the range of experiences of the Gambell people from which to make observations and reasoned inferences about the mainland culture is fairly restricted. Only certain segments of the outside world have impinged upon them. This is true not only of the people who have remained in the village, but also of most of those sent out to high school or hospital. Even for the latter there is usually only a limited chance to see some of the less desirable aspects of life on the mainland or the effects of a highly competitive social situation on those who are not properly qualified by training or skill for coping successfully with such a context. This is not to deny that some Sivokakmeit have apparently made successful adjustments to living outside or to deny that some have been exposed to a fuller spectrum of conditions in the white world than have others. Men who served in the armed forces fall in the former category, as do the few who have worked on the mainland in various capacities. But the great bulk of emigrants have lived on the mainland in favored circumstances (boarding school or hospital), and their perceptions of what life is like for most people on the mainland are perhaps overly colored by their experience. What has been shown to them is the power, the efficiency, the abundance, the wealth of the white world; and from these situations they have made their inferences about its general life conditions and have been led to its apotheosis.

If we may speak for a moment in somewhat more general terms, the same type of reasoning processes has been brought to bear on the acquisition of some of the basic wants in life, aside from those of technological detail, for instance. Insofar as the Gambell people, like people anywhere, want a steady food supply, sufficient warmth in their homes, health of body, enjoyment of recreation, and friendship of their fellows and insofar as they have drawn the conclusion from their contacts with mainland culture that these things are there to be had in abundant supply, many have been predisposed toward accepting the major life modes of that culture. In other words, it is a reasonable change of evaluation on their part, in view of the premises. Among the most vocal of the converted are the young, who have been most exposed and have then returned to the village, there to diffuse the new conceptions with all the force that interpersonal contact has in such culture transmission.[5] But that reason of itself is not sufficient to effect such a change of belief, and that it usually must work in conjunction with other factors is a topic that will require more discussion.

CONTACT WITH OTHER SYSTEMS OF BELIEF

To a considerable extent I have already sketched in some of the major features of contact with other systems of belief that have been experienced by Gambell people since 1940. Such contact has occurred mainly in the context of interpersonal relations, although nonpersonal types of acquaintance—e.g., schooling—have also been important.

That there has been, since 1940, much-increased contact in many forms with the mainland is one of the readiest of conclusions from examining the data of change. In the early 1940's only a few vessels came each spring or summer, and only three or four white people permanently lived in the village. But by 1955 there had been several hundred different individuals of the white world who visited the island itself and remained on at least a semipermanent basis. Moreover, some of this contact, e.g., that with the CAA, occurred under extremely favorable circumstances—in the homes. Other types of contact occurred in the village under conditions of impromptu friendship and mutual interest; and still other forms took place on the ice floes in situations of mutual help and at least overt equality.

In social science literature there are other hypotheses which are relevant to the patterns of interaction that occurred between the CAA people and the villagers. Williams, for instance (1947, p. 67), notes that

in intergroup relations, as in many others, the "propaganda of the deed" is especially likely to have effects upon attitudes and behavior.

Some of the strongest statements of positive sentiments which the Eskimo made regarding the CAA people referred to their help in

[5] In this connection, note a relevant proposition which is taken from the literature on intergroup relationships and modes of influence: "In intergroup relations, as in many others, word-of-mouth propaganda, especially that which appears spontaneous and informal, is more effective than visual or formal propaganda in influencing attitudes and behavior" (Williams, 1947, p. 66).

numerous instances, as when someone was lost or—in one case—a couple of children were buried under a snowslide. In less dramatic cases, the help of the white people in pulling boats up the beach after a day of hunting was also warmly remembered.

In another proposition, Williams notes that

lessened hostility will result from arranging intergroup collaboration on the basis of personal association of individuals as functional equals, on a common task jointly accepted as worthwhile. [*Ibid.*, p. 69]

A third relevant proposition states that

personal contacts between members of different groups are generally most effective in producing friendly relations when the individuals are of the same, or nearly the same, economic and social status and share similar interests and tastes. [*Ibid.*]

I have indicated that there obviously was not complete equality of status or in many cases overlap of interests between the CAA people and the Eskimos. But compared to most culture-contact situations, there was a striking amount of interaction of this type, with the St. Lawrence people intelligent and eager to learn about mechanical equipment, for instance, and the CAA people apparently tolerant, friendly, and helpful. Out on the ice floes, when some of the white men went along for the hunt, the technological skills were reversed; but in each instance representatives of both groups were working together at tasks in which they had joint interests, and it was by and large on a level of mutual respect.

With reference to this point Homans also hypothesizes that

the more frequently persons interact with one another, the more alike in some respects both their activities and their sentiments tend to become. [1951, p. 120]

A second relevant hypothesis is that

the more frequently persons interact with one another, the stronger their sentiments of friendship for one another are apt to be. [*Ibid.*, p. 133]

Although seemingly true in this case, Homans himself makes it clear that these particular two hypotheses must be seriously qualified by stating some of the sociopsychological conditions under which the contact is occurring. The necessity to bring in the qualifying context is particularly important here, for unquestionably there is as much contact between the village and the military base as there was between the village and the CAA. But the qualities of the interaction are very different and do not invariably lead to increased sentiments of friendship.

Relations with the military tended to be exploitative, in a personal and transitory way, on both sides. Some of this orientation may have come from the fact that the military did not need the Eskimos for the success of their task (which had been the case for the CAA). Contact with the military, beside being of a quality different from that with the CAA, also brings in another dimension which has been of importance—sheer frequency (as opposed to what we might call the intensity of the contact with the CAA and the few white people in the village in 1940). Practically every day since they have been near the village—six years—at least some soldiers or airmen were in the village, serving, whether they realized it or not, as models for many sentiments Gambell people were acquiring about the mainland.

One feature of recent contact situations is of considerable interest in pointing to some of the other mechanisms by means of which propensities toward change in sentiments were built up and compounded over the fifteen years. This feature is the "similarity of status attributes," to use the concept of Merton and Kitt (1950, p. 61). Those authors discuss the importance of likenesses in aspects of various statuses in the context of "reference group theory." In attempting to account for shifting standards of evaluation and justification in a group, they frame the hypothesis that "some similarity in status attributes between the individual and the reference group must be perceived or imagined, in order for comparison to occur at all." If the sermon is to be effective, a black man, for example, must somehow feel that he has a soul even as the white man who preaches to him about the necessity to take steps to save that soul by changing to the Christian religion.

What have been the means by which the Gambell people have been led to perceive sufficient similarities between themselves and people on the mainland such that they might conceivably adopt the central sentiments of the latter as being equally applicable to themselves? [6]

The means have been several. From the early years of United States suzerainty over the island, the St. Lawrence people have had held up to them the fact they are American citizens, and they have received instruction in language and other skills in an "American school," have saluted the flag of the United States, learned its pledge of allegiance, and celebrated its national holidays. Likewise, from the early years large numbers of them have intermittently been affiliated with the religious institutions of the mainland and have been included within the bond not only of national brotherhood, but also of the "universal brotherhood" proclaimed by the church and (more important) presented by white men.

With regard to these two features there was, then, a formal similarity in status attributes between Gambell people and the mainland for at least some thirty years prior to 1940. Since that time, however, there appears to have been a compounding of such status similarities on the basis of these minimal identities, such that now several more sets of experience have come on the scene to reinforce the sense of likeness.

On the one hand, the emphasis on being "Americans" has significantly increased, particularly during the postwar years of ideological conflict with the Soviet Union. The sense of sharp difference from ethnic relatives living across the 38 miles of water on the Siberian shore is underwritten at every opportunity. Propaganda from the radio and other mass media helps maintain such sentiments of Americanism. Although the sense of difference was present in 1940, it was not as sharp or as determined as now.

Furthermore, in terms of clear indices of increasingly similar "status attributes," Gambell people are entitled to vote (in territorial, now state and national, elections) and are subject to tax laws and other mainland legal sanctions, such as the insistence on monogamy.

The church has expanded its formal membership since 1940, spreading more thoroughly throughout the group its sense of a

---

[6] For a short statement of the use of reference group concepts in analyzing sociocultural change in Gambell, see my article "Reference Group Concepts in the Study of a Changing Eskimo Culture."

spiritual union with the mainland and the continental United States. Gambell people are aware that they participate in such widespread celebrations as the "World Day of Prayer" and that their congregation—being only a few miles from the international date line—is the last Presbyterian congregation to offer prayers on that day. The fact that one or two representatives attended church conferences on the mainland also underlines this sense of spiritual similarity.

Aside from the contacts with other systems of belief that have come to Gambell in the form of CAA and soldiers since 1940, there have been large numbers of Gambell people who have left the island and experienced contact on the mainland itself. And out on the mainland, school and hospital experiences have contributed their share in helping erase perceptual distinctions between Sivokakmeit and mainland people, as have some of the job experiences local men have had. The occasional opportunity to work side by side with white men (as in Nome, for instance) has been influential in inducing a sentiment of likeness.

Without question one of the most potent influences of this nature has been the military experience of Gambell people. The several men who had years in the armed forces during the war found that it was not the fact that they were Eskimos which was important in their contribution. Rather, it was that they were Americans.[7] Those who served in the home guard also did so with the realization that they were participating in a much wider conflict the extent of which went far beyond their island and which involved them only insofar as it involved American citizens. In addition, those who have served in the local National Guard unit in recent years well realize the many pressures to conform to a standardized—mainland—type of behavior. In this connection another of the Merton and Kitt hypotheses is relevant:

[In some cases] it is the institutional definitions of the social structure which may focus the attention of members of a group or occupants of a social status upon certain *common* reference groups. [1950, pp. 64–65]

---

[7] However, at least one of the Gambell men found that he was able to make a far better adjustment than did the white soldiers to the arctic conditions under which he had to fight when he was in the Aleutian campaign. His native background of contending with cold stood him well, and he said that he even wore his mukluks at times.

The mandatory order to speak English in all military operations of the National Guard is an extremely clear example of the proposition. In this case, therefore, the similarity in status attributes extends far deeper than the similarity in uniform.

In connection with the matter of contact with the outside world, some of the other "reference group hypotheses" discussed by Merton and Kitt (1950) are pertinent, i.e., those concerning what they call "anticipatory socialization." They hypothesize that "for the individual who adopts the values of a group to which he aspires but does not belong, this orientation may serve the twin functions of aiding his rise into that group and of easing his adjustment after he has become part of it" (p. 87); that "it appears . . . that anticipatory socialization is functional for the individual only within a relatively open social structure providing for mobility. . . . By the same token, the same pattern of anticipatory socialization would be dysfunctional for the individual in a relatively closed social structure, where he would not find acceptance by the group to which he aspires and would probably lose acceptance, because of his out-group orientation, by the group to which he belongs" (p. 88); and, finally, that "although anticipatory socialization may be functional for the *individual* in an open social system, it is apparently dysfunctional for the solidarity of the *group* or *stratum* to which he belongs" (p. 89). In short, an individual is trained for life elsewhere.

The experiences of many of the Gambell young people strongly support these propositions. Domestic jobs in the CAA homes, for instance, prepared several of the young girls for working and living on the mainland away from their own people. For the boys, the National Guard or army experience has functioned in a similar way. The mainland social structure can be described as quite open and tolerant compared to many which are the hosts for native groups around the world. For the Eskimo individual identifying with the mainland as a "reference culture," his anticipatory socialization can indeed be functional—under propitious conditions of sufficient education and skill. The only difficulty in the present case occurs when an individual identifies with the mainland culture and is "anticipatorily socialized" to it, yet cannot fully participate in it. This is the situation of several young people in Gambell, who for various reasons cannot leave the island for the mainland. Their deviant behavior (deviant to the elders) is the cause of considerable estrangement. This estrangement is the gist of the third hypothesis quoted above. To the extent that the young people do identify with models other than their elders, the collective sentiments of the group are disrupted and the anticipatory socialization is, in fact, "dysfunctional" for the solidarity of the Eskimo group. Perhaps most crucial in this respect are the drastically shifting standards of expectation which many girls have as to desirable marriage partners and their role as wives and daughters-in-law in an Eskimo (or white) household. Such tensions in human relations arising from divergence of views are also relevant to the discussion of stressful conditions in the life of the Gambell people (see below).

Before the third aspect of the general proposition under consideration here is taken up, discussion of the contact situation must be completed by mentioning the concomitant diminution of support of the older culture forms, which (in the absence of a nativistic movement) has lessened with the death of the old people since 1940. Two-thirds of the people who, fifteen years ago, were the "unique intermediary between the present and the past" have gone from the social environment in Gambell village. The knowledge, sentiments, and beliefs of the past have become progressively vitiated with the death of the older people; for, with the characteristic feature of all human life, each succeeding generation accomplishes new cultural syntheses from its transactions with an environment. The dynamic nature of man's imagination, his culture, and his social life means that no generation will ever exactly reproduce the cultural forms of its predecessor even under the most stable external conditions. The point of view has long since passed from anthropological thinking that "primitive," isolated cultures are arrested instances of various stages of cultural development. Change, even within the most isolated system, is seen to exist, although its rapidity and the pervasiveness of its effects may considerably vary. So, change inevitably occurring— be it only a slow and gradual diminution of past cultural forms in the face of a not too radically changed cultural and environmental situation—how much more profound will be the nature of the change when there is an intensive confrontation with different systems of belief while at the same time the most effective proponents of the older way, the elders, are steadily disappearing.

ALL TYPES OF STRESS

Running throughout Chapters III–VI is an account of change. Change of itself is not necessarily always stressful, but in many of the instances recorded above it would appear to be; for they were accomplished with such great rapidity that a gradual period of adjustment to them was not possible. The sudden loss of the reindeer herd is a good example of this type of change from a previous pattern.

But another type of change that produces stress and tensions is not sudden. Rather, it is prolonged—and in this very prolongation lie its stressful qualities.[8] I refer to the changing patterns of interpersonal expectation and obligation appropriate to certain statuses in the social system. The young people, for instance, who persistently throw in the face of their elders defiance of the old way are examples of this type of "stressor agent."

There have been many other types of stresses as well. The sheer deprivation of food and other basic wants is a stressful situation for the human organism, and such deprivation has occurred repeatedly during the fifteen-year time unit. Several bad hunting seasons have brought years of food scarcity and concern; the theretofore reliable reindeer herd is gone; the store is often empty of mainland food. In these years there has been nothing to do but go on a famine diet or try to obtain food from the mainland through welfare or similar agencies. In addition, stressful conditions have arisen out of the fact that a new set of wants has been adopted from the mainland which require money for satisfying them and yet there has been a concomitant irregularity and inadequacy of the monetary income of the village. The persistent search by some people for money to buy even a few gallons of fuel oil for their stoves during the coldest part of the winter vividly illustrated this point.

Illness has always been a problem directly causing considerable personal unhappiness and contributing to general social ineptitude. Over the fifteen years exceedingly high levels of morbidity and mortality have done their share to compound the general feelings

[8] In a recent study, Margaret Mead (1956) provides an example of a society which, by changing rapidly and in a wholesale manner, is said to have averted the disorganizing trends so often found in slow change elsewhere.

of insecurity and anxiety. The fact that here the rates of sickness and of death resulting from sickness are extremely high says a good deal about the realistic basis for the considerable anxiety over health in this group. There have also been stresses arising from practices of hospitalization. Not only are there the uncertainties and anxieties attendant on seeing a loved one go perhaps several hundred miles away with no assurance of his return and no way of visiting him during a prolonged period of hospitalization; there is also great concern over the loss of subsistence support at the beginning of hospitalization, before welfare assistance begins to come to the family, as well as afterward when it has stopped.

It should be clearly noted that in some cases these aforementioned types of stressful conditions are not new to the Sivokakmeit. For example, there has always been concern over the food supply, and poor health has no doubt been a persistent feature of their life situation for as long as Eskimo groups have lived in these regions. But it does seem that the fifteen years under study have been unusual in the striking confluence of many different types of stressful conditions in this small segment of time. What is even more crucial is the fact that although the stresses themselves might not be "objectively" new the standards of deprivation against which they are now being measured are different from traditional standards. The Sivokakmeit, that is to say, appear now to suffer as much or more from "relative deprivation" ( Merton and Kitt, 1950, pp. 45–46) as from the "objective" deprivation of good health, clothing, or food. I will not, by this statement, inadvertently deny the reality of malnutrition or drafty clothing in the group. But the inevitable marks of shifting standards of adequacy can be clearly seen in the turning away from the old cultural forms and in the dissatisfactions and disparagements expressed with regard to designs for living which were such a short time ago accepted as fully adequate. Perhaps the most vivid illustration of this is the discarding of seal and walrus blubber in favor of fuel oil, even though the animal fat was a most highly prized economic item in 1940.

Thus what happened in Gambell was not simply a psychocultural change (i.e., in sentiments toward the mainland), but a change of this nature complicated by (and contributed to) by periods of poor hunting. Part of the reaction to such poor hunting was that the

Eskimos wanted to live like white people, whom they considered immune to such misfortune. But during the research year this was not possible on the island, and the frustrations of goal attendant upon this situation were added stressful factors. It remains to be seen to what extent the newer orientation toward the mainland might be affected by beneficent changes in hunting and subsistence conditions on the island itself.

Aside from poor health and absolute deprivation from the economic inventory (such as the disappearance of the reindeer herd, poor hunting, etc.), there have been other features in this story of change which also have been of considerable significance in producing an environment of anxiety for the Gambell people. One of these, one noted repeatedly in studies of change in nonliterate groups, is the loss of a system of explanation for what happens in life—or as Redfield calls it, the "moral order" which governs life's activities and by which behavior is appraised and guided. Such a moral order interprets change, misfortune, unforeseen good luck, perhaps even arbitrary action on the part of outsiders, by reference to and integration into a basic set of orientations and convictions. Today the moral order characteristic of Gambell is fragmented: part is derived from the sustaining beliefs of an Eskimo past; part comes from the Christian religious sect in the village, from schoolteachers, from itinerant white specialists in medicine or the natural sciences, from soldiers and other white people. But a vast area is unattended; and, what is even more important, there is little in the situation that acts to synthesize and integrate these various fragments into an explanatory scheme appropriate to the complexity of the modern world.

Another stressful feature is related to that just mentioned. It is the decreasing amount of control which the people themselves have of the course of events affecting the village, a factor noted before. One example of such control is sheer knowledge of the modern world and its operations. The scope and scale of information required for successful management of one's life (or the life of a village) have suddenly increased at a rate with which the learning of relevant concepts and facts has not kept pace.

Still another example which may be cited is decrease in political autonomy. Until fairly recently, effective sociopolitical power was entirely in the hands of local people. But now political decisions and changes in policy made in offices thousands of miles away ultimately reach into Gambell village and dictate action one way rather than another. One may even see the same type of general process in the economy. For example, nothing can be done by Gambell people about long-term ecological effects deriving from interference by industrialized nations with the natural cycles of a subsistence economy—whether this be the mechanized hunting and excessive harvest of walrus by the Siberian Eskimos on the Chukotski shore or the disruption of traditional walrus migration routes caused by ships or aircraft spoiling the waters with oil slicks (as happened near the U.S. Air Force base at Thule, Greenland, thus frightening away seals and other maritime mammals) or by their noise and mere presence.

The summary image coming to mind to express this stressful shift is that of an energy system which is much more engaged in responding to exogenous changes than in fulfilling and manifesting endogenously derived lines of action. In terms of more concrete representations, over time this perception of being increasingly at the behest of outside events has been stressful for the Gambell people.

Yet there is another aspect of this matter of stressful conditions which needs to be especially pointed out, for perhaps it contributes as much to the over-all dimensions of anxiety in the village as does the direct deprivation of any of the basic wants. It has been noted before as a "descriptive generalization" of the pattern of sociocultural history of Gambell since 1940. This aspect consists in the dependability and stability of the environment, whether that be the physical environment of weather, the ecological environment of game supply, or the social environment of stable interpersonal expectations. It is one thing, for example, to know that there will be scarcity of food over a period of a few months; it is quite another to expect food and then be frustrated by poor hunting. Supposedly there is a broad area of relative stability of expectations about one's total environment, and added to this is the proposition that there is a range of permitted fluctuation in certain basic need areas outside of which such inconstancy is pathogenic for the organism. This does not mean that monotony must be the rule, nor does it mean that the fluctuating and in many ways unstable environment of the modern industrial society is not recognized. The fundamental point is that the unstable processes in Gambell strike more deeply—at subsistence, health, and mortality as well as basic social relations. Necessary stability of environment refers not only to such physical features as the weather or game supply. Insofar as the social environment constitutes one of the most crucial features of the "life space" of an individual, this also must be considered. A very broad swath is cut by the proposition, and the discussion here is indeed to be considered as only cursory statements of more far-reaching implications. But the extent to which aspects of this proposition underlie much thinking in the field of human behavior attests its importance.

In Chapter III the data on mortality patterns introduced a theme which was found to recur in the succeeding three chapters as well— the inconsistencies and unmanageable fluctuations in significant aspects of group life. It is obvious that there are fluctuations in the total environment of every group. A distinctive feature of the rise of technological civilization, however, lies in the fact that in the most crucial areas these fluctuations have been largely stabilized and brought under the control of society. The advances in technological agriculture, for example, assure a steady food supply; medicine brings more children into the world, keeps them healthier, and gives them more years than has been true for the great span of man's existence; and job placement bureaus, social security benefits, and unemployment insurance—to mention but a few stabilizing institutions—have the goal of making constant and somewhat expectable the monetary-subsistence area of modern industrialized life.

It would appear, then, that at least one of the functions of culture is to stabilize the environment in which men's behavior occurs. Such stabilization occurs with respect to two different realms of experience, each of which obviously contains many facets. The first realm is that of the series of outer conditions affecting the organism as these may be independently assessed; and the second, that of the inner coherence that is made of the organism's transactions with the environment. One might think of these as, in the first case, a *stabilization of process* and, in the second, a *stabilization of meaning*. One could also refer to the latter as the phenomenological dimension of human behavior. Another pair of terms for a distinction of this type is the "causal-functional" order and the "logico-meaningful" order.[9]

In brief terms, the technological and political institutions are given over to the stabilizing function of the first type, and the religious and philosophical orders are pre-eminently the locus of the stabilizing function of the second type. That man seems to require his social environment to be at least minimally dependable is seen, in the first instance, in the tendency to immediate restructuring and patterning of interaction that follows disruptions of various types, such as disasters, forced migrations, revolutions, and the like, and in the lines of authority and organization which soon emerge in a group that persists for any length of time. The "random scatter" of behavior is quickly drawn into some sort of pattern, however minimal. This need for ordering the disparate is seen in the second instance by man's versatile "mythmaking" potential, by his "pursuit of meaning" and the persistent organization of experiential input.[10]

The context in which the pathogenic consequences of too great a level of inconsistency of environment were first discussed was that of birth and death rates. In Gambell these have shown an undependability and inconstancy over the fifteen-year period. Living always on the thin edge of possible loss of a loved one by death, the Sivokakmeit are exposed to a considerable amount of stress simply by virtue of not knowing when sickness will strike. Coupled with the fluctuating character of the demographic equation are the additional stressful features stemming from the objective fact of high mortality rates characteristic of this population—the "static" stressful situation, as it were. Stress is therefore from the expected as well as the unforewarned loss of loved ones.

[9] See Sorokin, 1941, for this distinction. With reference to the "logico-meaningful" type of integration, see also Max Weber's discussion of "the problem of meaning" in Parsons, 1949, chap. vi, and 1951, chap. viii. Other references on this general problem of stabilization or "homeostatic" or "equilibrium" concepts include Bertalanffy, 1952; Campbell, 1927; Cottrell, 1955; Henderson, 1913; Leighton, 1946, 1959a; Leighton and Leighton, 1949; MacLeod, 1949; Meadows, 1957; and Stagner, 1954. These are but a few examples from many references dealing with concepts of homeostasis. Meadows points out the pervasiveness of the self-adjusting organismic model in current social research; concepts of equilibrium are crucial in Parsons' theoretical scheme; and Leighton's views on personality and social systems center on such a model. On the last see especially Leighton's *My Name Is Legion*.

[10] As examples, see Cantril, 1941, pp. 59–62, and 1950, and Festinger, 1957.

As noted before, sickness itself has always been one of the most serious of all stressful conditions for the St. Lawrence Eskimos. The basic problem has perhaps not changed since 1940. But there have been inconsistencies and instabilities in the treatment given or promised to those suffering. The lack of the white man's medical facilities which at one time will be offset by availability at another; the recurrent changes in medical personnel in the village itself; the bureaucratic procedures for hospitalization, which at times will speed a patient to the mainland and at other times delay his going until long past the time when hospitalization can save him—these fluctuating features of the treatment of sickness in Gambell have added a considerable measure of insecurity to the basic threats to life and longevity already present.

Similar stressful conditions of this nature are seen in the survey of subsistence patterns in Chapter V. Not only has there been the fact of objective deprivation, but also a recurrent theme over these years has been that of inconstancy of return and instability of expectation from the subsistence environment. One year's harvest may be the precursor of another; but it may just as likely be another year of famine. In this connection, it is also important to note that the physical environment in which the Gambell people seek their subsistence is one of fluctuating forces, undependable, unpredictable, and largely beyond their technological control. It is an environment that requires a full investment of work today against the uncertainties of tomorrow. Thus no matter what the time of day during the late spring, whenever the sea and weather permitted hunting the boat crews went out for meat. As the days wore on toward May and June, hunting could continue for 24 hours a day (if the men were able to stand the strain) because of the long hours of sunlight.

The white man's world has also contributed to this picture of inconstancy. The quadrupling of modal family income in the village in the space of a year and then a precipitate decline once more provide a companion piece to the fluctuations in walrus kill or fox trapping. Sometimes there were jobs, sometimes money. Often there were only the hope and unfounded expectation of work. Rumors were common, for instance, about "big construction jobs" coming to the island during 1955 or 1956. And when there is money, as from the occasional construction job or the sale of fox skins, it is quickly spent in the satisfaction of immediate goals and needs rather than stored away against an uncertain future. The wide variations in monthly store income testify to the inconstancy of cash return in the village. These inconstancies are in addition to the feelings of frustration about not now having jobs—frustrations which are the principal legacies of the several experiences that Gambell men have had with mass employment by the white world.

Stressful conditions in human relations have come with the breaking away from received cultural sentiments by the young people, who are no longer abiding by many of the kinship proscriptions that their parents feel are just and right. Yet the patterns are not yet crystallized into expected polarities, and there is much wandering in the middle phases of acculturation, wherein people are not quite cut off from the one set of standards or fully living by the other. The cross-purposes and divergent goals that exist between many parents and children react on the security and well-being of each. The old feel denied, with their teachings rebuffed; the young feel blocked, with their desires frustrated. Yet at the same time they are not sure where the right way lies. It is in this connection that some of the discussion above of "anticipatory socialization" is especially pertinent.

The theme of inconstancy of pattern has also been found in other areas of social life, and this section will be closed out by mentioning two or three of them. In the matter of recreation, for instance—the sheer lack of which causes the young people so much concern—there was a brief time in which their wants were satisfied. Ballroom dancing was common, and movies were being shown almost every day. Then both of these were abruptly stopped, and nothing has taken their place. The sense of vacuum existing in the area of recreational facilities during the entire year 1954–1955 was the source of many negative sentiments about those in power and control and of many positive sentiments exalting the mainland culture. The fact of once having been allowed dancing and then of having the decision reversed is one of the key features of the negative sentiments.

The military bases on the peripheries of Gambell have contributed their share to the stressful situation in which the village finds itself.

The history of village-military relations is marked with dissension and conflict over various matters, which in the beginning, at least, alternated with times of relative harmony. In addition, Gambell's leaders are pulled in different directions over the pattern of their relations with the military. They are aware that it is of considerable economic advantage to have so close a market for their ivory carving and skin sewing. But they cannot help being concerned over what is happening to their young people through contact with the army, particularly to the girls. The girls themselves feel the restraints on their conduct to be excessive and unfair and complain that they are not being allowed freedom to behave as they wish with the soldiers. Beyond all this is the feature of inconsistency. One week the curfew will be placed on visiting; it will remain in effect until laxity in enforcement brings about its subtle and unannounced lifting. Then it will suddenly be imposed once again on contacts with the military following a breech of the not-too-clear codes of behavior which the elders feel are necessary.

In effect, over the fifteen-year period the village of Gambell has experienced several types of stressful conditions in its total life situation. Such conditions are included in other propositions found in Leighton's *The Governing of Men.* The first proposition quoted below notes some of the specific situations, both physiological and psychosocial, which induce stress. The second is a summary of the ways in which such stressful factors may combine to impinge on the individual.

Principle 1. The following specific types of stress are disturbing to the emotions and thoughts of the individual:
- a. Threats to life and health;
- b. Discomfort from pain, heat, cold, dampness, fatigue and poor food;
- c. Loss of means of subsistence, whether in the form of money, jobs, business or property;
- d. Deprivation of sexual satisfaction;
- e. Enforced idleness;
- f. Restriction of movement;
- g. Isolation;
- h. Threats to children, family members and friends;
- i. Rejection, dislike and ridicule from other people;
- j. Capricious and unpredictable behavior on the part of those in authority upon whom one's welfare depends.

Principle 2. The following general types of stress are derived from the more specific types, but are in themselves particularly disturbing to the emotions and thoughts of the individual:

    a. Persistent frustration of goals, desires, needs, intentions and plans;

    b. Circumstances that promote the dilemma of conflicting and mu· tually incompatible desires and intentions;

    c. Circumstances creating confusion and uncertainty as to what is happening in the present and what can be expected in the future. [Leighton, 1946, pp. 252, 260]

These two principles, particularly the second, may be taken as summaries of many of the types of stressful factors which have been characteristic of the life situation of Gambell people from 1940 to 1955.

## NEW OPPORTUNITIES FOR ACHIEVING SECURITY AND SATISFYING ASPIRATIONS

This aspect of the proposition concerns the area of alternative roles and variant cultural patterns that have impinged upon Gambell in the fifteen-year time span. Although the fullest force of these new patterns and opportunities is felt among the young people, their impact is not entirely limited to that stratum of the population.

As indicated in Chapters IV–VI, through contact with the mainland since 1940 have come both practice in and knowledge of other ways of achieving security and satisfying aspirations—different subsistence patterns, different medical and health devices and facilities, different recreational forms, different religious beliefs. In religion there was perhaps not quite as much change as in other areas, for mainland religion was represented in the village in 1940. Nevertheless, even here the coming of the Seventh-Day Adventists significantly brought to the attention of Gambell people the alternatives that existed in this as in other areas of the mainland life. For a few Sivokakmeit the sect offered new ways to security through participation. For the remainder, however, it served mostly as a model of mainland religious diversification.

Many new opportunities for security have come in the form of jobs, most of them intermittent and only occasional, but many of them extremely lucrative while they lasted. Less well paying but nonetheless perhaps as effective in changing sentiments have been the increased opportunities for sale of carved ivory or skin sewing. Markets for this have greatly increased since 1940. Other actual opportunities have been the trips outside to attend school, which in some cases has given the young person the chance to learn a trade or other valuable skill.

The various construction jobs which Gambell people have had were outstandingly important in building up an exaggerated picture of the white world, even while they offered new opportunities for achieving security. But it must be noted that they were not long-range, sustained opportunities for establishing a stable basis of security and satisfying aspirations in a consistent manner with relation to the mainland. Rather, their effects have been more a foretaste of something else, and perhaps in part because of this some of their legacies in changing a system of belief have taken on the nature of parody, exaggeration of the elements of abundance and wealth. In this light, perhaps even more important, and surely more pervasive, than the actual opportunities for new ways of achieving security and satisfying aspirations have been new ideas of how to accomplish these ends.

In the images of the mainland culture that have been formed by the Sivokakmeit through their interaction with it during these fifteen years, one motif is common. Contributions to this have come both from those who left the island for the mainland and from the experiences of the people left behind. This theme is that of relatively greater freedom of activity on the mainland and more leeway of choice in deciding upon goals and means to them than exist in traditional Eskimo culture. This obviously means far more than the simple "political freedom" or some such restricted concept. It has, rather, to do with the wide gamut of social roles and complexes of institutionalized behavior. Whereas in inherited St. Lawrence culture there is nothing else for a boy to look forward to than becoming a hunter, with perhaps his only claim to distinction being that of a captain or striker, or, in exceptional cases, a shaman, in the mainland culture which he has now come to know there is a wide range of choice, and the differences between alternatives are wider than those existing between alternatives found in the native culture. The "job" with its many different forms presents an array of subsistence opportunity unequaled in the village traditional culture. In other words, the occupational structure offers a wider variety of legitimate choices and is more adjustable to many of the unique desires and needs of individuals than that of Gambell. Some men simply do not like to hunt as well as others do. They are not physically as able to endure the life, and they get less of a thrill from the chase and kill. They would perhaps prefer an occupational role that allowed them to remain indoors out of the weather, such as that of storekeeper. But in traditional St. Lawrence culture there is no place for such men.[11]

In other areas one can see many of the same processes. In the family, for instance, beginning with the choice of spouse, it is the romantic love complex that is found on the mainland, in contrast to that of traditional St. Lawrence culture in which the choice was not made by an individual himself. The residence pattern reinforced this lack of individual choice and freedom of action, for a married man lived with his parents and the latter were still in charge of the household. Furthermore, in the matter of treating kinsmen according to rigidly specified rules, much latitude and tolerance exist on the mainland by contrast to Sivokak.

It should be noted, of course, that a countervailing tendency to such restriction of choice was found in the fact that divorce formerly was much more easily accomplished than it is now. If, therefore, two young people could not live together amicably following a period of essentially trial marriage during the groom work, they could separate (with parents' consent) and begin again. Now, although the initial choice is much wider, its consequences are much more binding.

In religion, too, the possibility of choice has come into the picture. In common with other self-contained societies of the world, Gambell's native religion was for thousands of years the religion thought

[11] I say this without subscribing to the type of culture-personality theory which postulates that a particular range of constitutionally given temperamental patterns exists in any group and that if a person's basic pattern of temperament (or personality proclivities) happens to "fit" one which the culture exalts then personality adjustment and mental health are the result. See Benedict, 1934, and Mead, 1939. What I am saying is that in the present social circumstances of the Gambell people there are situations in which an individual is not qualified or able to hunt, yet that is the only role open to him. Take the case of a patient returned from a tuberculosis sanatorium with the injunction to "rest" and care for his body. Yet he must support his family—and how, in the matrix of the native culture, is he to do this without hunting?

appropriate to their relations with the supernatural world. It was therefore not a body of activity and belief to be lightly tampered with in the hope of experimentally finding a more utilitarian pattern, and it was not subject to the same ingeniously experimental modes of thought as was the subsistence environment. In the 1890's, Christianity had made its first inroads, but as late as 1940 there were many who quarreled with the relinquishment of the ancient faith and maintained the world view inherited from the past. Now the element of conforming with the religious norm—because it is the social norm as well—has passed, and one may or may not be a Presbyterian, depending upon personal choice. Some choose not to be, and no social sanctions like those of the past prevail to bring conformity.

In yet another way there has been enhancement of individual choice and freedom through the knowledge of (and some limited practice of) alternate ways of achieving security and satisfying aspirations. This way is more subtle than those just mentioned, but it deserves some discussion because of its generality. I point to the core meaning of freedom of choice, which consists in the exercise of decision and effectuation of action in the absence of external constraints of any nature seriously influencing that decision or behavior. It depends, in other words, upon a relatively controlled and unobtruding environmental situation or context in which the decision and action are occurring. This is obviously a relative matter, but there are empirical differences.

Looking at the materials thus, one can say that with regard to fundamental subsistence and economic problems the white mainland has presented a picture of almost unlimited freedom and enhancement of individual choice. For on the mainland there are envisioned no such external constraints on subsequent activity as the lack of food or money, lack of warmth and protection against cold, lack of health or of medical facilities if sickness occurs. In other words, in these basic terms (as well as in the more superficial ones mentioned above) the individual is relatively freer there than on the island to plan his life course and actually proceed toward the accomplishment of those goals.

Discussion of an individual's perception of freedom of choice can become confused with value statements and metaphysical, religious, or nationalistic overtones. What is freedom to one will be unconscionable constraint to another. The only point to be made is that to the Sivokakmeit, in terms of their perceptions and statements, there appears to be a far wider range of alternative behavior patterns open to people on the mainland than is true of the village with its traditional culture. What is perhaps most important, on the mainland these alternative patterns are equally legitimate and culturally valid. It is not a state of anomie, a situation in which an individual haphazardly seeks to satisfy his wants without reference to a set of normative standards deriving from group membership. Rather, what is presented to the percipient individual is a range of culturally legitimate patterns of behavior, and the choice is ostensibly being left to him.

The implications of much of the foregoing discussion might be summarized by saying that the "behavioral space" into which Gambell people are now moving is therefore phenomenologically much wider than that which characterized their culture a generation ago.[12] Whether such perceptions are in accord with reality is another question that might profitably be examined. It is not true that there was no chance to express individuality in the traditional culture, despite the obviously heavy weight of custom. In the old days, individual inclinations were shown in many small ways rather than in gross features of behavior pattern—perhaps in dress, the design of a tool, art work, or singing and dancing or, most of all, in the shamanistic complex with its encouragement of visionary experiences and commerce with the supernaturals. Today opportunities for expression of individuality are certainly different and in significant ways are "wider"; yet in their enthusiasm for the new, many of the Gambell people appear to have minimized the range of choice that existed traditionally. Very likely, of course, when juxtaposed against what is considered the range of behavioral choice today, memories of the past retreat into an appearance of bland uniformity and constriction of impulse.

At this point it is unnecessary to go into any of the potentially maladaptive consequences of this sudden release from patterns of

[12] At the Fifty-seventh Annual Meeting of the American Anthropological Association, Washington, D.C., 1958, I presented a paper discussing somewhat more fully this concept of "behavioral space."

social restriction that occurs when a young person makes the hour's airplane flight to Nome to find a job. It should be noted, however, that although those consequences are by no means always maladaptive, they frequently are so because of the rapidity with which the change is made, the lack of attitudinal preparation for making wise choices, and the sheer multiplicity of objects and modes of behavior from which the choice must be made.

## Interrelationships of the Four Aspects

There have always been many stressful conditions in the life of the Sivokakmeit—the concern over food, over health, over warmth being obvious examples. These have been documented even within fairly recent times (e.g., the great famine and epidemic of 1878), and there is little reason to feel that the St. Lawrence life situation was ever significantly different from this. It would therefore appear as though stressful conditions of themselves do not operate to induce such a change in belief.

This is likewise true of another of the four aspects of the proposition Leighton has mentioned. The Eskimos are ethnographically notorious as a people who have marvelously pieced together the smallest and seemingly most inutile bits of their environment to make a satisfying life.[18] Their powers of close observation of nature and reasoned thinking with a view to technological manipulation and invention (therefore change) demand the admiration even of white men from our own mechanized culture. There would therefore appear to be none of the "intellectual laziness" about these nonliterate people which Durkheim claimed was the general lot of the "primitive" (1915, p. 58). That this capacity for reasoned thinking is nothing new in St. Lawrence culture is attested by some of the ingenious implement types found in ancient archaeological sites on the island (Geist and Rainey, 1936; Collins, 1937). But it would also appear not to have been able of itself to change the system of belief about the white world even after knowledge that the latter existed

[18] Whenever a survey of the world's cultures is given the beginning student of anthropology, almost invariably the Eskimos are included and their ingenious adaptation to the environment stressed. As examples see Forde, 1934; Murdock, 1934; Goldenweiser, 1922 and 1937; Coon, 1948; Beals and Hoijer, 1953; Sanders *et al.*, 1953.

had come to the island. Other factors were apparently needed to bring about such a fundamental shift.

Two such factors were contact with the mainland of a greatly increased nature since 1940 and new opportunities for practicing alternative roles and for experiencing variant ways of achieving security. There was contact in 1940, obviously, but it was more a limited contact by idea than a contact by overwhelming firsthand pressure from that mainland world. Teachers and missionaries had been on the island for several decades, a nurse much less long. Traders had come in their small vessels with the melting of the spring sea, and the coast guard cutters paid annual visits. But all these representatives of the white world were no match for the momentum of the still basically Eskimo culture. They provided but limited models to copy; and they were too few—and other conditions were lacking —seriously to affect the transmission of St. Lawrence culture from one generation to the next. But the waves of contact since 1940 have very much altered the social environment. By contrast with the earlier years, Gambell has become a metropolitan place, with CAA families and technicians, soldiers, airmen, public health people, ANS people all coming in. Then, too, there has been emigration to the mainland, wholly a new feature in the lives of the Gambell people since 1940.

Concomitantly there have been theretofore unequaled opportunities for practicing the white man's culture since 1940, such as working over automobile motors at the CAA site and laying water pipe from the lake. The young have participated in the role of full-time student in the mainland high schools. Old and young have been convalescents in hospitals, and some have been placed in the permanent status of convalescent and receive monthly disability checks. Being welfare cases and receiving monthly checks for hardship gave to even more people a chance to participate in a portion of the mainland culture and to satisfy some of their aspirations through its social mechanisms. The young men with army experience and those of the National Guard unit have had given to them abundant new opportunities for achieving aspirations and certain of their security needs (such as those for subsistence and for the regard of one's fellows). Both these latter conditions (contact and opportunity) have increased to such a degree since 1940 when compared to the situation at that time and in the prior years that it can be said that they are new circumstances impinging upon Gambell.

In summary, therefore, it appears that sheer observation of fact, reasoned thinking, and the existence of stressful conditions are not sufficient of themselves to bring about a change of the type occurring here. Further, it also seems that a more intensive contact than that with just a few representatives of the outside world is necessary before a fundamental reorientation can take place, and this latter must be accompanied by actual opportunities for learning a wider variety of new skills and new goals and standards of behavior. In light of the St. Lawrence Island data, the beginning proposition may therefore be modified to read:

The things that alter a system of belief which a people holds are:
  a. Observation of fact and reasoned thinking, in addition to
  b. The persistence in the group of stressful conditions of all types, including those coming from too great a level of inconstancy in the physical and psychological environments; but these two conditions must be accompanied by
  c. At least neutral if not actually friendly face-to-face contact with large numbers of people exhibiting different systems of belief and (probably also)
  d. New opportunities for achieving security and satisfying aspirations. In some cases the latter will appear as a conception of greater institutionalized freedom of choice, or "behavioral space," with reference to a wide gamut of social roles and behavioral complexes.

# CHAPTER VIII

# "The Broken Tribe"

THE several previous chapters have brought us to a particular point in time and in the cultural life of a people. During the course of those chapters, data have been presented and analyzed in order to explain certain broad developments happening between 1940 and 1955. At this point a few considerations and speculations pertaining to the future of the village may be introduced, although these are not intended as the major goal or purpose of the book. They are simply statements of trends and probabilities seen up to 1955.

One feature of the present situation which will undoubtedly continue and probably increase in the immediate future is contact with the mainland. This will take many forms, including direct migration. There is little likelihood that the airline will stop its mail and passenger service or that the Alaska Native Service supply ship will cease its annual journeys to provision the native stores along the coast. The way will thus be set for more emigration to the mainland, by the young people leaving for high school and other types of training, by people leaving in search of jobs, and by villagers going to the mainland for hospitalization.[1]

---

[1] In an interesting instance of this type of development, it is reported in the journal *Alaska's Health* (published by the Alaska Department of Health) that recently some 54 children from St. Lawrence Island were airlifted to the Anchorage Medical Center for treatment of all types of ear, nose, throat, eye,

No doubt most of the emigrants leaving in search of work will be young people, both boys and girls. The older family heads, though they will similarly feel the strains attendant upon a sometimes uncertain economic base and a persistent self-disparaging evaluation coming from comparisons with new standards, will be less likely to go. The combination of deeper roots in Gambell and its cultural past, family responsibilities, and lack of language and other skills will all militate against their making the break.[2]

In this respect, it is significant that in 1958 several families from Gambell resolved to move to the mainland under provisions of the Department of the Interior's new policy of relocating Indian and Eskimo families in urban areas and helping them adapt to the modern world and its way of life. Some of the families went as far away as Chicago and Oakland, California; others remained closer to home in Seattle and in Fairbanks, Alaska. According to reports, however, all but one family of these first emigrants shortly returned to Gambell, apparently out of some sense of disillusionment with what they found on the mainland. Their returning is said to have cooled the enthusiasm of several other family heads who were ready to leave for the States. How long that hesitancy will remain, however, is problematical.

Another important feature of the situation in 1955 which will likely continue for some years to come—and which no doubt lies behind thoughts of movement to the mainland—is the increased intensity of stresses arising from sentiments of relative deprivation. Once the initial breakthroughs have been made in terms of accepting other standards, it is not so much the fact, for example, that hunting is either good or bad (and it has been better in some of the years since 1955), but simply the fact that hunting has to be done instead of working at a steady job, which produces feelings of self-disparage-

---

and other crippling conditions. These conditions had all been diagnosed previously by physicians visiting the island, but there were no facilities for treating them short of a 1,500-mile round trip to southern Alaska. See *Alaska's Health*, vol. XVI (April, 1959).

[2] For a short firsthand account of the experiences of a young Eskimo from Pt. Hope, Alaska, in the world of Fairbanks and Anchorage see James W. Van-Stone, "The Autobiography of an Alaskan Eskimo," *Arctic*, vol. X, no. 4 (1957). This young man's experiences are very similar to those of young men from Gambell, and his reactions are much the same.

ment relative to the mainland. As more contact with and exposure to the mainland increases, the Eskimo way is seen in a new light—a new cultural "anchorage" has been formed, to adapt a term used by Newcomb (1950) and Sherif and Cantril (1947)—and the things which even recently were sufficient and gave satisfaction will now be seen to fall short of being adequate, even when they are at their best. They will fall short because of now being judged according to different (and often, lamentably, quite irrelevant) standards. The use of more prestigeful but less windproof white man's clothing is a case in point. Eating walrus meat—even when one's meat cellar is full after a rich hunting season—will not yield the security it once did; for now it will not be walrus, but bread, canned meat, and canned fruit that is felt to be the only acceptable meal.

It is furthermore unlikely that after 1955 Gambell will have been free from the effects of many stressful conditions of other types than those deriving from shifts in cultural standards. Some of these conditions will be solidly rooted in "objective fact"; that is to say, they will still be stressful even after the qualifying effects of different sentiments and values have been taken into account. Sickness, for example, for some time to come will no doubt continue to be a serious problem threatening the village and its people, although as mentioned before strenuous efforts are beginning to be made to improve public health, particularly in the problem of tuberculosis. The fight for food will go on in this exacting arctic environment, with the greatest part of subsistence necessarily still based on the hunting of the walrus, whale, and seal in the vicissitudes of arctic weather. Even when the hunt proves relatively bountiful, there is still the uncertainty of next year. Furthermore, at the present time there appears to be nothing of the white world that could act as functional equivalent to hunting and provide sufficiently steady jobs to support a village economy linked with the mainland. No construction jobs of a permanent nature seem likely, for instance, and since St. Lawrence Island falls outside the perimeter of the "DEW" line radar stations stretching across the top of North America, there are no jobs available for Eskimo maintenance men, as is the case in some Alaskan and Canadian Eskimo communities. An insufficient cash return from the ivory sales, fox trapping, and skin sewing is apt to be the principal source of income for some time to come.

These features of the relationship to the mainland economy, if they are not altered by some totally unexpected development, will no doubt add their portion to the stresses under which the Gambell people will live.

Further, regarding the matter of stressful conditions, at the end of the research year in 1955 it appeared that the army camp was likely to remain near the village for many years. Had this been the case, problems arising from increased contact between the young people and the soldiers stationed nearby would probably have been exacerbated, particularly if the ratio of soldiers to villagers had increased over what it was up to that point. In fact, however, the base was abandoned two years after our departure from the island, and thus the matter of disruptive consequences of this intergroup contact to some extent solved itself. An excerpt from a letter written by a villager then living on the mainland describes some of the after-effects of the army's departure that he noted on a visit to the village:

Lots of changes have been taken place in that tiny village in the four years I've been away. The Army camp made lots of differences and I was told it was torn down in nearly one day. You know the people of the village are not anyones to let a handout go, which is one of the vices of the people up there. If they had divide it equally among themselves and tear it down carefully they would improve the village the great deal. Instead they had ruined most of the good material trying to get all they can. I was proud of them, though. I walked around the village and wherever I went men, some women, even children were banging away with hammers building new houses, adding new sections to the one they have or repairing their homes. I joined the busy beavers by adding a section to our tiny house and my father had built a warehouse by himself after I left. Another thing I was amazed at was some people are driving Army weasels. I rode one from runway to the village . . . a free taxi service. The leaving of the Army did some bad too. They had left liquor buried somewhere; there must be tons of it. The young people dug it out and made themselves alcoholic addicts. Even young fine girls made themselves bums by getting drunkards.

Some other implications of types of behavior noted in this excerpt will be discussed below. At this point it may be noted that the leaving of the army base may in the long run produce more stress and anxiety than would have been the case had it remained; for the village had clearly grown dependent on the camp in many ways, not the least of which was reliance on it for steady sales of ivory carving and skin sewing. The contributions of the base in terms of scrap materials for building and other uses, as well as surplus food, have been noted in previous chapters. It is very likely, therefore, that further feelings of frustration and stresses arising from relative deprivation will have been heightened by the departure of the army base.

Some other considerations of sociocultural development may be mentioned as well. To persist as a recognizably Eskimo village, Gambell will almost necessarily have to continue some form of its ancient hunting pattern. Thus the problem of principles underlying membership in the boat crew is one that must be solved, and it is probable that these principles will continue to be based primarily on kinship criteria, rather than on those of money or some other form of negotiable goods in return for service. For example, not until cash is more easily acquired than it is now could this form of payment be satisfactorily instituted. Moreover, it would violate basic cultural sentiments relating to kinship. Unless the idea were strongly imposed from the outside, there would seem to be little chance that "workers' groups" on a primarily nonkinship basis will develop here, as has happened among the Siberian Eskimos on the shore opposite St. Lawrence Island (see Hughes, 1959).

This is not to say that the kinship institutions of the culture will remain as viable in all respects as they might in hunting, however, for they have begun to change in the areas of interpersonal relations and obligations, treatment of the old people, patterns of sharing and reciprocity, and so forth. But the kinship basis of the boat crew will probably be the last to change in terms of a nonimposed, functionally derived shift. And when it does, it will probably do so only by dint of an over-all change in economic structure. Furthermore, the tenacity of the kinship system generally, particularly the extended family but also the clan system, may surprise the expectant social scientist.[3]

In the matter of dependence on outside sources of supply as well

[3] See Vogt's study of Navaho veterans, for example; he points out that it is the area of kinship and social organization which is most resistant to culture change, even more than matters of religion, often thought the most deeply rooted and difficult to change (Vogt, 1951, pp. 113–115).

as outside direction, there might be more behavior of this type in the future than has been true up to now. When hunting is poor and the meat cellars low, the request for relief supplies will be quicker and will be made with less hesitation. Welfare aid of various types will be used wherever possible, and other sources of funds will be investigated; for they help to fill an ever-increasing need now that the shift to a money standard and mainland conceptions of life have occurred. That behavior patterns when rewarded tend to persist is a commonplace of relevance here.

One might also, somewhat paradoxically, expect a greater secularization of life in Gambell. Although it is true that now the entire village is Christian, steady attendance at church does not by any means include the entire village. Even if this were to have been the case after 1955, the basic conflicting nature of the two religious systems point in a determinate direction. In a very real sense the replacement of the old religion by Christianity has meant a great reduction in the scope of practice and belief pertaining to the supernatural world. There are no legitimate Christian practice and justifying belief, for instance, to accompany the cutting up of animals out on the ice, as there were in the ancient Eskimo religion. Since there is no functional substitute in the newer religion, certain ancient practices relating to the proper treatment of animals which man must kill for food have tended to persist, even among the most devout of Christians. Evidently the sentiments concerning the bringing of the natural order into the moral order of man were too well laid for them to disappear with a change in formal belief. But with the dying off of the old people even these practices—not torturing dying animals, for example, and dropping back into the sea all unwanted parts after the butchering—will very likely disappear, for the young will not have the foundation in memory and practice which now gives meaning to these customs.

In still another dimension, contact with the white world sets up influences toward secularization. St. Lawrence Islanders who journey to Nome and other mainland towns see that the practice of not attending church is a legitimate (at least unpunishable) alternative behavior pattern. Such behavior is part of the general profile of "independence" and multiple alternatives which is presented to the percipient individual, part of the wider "behavioral space" discussed in the last chapter. Already one sees "secularized" trends in Gambell village coming from such a vindicating perception of the mainland. For instance, some of the white men with whom the young Gambell people have come into contact include quite outspoken nonchurchgoing soldiers. Such people seem to them as representative of the white world as the missionary.

But in a larger sense, even this process of contact is probably not as important as the progressive specialization of religion into the delimited Sunday service and the spectator role, which is the way religion appears to most of the Gambell people. With this specialization, mainland religion would appear to have lost its place as a functional analogue of the pervasive and widespread aboriginal religion oriented to the animals, the spirits and the winds, and the multiple souls of men.

Under further conditions of stress, the development of intragroup hostilities is probable. Many Alaskan Eskimo groups, including those of St. Lawrence Island, traditionally kept antagonisms in the village under control through hostile gossip and witchcraft activity (Lantis, manuscript). Others were more open and direct, and in some places murder was a common means of settling hostilities. The Central tribes of Canada provide examples of this practice. In Gambell for at least the past fifty years sustained intergroup conflict among the patriclans has not occurred, although in previous centuries it apparently did so. But given the perception of increasing shortage of scarce goods (food, jobs, material goods, etc.), one might expect harsher competition among the family groups and clans, with none of the heretofore ameliorative effects of the cultural insistence regarding sharing. Soon, indeed, there may be reached that critical divide beyond which the ancient sentiment oriented toward sharing breaks before the array of forces now tending to undermine it. In addition to the shortage of goods, a factor influencing the disappearance of older sharing patterns is the realization on the part of people that in the mainland culture the sharing of one's goods is not a primary value.

One might also expect more open violence in the village if liquor becomes more prominent and easily obtained than it has been up to this point. In the past two generations or so, such violence has been absent from St. Lawrence culture, although before that time these people shared the Eskimo traits of aggressiveness toward those defined as outside one's group. Now, however, sentiments of at least overt hospitality and friendliness toward all other villagers have been strongly developed, and it would require a dissolver of inhibition such as liquor provides to give release to some of the sentiments of antagonism which exist and will probably increase with shortage of desirable goods and privileges. The excerpt from a letter quoted above, in which is described the enthusiasm that some of the young people had for liquor found in the abandoned army camp site, is probably indicative both of present concerns and of future developments.[4] The hostility may also turn away from the old people and nonclan members to include white people, a state of affairs which generally has not been true up to this point.

Something else that might very well occur is the breaking of formal village rules, aside from the informal shared sentiments which provide the structure for ongoing daily life. Edicts of the village council, especially those concerning liquor, the curfew hours for visitors, and the relationship of the young girls with outsiders, may increasingly tend to be thwarted. There may also be a rise in petty thievery, although up to recent times this type of behavior had been rare in the village. Perhaps it is beginning, however, for in a letter received from Gambell in 1956, it was noted that there had been some thefts of fuel oil from the army base. Nothing of this sort had happened during 1954–1955, and apparently there had been little of it in the years since 1940. In 1940 the council had dealt firmly with theft when it occurred in the village, and its use of

---

[4] That this prediction may prove at least partially true is indicated in a recent news release which concerns some 7,000 cases of beer "on St. Lawrence Island in the Bering Sea between the Soviet Union and Alaska. Two years ago, medical officers declared it unfit. And the Army stacked the beer cans in pits, poured oil and gasoline on them, burned them, ran them over with a tractor, and then buried them. But somehow natives salvaged some of the beer. They have been pulling cans out of the pits and drinking their contents. Then, in high spirits, they have destroyed property in the nearby village of Gambell. The Village Council of that community has complained to Sen. E. L. (Bob) Bartlett (D-Alaska). Bartlett relayed the complaint to Lt. Gen. Frank A. Armstrong, head of the Unified Alaskan Command. And after a series of telegrams, Bartlett reported Friday, Armstrong promised to airlift a platoon to the island. Its officer would be under orders 'to certify as to complete destruction,' Armstrong said" (Associated Press, reported in Ithaca *Journal*, August 1, 1959).

public sanctions by which the offenders voluntarily surrendered themselves was very effective (Hughes, 1953). The development of strong in-group sentiments against thievery was probably greatly aided by the formation of the council in the 1920's, and up to that point thefts may have been part of the general relationship between clans. It is known that, in the early days of contact with the outside, whaling ships were considered legitimate targets for theft, being part of the "out-group." But as Lantis has stated in this regard, generalizing about the Alaskan Eskimos, theft is a serious crime within the village, although stealing from an enemy falls outside the scope of such a moral code. Moreover, "thievery within the community, which is increasing apparently, indicates that the old concepts and code are breaking" (Lantis, manuscript).

It may very well be that, unless the village council begins to take far stronger steps and to act in a more decisive and farsighted manner than it did during 1954–1955, it will see a gradual whittling away of its scope of authority and power in village life through being undercut by persistent and successful violation of its codes.

The picture thus outlined is familiar to social scientists as one of disintegration in the life of a village or at least the beginnings of the gradual dissolution of a community as an organized, functioning social unit. This does not necessarily refer to the constituent personalities whose patterned behavior composes the social unit or to their potentialities for reaching satisfactory adjustments to new environments should Gambell as a sociocultural integrate dissolve, although these phenomena are often related (see Leighton, 1959b, for example).

Instances of social and cultural disintegration of nonliterate groups following contact with an overwhelming outside group are common in the anthropological literature. Disruption of a traditional economy and no adequate functional substitute; destruction, often harshly done, of political autonomy; breakdown in family, clan, and tribal social control and guidance; disagreements and lack of congruence concerning sentiments necessary to the functional integrity of the group; decline and confusion in religious systems and orientations toward the supernatural; disappearance or lack of development of stabilizing and equilibrating institutions—these are familiar themes found in culture-contact literature from all continents.[5] One of the most poignant statements of this phenomenon, however, is contained in Alan Paton's novel *Cry, the Beloved Country;* in this the full depth of the shattering experience for the people themselves takes on new meaning:

Cry for the broken tribe, for the law and the custom that is gone. . . . Cry, the beloved country, that these things are not yet at an end. The sun pours down on the earth, on the lovely land that man cannot enjoy. He knows only the fear of his heart. . . . Cry, the beloved country, for the unborn child that is the inheritor of our fear. Let him not love the earth too deeply. Let him not laugh too gladly when the water runs through his fingers, nor stand too silent when the setting sun makes red the veld with fire. Let him not be too moved when the birds of his land are singing, nor give too much of his heart to a mountain or a valley. For fear will rob him of all if he gives too much.

Yes, it was true, then. He had admitted it to himself. The tribe was broken, and would be mended no more. He bowed his head. It was as though a man borne upward into the air felt suddenly that the wings of miracle had dropped away from him, so that he looked down upon the earth, sick with fear and apprehension. The tribe was broken, and would be mended no more. The tribe that had nurtured him, and his father and his father's father, was broken. For the men were away, and the young men and the girls were away, and the maize hardly reached to the height of a man.

Frequently out of such conditions of prolonged and widespread deprivation, frustration, and destruction of life's meaning, there has arisen a forceful, integrated social and ideological movement which seeks to re-establish the hegemony of a moral order and a feeling of political autonomy in directing processes of sociocultural change. These appear to be organized attempts at laying down a new charter for life, a clear definition of goals and means of reaching them. Such movements have in common that they attempt to block and divert the current tendencies in sociocultural change and development, to rechannel the social process; they may be seen as "drift-denying movements"—conscious feeling on the part of the

[5] The best bibliography of contact literature is Keesing, 1953; see also Siegel, 1955, in which are found abstracts of studies of contact between North American Indian groups and the white world that in many cases has led to various types of disintegration of the group.

people and their leaders that life has made them its victims and a consequent attempt to reclaim proprietorship in setting goals.

Such processes are variously labeled "nativistic," "messianic," or "revivalistic" movements, "cargo cults," or, in Wallace's recent phrase which attempts to summarize all these other terms, "revitalization movements" (1956, p. 264). This is defined as "a deliberate organized, conscious effort by members of a society to construct a more satisfying culture." Some of the more familiar examples are found in the Ghost Dance of the Plains area of North America during the late nineteenth century; the Peyote Cult of the same area; the Vailala Madness of New Guinea; and the more recent Cargo Cults of Melanesia. In addition, however, most of the revolutionary ideologies of Western European history have partaken of the revitalization theme, and one sees this phenomenon today as well, both in modern cultural movements stemming from real or perceived deprivation, such as the Celtic Revival or the Acadian Revival of northeastern North America, and in some of the extremely nationalistic political movements, such as those in the Middle East or Africa.[6]

The following propositions may be said to outline the natural history of many such movements:

In communities undergoing stress it is common for belief systems to:
    Become more emotional and less rational,
    Increase in number and variety,
    Increase in tendency to conflict,
    Become plastic and changeable.

The longer and more intense the stress, the more extensive will be the changes in the systems of belief until some new equilibrium is established.

As systems of belief in a community under stress become more emotional, unstable and conflicting, the community becomes less able to deal with its stresses.

Out of the confusion of a community under stress there is likely to arise a single radical system of belief which may or may not bring a new stability, but which will bring to a large section of the population a sense of at least temporary relief from stress.

[6] For fuller statements of various such "drift-denying movements" see Firth, 1951, chap. iii; Linton, 1943; Mead, 1956; Mooney, 1892; Nash, 1955; Siegel, 1955; Wallace, 1956; Wallis, 1943; or Williams, 1923, 1934.

After a period of stress, there is a drift back toward former systems of belief, but the return is rarely, if ever, complete. [From Leighton, 1946, pp. 299, 302, 303]

Among the stressful conditions leading to the development of such a movement, feelings of both deprivation and frustration of meaningful goals in life are critical. Nash has phrased this in the form of a hypothesis and, with relevance to the problem of contact between two groups, indicated that such a movement may arise within the context of either the acceptance or the rejection of the alien culture (Nash, 1955, p. 442). The important gap is that between aspirations and accomplishment, no matter what the cultural content.[7]

In light of these considerations, it is relevant to ask whether the present sociocultural trends seen in Gambell up to 1955 and more recently point inevitably in the direction of the disintegration of the village as a sociocultural unit and whether there could develop out of such a situation a "psychology of rebuff" and of disillusionment with the white world that would be sufficiently intense to lead to a reactive movement of the type described above.

It is of course not inevitable that a native village become disintegrated under the impact of the white world; change is not synonymous with disintegration.[8] But the fact that so many groups have become severely disrupted through intensive exposure indicates that unless there are cogent reasons for thinking the contrary one should expect this to occur in any given case. What might be some of those contrary reasons? What are some of Gambell's liabilities with respect to maintaining itself as a recognizably Eskimo village in the modern world? And what resources might it have which would work toward its integrity as a self-contained village, albeit one which had a different pattern of extensions into the white world?

Of considerable importance in this respect is the question of the

---

[7] A proposition from studies of intergroup relations is also pertinent to this matter of relative deprivation, frustrated goals, and an organized reaction of this type: "A militant reaction from a minority group is most likely when (a) the group's position is rapidly improving or (b) when it is rapidly deteriorating, especially if this follows a period of improvement" (Williams, 1947, Proposition 43).

[8] Spencer, 1959, also points this out in his recent study of the Point Barrow and other North Alaskan Eskimo groups.

relative permeability of the restraining social boundaries of the village. If the existence of many sentiments leading to thoughts of emigration from the village are granted, how easy is it for an individual to leave the social unit? In Gambell at the present time it is fairly easy. There are no obvious bars placed in the way of emigration and of leaving the stressful field—no quotas on immigration, for instance, and no official discriminatory regulations which would set up a ring of measures keeping Gambell people in their stressful situation, such as are found in South Africa with its apartheid. One of the factors preventing migration in some cases might be lack of knowledge of conditions to be encountered on the mainland; but for many, such lack of knowledge is counterbalanced by hope and high expectation. The main barrier preventing large-scale migration is financial, and as noted above this is being erased through the active assistance and encouragement given by the government in its relocation program. Thus, even if many stressful conditions shall have continued to impinge on Gambell in the years after 1955, it seems unlikely that there could be reached a point of despair sufficiently strong to generate anything resembling a revitalization movement in the village itself. It is more likely that many of the people would already have left Gambell before that time through the escape route provided by social and economic circumstances.

This is not to say that they will completely escape some of the sociopsychological effects attendant upon trying to cross the wide gap between cultural systems in too short a time. Many of the people who will leave for the mainland are not prepared, either in terms of intellectual and cognitive skills or in terms of values and sentiment patterns, quickly to effect that metamorphosis. Adaptation is difficult to achieve even under the best circumstances, but particularly so when the emigrants lack the requisite skills for successfully competing on the mainland occupational market: education, mechanical or intellectual training, experience in working and household routines appropriate to the new situation. These problems are increased when the mainland economy itself is on an insubstantial base even for the white population.[9]

The common effect of an attempt at more successful personal

[9] In connection with this problem, see Lantis, "American Arctic Populations: Their Survival Problems."

adjustment to life through emigration is to find, instead, a demoralizing situation of inconstant economic opportunity, social isolation and discrimination, encouragement toward excessive drinking, and disadvantaged housing and standard of living. During World War II, for instance, many Eskimos from western Alaskan villages migrated to urban centers (especially Nome, Kotzebue, and Fairbanks) where they found jobs. But they also found extremely disruptive economic and social conditions (Lantis, manuscript). The principal target for many of the Eskimos of the arctic coastal regions is still Nome, which has, even for most of its white population, only an intermittently stable economic base. Such undependable subsistence is more disruptive for the Eskimo immigrants, and the conditions under which they live for the most part are the familiar ones of disease, squalor, and social breakdown.[10]

Relevant to this, it is of interest to note that one can find Eskimo people strongly supporting social institutions which in many ways fulfill certain of the features of nativistic or revitalization movements. These are the evangelical Christian sects, stressing simple alternatives to the complex questions of life and much social companionship among the congregation. Such sects are presumably an answer to deep feelings of being uprooted in social experiences by the demoralizing conditions of life in the town. It is conceivable that something of this nature could happen in Gambell, too, if the stressful conditions were to continue for many years and no escape to the mainland seemed possible. An emphasis on a radical religious movement is one alternative expression of a revitalization movement based on only a political or nationalistic foundation; in fact, religion is the most characteristic feature of such movements.

It is not being suggested here that successful adaptation to mainland life is impossible for the Gambell people, any more than for any other native people taken as individuals. Quite obviously some Eskimos have made noteworthy contributions and extremely useful adjustments to the conditions of mainland life. But the way is very difficult, and it is understandable that many fail. In this connection, one of the most valuable steps that might be taken to prevent such

---

[10] The effects of such "interference with striving" can be quite profound and lead to persistent maladaptive patterns of response, or psychiatric disorder; for a discussion of this type of development, see Leighton, 1959a.

tragedy is education of the people in the village as to the real conditions of housing, joblessness, and discrimination which they are likely to find on the mainland.

But it appears that the time has passed when entire groups or communities of Eskimos can successfully relate to the mainland economy and social structure. In short, the day of the hunter has passed. The industrialized world has moved too much into the arctic regions and has disturbed ancient animal migration routes; it has destroyed plant and animal life on which an Eskimo economy is based; and through the medium of contact and presentation of alternative models for behavior, it has sapped the strength of sentiments supporting the old way of life. Thus for those Eskimos who are successful in adapting themselves to the mainland, that adaptation consists in a metamorphosis, not a symbiotic relationship, the mode of adaptation when fox skins or baleen could be traded to the white world and the Eskimo way of life go on relatively undisturbed. The people who adapt themselves are no longer Eskimos, no longer people who retain a cultural tradition of their own, fitting only certain aspects of their social and economic cycles with those of the mainland. They perforce have to forsake the overarching structure of Eskimo belief and practice if they, as separable human personalities, are to attain that maximum of satisfaction from their life situation which one may call security. In effect, if they are to adjust to the white world, they must become as much like white men as possible. And the more that people move in that direction, obviously the more Gambell, as an Eskimo village, disappears from the human scene.[11]

In the meantime, some steps might be taken to improve the situation of Gambell as an Eskimo village based on hunting and to search out either alternative resources for those which are now failing or will do so or new uses of materials or advantages which are found in the environment. The greater utilization of local products to satisfy current needs, such as development of a modern burner for seal oil, is one example. Something might also be done toward developing greater commercial use of walrus hides from this area, for these unusually tough and adhesive skins have been

[11] For an account of a similar development in a modern Aleut village, see Berreman, 1955.

found useful in some aspects of modern industry (see General Motors, n.d.). With regard to the walruses per se, there are steps that could be taken to improve the harvest of these animals (as well as other sea mammals) and augment the food supply. Fay has suggested a number of things, ranging from thorough study of the distribution and movements of the herds to teaching people the fundamentals of wildlife conservation (which could include placing a limit on number of animals killed), use of more efficient hunting weapons, greater utilization of carcasses, and better storage facilities (1958, pp. 34–39). Certainly one of the basic needs is to establish a more stable economy if the village is to maintain itself in any sort of self-subsistent and integrated fashion. The Parran report (Alaska Health Survey Team, 1954), mostly concerned with health, also points up the critical need for a stable food supply as a fundamental requisite for the health of native villages in Alaska. Lantis also emphasizes this in another of her recent articles on the condition of the Alaskan Eskimos (1952b).

Yet it is difficult to see what could be done to stabilize in any long-term manner Gambell's ancient patterns of hunting and trapping. Man's technological development is still not of sufficient order that it can control weather and the ecological cycle, and international agreements that will regulate the protection of walruses have not yet been reached. The principal adaptive pattern seems to be that of conserving resources which are available and taking advantage of opportunities which are offered by nature. Perhaps one answer might be the adoption of larger boats which could more efficiently hunt walruses on the ice floes during the open spring sea, traveling with the herds and getting a much larger kill each hunting trip. This has been done on the Siberian coast, where in recent years there were numerous rendering stations to process seal, walrus, and whale oil for local use (Krypton, 1956, p. 66). St. Lawrence people claim, in fact, that one reason their hunting has grown worse in recent years is because of the greater animal harvest possible on the Siberian coast by the larger and more mechanized boats. This may be true, and indeed more efficient means of harvest would, if not controlled, ever more quickly deplete the herds and destroy the native economy. Another difficulty in the use of such boats would be the formidable problem of pier and beaching facilities and of proper storage of the meat brought home.

If the problem is examined in terms of a still closer co-ordination of St. Lawrence Island with the mainland economy, as noted above, there appears to be very little at the present time which would make the island a valuable economic site in production of materials needed by the white world. There has been prospecting for minerals to some extent, but apparently nothing was discovered of sufficient value to justify further exploitation. And it is not likely that, aside from military and defense establishments (which, as indicated earlier, are also transitional and undependable), any other economic institutions of the mainland would come to the island and serve as the basis of a stable economy. Because of cost, tourists, for instance, would probably not find much on St. Lawrence Island that they had not already seen on the mainland in their guided tours, where they see Eskimos carving ivory and performing native dances.

The commercial raising of reindeer, once thought to be an extremely feasible plan because of St. Lawrence's insular position (by which the herd would be protected from wolves and other predators), proved to be unrealizable because a large Stateside market for the meat did not develop. This was, in fact, one of the reasons for the failure of the reindeer industry throughout Alaska (Lantis, 1952a). Yet even if there were a market for the deer, the St. Lawrence people would not be any better off, since their range lands would be unexploitable for many years to come because of having been overgrazed by the herd that flourished upon them as recently as 1944–1945.

The story of Gambell, modern descendant of the ancient Eskimo village of Sivokak, is apparently another instance of a small community which from 1940 through the middle years of the 1950's has been irrevocably swept up in the world-wide transition from a subsistence economy and ethnocentric moral order to a closer relationship with the pervasive industrialized economy of the modern world and the abstract moral order which seems to be a feature of that world. Whether the people whose current patterns of interaction and interdependence comprise Gambell as a social unit can successfully adapt their personal lives and habits to the new conditions imposed by the mainland world is one question. Whether Gambell village as a sociocultural system in its own right will continue to survive and function with anything resembling an integrated, cohesive, and relatively perduring community is quite another matter. The unique contribution which, through several thousand years, the Sivokakmeit have made to the infinite variety of man's cultures will soon, in all probability, pass from practice to the written page.

# APPENDIX

# Method Used for
# Health Study

WITH a 1940 census of the village as a base, interviews with a key informant were conducted to obtain a picture of what had happened to that 1940 population (293 individuals) in the fifteen-year period which had elapsed. Interest was primarily in learning of deaths, births, types of sicknesses experienced during lifetime, types of sicknesses that proved fatal, and, if possible, data on migration, jobs, etc. In other words, what has been the pattern of health in this society during the last fifteen years? The data are not limited to answering just this question, however; they are useful also to some extent in ascertaining population turnover, birth rates, and infant mortality rates.

Health records, when found for a dead individual, were also used to help fill out the picture of sickness and cause of death. A final source of data for our particular purposes was our own knowledge of such facts as sociological status (e.g., family situation or clan affiliation).

The data in the interviews with the key informant, plus the scanty health records and the sociological data we added, were transferred to punch cards for analysis.

There are, of course, advantages and disadvantages in the use of a key informant for obtaining village-wide data on such topics as health. Where feasible, a wide survey is the better tool for such a topic as this. But it is not always possible. In addition, the key-informant technique has proved itself very useful in traditional anthropological field work, and for at least two reasons we placed the main reliance on it to obtain our gross systematic health data, particularly that pertaining to dead individuals. In the first place, in a small community such as Gambell, contact with other people is extensive and frequent. Few significant personal facts escape the wide net of gossip and talk that is thrown over the village. This is especially true in matters of health, which is (and always has been) one of the central objects of concern and attention in this and other Eskimo villages. There is the additional fact that our key informant (a 36-year-old Gambell woman) was herself bothered with health problems and sensitized to them in other people.

A second, and more cogent, reason for using the key informant was that our problem called for finding health patterns over a fifteen-year period in which many of the original 1940 population unit had died. Health records with adequate data on deceased respondents are lacking, and we were faced with a choice either of foregoing the chance to say anything systematic concerning sickness and mortality or of devising another method. We chose to question a highly motivated, intelligent and responsive person in the village as to the principal types of sickness experienced by people listed on that census and by all those born in the village since 1940. On the basis of her essential agreement in diagnosis and symptom patterns with the health records that were found and used (roughly two-thirds of the dead population), one can have a high degree of confidence in the probability of accurate reporting on those where health records are lacking. With regard to living people, as mentioned earlier, I felt that the health survey with the 25 respondents was the more useful instrument, although it complemented the key informant's data. The latter could give only the salient sicknesses that the respondent suffered and could not, of course, go into fine details.

In Table 1 the informant's data are compared with the health records. The phrase "no essential contradiction" takes account of the informant's lack of medical knowledge and medical terms; in general she spoke in lay terms of the principal bodily system involved in the death.

Table 1. Contradiction between informant's data and health records for dead individuals

|  | Cases | % |
|---|---|---|
| No essential contradiction | 91 | 85 |
| Contradiction in main cause of death | 7 | 6 |
| Contradiction in hospitalization history | 1 | 1 |
| Contradiction in dates | 5 | 5 |
| Contradiction in major experience of sickness in lifetime | 3 | 3 |
| Total | 107 | 100 |

But the fact that there were health record forms for two-thirds of the dead individuals does not mean that we could derive any benefit from that many records. The necessity to rely on a key informant's knowledge rather than health records in attempting a study of sicknesses of currently dead people is emphasized by the generally inadequate and poorly kept records for duration, intensity, dates, etc., of illnesses. Some of the records were copied *in toto* for dead people; main causes of death and illness immediately preceding death were abstracted for the rest. Health records for living people were not available for use, according to the nurse's own testimony; and the unusable nature of the current records was underscored by several doctors who visited the island during 1954–1955 and tried to consult them for use in treating sick patients. Thus, it was necessary to rely on other sources of data for a study of the health of deceased—as well as living—people. As shown in Table 2, it would be less than satisfactory to rely only on the records.

Table 2. Adequacy of health records for dead individuals

|  | Cases | % |
|---|---|---|
| Some health history, but no mention of death | 2 | 1 |
| Some health history; statement that death occurred; no diagnosis or symptoms | 47 | 33 |
| Some health history; mention of death; symptoms and diagnosis | 34 | 24 |
| Only fact of death on record | 10 | 7 |
| No records found | 48 | 34 |
| Named record found, but no data recorded | 2 | 1 |
| Total | 143 | 100 |

The conclusion one comes to, even with all the necessary qualifications added, is that the health records for Gambell village since 1940 do not constitute a reliable source for mortality estimates. One thus is forced to rely on some other method, such as the key informant, for the bulk of data concerning morbidity and mortality, as Table 3 shows. For one-third of the cases we used only the informant; for two-thirds we used both the informant and the records —nevertheless, interpretations based only on the records would be seriously crippled without the corroboration of the informant.

One other word might be added. Table 3 does not tell the whole

*Table 3.* Source of health data for dead individuals

|  | Cases | % |
|---|---|---|
| Records only | 5 | 2 |
| Informant only | 40 | 28 |
| Both records and informant | 98 | 69 |
| Health data supplied by C.C.H. or J.M.H. | 2 | 1 |
| Total | 145 * | 100 |

* This total is higher than actual cases, for the data overlapped in a couple of cases.

story, for when we include all the living individuals on whom we had only the informant's testimony and no health record (although, to be sure, there was the health survey on 25 cases), the extent of the inadequacy of the records is more cogently seen. For the total number of cases included in the interviewing (599), our information came only from the informant 80 per cent of the time.

*Table 4.* Relationship between mortality status in 1955 and age in 1940

| | Age in 1940 | | | | | | | | | | | | | |
|---|---|---|---|---|---|---|---|---|---|---|---|---|---|---|
| | 0–3 | | 4–9 | | 10–15 | | 16–30 | | 31–55 | | 56–57 | | 76 & over | Not ascert. | |
| | No. | % | No. | % | No. | % | No. | % | No. | % | No. | % | No. | No. | Total |
| Living in 1940; died before 1955 | 13 | 39 | 10 | 22 | 14 | 29 | 20 | 30 | 23 | 34 | 19 | 58 | 2 | 4 | 105 |
| Living in 1940; still living | 20 | 61 | 36 | 78 | 34 | 71 | 47 | 70 | 45 | 66 | 14 | 42 | | 3 | 199 |
| Totals | 33 | 100 | 46 | 100 | 48 | 100 | 67 | 100 | 68 | 100 | 33 | 100 | 2 | 7 | 304 * |

* This figure includes 11 people now living who immigrated to Gambell since 1940.

# Glossary of Frequently

# Used Eskimo Terms

*aliginalre:* shaman, religious practitioner

*angyaellk:* captain of the boat crew

*angyak:* walrus-hide covered hunting boat

*chkwaek:* boat captain's ceremony at the first launching of the whaleboat in the spring

*ilaekwaekothreit:* group of kinsmen tracing their relationship through males; a patriclan

*kaezivae:* a trading ceremonial

*kaiyootak:* wooden trencher used for family meal

*kamukrak:* term for "flesh"; also used to indicate closest kinship relationship

*kamukrakothreit:* ego's "very closest" kin; more generally, clansmen of one's own generation

*mangtak:* whale skin

*noonivak:* a plant, *Rhodiola rosea*

*ramka:* group of kinsmen tracing their relationship through males; a patriclan

*Sivokakmeit* (sing., *Sivokakme*): "the people belonging to Sivokak" (i.e., Gambell village or, in the old days, St. Lawrence Island as a whole)

*Clan names:* Aemagagomeit, Aimaramka, AmIchtowaet, Avaetmeit, Laelkaegameit, Meruchtameit, Naeskaegomeit, OongwaezIgameit, Puwowalagameit.

See also the key to Chart 12 for a list of kinship terms (p. 231) and p. 258 for the names of various members of the boat crew.

# References

Adams, Donald K.  1953  The organs of perception: sentiments. Journal of personality, XXII, no. 1, 52–59.

Alaska Health Survey Team, Thomas Parran, Chief  1954  Alaska's health: a survey report to the United States Department of the Interior. Pittsburgh, Graduate School of Public Health, University of Pittsburgh.

Alaska's Health  1959  "Air lifted clinic wings 1500 miles from St. Lawrence Island across Bering Sea," Alaska's health, XVI, April, 1–3.

Anderson, Edgar  1956  Natural history, statistics, and applied mathematics. American journal of botany, XLIII, no. 10, 882–889.

Anderson, Odin W.  1958  Infant mortality and social and cultural factors: historical trends and current patterns. In E. Gartly Jaco, ed., Patients, physicians, and illness, pp. 10–24. Glencoe, Free Press.

Aronson, Joseph D.  1940  The history of disease among the natives of Alaska. Transactions and studies of the College of Physicians of Philadelphia, VIII, no. 1, 27–34.

Bacon, Sir Francis  In E. A. Burtt, ed., The English philosophers from Bacon to Mill. New York, Modern Library, 1939.

——  In Richard F. Jones, ed., Francis Bacon: essays, advancement of learning, New Atlantis, and other pieces. New York, Odyssey Press, 1937.

Barnett, Homer G.  1953  Innovation. New York, McGraw-Hill.

Barrett, William  1958  Irrational man: a study in existential philosophy. Garden City, Doubleday.

Beals, Ralph, and Harry Hoijer  1953  An introduction to anthropology. New York, Macmillan.

Beddard, F. E.  1900  A book of whales. New York, Putnam's.

Benedict, Ruth  1934  Patterns of culture. Boston, Houghton Mifflin.

Berreman, Gerald D.  1955  Inquiry into community integration in an Aleutian village. American anthropologist, LVII, no. 1, 49–59.

Birket-Smith, Kaj  1936  The Eskimos. New York, Dutton.

—— 1959  The Eskimos. Rev. ed. London, Methuen.

Bowlby, John  1957  Child care and the growth of love. Penguin Books.

Brockington, Fraser  1958  World health. Penguin Books.

Byers, Douglas S.  1957  The Bering bridge—some speculations. Ethnos, I–II, 20–26.

Cameron, Norman D.  1947  The psychology of behavior disorders. Cambridge, Houghton Mifflin.

Campbell, Charles MacFie  1926  Delusion and belief. Cambridge, Harvard University Press.

Cantril, Hadley  1941  The psychology of social movements. New York, Wiley.

—— 1950  The "why" of man's experience. New York, Macmillan.

—— 1958  The politics of despair. New York, Basic Books.

Carpenter, Edmund S.  1954  Eternal life and self-definition among the Aivilik Eskimo. American journal of psychiatry, CX, no. 11, 841–843.

Collins, Henry B.  1937  Archaeology of St. Lawrence Island, Alaska. Smithsonian miscellaneous collections 96, no. 1. Washington.

Coon, Carleton  1948  A reader in general anthropology. New York, Henry Holt.

Cottrell, Fred  1955  Energy and society. New York, McGraw-Hill.

Davis, Kingsley  1949  Human society. New York, Macmillan.

—— 1951  The population of India and Pakistan. Princeton, Princeton University Press.

De Coccola, Raymond, and Paul King  1956  Ayorama. New York, Oxford.

Diethelm, Oskar  1955  Treatment in psychiatry. Springfield, Ill., Charles C. Thomas.

Dollard, John, Leonard Doob, *et al.*  1939  Frustration and aggression. New Haven, Yale University Press.

Doty, W. F.  1900  Eskimos on St. Lawrence Island. *In* Sheldon Jackson, Ninth annual report on introduction of domestic reindeer into Alaska, 1899, pp. 186–256. Washington, Government Printing Office.

—— 1901  Supplementary report. *In* Sheldon Jackson, Tenth annual report on introduction of domestic reindeer into Alaska, 1900, pp. 133–134. Washington, Government Printing Office.

Driver, Harold E., and William C. Massey 1957 Comparative studies of North American Indians. Transactions of the American Philosophical Society, n.s., vol. XLVII, pt. 2.

Dunning, R. W. 1959 Ethnic relations and the marginal man in Canada. Human organization, XVIII, no. 3, 117–122.

Durkheim, Emile 1915 The elementary forms of the religious life (trans. Joseph Swain). London, George Allen.

—— 1933 On the division of labor in society (trans. George Simpson). New York, Macmillan.

Elliott, Henry W. 1875 A report upon the condition of affairs in the Territory of Alaska. Washington, Government Printing Office.

—— 1898 The seal islands of Alaska. *In* Seal and salmon fisheries and general resources of Alaska, III, 3–288. Washington, Government Printing Office.

Fay, Francis H. 1955a The Pacific walrus (*Odobenus rosmarus divergens*): spatial ecology, life history, and population. Ph.D. dissertation, University of British Columbia.

—— 1955b Personal communication.

—— 1956 Personal communication.

—— 1957 History and present status of the Pacific walrus population. Transactions of the twenty-second North American wildlife conference, pp. 431–445. Washington, Wildlife Management Institute.

—— 1958 Pacific walrus investigations on St. Lawrence Island, Alaska. Anchorage, Alaska, Arctic Health Research Center, U.S. Public Health Service.

Fay, Francis H., and Tom J. Cade 1959 An ecological analysis of the avifauna of St. Lawrence Island, Alaska. University of California Publications in Zoology, LXIII, no. 2, 73–150.

Fellows, F. S. 1934 Mortality in the native races of Alaska, with special reference to tuberculosis. Public health reports, XLIX (March 2), 289–298.

Festinger, Leon 1957 A theory of cognitive dissonance. Evanston, Ill., Row, Peterson.

Fey, Harold 1955 Alaska Native Brotherhood. Christian century, Dec. 28, pp. 1521–1523.

Firth, Raymond 1951 Elements of social organization. London, Watts.

—— 1955 Function. *In* William L. Thomas, Jr., ed., Current anthropology. Chicago, University of Chicago.

Forde, C. Daryll 1934 Habitat, economy, and society. New York, Dutton.

Friedmann, Herbert 1932 The birds of St. Lawrence Island, Bering Sea. Proceedings of the United States National Museum, LXXX, art. 12, 1–31.

Gambell, V. C. 1900 The school house farthest west. Youth's companion, vol. LXXIV, nos. 16, 17, 18, 19, pp. 197–198, 213–214, 225–226, 240–241.

Geist, Otto W. 1937 The spy in the igloo. Alaska sportsman, III, no. 12, 8–9, 22.

Geist, Otto W., and Froelich G. Rainey 1936 Archeological excavations at Kukulik, St. Lawrence Island, Alaska. Miscellaneous publications of the University of Alaska, vol. II. Washington, Government Printing Office.

General Motors n.d. 26,000 "partners." Detroit.

Giddings, J. L., Jr. 1952 Observations on the "Eskimo type" of kinship and social structure. Anthropological papers of the University of Alaska, I, no. 1, 5–10.

Goldenweiser, A. A. 1922 Early civilization. New York, Alfred Knopf.
—— 1937 Anthropology. New York, Crofts.

Golder, F. A. 1922 Bering's voyages: an account of the efforts of the Russians to determine the relation of Asia and America. 2 vols. New York, American Geographical Society.

Goode, William J., and Paul Hatt 1952 Methods in social research. New York, McGraw-Hill.

Grene, Marjorie 1959 Introduction to existentialism. Phoenix Books. Chicago, University of Chicago.

Hallowell, A. I. 1951a Culture, personality, and society. *In* A. L. Kroeber, ed., Anthropology today. Chicago, University of Chicago Press.
—— 1951b Cultural factors in the structuralization of perception. *In* John H. Rohrer and Muzafer Sherif, eds., Social psychology at the crossroads. New York, Harper.
—— 1955a Culture and experience. Philadelphia, University of Pennsylvania Press.
—— 1955b Personality structure and the evolution of man. *In* A. I. Hallowell, Culture and experience. Philadelphia, University of Pennsylvania Press.
—— 1955c The self and its behavioral environment. *In* A. I. Hallowell, Culture and experience. Philadelphia, University of Pennsylvania Press.

Hartley, Eugene 1951 Psychological problems of multiple group membership. *In* John H. Rohrer and Muzafer Sherif, eds., Social psychology at the crossroads. New York, Harper.

Heller, Christine A. 1953 Edible and poisonous plants of Alaska. College, Alaska, Extension Service, University of Alaska.

Henderson, L. J. 1913 The fitness of the environment. New York, Macmillan.

Herskovits, Melville J. 1959 Past developments and present currents in ethnology. American anthropologist, LXI, no. 3, 389–397.

Hohman, Elmo Paul 1928 The American whaleman. New York, Longmans, Green.

Homans, George 1950 The human group. New York, Harcourt.

Hooper, Capt. C. L. 1881 Report of the cruise of the U.S. Revenue-Steamer Corwin in the Arctic Ocean, 1880. Washington, Government Printing Office.

Hopkins, D. M. 1959 Cenozoic history of the Bering land bridge. Science, CXXIX, no. 3362, 1519–1527

Hughes, Charles C. 1953 A preliminary ethnography of the Eskimo of St. Lawrence Island, Alaska. M.A. thesis, Cornell University.

—— 1957a Reference group concepts in the study of a changing Eskimo culture. In Verne F. Ray, ed., Cultural stability and cultural change. Proceedings of the 1957 annual spring meetings of the American Ethnological Society.

—— 1957b Sivuokakh: an Eskimo village and the modern world. Ph.D. dissertation, Cornell University.

—— 1958a An Eskimo deviant from the "Eskimo" type of social organization. American anthropologist, LX, no. 6, 1140–1147.

—— 1958b The patterning of recent cultural change in a Siberian Eskimo village. Journal of social issues, XIV, no. 4, pp. 25–35.

—— 1959 Translation of I. K. Voblov's "Eskimo Ceremonies." Anthropological papers of the University of Alaska, VII, no. 2, 71–90.

Hughes, Charles C., Marc-Adelard Tremblay, Robert N. Rapoport, and Alexander H. Leighton 1960 People of cove and woodlot. Vol. II of the Stirling County Study in Psychiatric Disorder and Sociocultural Environment. New York, Basic Books.

Hughes, Jane Murphy 1960 An epidemiological study of psychopathology in an Eskimo village. Ph.D. dissertation, Cornell University.

Jackson, Sheldon 1900 Ninth annual report on introduction of domestic reindeer into Alaska, 1899, esp. pp. 37–38, 60. Washington, Government Printing Office.

—— 1901 Tenth annual report on introduction of domestic reindeer into Alaska, 1900, esp. pp. 17–18, 37. Washington, Government Printing Office.

—— 1902 Eleventh annual report on introduction of domestic reindeer into Alaska, 1901, esp. p. 12. Washington, Government Printing Office.

Jaco, E. Gartly, ed.    1958    Patients, physicians, and illness. Glencoe, Free Press.

Keesing, Felix M.    1953    Culture change. Stanford, Stanford University Press.

Kenyon, Karl W., and Victor B. Scheffer    1955    The seals, sea-lions, and sea otter of the Pacific coast. Fish and Wildlife Service, U.S. Department of the Interior, circular 32. Washington, Government Printing Office.

Kluckhohn, Clyde    1945a    The concept of culture. *In* Ralph Linton, ed., The science of man in the world crisis. New York, Columbia University Press.

—— 1945b    The problem of communication between cultures seen as integrated wholes. *In* L. Bryson, ed., Approaches to national unity. New York, Harper.

—— 1951    Values and value-orientations in the theory of action: an exploration in definition and classification. *In* Talcott Parsons and Edward A. Shils, eds., Toward a general theory of action. Cambridge, Harvard University Press.

Kluckhohn, Clyde, and Dorothea C. Leighton    1946    The Navaho. Cambridge, Harvard University Press.

Krypton, Constantine    1956    The northern sea route and the economy of the Soviet north. New York, Praeger.

La Barre, Weston    1954    The human animal. Chicago, University of Chicago Press.

Lantis, Margaret    1946    The social culture of the Nunivak Eskimo. Transactions of the American Philosophical Society, n.s., XXXV, pt. III, 156–323.

—— 1947    Alaska Eskimo ceremonialism. Monographs of the American Ethnological Society, vol. XI.

—— 1950    The reindeer industry in Alaska. Arctic, III, no. 1, 27–44.

—— 1952a    Eskimo herdsmen. *In* Edward H. Spicer, ed., Human problems in technological change. New York, Russell Sage.

—— 1952b    Present status of the Alaskan Eskimos. *In* Science in Alaska, Arctic Institute of North America, pp. 38–51.

—— 1953    Nunivak Eskimo personality as revealed in the mythology. Anthropological papers of the University of Alaska, II, no. 1, 109–174.

—— 1957    American Arctic populations: their survival problems. Proceedings of the 18th annual biology colloquium, pp. 119–130. Corvallis, Oregon, Oregon State College.

—— n.d.    Alaska Eskimo acculturation. Manuscript.

Leif, Alfred, ed. 1948 The commonsense psychiatry of Dr. Adolf Meyer. New York, McGraw-Hill.

Leighton, Alexander H. 1946 The governing of men. Princeton, Princeton University Press.

—— 1949 Human relations in a changing world. New York, Dutton.

—— 1959a My name is Legion: foundations for a theory of man in relation to culture. Vol. I of the Stirling County Study in Psychiatric Disorder and Sociocultural Environment. New York, Basic Books.

—— 1959b Mental illness and acculturation. *In* Iago Galdston, ed., Medicine and anthropology. New York, International Universities Press.

Leighton, Alexander H., John A. Clausen, and Robert N. Wilson, eds. 1958 Explorations in social psychiatry. New York, Basic Books.

Leighton, Alexander H., and Charles C. Hughes 1955 Notes on Eskimo patterns of suicide. Southwestern journal of anthropology, XI, no. 4, 327–338.

Leighton, Alexander H., and Dorothea C. Leighton 1949 Gregorio, the hand-trembler. Papers of the Peabody Museum of American Archaeology and Ethnology, Harvard University, vol. XL, no. 1.

Leighton, Alexander H., Dorothea C. Leighton, Charles C. Hughes, and Jane M. Hughes 1956 Suggestions for improving public health in Gambell, St. Lawrence Island, Alaska. Typewritten memorandum.

Leighton, Alexander H., and Robert J. Smith 1955 A comparative study of social and cultural change. Proceedings of the American Philosophical Society, XCIX, no. 2, 79–88.

Lerrigo, P. H. J. 1901 Report from St. Lawrence Island (pp. 98–114), Abstract of journal, Gambell, St. Lawrence Island (pp. 114–132), and Supplementary report (pp. 132–133). *In* Sheldon Jackson, Tenth annual report on introduction of domestic reindeer into Alaska, 1900. Washington, Government Printing Office.

—— 1902 Annual report, Presbyterian reindeer station, Gambell, St. Lawrence Island (pp. 88–96), Daily journal on St. Lawrence Island (pp. 97–123). *In* Sheldon Jackson, Eleventh annual report on introduction of domestic reindeer into Alaska, 1901. Washington, Government Printing Office.

Linton, Ralph 1936 The study of man. New York, Appleton-Century.

MacLeod, Robert B. 1947 The phenomenological approach to social psychology. Psychological review, LIV, no. 4, 193–210.

—— 1949a The new psychologies of yesterday and today. Canadian journal of psychology, III, 199–212.

—— 1949b Perceptual constancy and the problem of motivation. Canadian journal of psychology, III, no. 2, 57–66.

MacLeod, Robert B. 1951 The place of phenomenological analysis in social psychological theory. In John H. Rohrer and Muzafer Sherif, eds., Social psychology at the crossroads. New York, Harper.

Malinowski, Bronislaw 1953 Argonauts of the western Pacific. New York, Dutton.

Mandelbaum, David, ed. 1949 Selected writings of Edward Sapir. Berkeley, University of California Press.

Masserman, Jules 1946 Principles of dynamic psychiatry. Philadelphia, Saunders.

May, Rollo 1958 The origins and significance of the existential movement in psychology *and* Contributions of existential psychotherapy. *In* Rollo May, Ernest Angel, and Henri F. Ellenberger, eds. Existential psychiatry, pp. 3–91. New York, Basic Books.

Mead, Margaret 1939 Sex and temperament. *In* Margaret Mead, From the south seas. New York, Morrow.

—— 1956 New lives for old. New York, Morrow.

Meadows, Paul 1957 Models, systems, and science. American sociological review, XXII, no. 1, 3–9.

Merton, Robert K. 1949 Social theory and social structure. Glencoe, Free Press.

—— 1957 Social theory and social structure. Rev. ed. Glencoe, Free Press.

Merton, Robert K., and Alice Kitt 1950 Contributions to the theory of reference group behavior. *In* Robert K. Merton and Paul F. Lazarsfeld, eds., Continuities in social research. Glencoe, Free Press.

Meyer, Adolf 1957 Psychobiology: a science of man. Springfield, Ill., Charles C. Thomas.

Mooney, James 1892 The Ghost Dance religion. *In* Fourteenth annual report of the Bureau of American Ethnology, pt. II. Washington, Government Printing Office.

Moore, Riley D. 1923 Social life of the Eskimo of St. Lawrence Island. American anthropologist, XXV, no. 3, 339–375.

Muir, John 1917 The cruise of the Corwin: journal of the Arctic expedition of 1881 in search of De Long and the Jeannette. Boston, Houghton Mifflin.

Muncie, Wendell 1939 Psychobiology and psychiatry. St. Louis, Mosby.

Murdock, G. P. 1934 Our primitive contemporaries. New York, Macmillan.

—— 1949 Social structure. New York, Macmillan.

Murdoch, John 1892 Ethnological results of the Point Barrow Expedition. In Ninth annual report of the Bureau of American Ethnology. Washington, Government Printing Office.

Murie, Olaus J. 1936a Notes on the mammals of St. Lawrence Island, Alaska. *In* Otto W. Geist and Froelich G. Rainey, Archeological excavations at Kukulik, St. Lawrence Island, Alaska, Appendix III. Washington, Government Printing Office.

—— 1936b The birds of St. Lawrence Island, Alaska. *In* Otto W. Geist and Froelich G. Rainey, Archeological excavations at Kukulik, St. Lawrence Island, Alaska, Appendix V. Washington, Government Printing Office.

Nash, Philleo 1955 The place of religious revivalism in the formation of the intercultural community on Klamath reservation. *In* Fred Eggan, ed., Social anthropology of North American tribes. Chicago, University of Chicago.

Nelms, Paul H. 1945 Saint Lawrence Island. Alaska sportsman, XI, 10–11, 34–39.

—— 1946 On St. Lawrence Island. Alaska life, IX, 11–13, 21–22.

Nelson, E. W. 1899 The Eskimo about Bering Strait. *In* Eighteenth annual report of the Bureau of American Ethnology, pt. 1. Washington, Government Printing Office.

Newcomb, Theodore 1950 Social psychology. New York, Dryden.

Northrop, F. S. C. 1947 The logic of the sciences and the humanities. New York, Macmillan.

Oswalt, W. H. 1957 A western Eskimo ethnobotany. Anthropological papers of the University of Alaska, VI, no. 1, 17–36.

Parran Report. *See* Alaska Health Survey Team.

Parsons, Talcott 1949 The structure of social action. Glencoe, Free Press.

—— 1951 The social system. Glencoe, Free Press.

Paton, Alan 1948 Cry, the beloved country. New York, Charles Scribner's.

Porsild, A. E. 1953 Edible plants of the arctic. Arctic, VI, no. 1, 15–34.

Radcliffe-Brown, A. R. 1952 On joking relationships. *In* A. R. Radcliffe-Brown, Structure and function in primitive society. Glencoe, Free Press.

—— 1957 The natural science of society. Glencoe, Free Press.

Rausch, Robert 1953 On the land mammals of St. Lawrence Island, Alaska. Murrelet, XXXII, no. 2, 18–26.

Redfield, Robert 1955 The little community. Chicago, University of Chicago Press.

Rivers, W. H. R. 1922 The psychological factor. *In* W. H. R. Rivers, ed., Essays on the depopulation of Melanesia. Cambridge, Cambridge University Press.

Sanders, Irwin T., Richard B. Woodbury, *et al.* 1953 Societies around the world. Vol. I. New York, Dryden.

Semushkin, Tikhon 1948 Alitet Ukhodit v Gory. Moscow.

Sherif, Muzafer 1953 The concept of reference groups in human relations. *In* Muzafer Sherif and M. O. Wilson, eds., Group relations at the crossroads. New York, Harper.

Sherif, Muzafer, and Hadley Cantril 1947 The psychology of ego-involvements. New York, Wiley.

Sherif, Muzafer, and Carolyn W. Sherif 1953 Groups in harmony and tension, chap. vii. New York, Harper.

Siegel, Bernard J. 1955 Acculturation. Stanford, Stanford University Press.

Smith, N. Leighton 1937 Eskimos hunt whales ceremoniously. Alaska sportsman, III, 16–18.

Smith, Robert J. 1957 Comparative studies in anthropology of the interrelations between social and technological change. Human organization, XVI, no. 1, 30–36.

Smith, T. Lynn 1948 Population analysis. New York, McGraw-Hill.

Snodgrass, Roland 1936 Notes on the geography and geology of western St. Lawrence Island, Alaska. *In* Otto W. Geist and Froelich G. Rainey, Archeological excavations at Kukulik, St. Lawrence Island, Alaska, Appendix II. Washington, Government Printing Office.

Social Science Research Council Summer Seminar on Acculturation 1954 Acculturation: an explanatory formulation. American anthropologist, LVI, no. 6, 973–1000.

Sorokin, P. A. 1941 Social and cultural dynamics, vol. IV. New York, American Book.

Spencer, Robert F. 1959 The North Alaskan Eskimo: a study in ecology and society. Smithsonian Institution, Bureau of American Ethnology, Bulletin 171. Washington, Government Printing Office.

Spier, Leslie 1925 The distribution of kinship systems in North America. University of Washington publications in anthropology, I, no. 2, 69–88.

Stagner, Ross 1954 Homeostasis as a unifying concept in personality theory. *In* William E. Martin and Celia B. Stendler, eds., Readings in child development. New York, Harcourt.

Steffen, Ed 1958 Personal communication.

Stone, Kirk H. 1952 Some geographic bases for planning new Alaska settlement. Science in Alaska, Arctic Institute of North America, pp. 136–150.

Swadesh, Morris 1951 Kleinschmidt centennial III: Unaaliq and proto Eskimo. International journal of American linguistics, XVII, 66–70.

Tillich, Paul 1944 Existential philosophy. Journal of the history of ideas, V, no. 1, 44–70.

Tremblay, Marc-Adelard 1957 The key-informant technique: a non-ethnographic application. American anthropologist, LIX, 688–701.

United Nations Organization 1954 Demographic Yearbook. New York.

—— 1955 Statistical Yearbook. New York.

United States Department of Commerce 1952 Local climatological data, Gambell, Alaska. Washington, Government Printing Office.

United States Department of Health, Education, and Welfare 1956 Vital statistics—special reports, vol. XLIV, no. 10 (Aug.). Washington, Government Printing Office.

VanStone, James W. 1957 The autobiography of an Alaskan Eskimo. Arctic, X, no. 4, 195–210.

—— 1958a Commercial whaling in the Arctic Ocean. Pacific North-west quarterly, Jan., pp. 1–10.

—— 1958b An Eskimo community and the outside world. Anthro-pological papers of the University of Alaska, VII, no. 1, 27–38.

Voblov, I. K. 1952 Eskimosskie Prazdniki. Sibirskii Etnograficheskii Sbornik. Trudy Instituta Etnografii, Akademia Nauk SSSR. Novaia Seria, vol. XVIII.

Vogt, Evon Z. 1951 Navaho veterans. Papers of the Peabody Museum of American Archaeology and Ethnology, Harvard University, vol. XLI, no. 1.

Wallace, A. F. C. 1956 Revitalization movements. American anthro-pologist, LVIII, no. 2, 264–281.

Wallis, W. D. 1943 Messiahs: their role in civilization. Washington, D.C., American Council on Public Affairs.

Weyer, Edward M. 1932 The Eskimos. New Haven, Yale University Press.

Whitehorn, John C. 1932 Concerning emotion as impulsion and in-stinct as orientation. American journal of psychiatry, XI (May), 1093–1106.

Williams, F. E. 1923 The Vailala madness and the destruction of native ceremonies in the Gulf division. Port Moresby, Territory of Papua, Anthropology report no. 4.

—— 1934 The Vailala madness in retrospect. *In* E. E. Evans-Pritchard,

Raymond Firth, Bronislaw Malinowski, and Isaac Schapera, eds., Essays presented to C. G. Seligman. London, Paul, Trench, Trubner.

Williams, Robin M., Jr. 1947 The reduction of intergroup tensions. New York, Social Science Research Council.

—— 1951 American society. New York, Knopf.

Williams, William F. 1902 Loss of the Arctic fleet. *In* William F. Williams, Famous fleets in New Bedford's history: stories of wooden ships and iron men. New Bedford, Reynolds.

# Index

I
I